Praise for Arundhati Roy:

"Arundhati Roy is incandescent in her brilliance and her fearlessness. And in these extraordinary essays—which are clarions for justice, for witness, for a true humanity—Roy is at her absolute best."
—Junot Díaz

"Her incomparable divining rod picks up the cries of the despised and the oppressed in the most remote corners of the globe; it even picks up the cries of rivers and fish. With an unfailing charm and wit that makes her writing constantly enlivening to read, her analysis of our grotesque world is savagely clear, and yet her anger never obscures her awareness that beauty, joy, and pleasure can potentially be part of the life of human beings."

—Wallace Shawn

"Arundhati Roy combines her brilliant style as a novelist with her powerful commitment to social justice in producing these eloquent, penetrating essays."

—Howard Zinn

"Arundhati Roy is one of the most confident and original thinkers of our time."

—Naomi Klein

"The fierceness with which Arundhati Roy loves humanity moves my heart."

—Alice Walker

"Arundhati Roy calls for 'factual precision' alongside of the 'real precision of poetry.' Remarkably, she combines those achievements to a degree that few can hope to approach."

—Noam Chomsky

"[Roy is] an electrifying political essayist.... So fluent is her prose, so keen her understanding of global politics, and so resonant her objections to nuclear weapons, assaults against the environment, and the endless suffering of the poor that her essays are as uplifting as they are galvanizing."

—Booklist

The End of Imagination

Arundhati Roy

Haymarket Books
Chicago, Illinois

Published in 2016 by
Haymarket Books
P.O. Box 180165
Chicago, IL 60618
773-583-7884
www.haymarketbooks.org
info@haymarketbooks.org

ISBN: 978-1-60846-619-1

Trade distribution:
In the US, Consortium Book Sales and Distribution, www.cbsd.com
In Canada, Publishers Group Canada, www.pgcbooks.ca

This book was published with the generous support of
Lannan Foundation and Wallace Action Fund.

Cover design by Abby Weintraub.

Printed in Canada by union labor.

Library of Congress Cataloging-in-Publication data is available.

10 9 8 7 6 5 4 3 2 1

Contents

Part III

My Seditious Heart

An Unfinished Diary of Nowadays

On a balmy February night, aware that things were not going well, I did what I rarely do. I put in earplugs and switched on the television. Even though I had said nothing about the spate of recent events—murders and lynchings, police raids on university campuses, student arrests, and enforced flag-waving—I knew that my name was still on the A-list of "anti-nationals." That night, I began to worry that, in addition to the charge of criminal contempt of court I was already facing (for "interfering in the administration of justice," "bashing the Central Government, State Governments, the Police Machinery, so also [the] Judiciary," and "demonstrating a surly, rude and boorish attitude"),[1] I would also be charged with causing the death of the eternally indignant news anchor on Times Now. I thought he might succumb to an apoplectic fit as he stabbed the air and spat out my name, suggesting that I was a part of some shadowy cabal that was behind the ongoing "anti-national" activity in the country. My crime, according to him, is that I have written about the struggle for freedom in Kashmir, questioned the execution of Mohammad Afzal Guru, walked with the Maoist guerrillas ("terrorists" in television-speak) in the forests of Bastar, connected their armed rebellion to my reservations about India's chosen model of "development," *and*—with a hissy, sneering pause—even questioned the country's nuclear tests.

Now it's true that my views on these matters are at variance with those of the ruling establishment. In better days, that used to be known as a critical perspective or an alternative worldview. These days in India, it's called sedition.

Sitting in Delhi, somewhat at the mercy of what looks like a democratically elected government gone rogue, I wondered whether I should rethink some of my opinions. I thought back, for instance, on a talk I gave in 2004 at the annual meeting of the American Sociological Association, just before the Bush-versus-Kerry election, in which I joked about how the choice between the Democrats and the Republicans—or their equivalents in India, the Congress and the Bharatiya Janata Party (BJP)—was like having to choose between Tide and Ivory Snow, two brands of washing powder both actually owned by the same company. Given all that is going on, can I honestly continue to believe that?

On merit, when it comes to pogroms against non-Hindu communities, or looking away while Dalits are slaughtered, or making sure the levers of power and wealth remain in the hands of the tiny minority of dominant castes, or smuggling in neoliberal economic reforms on the coattails of manufactured communal conflict, or banning books, there's not much daylight between the Congress and the BJP. (When it comes to the horrors that have been visited upon places like Kashmir, Nagaland, and Manipur, all the parliamentary parties, including the two major Left parties, stand united in their immorality.)

Given this track record, does it matter that the stated ideologies of the Congress and the BJP are completely different? Whatever its practice, the Congress *says* it believes in a secular, liberal democracy, while the BJP mocks secularism and believes that India is essentially a "Hindu Rashtra" —a Hindu nation. Hypocrisy, Congress-style, is serious business. It's clever—it smokes up the mirrors and leaves us groping around. However, to proudly declare your bigotry, to bring it out into the sunlight as the BJP does, is a challenge to the fundamental social, legal, and moral foundations on which modern India (supposedly) stands. It would be an error to imagine that what we are witnessing today is just business as usual between unprincipled, murderous political parties.

Although the idea of India as a Hindu Rashtra is constantly being imbued with an aura of ancientness, it's a surprisingly recent one. And, ironically, it has more to do with representative democracy than it does with religion. Historically, the people who now call themselves Hindu only identified themselves by their *jati*, their caste names. As a community, they functioned as a loose coalition of endogamous castes organized in a strict hierarchy. (Even today, for all the talk of unity and nationalism, only 5 percent of marriages in India cut across caste lines. Transgression can still get young people beheaded.) Since each caste could dominate the ones below it, all except those at the very bottom were inveigled into being a part of the system. *Brahmanvaad*—Brahminism—is the word that the anti-caste movement has traditionally used to describe this taxonomy. Though it has lost currency (and is often erroneously taken to refer solely to the practices and beliefs of Brahmins as a caste group), it is, in fact, a more accurate term than "Hinduism" for this social and religious arrangement, because it is as ancient as caste itself and predates the idea of Hinduism by centuries.

This is a volatile assertion, so let me shelter behind Bhimrao Ambedkar. "The first and foremost thing that must be recognised," he wrote in *Annihilation of Caste* in 1936, "is that Hindu society is a myth. The name Hindu is itself a foreign name. It was given by the Mohammedans to the natives [who lived east of the river Indus] for the purpose of distinguishing themselves."[2]

So how and why did the people who lived east of the Indus begin to call themselves Hindus? Towards the end of the nineteenth century, the politics of representative governance (paradoxically, introduced to its colony by the imperial British government) began to replace the politics of emperors and kings. The British marked the boundaries of the modern nation-state called India, divided it into territorial constituencies, and introduced the idea of elected bodies for local self-government. Gradually, subjects became citizens, citizens became voters, and voters formed constituencies that were assembled from complicated networks of old as well as new allegiances, alliances, and loyalties. Even as it came into existence, the new nation began to struggle against its rulers. But it was no longer a question of overthrowing a ruler militarily and taking the throne. The new rulers, whoever they were, would need to be legitimate representatives of the people. The politics of representative governance set up a new anxiety: Who could legitimately claim to represent the aspirations of the freedom struggle? Which constituency would make up the majority?

This marked the beginning of what we now call "vote bank" politics. Demography turned into an obsession. It became imperative that people who had previously identified themselves only by their caste names band together under a single banner to make up a majority. That was when they began to call themselves Hindu. It was a way of crafting a political majority out of an impossibly diverse society. "Hindu" was the name of a political constituency more than of a religion, one that could define itself as clearly as other constituencies—Muslim, Sikh, and Christian—could. Hindu nationalists, as well as the officially "secular" Congress Party, staked their claims to the "Hindu vote."

It was around this time that a perplexing contestation arose around the people then known as "Untouchables" or "Outcastes," who, though they were outside the pale of the caste system, were also divided into separate castes arranged in a strict hierarchy. To even begin to understand the political chaos we are living through now, at the center of which is the suicide of the Dalit scholar Rohith Vemula—it's important to understand, at least conceptually, this turn-of-the-century contestation.

Over the previous centuries, in order to escape the scourge of caste, millions of Untouchables (I use this word only because Ambedkar used it too) had converted to Buddhism, Islam, Sikhism, and Christianity. In the past, those conversions had not been a cause of anxiety for the privileged castes. However, when the politics of demography took center stage, this hemorrhaging became a source of urgent concern. People who had been shunned and cruelly oppressed were now viewed as a population that could greatly expand the numbers of the Hindu constituency. They had to be courted and brought into the "Hindu fold." That was the beginning of Hindu evangelism. What we know today as *ghar wapsi*, or "returning home," was a ceremony that dominant castes devised to "purify" Untouchables and Adivasis, whom they considered "polluted." The idea was (and is) to persuade these ancient and autochthonous peoples that they were formerly Hindus, and that Hinduism was the original, indigenous religion of the subcontinent. It was not only Hindu nationalists among the privileged castes who tried to embrace the Untouchables politically while continuing to valorize the caste system. Their counterparts in the Congress did the same thing too; this was the reason for the legendary standoff between Bhimrao Ambedkar and Mohandas Gandhi, and continues to be cause of serious disquiet in Indian politics. Even today, to properly secure its idea of a Hindu Rashtra, the BJP has to persuade a majority of the Dalit population to embrace a religion that stigmatizes and humiliates them. It has been surprisingly successful, and has even managed to draw in some militant Ambedkarite Dalits. It is this paradox that has made the political moment we are living through so incandescent, so highly inflammable, and so unpredictable.

Ever since the Rashtriya Swayamsevak Sangh (RSS) was founded, in 1925, this ideological holding company of Hindu nationalism (and of the BJP) has set itself the task of making myriad castes, communities, tribes, religions, and ethnic groups submerge their identities and line up behind the banner of the Hindu Rashtra. Which is a little like trying to sculpt a gigantic, immutable stone statue of Bharat Mata—the Hindu right's ideal of Mother India—out of a stormy sea. Turning water into stone may not be a practical ambition, but the RSS's long years of trying have polluted the sea and endangered its flora and fauna in irreversible ways. Its ruinous ideology—known as Hindutva, and inspired by the likes of Benito Mussolini and Adolf Hitler—openly proposes Nazi-style purges of Indian Muslims. In RSS doctrine (theorized by M. S. Golwalkar, the organization's second *sarsanghchalak*, or supreme leader), the three main enemies obstructing the path to the Hindu Rashtra are Muslims, Christians, and Communists. And now, as the RSS races towards that goal, although what's happening around us may look like chaos, everything is actually going strictly by the book.

Of late, the RSS has deliberately begun to conflate nationalism with Hindu nationalism. It uses the terms interchangeably, as though they mean the same thing. Naturally, it chooses to gloss over the fact that it played absolutely no part in the struggle against British colonialism. But while the RSS left the battle of turning a British colony into an independent nation to other people, it has, since then, worked far harder than any other political or cultural organization to turn this nation into a Hindu nation. Before the BJP was founded in 1980, the political arm of the RSS was the Bharatiya Jan Sangh. However, the RSS's influence cut across party lines, and in the past its shadowy presence has even been evident in some of the more violent and nefarious activities of the Congress Party. The organization now has a network of tens of thousands of *shakhas* (branches) and hundreds of thousands of workers. It has its own trade union, its own educational institutions where millions of students are indoctrinated, its own teachers' organization, a women's wing, a media and publications division, its own organizations dedicated to Adivasi welfare, its own medical missions, its own sad stable of historians (who produce their own hallucinatory version of history), and, of course, its own army of trolls on social media. Its sister concerns, the Bajrang Dal and the Vishwa Hindu Parishad, provide the stormtroopers who carry out organized attacks on anyone whose views they perceive to be a threat. In addition to creating its own organizations (which, together with the BJP, make up the Sangh Parivar—the Saffron Family), the RSS has also worked patiently to place its chessmen in public institutions: on government committees, in universities, the bureaucracy, and, crucially, the intelligence services.

That all this farsightedness and hard work were going to pay off one day was a foregone conclusion. Still, it took imagination and ruthlessness to come this far. Most of us know the story, but given the amnesia that is being pressed upon us, it might serve to put down a chronology of the recent present. Who knows, things that appeared unconnected may, when viewed in retrospect, actually be connected. And vice versa. So forgive me if, in an attempt to decipher a pattern, I go over some familiar territory.

The journey to power began with the Ram Janmabhoomi movement. In 1990, L. K. Advani, BJP leader and a member of the RSS, traveled the length and breadth of the country in an air-conditioned *rath*—chariot—exhorting "Hindus" to rise up and build a temple on the hallowed birthplace of Lord Ram. The birthplace, people were told, was the exact same spot on which a sixteenth-century mosque, the Babri Masjid, stood, in the town of Ayodhya. In 1992, just two years after his *rath yatra* (chariot procession), Advani stood by and watched as an organized mob reduced the Babri Masjid to rubble. Riots, massacres, and serial bomb-ings followed. The country was polarized in a way it had not been since Partition. By 1998, the BJP (which had only two seats in Parliament in 1984) had formed a coalition government at the center.

The first thing the BJP did was to realize a long-standing desire of the RSS by conducting a series of nuclear tests. From being an organiza-tion that had been banned three times (after the assassination of Gandhi, during the Emergency, and after the demolition of the Babri Masjid), the RSS was finally in a position to dictate government policy. We can call it the Year of the Ascension.

It wasn't the first time India had conducted nuclear tests, but the exhibitionism of the 1998 ones was different. It was like a rite of passage. The "Hindu bomb" was meant to announce the imminent arrival of the Hindu Rashtra. Within days, Pakistan (already ahead of the curve, hav-ing declared itself an Islamic republic in 1956) showed off its "Muslim bomb." And now we're stuck with these two strutting, nuclear-armed roosters, who are trained to hate each other, who hold their minority populations hostage as they mimic each other in a competing horror show of majoritarianism and religious chauvinism. And they have Kash-mir to fight over.

The nuclear tests altered the tone of public discourse in India. They coarsened and, you could say, weaponized it. In the months that fol-lowed, we were force-fed Hindu nationalism. Then, like now, articles circulated, predicting that a mighty, all-conquering Hindu Rashtra was about to emerge—that a resurgent India would "burst forth upon its former oppressors and destroy them completely." Absurd as it all was, having nuclear weapons made thoughts like these seem feasible. It *creat-ed* thoughts like these.

You didn't have to be a visionary to see what was coming.

The Year of the Ascension, 1998, witnessed gruesome attacks on Christians (essentially Dalits and Adivasis), Hindutva's most vulnerable foes. Swami Aseemanand, the head of the RSS-affiliated Vanvasi Kalyan Ashram's religious wing (who would make national news as the main accused in the 2007 Samjhauta Express train bombing), was sent to the remote, forested Dangs district in western Gujarat to set up a headquarters. The violence began on Christmas Eve. Within a week, more than twenty churches in the region were burned down or otherwise destroyed by mobs of thousands led by the Hindu Dharma Jagran Manch, an organization affiliated to the Vishwa Hindu Parishad and the Bajrang Dal. Soon, Dangs district became a major center of *ghar wapsi*. Tens of thousands of Adivasis were "returned" to Hinduism. The violence spread to other states. In Keonjhar district in Odisha, an Australian Christian missionary, Graham Staines, who had been working in India for thirty-five years, was burned alive along with his two sons, ages six and ten. The man who led the attack was Dara Singh, a Bajrang Dal activist.

In April 2000, the US president Bill Clinton was on an official visit to Pakistan, after which he was due in Delhi. It was less than a year since the war in the Kargil district of Ladakh, in which India had pushed back the Pakistani army after it, in an aggressive, provocative move, sent soldiers across the Line of Control to occupy a strategic post. The Indian government was keen for the international community to recognize that Pakistan was a "terrorist state." On April 20, the night before Clinton was expected to arrive, thirty-five Sikhs were shot down in cold blood in Chittisinghpora, a village in south Kashmir. The killers were said to be Pakistan-based militants disguised in Indian Army uniforms. It was the first time Sikhs had been targeted by militants in Kashmir. Five days later, the Special Operations Group and the Rashtriya Rifles claimed to have tracked down and killed five of the militants. The burned, disfigured bodies of the dead men were dressed in fresh, unburned army uniforms. It turned out they were all local Kashmiri villagers who had been abducted by the army and killed in a staged encounter.

In October 2001, just weeks after the 9/11 attacks in the United States, the BJP installed Narendra Modi as the chief minister of Gujarat. At the time, Modi was more or less unknown. His main political credential was that he had been a long-time and loyal member of the RSS.

On the morning of December 13, 2001, in Delhi, when the Indian Parliament was in its winter session, five armed men in a white Ambassador car fitted with an improvised explosive device drove through its gates. Apparently, they got through security because they had a fake Home Ministry sticker on their windscreen, the back of which read:

INDIA IS A VERY BAD COUNTRY AND WE HATE IN-
DIA WE WANT TO DESTROY INDIA AND WITH THE
GRACE OF GOD WE WILL DO IT GOD IS WITH US AND
WE WILL TRY OUR BEST. THIS EDIET WAJPEI AND AD-
VANI WE WILL KILL THEM. THEY HAVE KILLED MANY
INNOCENT PEOPLE AND THEY ARE VERY BAD PER-
SONS. THERE BROTHER BUSH IS ALSO A VERY BAD
PERSON HE WILL BE NEXT TARGET HE IS ALSO THE
KILLER OF INNOCENT PEOPLE HE HAVE TO DIE AND
WE WILL DO IT

When the men were eventually challenged, they jumped out and
opened fire. In the gun battle that ensued all the attackers, eight security personnel, and a gardener were killed. The then–prime minister,
A. B. Vajpayee (also a member of the RSS), had, only the previous day,
expressed a worry that the Parliament might be attacked. L. K. Advani,
who was the home minister by then, compared the assault to the 9/11
attacks. He said the men "looked like Pakistanis." Fourteen years later,
we still don't know who they really were. They are yet to be properly
identified.

Within days, on December 16, the Special Cell of the Delhi Police
announced that it had cracked the case. It said that the attack was a joint
operation by two Pakistan-based terrorist outfits, Lashkar-e-Taiba and
Jaish-e-Mohammad. Three Kashmiri men, S. A. R. Geelani, Shaukat
Hussain Guru, and Mohammed Afzal Guru, were arrested. Shaukat's
wife, Afsan Guru, was arrested too. The mastermind at the Indian end,
the Special Cell told the media, was Geelani, a young professor of Arabic
at Delhi University. (He was subsequently acquitted by the courts.) On
December 21, based on these intelligence inputs, the Government of
India suspended air, rail, and bus communications with Pakistan, banned
overflights, and recalled its ambassador. More than half a million troops
were moved to the border, where they remained on high alert for several
months. Foreign embassies issued travel advisories to their citizens and
evacuated their staff, apprehending a war that could turn nuclear.

On February 27, 2002, while Indian and Pakistani troops eyeballed
each other on the border and communal polarization was at a fever pitch,
fifty-eight *kar sevaks*—Hindu pilgrims—traveling home from Ayodhya

were burned alive in their train coach just outside the train station in the town of Godhra, Gujarat. The Gujarat police said the coach had been firebombed from the outside by an angry mob of local Muslims. (Later, a report by the State Forensic Lab showed that this was not the case.) L. K. Advani said that "outside elements" may have also been involved. The *kar sevaks'* bodies, burned beyond recognition, were transported to Ahmedabad for the public to pay their respects.

What happened next is well known. (And well forgotten too, because the bigots of yesterday are being sold to us as the moderates of today.) So, briefly: In February and March 2002, while police stood by, Gujarat burned. In cities and in villages, organized Hindutva mobs murdered Muslims in broad daylight. Women were raped and burned alive. Infants were put to the sword. Men were dismembered. Whole localities were burned down. Tens of thousands of Muslims were driven from their homes and into refugee camps. The killing went on for several weeks.

There have been pogroms in India before, equally heinous, equally unpardonable, in which the numbers of people killed have been far higher: the massacre of Muslims in Nellie, Assam, in 1983, under a Congress state government (estimates of the number killed vary between two thousand, officially, and more than double that figure, unofficially); the massacre of almost three thousand Sikhs following the assassination of Indira Gandhi in 1984, by Congress-led mobs in Delhi (which Rajiv Gandhi, who then went on to become prime minister, justified by saying, "When a big tree falls, the ground shakes"); the massacre, in 1993, of hundreds of Muslims by the Shiv Sena in Mumbai, following the demolition of the Babri Masjid. In these pogroms too, the killers were protected and given complete impunity.

But Gujarat 2002 was a massacre in the time of mass media. Its ideological underpinning was belligerently showcased, and the massacre justified in ways that marked a departure from the past. It was perpetuation, as well as a commencement. We, the public, were being given notice in no uncertain terms. The era of dissimulation had ended.

The Gujarat pogrom dovetailed nicely with the international climate of Islamophobia. The War on Terror had been declared. Afghanistan had been bombed. Iraq was already on the radar. Within months of the massacre, a fresh election was announced in Gujarat. Modi won it hands down. A few years into his first tenure, some of those involved in the 2002 pogrom were caught on camera boasting about how they had hacked, burned, and speared people to death. The footage was broadcast on the national news. It only seemed to enhance Modi's popularity in the state, where he won the next two elections as well, securing the backing of several heads of major corporations along the way, and remained chief minister for twelve years.

While Modi moved from strength to strength, his party faltered at the center. Its "India Shining" campaign in the 2004 general election was received by people as a cruel joke, and the Congress made a stunning comeback. The BJP remained out of power at the center for the next ten years.

The RSS showed itself to be an organization that thrives in the face of adversity. The climate was what is known as "vitiated." Between 2003 and 2009, a series of bombings and terror strikes on trains, buses, marketplaces, mosques, and temples by what were thought to be Islamist terror groups killed scores of innocent people. The worst of them all were the 2008 Mumbai attacks, in which Lashkar-e-Taiba militants from Pakistan shot 164 people and wounded more than 300.

Not all the attacks were what they were made out to be. What follows is just a sampling, an incomplete list of some of those events: On June 15, 2004, a young woman called Ishrat Jahan and three Muslim men were shot dead by the Gujarat police, who said they were Lashkar-e-Taiba operatives on a mission to assassinate Modi. The Central Bureau of Investigation has since said that the "encounter" was staged, and that all four victims were captured and then killed in cold blood. On November 23, 2005, a Muslim couple, Sohrabuddin Sheikh and his wife Kauser Bi, were taken off a public bus by the Gujarat police. Three days later, Sheikh was reported killed in an "encounter" in Ahmedabad. The police said that he worked for Lashkar-e-Taiba, and that they suspected he was on a mission to assassinate Modi. Kauser Bi was killed two days later. A witness to the Sheikh killing, Tulsiram Prajapati, was also shot dead a year later, also in a police encounter. Several senior police officers of the Gujarat police are standing trial for these killing. (One of them, P. P. Pandey, was appointed as the director general of police for Gujarat in April 2016.) On February 18, 2007, the Samjhauta Express, a "friendship train" that ran twice a week between Delhi and Attari in Pakistan, was bombed, killing sixty-eight people, most of them Pakistanis. In September 2008, three bombs went off in the towns of Malegaon and Modassa. Several of those arrested in these cases, including Swami Aseemanand of the Vanvasi Kalyan Ashram, were members of the RSS. (Hemant Karkare, the police officer who headed the Maharashtra Anti-Terrorism Squad, which led the investigations, was shot dead in 2008 during the course of the Mumbai attacks. For the story within the story, read *Who Killed Karkare?* by S. M. Mushrif, a retired inspector general of the Maharashtra police.)

The assaults on Christians continued too. The most ferocious of them was in Kandhamal, Odisha, in 2008. Ninety Christians (all Dalits) were murdered, and more than fifty thousand people were displaced. Tragically, the mobs that attacked them were made up of newly "Hinduized" Adivasis freshly dragooned into the Sangh Parivar's vigilante militias. Kandhamal's Christians continue to live under threat, and most of them cannot return to their homes. In other states too, like Chhattisgarh and Jharkhand, Christians live in constant danger.

In 2013, the BJP announced that Modi would be its prime ministerial candidate for the 2014 general election. During his campaign, he was asked if he regretted what had happened on his watch in Gujarat in 2002. "Any person if we are driving a car, we are a driver, and someone else is driving a car and we're sitting behind," he told a Reuters journalist, "even then if a puppy comes under the wheel, will it be painful or not? Of course it is. If I'm a chief minister or not, I'm a human being. If something bad happens anywhere, it is natural to be sad."

The media dutifully filed the Gujarat pogrom away as old news. The campaign went well. Modi was allowed to reinvent himself as the architect of the "Gujarat model"—supposedly an example of dynamic economic development. He became corporate India's most favored candidate—the embodiment of the aspirations of the new India, architect of an economic miracle waiting to happen. His election broke the bank, costing more than Rs 700 crore—$115 million—according to the election commission.

But behind the advertising blitz and the 3D dioramas, things hadn't really changed all that much. In a district called Muzaffarnagar, in Uttar Pradesh, the tried and tested version of the *real* Gujarat model was revived as a poll strategy. Technology played a part. (This would become a recurring theme.) It began with an altercation over what was, at the time, being called "love-jihad"—a notion that played straight into that old anxiety about demography. The Muslim "love-jihad" campaign, Hindus were told, involved entrapping Hindu girls romantically and persuading them to convert to Islam. In August 2013, a Muslim boy accused of teasing a Hindu girl was killed by two Jats. Two Jats were killed in retaliation. A video of an obviously Muslim mob beating a man to death began to circulate on Facebook and over cell-phone networks. In reality, the incident had taken place in Sialkot, Pakistan. But it was put about that the video documented a local incident in which Muslims had beaten a Hindu boy to death. Provoked by the video, Hindu Jat farmers armed with swords and guns turned on local Muslims, with whom they had lived and worked for centuries. Between August and September 2013, according to official estimates, sixty-two people were killed—forty-two Muslims and twenty Hindus. Unofficial estimates put the number of Muslims killed at two hundred.[3] Tens of thousands of Muslims were forced off their lands and into refugee camps. And, of course, many women were raped.

In April 2014, just before the general election, Amit Shah, a general secretary of the BJP at the time and now the party president (he had been arrested in the Sohrabuddin Sheikh case, but was discharged by a special court), spoke at a meeting of Jats in a district bordering Muzaffarnagar. "In Uttar Pradesh, especially western UP, it is an election for honor," he said. "It is an election to take revenge for the insult. It is an election to teach a lesson to those who have committed injustice." Once again, the strategy paid off. The BJP swept Uttar Pradesh—the state with the largest share of seats in Parliament.

In the midst of all this, the slew of genuinely progressive legislation which the Congress-led government had pushed through—like the Right to Information Act and the National Rural Employment Guarantee Act, which brought a modicum of real relief to the poorest of the poor—seemed to count for nothing. After ten years out of power at the center, the BJP won a massive single-party majority. Narendra Modi became the prime minister of the world's largest democracy. In an election campaign in which optics was everything, he flew from Ahmedabad to Delhi for his swearing-in on a private jet belonging to the Adani Group.

The victory was so decisive, the celebrations so aggressive, that it seemed the establishment of the Hindu Rashtra was only weeks away.

Modi's ascent to power came at a time when much of the rest of the world was descending into chaos. There was civil war in Afghanistan, Iraq, Libya, Somalia, South Sudan, and Syria. The Arab Spring had happened and un-happened. Islamic State of Iraq and Syria (more commonly known as ISIS or ISIL), the macabre progeny of the War on Terror which makes even the Taliban and Al-Qaida seem like moderates, was on the rise. The European refugee crisis had begun, even if it had not yet peaked. Pakistan was in serious trouble. In contrast, India looked like the warm, cuddly, unruly, Bollywoody, free-market-friendly democracy that *works*. But that was the view from the outside.

As soon as he was sworn in, the new prime minister began to display the kind of paranoia you might expect from a man who knows he has a lot of enemies and who does not trust his own organization. His first move was to disempower and make redundant a faction within the BJP led by Advani, whom he now viewed as a threat. He usurped a great deal of the decision-making in the government, and then set off on a dizzying world tour (which hasn't ended yet), with a few pit stops in India. Modi's personal ambition, his desire to be seen as a global leader, soon began to overshadow the organization that had mentored him, and which does not take kindly to self-aggrandizement. In January 2015, he greeted the visiting US president, Barack Obama, in a suit that cost over a million rupees, with his name woven into the pin stripes: narendradamodardasmodinarendradamodardasmodi. This was clearly a man who was in love with himself—no longer just a worker bee, no longer merely a humble servant. It began to look as though the ladders that had been used to climb into the clouds were being kicked away.

The ModiModi suit was eventually auctioned and bought by an admirer for Rs 4.3 crore (roughly $647,000). Meanwhile, it became the delight of cartoonists and the butt of some seriously raucous humor on social media. A man who had been feared was being laughed at for the first time. A month after his wardrobe malfunction, Modi experienced his first major shock. In the February 2015 Delhi State election, even though he campaigned tirelessly, the fledgling Aam Admi Party won sixty-seven of seventy seats. It was the first election Modi had lost since 2002. Suddenly, the new leader began to look brittle and unsure of himself.

Nevertheless, in the rest of the country, thugs and vigilante assassins, sure of political backing from the people they had brought into power, continued about their bloody business. In February 2015, Govind Pansare, a writer and a prominent member of the Communist Party of India, was shot dead in Kolhapur, in Maharashtra. On August 30, 2015, M. M. Kalburgi, a well-known Kannada rationalist, was assassinated outside his home in Dharwad, in Karnataka. Both men had been threatened several times by extremist right-wing Hindu organizations and told to stop their writing.

In September 2015, a mob gathered outside the home of a Muslim family in Dadri, a village near Delhi, claiming that they had been eating beef (a violation of the ban on cow slaughter that had been imposed in Uttar Pradesh as well as in several other states). The family denied it. The mob refused to believe them. Mohammad Akhlaq was pulled out of his home and bludgeoned to death. The thugs of the new order were unapologetic. After the murder, when the Sangh Parivar's apparatchiks spoke to the press about "illegal slaughter," they meant the imaginary cow. When they talked about "taking evidence for forensic examination," they meant the food in the family's fridge, not the body of the lynched man. The meat taken from Akhlaq's house turned out not to be beef after all. But so what?

For days after that, the Twitter-loving prime minister said nothing. Under pressure, he issued a weak, watery admonishment. Since then, similar rumors have led to others being beaten to within an inch of their lives, even hanged. With their tormentors assured of complete impunity, Muslims now know that even a minor skirmish can ignite a full-scale massacre. A whole population is expected to hunch its shoulders and live in fear. And that, as we know, is not a feasible proposition. We are talking about approximately 170 million people.

Then, quite suddenly, just when hope was failing, something extraordinary began to happen. Despite, or perhaps *because* of, the fact that the BJP's massive majority in Parliament had reduced the opposition to a rump, a new kind of resistance made itself known. Ordinary people began to show discomfort with what was going on. That feeling soon hardened into a stubborn resilience. In protest against the lynching of Akhlaq, and the murders of Kalburgi and Pansare, as well as that of the rationalist and author Narendra Dabholkar, murdered in Pune in 2013, one by one, several well-known writers and filmmakers began to return various national-awards they had received. By the end of 2015, dozens of them had done so. The returning of awards—which came to be known as *award-wapsi*, an ironic reference to *ghar wapsi*—was an unplanned, spontaneous, and yet deeply political gesture by artists and intellectuals who did not belong to any particular group or subscribe to any particular ideology, or even agree with each other about most things. It was powerful and unprecedented, and probably has no historical parallel. It was politics plucked out of thin air.

Award-wapsi was widely reported by the international press. Precisely because it was spontaneous, and could not be painted into a corner as any sort of conspiracy, it enraged the government. If this was not enough, around the same time, in November 2015, the BJP suffered another massive electoral defeat, this time in the state of Bihar, at the hands of two wily, old-school politicians—Nitish Kumar and Lalu Prasad Yadav. Lalu is a doughty foe of the Sangh Parivar, and, way back in 1990, he was one of the few politicians to show some steel and arrest Advani when the *rath yatra* passed through Bihar. Losing the Bihar election was a personal as well as political humiliation for Modi, who had spent weeks campaigning there. The BJP was quick to suggest some sort of collusion between its opponents and "anti-national" intellectuals.

In a party that can mass-produce trolls but finds it hard to produce a single real thinker, this humiliating setback sharpened its instinctive hostility towards intellectual activity. It was never just dissent that our current rulers wished to crush. It was thought—intelligence—itself. Not surprisingly, the prime targets in the attack on our collective IQ have been some of India's best universities.

The first signs of trouble came when, in May 2015, the administration of the Indian Institute of Technology in Chennai "de-recognized" a student organization called the Ambedkar-Periyar Study Circle (APSC). Its members are Dalit Ambedkarites, who have a sharp critique of Hindutva politics but also of neoliberal economics, and of the rapid corporatization and privatization that is putting higher education out of the reach of the poor. The order banning the APSC accused it of trying to "de-align" Dalit and Adivasi students, to "make them protest against the . . . Central government" and create hatred against the "Prime Minister and Hindus."[4] Why should a tiny student organization with only a couple of dozen members have been seen as such a threat? Because by making connections between caste, capitalism, and communalism, the APSC was straying into forbidden territory—the sort of territory into which the South African anti-apartheid activist Steve Biko and the US civil rights leader Martin Luther King Jr. had strayed, and paid for with their lives. The de-recognition led to public protests and was quickly rescinded, although the APSC continues to be harassed and its activity remains seriously impeded.

The next confrontation came at India's best-known film school, the Film and Television Institute of India (FTII) in Pune, where BJP and RSS cronies were appointed to the institute's governing council. Among these "persons of eminence," one had until recently been the state president of the Akhil Bharatiya Vidyarthi Parishad (ABVP), the student wing of the RSS. Another was a filmmaker who had made a documentary called *Narendra Modi: A Tale of Extraordinary Leadership*. An actor by the name of Gajendra Chauhan was appointed the council's chairman. His credential for the post, apart from his loyalty to the BJP, was his less-than-mediocre performance as Yudhishthira in a television version of the Mahabharata. (Of the rest of his acting career, the less said the better. You can find him on YouTube.)

The students went on strike, demanding to know on what basis a chairman with no qualifications for the job could be foisted on them. They demanded that Chauhan be removed from his post. Their real fear was that, by stacking the governing council with its cohorts, the government was setting up a coup, preparing (for the nth time) to privatize the FTII and turn it into yet another institution exclusively for the rich and privileged.

The strike lasted for 140 days. The students were attacked by off-campus Hindutva activists, but were supported by trade unions, civil-society groups, filmmakers, artists, intellectuals, and fellow students from across the country. The government refused to back down. The strike was eventually called off, but the unrest just moved to a bigger arena.

For several years now, the University of Hyderabad (UOH) has been a charged place, particularly around Dalit politics. Among the many student groups active on the campus is the Ambedkar Students Association (ASA). As a formation of Ambedkarites, like the APSC in Chennai, the ASA was asking some profound and disturbing questions. For obvious reasons, the ASA's main antagonist on campus was the ABVP, which is emerging as the eyes and ears of the RSS, and its agent provocateur, on almost every campus in the country. When, in August, the ASA, quoting Ambedkar's views on capital punishment, protested the hanging of Yakub Memon—convicted for the 1993 serial blasts in Mumbai that followed the Shiv Sena–led pogrom against Muslims—the ABVP branded them "anti-national." Following a head-on confrontation between the two groups over the documentary film *Muzaffarnagar Baqi Hain* (Muzaffarnagar Is Still Standing), which the ASA wanted to screen on campus, five students—all Dalits, and all members of the ASA—were suspended and asked to vacate the hostel. Young Dalits reaching out in solidarity to the Muslim community was not something the Sangh Parivar was going to allow if it could help it.

These were first-generation students, whose parents had toiled all their lives to scrape together enough money to get their children an education. It's hard for middle-class people who take the education of their children for granted to imagine what it means to have such painstakingly cultivated hope so callously snuffed out.

One of the five expelled students was Rohith Vemula, a PhD scholar. He was the son of a poor single mother, and had no means of supporting himself without his scholarship. Driven to despair, on January 17, 2016, he hanged himself. He left behind a suicide note of such extraordinary power and poignancy that—like a piece of great literature should—his words ignited a tinderbox of accumulated fury. Rohith wrote,

> I always wanted to be a writer. A writer of science, like Carl Sagan.
> I loved Science, Stars, Nature, but then I loved people without knowing that people have long since divorced from nature. Our feelings are second handed. Our love is constructed. Our beliefs colored.

Our originality valid through artificial art. It has become truly difficult to love without getting hurt.

The value of a man was reduced to his immediate identity and
nearest possibility. To a vote. To a number. To a thing. Never was a
man treated as a mind. As a glorious thing made up of star dust. In
every field, in studies, in streets, in politics, and in dying and living.

I am writing this kind of letter for the first time. My first time
of a final letter. Forgive me if I fail to make sense.

Maybe I was wrong, all the while, in understanding [the] world.
In understanding love, pain, life, death. . . . My birth is my fatal accident. I can never recover from my childhood loneliness. The unap-
preciated child from my past.[5]

Imagine this. We live in a culture that shunned a man like Rohith Vemu
la and treated him as an Untouchable. A culture that shut him down and
made a mind like his extinguish itself. Rohith was a Dalit, an Ambedkarite, a Marxist (who was disillusioned by the Indian Left), a student of
science, an aspiring writer, and a seasoned political activist. But beyond
all these identities, he was, like all of us, a unique human being, with
a unique set of joys and sorrows. We might never know what that last
secret sadness was that made him take his life. Perhaps that's just as well.
We must make do with his farewell letter.

The things that make it revolutionary might not be immediately
obvious. Despite all that was done to him, it contains sorrow but not
victimhood. Though everything we know about him tells us that he was
ferocious about his identity and his politics, he refuses to box himself
in and define himself by the tags that others have given him. Despite
bearing the weight of an oppression and cultural conditioning that is
centuries old, Rohith gives himself—wrests for himself—the right to be
magnificent, to dream of being stardust, of being loved as an equal, as all
men and women ought to be.

Rohith was only the latest of the many Dalit students who end their
lives every year. His story resonated with thousands of Dalits in universities across the country—students who had been traumatized by the medieval horrors of the caste system, and the segregation, discrimination,
and injustice that follow them into the most modern university campuses, into India's premier medical and engineering colleges, into their

hostels, canteens, and lecture rooms. (About half of all Dalit students drop out of school before they matriculate. Under 3 percent of the Dalit population are graduates.) They saw Rohith Vemula's suicide for what it was—a form of institutionalized murder. His suicide—and, it has to be said, the power of his prose—made people stop in their tracks and think and rage about the criminal arrangement known as the caste system, that ancient engine that continues to run modern Indian society.

The fury over Vemula's suicide was, and is, an insurrectionary moment for a thus-far marginalized, radical political vision. It saw Ambedkarites, Ambedkarite Marxists, a coalition of Left parties and social movements march together. Alert to the fact that if this configuration was allowed to consolidate it could grow into a serious threat, the BJP moved to defuse it. Its clumsy, outrageous response—claiming that Rohith Vemula was not a Dalit—backfired badly, and pushed the party into what looked like (and could still turn out to be) a tailspin.

Attention had to be diverted. Another crisis was urgently required. The gunsights swung around. The target had been marked a while ago.

Jawaharlal Nehru University (JNU), long known to be a "bastion of the Left," was the focus of a front-page story in the November 2015 issue of *Panchajanya*, the RSS's weekly paper. It described JNU as a den of Naxalites, a "huge anti-national block which has the aim of disintegrating India." Naxalites had been a long-standing problem for the Sangh Parivar—Enemy Number Three in its written doctrine. But now, evidently, it had another, more worrying enemy, too.

Over the last few years, the student demography in JNU has changed dramatically. From being in a small minority, students from disadvantaged backgrounds—Dalits, Adivasis, and the many castes and sub-castes that come under the capacious category known as Other Backward Castes (OBC), formerly called Shudras—now make up almost half the student body. This has radically changed campus politics. What troubles the Parivar more than the presence of the Left on the JNU campus, perhaps, are the rising voices of this section of students. They are, for the most part, followers of Ambedkar, of the Adivasi hero Birsa Munda, who fought the British and died in prison in 1900, and of the radical thinker and reformer Jotirao Phule, who was a Shudra and called himself a *mali*, a gardener. Phule renounced, in fact denounced, Hinduism—most trenchantly in his famous book *Gulamgiri* (Slavery), published in 1873. In much of his writing and poetry, Phule deconstructs Hindu myths to show how they are really stories grounded in history, and how they glorify the idea of an Aryan conquest of an indigenous, Dravidian culture. Phule writes of how Dravidians were demonized and turned into *asuras*, while the conquering Aryans were exalted and conferred divinity. In effect, he frames Hinduism as a colonial narrative.

In 2012, an organization of Dalit and OBC students in JNU began to observe what it calls Mahishasur Martyrdom Day. Mahishasur, Hindus believe, is a mythical half-human, half-demon entity whom the goddess Durga vanquished in battle—a victory that is celebrated every year during Durga Puja. These young intellectuals said that Mahishasur was actually a Dravidian king, beloved of the Asur, Santhal, Gond, and Bhil tribes in West Bengal and Jharkhand. The students declared that they would mourn the day Mahishasur was martyred, not celebrate it. Another group, that called itself the "New Materialists," began to hold a "free food festival" on Mahishasur Martyrdom Day, at which it served beef and pork, saying these were the traditional foods of the oppressed castes and tribes of India.

OBCs make up the majority of India's population and are vitally important to every major political party. It is for this reason that Modi, in his 2014 election campaign, went out of his way to foreground the fact that he was an OBC. (Most people think of "Modi" as a surname associated with the Banias.) OBCs have traditionally been used by the dominant castes as henchmen, to hold the line against Dalits (just as Dalits have been used as foot soldiers in attacks on Muslims, and Adivasis are pitted against Dalits—as they were in Kandhamal in 2008.) These signs of a section of OBCs breaking rank with Hinduism set off the RSS's extremely alert early-warning system.

If this were not trouble enough, a tentative conversation (or perhaps just an argument that was prelude to a conversation) had started between some young communists—who seemed to have begun to understand the past errors of India's major communist parties—and the followers of Birsa Munda, Ambedkar, and Phule. These groups have a vexed history, and had every reason to be wary of each other. As long as each of these loose constituencies remained hostile to the others, they did not constitute a real threat to the Sangh Parivar.

The RSS recognized that if what was going on in JNU was not stopped, it could one day pose an intellectual and existential threat to the fundamental principles and politics of Hindutva. Why so? Because such an alliance proposes, even if only conceptually, the possibility of a counter-mobilization, a sort of reverse engineering of the Hindutva project. It envisions an altogether different coalition of castes, one that is constituted from the ground up, instead of organized and administered from the top down: Dalit-Bahujanism instead of Brahminism. A powerful movement, contemporary and yet rooted in India's unique social and cultural context, that has people like Ambedkar, Jotiba Phule, Savitribai Phule, Periyar, Ayyankali, Birsa Munda, Bhagat Singh, Marx, and Lenin as the stars in its constellation. A movement that challenges patriarchy, capitalism, and imperialism, that dreams of a casteless, classless society, whose poets would be the poets of the people, and would include Kabir, Tukaram, Ravidas, Pash, Gaddar, Lal Singh Dil, and Faiz. A movement of Adivasi-Dalit-Bahujans in the sense championed by the Dalit Panthers (who, in the 1970s, took "Dalit" to connote "members of the scheduled castes and tribes, neo-Buddhists, the working people, the landless and poor peasants, women and all those who are being exploited politically, economically and in the name of religion").[6] A movement whose comrades would include those from the privileged castes who no longer want to claim their privileges. A movement spiritually generous enough to embrace all those who believe in justice, whatever their creed or religion.

Small wonder, then, that the *Panchajanya* story went on to say that JNU was an institution where "innocent Hindu youth are lured after being fed wrong facts about the Varna system, which is an integral part of Hindu society." It wasn't really the "disintegrating" of India that the RSS was worried about. It was the disintegration of Hindutva. And not by a new political party, but by a new way of thinking. Had all this hinged on a formal political alliance, its leaders could have been killed or jailed. Or simply bought out, like any number of *swamis, sufis, maulanas,* and other charlatans have been. But what do you do with an idea that has begun to drift around like smoke?

You try and snuff it out at its source.

The battle lines could not have been marked more clearly. It was to be a battle between those who dream of equality and those who believe in institutionalizing inequality. Rohith Vemula's suicide made the conversation that had begun in JNU more important, more urgent, and very real. And it probably brought forward the date of an attack that was already in the cards.

The ambush was built around an obstinate old ghost that refuses to go away. The harder they try to exorcise it, the more stubbornly it persists with its haunting.

The third anniversary of the hanging of Mohammed Afzal Guru fell on February 9, 2016. Although Afzal was not accused of direct involvement in the 2001 attack on the Indian Parliament, he was convicted by the Delhi High Court and given three life sentences and a double death sentence for being part of the conspiracy. In August 2005, the Supreme Court upheld this judgment and famously said,

> As is the case with most conspiracies, there is and could be no direct evidence amounting to criminal conspiracy. . . . The incident which resulted in heavy casualties had shaken the entire nation, and the collective conscience of the society will only be satisfied if capital punishment is awarded to the offender.[7]

The controversy over the Parliament attack, over the Supreme Court judgment, and over Afzal's sudden, secret execution is by no means a new one. Several books and essays by scholars, journalists, lawyers, and writers (including me) have been published on the subject. Some of us believe that there are grave questions about the attack that remain unanswered, and that Afzal was framed and did not receive a fair trial. Others believe that the manner of his execution was a miscarriage of justice.

After the Supreme Court judgment, Afzal remained in solitary confinement in Tihar Jail for several years. The BJP, which was out of power at the center during those years, made frequent and aggressive demands that he be pulled out of the queue of those awaiting execution and hanged. The issue became a central theme in its election campaigns. Its slogan was: *Desh abhi sharminda hai, Afzal abhi bhi zinda hai.* (The country hangs its head in shame because Afzal is still alive.)

As the 2014 general election approached, the Congress-led government in power at the center—weakened by a series of corruption scandals and terrified of being outflanked by the BJP in this contest of competitive nationalism, one that the Congress is doomed to lose—pulled Afzal out of his cell one morning and hurriedly hanged him. His family was not even informed, let alone permitted a last visit. For fear that his grave would become a monument and a political rallying point for the struggle in Kashmir, he was buried inside Tihar Jail, next to Maqbool Butt, the Kashmiri separatist hero who was hanged in 1984. (P. Chidambaram, who served the Congress-led government as home minister from 2008 to 2012, now says that Afzal's case was "perhaps not correctly decided." When I was in Class IV, we had a saying: Sorry doesn't make a dead man alive.)

Every year since then, on the anniversary of Afzal Guru's hanging, the Kashmir valley shuts down in protest. Leave alone the Kashmiri nationalists, even the mainstream, pro-India Peoples Democratic Party, currently the BJP's coalition partner in the state of Jammu and Kashmir, continues to demand that Afzal's mortal remains be returned to his family for a proper burial.

A few days prior to the third anniversary of his death, notices appeared on the JNU campus inviting students to a cultural evening "against the Brahmanical 'collective conscience,' against the judicial killing of Afzal Guru and Maqbool Butt" and "in solidarity with the struggle of Kashmiri people for their democratic right to self-determination."

It was not the first time JNU students had met to discuss these issues. Only this time, the February 9 anniversary fell three weeks after Rohith Vemula's suicide. The atmosphere was politically charged. Once again, the ABVP was the cat's paw. It complained to the university authorities, then invited the Delhi police to intervene in what it said was "anti-national activity." A camera crew from Zee TV was on hand to record the event. The first batch of footage in that Zee broadcast showed two groups of students confronting each other on the JNU campus, shouting slogans. In response to the ABVP's *Bharat Mata ki jai!* (Victory to Mother India!), another group of students, most of them Kashmiris, some of them wearing masks, began to chant what Kashmiris chant every day at every street-corner protest and at every militant's funeral in Kashmir:

Hum kya chahatey?
Azadi!
Chheen ke lengey—
Azadi!
What do we want?
Freedom!
We will snatch it—
Freedom!

There were also some less familiar slogans:

Bandook ke dum pe!
Azadi!
At gunpoint if need be!
Freedom!

Kashmir ki azadi tak, Bharat ki barbaadi tak,
Jung ladengey! Jung ladengey!
Until freedom comes to Kashmir, until destruction comes to India
War will be waged! War will be waged!

And:

Pakistan Zindabad!
Long live Pakistan!

From the Zee TV footage, it wasn't clear who the students actually chanting the slogans were. Sure, it riled viewers, but winding people up about Kashmir or getting them to rail at unknown students who looked and sounded like Kashmiris was not the point, and would have served no purpose. Especially not when the BJP's negotiations with the Peoples Democratic Party about forming a new government in Jammu and Kashmir had run into rough weather. (That problem has subsequently been resolved.) In the JNU ambush, Kashmir was just the trigger-wire. The real goal was (and is) to tarnish the reputation of JNU, in order to eventually shut it down.

It was an easy problem to solve. The soundtrack of the confrontation was grafted onto the video of another meeting that took place two days later, this one addressed by Kanhaiya Kumar, president of the JNU

Students' Union. Kanhaiya belongs to the All India Students Federation, the student wing of the Communist Party of India. At the meeting he addressed, the refrain of *"Azadi!"* was the same, only the slogans raised were completely different. They demanded *azadi* from poverty, from caste, from capitalism, from the Manusmriti, from Brahminism. It was a whole other ball of wax.

The doctored video was broadcast to millions by major news channels, including Zee TV, Times Now, and News X. It was shameful, unprofessional, and possibly criminal. The broadcast set off a frenzy. First Kanhaiya Kumar, and then, two weeks later, two other students accused of organizing the Afzal Guru meeting, Umar Khalid and Anirban Bhattacharya, formerly members of the left-wing Democratic Students Union, were arrested and charged with sedition. Posters went up across Delhi putting a price on these students' heads. One even offered a cash reward for Kanhaiya Kumar's tongue.

The Kashmiri students who were actually seen raising slogans in the Zee TV footage remained unidentified. But they were only doing what thousands of people do every day in Kashmir. Can there be separate standards for sloganeering in Delhi and Srinagar? Perhaps you could say yes, if you argue, as many Kashmiris do, that all of Kashmir is a giant prison, and you can't arrest the already incarcerated. In any case, did those students' slogans really deliver a mortal blow to this mighty, nuclear-powered Hindu nation?

Matters continued to escalate in ever more ludicrous ways. Based on a joke on a parody Twitter account ("Hafeez Muhamad Saeed"), the home minister Rajnath Singh announced that the protest at JNU was backed by Hafiz Saeed, the head of Lashkar-e-Taiba and India's equivalent of Osama bin Laden. Television channels began to suggest that Umar Khalid, a self-declared Marxist-Leninist, was a Jaish-e-Mohammad terrorist. (The hard evidence this time was that his name was Umar.)

Smriti Irani, the unstoppable minister of human resource development, who is in charge of higher education, said the nation would not tolerate an insult to Mother India. The saffron-robed Yogi Adityanath, a BJP Member of Parliament (MP) from Gorakhpur, said that "JNU has become a blot on education," and that it "should be closed down in the interest of the nation." Another self-styled man of god, the BJP MP Sakshi Maharaj, also clad in saffron, called them "traitors" and said they "should be hanged instead of being lodged in jail for life or they should be killed by police bullet."[8] Gyandev Ahuja, a BJP member of the Rajasthan legislative assembly and an empiricist extraordinaire, informed the world, "More than 10,000 butts of cigarettes and 4,000 pieces of *beedis* are found daily in the JNU campus. Fifty thousand big and small pieces of bones are left by those eating non-vegetarian food. They gorge on meat . . . these anti-nationals. Two thousand wrappers of chips and *namkeen* are found, as also 3,000 used condoms—the misdeeds they commit with our sisters and daughters there. And 500 used contraceptive injections are also found." In other words, JNU students were meat-eating, chip-crunching, cigarette-smoking, beer-swilling, sex-obsessed anti-nationals. (Does that sound so terrible?)

The prime minister said nothing.

The students of JNU and Hyderabad Central University, on the other hand, had plenty to say. The protests on those campuses spread to the streets. And then to universities in other parts of the country. In Delhi, on the day Kanhaiya Kumar was to be produced before a magistrate, the war zone shifted to the courts. On two days in a row, sheltering under an oversized national flag, a group of lawyers who boasted openly of their affiliation to the BJP beat up students, professors, journalists, and finally Kanhaiya Kumar himself inside a courthouse. They threatened and abused a committee of senior lawyers that the Supreme Court had urgently constituted to look into the matter. The police stood by and watched. The Delhi police chief called it a minor scuffle. The lawyers gloated to the press about how they "thrashed" Kanhaiya and forced him to say "Bharat Mata ki jai." For a few days it looked as though every last institution in the country was helpless in the face of this insane attack.

The RSS has now declared that anybody who refuses to say "Bharat Mata ki jai!" is an anti-national. The yoga and health-food tycoon Baba Ramdev announced that, were it not illegal, he would behead anybody who refused to say it.

What would these people have done to Ambedkar? In 1931, when questioned by Gandhi about his sharp critique of the Congress—which was seen as a critique of the party's struggle for an independent homeland—Ambedkar said, "Gandhiji, I have no homeland. No Untouchable worth the name would be proud of this land." Would they have charged him with sedition? (On the other hand, garlanding portraits of Ambedkar, as the Sangh Parivar has done, and suggesting that he—the man who called Hinduism "a veritable chamber of horrors"—is one of the founding fathers of the Hindu Rashtra is probably much worse.)

The other tactic the BJP and its media partners have used to silence people is an absurd false binary—the Brave Soldiers versus the Evil Anti-nationals. In February, just when the JNU crisis was at its peak, an avalanche on the Siachen Glacier killed ten soldiers, whose bodies were flown down for military funerals. For days and nights, screeching television anchors and their studio guests inserted their own words into the mouths of the dead men and grafted their tinpot ideologies onto lifeless bodies that couldn't talk back. Of course they neglected to mention that most Indian soldiers are poor people looking for a means of earning a living. (You don't hear the patriotic rich asking for the draft, so that they and their children are forced to serve as ordinary soldiers.)

They also forgot to tell their viewers that soldiers are not just deployed on the Siachen Glacier or on the borders of India. That there has not been a single day since Independence in 1947 when the Indian Army and other security forces have not been deployed *within* India's borders against what are meant to be their "own" people—in Kashmir, Nagaland, Manipur, Mizoram, Assam, Junagadh, Hyderabad, Goa, Punjab, Telangana, West Bengal, and now Chhattisgarh, Orissa, and Jharkhand.

Tens of thousands of people have lost their lives in conflicts in these places. An even greater number have been brutally tortured, leaving many of them crippled for life. There have been documented cases of mass rape in Kashmir in which the accused have been protected by the Armed Forces Special Powers Act, as though rape is a necessary and unavoidable part of battle.[9] The aggressive insistence on unquestioning soldier-worship, even by self-professed "liberals," is a sick, dangerous game that's been dreamt up by a cynical oligarchy. It doesn't help either soldiers or civilians. And if you take a hard look at the list of places within India's current borders in which its security forces have been deployed, an extraordinary fact emerges—the populations in those places are mostly Muslim, Christian, Adivasi, Sikh, and Dalit. What we are being asked to salute obediently and unthinkingly is a reflexively dominant-caste Hindu state that nails together its territory with military might.

What if some of us dream instead of creating a society to which people *long* to belong? What if some of us dream of living in a society that people of which are not *forced* to be part? What if some of us don't have colonialist, imperialist dreams? What if some of us dream instead of justice? Is it a criminal offense?

So what is this new bout of flag-waving and chest-thumping all about, really? What is it trying to hide? The usual stuff: A tanking economy and an abject betrayal of the election promises the BJP made to gullible people, as well as to its corporate sponsors. During his election campaign, Modi burned his candle at both ends. He vulgarly promised poor villagers that Rs 15 lakh would magically appear in their bank accounts when he came to power. He was going to bring home the illegal billions that rich Indians had parked in offshore tax havens and distribute it to the poor. How much of that illegal money was brought back? Not a lot. How much was redistributed to the poor? Approximately zero point zero zero, whatever that is in rupees. Meanwhile, corporations were eagerly looking forward to a new Land Acquisition Act that would make it easier for businessmen to acquire villagers' land. That legislation did not make it past the upper house. In the countryside, the crisis in agriculture has deepened. While big business has had tens of thousands of crore of rupees worth of loans written off, tens of thousands of small farmers trapped in a cycle of debt—that will never be written off—continue to kill themselves. In 2015, in the state of Maharashtra alone, more than 3,200 farmers committed suicide. Their suicides too are a form of institutionalized murder, just as Rohith Vemula's was.

What the new government has to offer in lieu of its wild election promises is the kind of deal that is usually available only on the Saffron stock exchange: Trade in your hopes for a decent livelihood and buy into an exciting life of perpetual hysteria. A life in which you are free to hate your neighbor, and if things get really bad, and if you really want to, you can get together with friends and even beat her or him to death.

The manufactured crisis in JNU has also, extremely successfully, turned our attention away from a terrible tragedy that has befallen some of the most vulnerable people in this country. The war for minerals in Bastar, Chhattisgarh, is gearing up again. Operation Green Hunt—the previous government's attempt at clearing the forest of its troublesome inhabitants in order to hand it over to mining and infrastructure companies—was largely unsuccessful. Many of the hundreds of memorandums of understanding that the government signed with private companies regarding this territory have not been actualized. Bastar's people, among the poorest in the world, have, for years, stopped the richest corporations in their tracks. Now, in preparation for the as-yet-unnamed Operation Green Hunt II, thousands of Adivasis are in jail once again, most of them accused of being Maoists. The forest is being cleared of all witnesses—journalists, activists, lawyers, and academics. Anybody who muddies the tidy delineation of the state-versus–"Maoist terrorists" paradigm is in a great deal of danger. The extraordinary Adivasi schoolteacher and activist Soni Sori, who was imprisoned in 2011 but went straight back to her organizing work after being released in 2014, was recently attacked and had her face smeared with a substance that burned her skin. She has since gone back to work in Bastar once again. With a burned face. The Jagdalpur Legal Aid Group, a tiny team of women lawyers that offered legal aid to incarcerated Adivasis, and Malini Subramaniam, whose series of investigative reports from Bastar were a source of embarrassment to the police, have been evicted and forced to leave. Lingaram Kodopi, Bastar's first Adivasi journalist, who was horribly tortured and imprisoned for three years, is being threatened, and has despairingly announced that he will kill himself if the intimidation does not stop. (Four other local journalists have been arrested on specious charges, including for posting comments against the police on WhatsApp.) Bela Bhatia, a researcher, has had the village she lives in visited by mobs shouting slogans against her and threatening her landlords. Paramilitary troops and vigilante militias, confident of impunity, have once again begun to storm villages and terrorize people, forcing them to abandon their homes and flee into the forest as they did in the time of Operation Green Hunt I. Horrific accounts of rape, molestation, looting, and robbery are trickling in. The Indian Air Force has begun "practicing" air-to-ground firing from helicopters.

Anybody who criticizes the corporate takeover of Adivasi land is called an anti-national "sympathizer" of the banned Maoists. Sympathy is a crime too. In television studios, guests who try to bring a semblance of intelligence into the debate are shouted down and compelled to demonstrate their loyalty to the nation. This is a war against people who have barely enough to eat one square meal a day. What particular brand of nationalism does this come under? What exactly are we supposed to be proud of?

Our lumpen nationalists don't seem to understand that the more they insist on this hollow sloganeering, the more they force people to say, "Bharat Mata ki jai!" and to declare that "Kashmir is an integral part of India," the less sure of themselves they sound. The nationalism that is being rammed down our throats is more about hating another country—Pakistan—than loving our own. It's more about securing territory than loving the land and its people. Paradoxically, those who are branded anti-national are the ones who speak about the deaths of rivers and the desecration of forests. They are the ones who worry about the poisoning of the land and the falling of water tables. The "nationalists," on the other hand, go about speaking of mining, damming, clear-cutting, blasting, and selling. In their rulebook, hawking minerals to multinational companies is patriotic activity. They have privatized the flag and wrested the microphone.

The three JNU students who were arrested are all out on interim bail. In Kanhaiya Kumar's case, the bail order by a High Court judge caused more apprehension than relief: "Whenever some infection is spread in a limb, effort is made to cure the same by giving antibiotics orally and if that does not work, by following second line of treatment. Sometimes it may require surgical intervention also. However, if the infection results in infecting the limb to the extent that it becomes gangrene, amputation is the only treatment."[10] *Amputation?* What could she mean?

As soon as he was released, Kanhaiya appeared on the JNU campus and gave his now-famous speech to a crowd of thousands of students. It doesn't matter whether or not you agree with every single thing he said. I didn't. But it's the spirit with which he said it that was so enchanting. It dissipated the pall of fear and gloom that had dropped on us like a fog. Overnight, Kanhaiya *and* his cheeky audience became beloved of millions. The same thing happened with the other two students, Umar Khalid and Anirban Bhattacharya. Now, people from all over the world have heard the slogan the BJP wanted to silence: *"Jai Bhim! Lal salam!"* (Salute Bhimrao Ambedkar! Red salute!)

And with that call, the spirit of Rohith Vemula and the spirit of JNU have come together in solidarity. It's a fragile, tenuous coming together that will most likely—if it hasn't already—come to an unhappy end, exhausted by mainstream political parties, NGOs, and its own inherent contradictions. Obviously, neither the "Left" nor the "Ambedkarites" nor the "OBCs" are remotely homogenous categories in themselves. However, even broadly speaking, the present Left, is for the most part, doctrinally opaque to caste and, by *unseeing* it, perpetuates it. (The outstanding exception to this, it must be said, are the writings of the late Anuradha Gandhy.) This has meant that many Dalits and OBCs who do lean towards the Left have had bitter experiences and are now determined to isolate themselves, thereby inadvertently deepening caste divisions and strengthening a system that sustains itself by precluding all forms of solidarity.

All these old wounds will act up, we'll tear each other to shreds, arguments and accusations will fly around in maddening ways. But even after this moment has passed, the radical ideas that have emerged from this confrontation with the agents of Hindutva are unlikely ever to go away. They will stay around, and will continue to be built upon. They must, because they are our only hope.

Already the real meanings, the real politics behind the refrain of *"Azadi,"* are being debated. Did Kanhaiya pinch the slogan from the Kashmiris? He did. (And where did the Kashmiris get it? From the feminists or the French Revolution, maybe.) Is the slogan being diluted? Most definitely, as far as those who chant it in Kashmir are concerned. Is it being deepened? Yes, that too. Because fighting for *azadi* from patriarchy, from capitalism, and from *Brahminvaad* is as radical as any struggle for national self-determination.

Perhaps while we debate the true, deep meanings of freedom, those who have been so shocked by what is happening in the mainland over the last few months will be moved to ask themselves why, when far worse things happen in other places, it leaves them so untroubled. Why is it all right to for us to ask for *azadi* in our university campuses while the daily lives of ordinary people in Kashmir, Nagaland, and Manipur are overseen by the army and their traffic jams managed by uniformed men waving AK-47s? Why is it easy for most Indians to accept the killing of 112 young people on the streets of Kashmir in the course of a single summer? Why do we care so much about Kanhaiya Kumar and Rohith Vemula, but so little about students like Shaista Hameed and Danish Farooq, who were shot dead in Kashmir the day before the smear campaign against JNU was launched? *Azadi* is an immense word, and a beautiful one too. We need to wrap our minds around it, not just play with it. This is not to suggest some sort of high-mindedness in which we all fight each other's battles side by side and feel each other's pain with equal intensity. Only to say that if we do not acknowledge each other's yearning for *azadi*, if we do not acknowledge injustice when it is looking us straight in the eye, we will all go down together in the quicksand of moral turpitude.

The end result of the BJP's labors is that students, intellectuals, and even sections of the mainstream media have seen how we are being torn apart by its manifesto of hate. Little by little, people have begun to stand up to it. Afzal's ghost has begun to travel to other university campuses.

As often happens after episodes like this, everybody who has been involved can, and usually does, claim victory. The BJP's assessment seems to be that the polarization of the electorate into "nationalists" and "anti-nationals" has been successful, and has brought it substantial political gain. Far from showing signs of contrition, it has moved to turn all the knobs to high.

Kanhaiya, Umar, and Anirban's lives are in real danger from rogue assassins seeking approbation from the Sangh Parivar's high command. Thirty-five students of the FTII (one in every five) have had criminal cases filed against them. They're out on bail, but are required to report regularly to the police. Appa Rao Podile, the much-hated vice chancellor of UOH who went on leave in January and had a case filed against him, laying responsibility at his door for the circumstances that led to Rohith Vemula's suicide, has reappeared on the campus, enraging students. When they protested, police invaded the campus, brutally beat them, arrested twenty-five students and two faculty members, and held them for days. The campus is cordoned off by police—ironically the police of the Telangana State that so many of the students on this same campus fought so long and so hard to create. The arrested UOH students too have serious cases filed against them now. They need lawyers, and money to pay them with. Even if they are eventually acquitted, their lives can be destroyed by the sheer harassment involved.

It isn't just students. All over the country, lawyers, activists, writers, and filmmakers—anybody who criticizes the government—is being arrested, imprisoned, or entangled in spurious legal cases. We can expect serious trouble, all sorts of trouble, as we head toward state elections—in particular the 2017 contest in Uttar Pradesh—and the general election in 2019. We must anticipate false-flag terrorist strikes, and perhaps even what is being optimistically called a "limited war" with Pakistan. At a public meeting in Agra, on February 29, Muslims were warned of a "final battle." A fired-up, five-thousand-strong crowd chanted: *"Jis Hindu ka khoon na khaule, khoon nahin woh pani hai."* (Any Hindu whose blood isn't boiling has water in the veins, not blood.) Regardless of who wins elections in the years to come, can this sort of venom be counteracted once it has entered the bloodstream? Can any society mend itself after having its fabric slashed and rent apart in this way?

What is happening right now is actually a systematic effort to *create* chaos, an attempt to arrive at a situation in which the civil rights enshrined in the constitution can be suspended. The RSS has never accepted the constitution. It has now, finally, maneuvered itself into a position where it has the power to subvert it. It is waiting for an opportunity. We might well be witnessing preparations for a coup—not a military coup, but a coup nevertheless. It could be only a matter of time before India will officially cease to be a secular, democratic republic. We may find ourselves looking back fondly on the era of doctored videos and parody Twitter handles.

Our forests are full of soldiers and our universities full of police. The University Grants Commission's new guidelines for higher educational institutions suggests that campuses have high boundary walls topped by concertina wire, armed guards at entrances, police stations, biometric tests, and security cameras. Smriti Irani has ordered that all public universities must fly the national flag from 207-foot-high flagpoles for students to "worship." (Who'll get the contracts?) She has also announced plans to rope in the army to instill patriotism in the minds of students.

In Kashmir, the presence of an estimated half a million troops ensures that whatever its people may or may not want today, Kashmir has been made an integral part of India. But now, with soldiers and barbed wire and enforced flag-worshipping in the mainland, it looks more and more as though India is becoming an integral part of Kashmir.

As symbols of countries, flags are powerful objects, worthy of contemplation. But what of those like Rohith Vemula, who have imaginations that predate the idea of countries by hundreds of thousands of years? The earth is 4.5 billion years old. Human beings appeared on it about two hundred thousand years ago. What we call "human civilization" is just a few thousand years old. India as a country with its present borders is less than eighty years old. Clearly, we could do with a little perspective.

Worship a flag? My soul is either too modern or too ancient for that. I'm not sure which.

Maybe both.

Map of India

Siachen

LINE OF CONTROL

Kupwara
Chattisinghpora
Srinagar
Jammu & Kashmir
Jammu

N

PAKISTAN

Punjab

Uttarakhand

CHINA

New Delhi

NEPAL

Pokaran
Jaipur
Uttar Pradesh
Ayodhya

Rajasthan

Bihar

Guwahati
Assam
Nagaland

Manipur

Ahmedabad
Vadodara
Godhra
Madhya Pradesh

Jharkhand
West Bengal
Singur

Mizoram
Tripura

Narmada River

Koel River

Gujarat
Mehndi Kheda
Chhattisgarh
Lalgarh
Kolkata

Umergaon

Orissa
Nandigram

Mumbai
Malegaon

Kandhamal

Maharashtra
Dantewara
Rayagarha
Chilika Lake

Hyderabad

Andhra Pradesh

Karnataka

Mangalore
Bangalore
Chennai

Tamil Nadu

Kerala

SRI LANKA

Map not to scale

Glossary

Adivasis: tribal, but literally original inhabitants of India.

Adivasi Mukti Sangathan: activist group in Madhya Pradesh; literally, Adivasi Liberation Group.

L. K. Advani: former Indian deputy prime minister who has close associations with right-wing Hindu fundamentalist groups in India and led the Rath Yatra in 1990.

Babri Masjid: On December 6, 1992, violent mobs of Hindu fundamentalists converged on the town of Ayodhya and demolished the Babri Masjid, an old Muslim mosque. Initiated by the Bharatiya Janata Party (BJP) leader L. K. Advani, this was the culmination of a nationwide campaign to "arouse the pride" of Hindus. Plans for replacing the mosque with a huge Hindu temple are under way.

Bajrang Dal: militant Hindu fundamentalist organization named after the Hindu god Hanuman; allied with the BJP and the Vishwa Hindu Parishad (VHP), and with them instrumental in the destruction of the Babri Masjid in Ayodhya in 1992.

beedi: a mixture of blended tobacco wrapped in beedi leaves.

Beej Bachao Andolan: a farmers' movement promoting the use of indigenous crops, cropping systems, and agricultural methods.

Bharatiya Janata Party: literally, the Indian People's Party, at present the largest single party of the governing coalition since the elections

of 1998. It espouses a Hindu nationalist ideology, and its support is
concentrated mostly in northern India.

Chhattisgarh Mukti Morcha: a trade union group in the mining areas
of Chhattisgarh (literally, the Chhattisgarh Liberation Front).

Dalit: those who are oppressed or literally "ground down"; the preferred term for those people who used to be called "Untouchables" in India. Gandhi coined the term *harijan* (children of God)
as a euphemism for these castes, but "Dalits" is preferred today by
the more militant among them and has a more explicit political
meaning.

Dandi March: In March 1930, Gandhi and more than seventy other
activists began a twenty-three-day march to the coastal Indian village of Dandi; it was called the "Salt March" because Gandhi called
for the illegal production and purchase of salt by the native population. He called the march, widely considered a major turning point
in the struggle for Independence, "the final struggle of freedom."

dargah: Muslim tomb.

dharna: peaceful protest or sit-in.

EIAs: Environmental Impact Assessments, usually done by private
consultants hired by project authorities for projects such as dams,
mines, and large-scale irrigation projects.

S. A. R. Geelani: teacher of Arabic at Delhi University, implicated
in the conspiracy behind the attack on the Indian Parliament in
December 2002, and sentenced to death. He was acquitted and
released after nearly two years in jail.

goondas: thugs.

Hindutva: ideology seeking to strengthen "Hindu identity" and create
a Hindu state, advocated by the BJP, Shiv Sena, and other commu-
nalist parties.

hydel: hydroelectric power.

ISI: Inter Services Intelligence, the Pakistani intelligence agency.

Jain Hawala case: a scandal involving twenty-four politicians charged
with taking bribes from businessman Surendra Kumar Jain.

jamadarni: a sweeper woman, usually used pejoratively.

Kahars: a caste whose main occupation is fishing.

khadi: hand-spun cotton cloth popularized by Gandhi during the Independence movement as a defiant statement of self-reliance and a badge of membership in the Congress movement. Khadi is still worn today by many politicians and Gandhian workers.

Kevats: a caste whose main occupation is plying boats.

khichdi: a rice and lentil dish.

Kinara Bachao Andolan: activist group working in coastal Gujarat (literally, Movement to Save the Coast).

Koel Karo Sangathan: a movement against a proposed dam on the Koel and Karo Rivers in the state of Bihar.

Kumbh Mela: a Hindu festival in which millions gather to ritually bathe in sacred rivers.

Lal Johar: salutation of the Chhattisgarh Mukti Morcha: literally, Red Salute.

Lord Linlithgow: governor-general of India from April 1936 to April 1943.

LTTE: Liberation Tigers of Tamil Eelam, Sri Lankan Tamil separatist guerrilla group.

Malimath Committee: the Committee on Reforms of the Criminal Justice System, constituted by the government of India in November 2000 and headed by retired justice V. S. Malimath, former chief justice of Kerala and Karnataka.

Mandal Commission: commission constituted by the Janata Party government under the chairmanship of B. P. Mandal in 1977 to look into the issue of reservations for "backward" castes in government jobs and educational institutions. The report was submitted in 1980, and its recommendations led to a huge backlash from upper castes, with violence and agitation across the country.

mandir: temple.

Manusmriti: an ancient code of conduct, attributed to Manu, sometimes viewed as a book of Hindu laws.

masjid: mosque.

Mazdoor Kisan Shakti Sangathan: literally, Organization for the Empowerment of Workers and Farmers, active in the right-to-information campaigns in Rajasthan.

MCC: Maoist Coordination Committee, extreme left-wing armed group, present in many states in India.

Mehndi Kheda: village in the state of Madhya Pradesh, the site of a clash between Adivasis and the police.

Narendra Modi: Chief Minister of Gujarat; presided over the state government when violent riots took more than two thousand Muslim lives in 2002.

Muthanga: wildlife sanctuary in the state of Kerala, the site of a clash between Adivasis and the police.

Naga Sadhu: the naked warrior-ascetics of the Shaiva sect.

Narmada Bachao Andolan: Save the Narmada Movement.

Nimad Malwa Kisan Mazdoor Sangathan: alliance of activist groups working in Madhya Pradesh on issues of water, power, and privatization of resources (literally, the Nimad Malwa Peasants' and Workers' Organization).

Shankar Guha Niyogi: trade union leader of the Chhattisgarh Mukti Morcha, killed in September 1991 by hired assassins.

Parsis: Persian-descended Zoroastrians.

Prasad: Sacred food, is shared by devotees in an act of seeking benediction.

PWG: Peoples' War Group, an extreme left-wing armed group, present in many states in India.

Ram Mandir: see Babri Masjid, above.

Rashtrapati Bhavan: the residence of the president of India, formerly the viceroy's residence.

Rashtriya Swayamsevak Sangh (RSS): literally, the National Self-Help Group; a right-wing militaristic organization with a clearly articulated anti-Muslim stand and a nationalistic notion of Hindutva. The RSS is the ideological backbone of the BJP.

Rath Yatra: literally, the Chariots' Journey, a long road rally led by an ornamental bus dressed up as a chariot, undertaken first in 1990 by L. K. Advani to "mobilize Hindu sentiment" for the building of the Ram Mandir at Ayodhya. It culminated in widespread violence in many parts of northern India.

Sangh Parivar: the group of closely linked right-wing Hindu fundamentalist organizations in India that includes the Bajrang Dal, BJP, RSS, and VHP (literally, family group).

Saraswati shishu mandirs: literally, temples for children, named after

Saraswati, the Hindu goddess of learning.

Satyagraha: literally "life force," was Gandhi's term for civil disobedience. The term is now commonly applied to any movement that confronts its foe—typically, the State—nonviolently.

Savarna Hinduism: that part of caste Hindu society which excludes the Dalits and so-called backward castes.

shakha: an RSS branch (literally) or center. RSS shakhas are training camps or cells.

Shiv Sena: a rabid right-wing regional Hindu chauvinist party in the state of Maharashtra.

shloka: stanzas, or verse in general, that are prayers to the deities.

stupa: a Buddhist religious monument.

swadeshi: nationalist.

Pravin Togadia: former surgeon, rabble-rousing demagogue of the Hindu right wing, synonymous with inflammatory hate speech against Muslims.

Tehelka case: an exposé by the Tehelka website, in which senior Indian politicians, defense officers, and government servants were secretly filmed accepting bribes from journalists posing as arms dealers.

VHP: Vishwa Hindu Parishad, literally the World Hindu Council, self-appointed leaders of the Hindu community and part of the "Sangh" family of Hindu nationalist organizations to which the BJP also belongs. The VHP was in the forefront of the move to destroy the Babri Masjid and build a Ram temple at Ayodhya.

Yatra: (literally, pilgrimage) can be translated as any journey "with purpose."

Part I

1. The End of Imagination

*For marmots and voles and everything else on earth that is threat-
ened and terrorized by the human race*

"The desert shook," the government of India informed us (its people).

"The whole mountain turned white," the government of Pakistan replied.

By afternoon the wind had fallen silent over Pokhran. At 3:45 p.m., the timer detonated the three devices. Around 200 to 300 meters deep in the earth, the heat generated was equivalent to a million degrees centigrade—as hot as temperatures on the sun. Instantly, rocks weighing around a thousand tons, a mini-mountain underground, vaporized . . . shock waves from the blast began to lift a mound of earth the size of a football field by several meters. One scientist on seeing it said, "I can now believe stories of Lord Krishna lifting a hill" (*India Today*).

May 1998. It'll go down in history books, provided of course we have history books to go down in. Provided, of course, we have a future. There's nothing new or original left to be said about nuclear weapons. There can be nothing more humiliating for a writer of fiction to have to do than restate

First published in *Outlook* (India) and *Frontline* magazines, July 27, 1998.

a case that has, over the years, already been made by other people in other parts of the world, and made passionately, eloquently, and knowledgeably.

I am prepared to grovel. To humiliate myself abjectly, because, in the circumstances, silence would be indefensible. So those of you who are willing: let's pick our parts, put on these discarded costumes, and speak our secondhand lines in this sad secondhand play. But let's not forget that the stakes we're playing for are huge. Our fatigue and our shame could mean the end of us. The end of our children and our children's children. Of everything we love. We have to reach within ourselves and find the strength to think. To fight.

Once again we are pitifully behind the times—not just scientifically and technologically (ignore the hollow claims), but more pertinently in our ability to grasp the true nature of nuclear weapons. Our Comprehension of the Horror Department is hopelessly obsolete. Here we are, all of us in India and in Pakistan, discussing the finer points of politics, and foreign policy, behaving for all the world as though our governments have just devised a newer, bigger bomb, a sort of immense hand grenade with which they will annihilate the enemy (each other) and protect us from all harm. How desperately we want to believe that. What wonderful, willing, well-behaved, gullible subjects we have turned out to be. The rest of humanity (yes, yes, I know, I *know*, but let's ignore them for the moment. They forfeited their votes a long time ago), the rest of the rest of humanity may not forgive us, but then the rest of the rest of humanity, depending on who fashions its views, may not know what a tired, dejected heartbroken people we are. Perhaps it doesn't realize how urgently we need a miracle. How deeply we yearn for magic.

If only, if *only*, nuclear war was just another kind of war. If only it was about the usual things—nations and territories, gods and histories. If only those of us who dread it are just worthless moral cowards who are not prepared to die in defense of our beliefs. If only nuclear war was the kind of war in which countries battle countries and men battle men. But it isn't. If there is a nuclear war, our foes will not be China or America or even each other. Our foe will be the earth herself. The very elements—the sky, the air, the land, the wind and water—will all turn against us. Their wrath will be terrible.

Our cities and forests, our fields and villages will burn for days. Rivers will turn to poison. The air will become fire. The wind will spread the flames. When everything there is to burn has burned and the fires die, smoke will rise and shut out the sun. The earth will be enveloped in darkness. There will be no day. Only interminable night. Temperatures will drop to far below freezing and nuclear winter will set in. Water will turn into toxic ice. Radioactive fallout will seep through the earth and contaminate groundwater. Most living things, animal and vegetable, fish and fowl, will die. Only rats and cockroaches will breed and multiply and compete with foraging, relict humans for what little food there is.

What shall we do then, those of us who are still alive? Burned and blind and bald and ill, carrying the cancerous carcasses of our children in our arms, where shall we go? What shall we eat? What shall we drink? What shall we breathe?

The head of the Health, Environment and Safety Group of the Bhabha Atomic Research Center in Bombay has a plan. He declared in an interview (*Pioneer*, April 24, 1998) that India could survive nuclear war. His advice is that if there is a nuclear war, we take the same safety measures as the ones that scientists have recommended in the event of accidents at nuclear plants.

Take iodine pills, he suggests. And other steps such as remaining indoors, consuming only stored water and food and avoiding milk. Infants should be given powdered milk. "People in the danger zone should immediately go to the ground floor and if possible to the basement."

What do you do with these levels of lunacy? What do you do if you're trapped in an asylum and the doctors are all dangerously deranged?

Ignore it, it's just a novelist's naiveté, they'll tell you, Doomsday Prophet hyperbole. It'll never come to that. There will *be* no war. Nuclear weapons are about peace, not war. "Deterrence" is the buzzword of the people who like to think of themselves as hawks. (Nice birds, those. Cool. Stylish. Predatory. Pity there won't be many of them around after the war. "Extinction" is a word we must try and get used to.) Deterrence is an old thesis that has been resurrected and is being recycled with added local flavor. The Theory of Deterrence cornered the credit for having prevented the Cold War from turning into a Third World War. The only immutable fact about the Third World War is that if there's going to be one, it will be fought after the Second World War. In other words, there's no fixed schedule. In other words, we still have time. And perhaps the pun (the Third World War) is prescient. True, the Cold War is over, but let's not be hoodwinked by the ten-year lull in nuclear posturing. It was just a cruel joke. It was only in remission. It wasn't cured. It proves no theories. After all, what is ten years in the history of the world? Here it is again, the disease. More widespread and less amenable to any sort of treatment than ever. No, the Theory of Deterrence has some fundamental flaws.

Flaw Number One is that it presumes a complete, sophisticated understanding of the psychology of your enemy. It assumes that what deters you (the fear of annihilation) will deter them. What about those who are *not* deterred by that? The suicide-bomber psyche—the "We'll take you with us" school—is that an outlandish thought? How did Rajiv Gandhi die?

In any case who's the "you" and who's the "enemy"? Both are only governments. Governments change. They wear masks within masks. They molt and reinvent themselves all the time. The one we have at the moment, for instance, does not even have enough seats to last a full term in office, but demands that we trust it to do pirouettes and party tricks with nuclear bombs even as it scrabbles around for a foothold to maintain a simple majority in Parliament.

Flaw Number Two is that deterrence is premised on fear. But fear is premised on knowledge. On an understanding of the true extent and scale of the devastation that nuclear war will wreak. It is not some inherent, mystical attribute of nuclear bombs that they automatically inspire thoughts of peace. On the contrary, it is the endless, tireless, confrontational work of people who have had the courage to openly denounce them, the marches, the demonstrations, the films, the outrage—*that* is what has averted, or perhaps only postponed, nuclear war. Deterrence will not and cannot work given the levels of ignorance and illiteracy that hang over our two countries like dense, impenetrable veils. (Witness the Vishwa Hindu Parishad—VHP—wanting to distribute radioactive sand from the Pokhran desert as prasad all across India. A cancer yatra?) The Theory of Deterrence is nothing but a perilous joke in a world where iodine pills are prescribed as a prophylactic for nuclear irradiation.

India and Pakistan have nuclear bombs now and feel entirely justified in having them. Soon others will, too. Israel, Iran, Iraq, Saudi Arabia, Norway, Nepal (I'm trying to be eclectic here), Denmark, Germany, Bhutan, Mexico, Lebanon, Sri Lanka, Burma, Bosnia, Singapore, North Korea, Sweden, South Korea, Vietnam, Cuba, Afghanistan, Uzbekistan . . . and why not? Every country in the world has a special case to make. Everybody has borders and beliefs. And when all our larders are bursting with shiny bombs and our bellies are empty (deterrence is an exorbitant beast), we can trade bombs for food. And when nuclear technology goes on the market, when it gets truly competitive and prices fall, not just governments, but anybody who can afford it can have their own private arsenal—businessmen, terrorists, perhaps even the occasional rich writer (like myself). Our planet will bristle with beautiful missiles. There will be a new world order. The dictatorship of the pro-nuke elite. We can get our kicks by threatening each other. It'll be like bungee jumping when you can't rely on the bungee cord, or playing Russian roulette all day long. An additional perk will be the thrill of Not Knowing What to Believe. We can be victims of the predatory imagination of every green card–seeking charlatan who surfaces in the West with concocted stories of imminent missile attacks. We can delight at the prospect of being held to ransom by every petty troublemaker and rumormonger, the more the merrier if truth be told, anything for an excuse to make more bombs. So you see, even without a war, we have a lot to look forward to.

But let us pause to give credit where it's due. Whom must we thank for all this?

The Men who made it happen. The Masters of the Universe. Ladies and gentlemen, the United States of America! Come on up here, folks, stand up and take a bow. Thank you for doing this to the world. Thank you for making a difference. Thank you for showing us the way. Thank you for altering the very meaning of life.

From now on it is not dying we must fear, but living.

It is such supreme folly to believe that nuclear weapons are deadly only if they're used. The fact that they exist at all, their very presence in our lives, will wreak more havoc than we can begin to fathom. Nuclear weapons pervade our thinking. Control our behavior. Administer our societies. Inform our dreams. They bury themselves like meat hooks deep in the base of our brains. They are purveyors of madness. They are the ultimate colonizer. Whiter than any white man that ever lived. The very heart of whiteness.

All I can say to every man, woman, and sentient child here in India, and over there, just a little way away in Pakistan, is: take it personally. Whoever you are—Hindu, Muslim, urban, agrarian—it doesn't matter. The only good thing about nuclear war is that it is the single most egalitarian idea that man has ever had. On the day of reckoning, you will not be asked to present your credentials. The devastation will be undiscriminating. The bomb isn't in your backyard. It's in your body. And mine. *Nobody*, no nation, no government, no man, no god, has the right to put it there. We're radioactive already, and the war hasn't even begun. So stand up and say something. Never mind if it's been said before. Speak up on your own behalf. Take it very personally.

The Bomb and I

In early May (before the bomb), I left home for three weeks. I thought I would return. I had every intention of returning. Of course, things haven't worked out quite the way I had planned.

While I was away, I met a friend of mine whom I have always loved for, among other things, her ability to combine deep affection with a frankness that borders on savagery.

"I've been thinking about you," she said, "about *The God of Small Things*—what's in it, what's over it, under it, around it, above it . . ."

She fell silent for a while. I was uneasy and not at all sure that I wanted to hear the rest of what she had to say. She, however, was sure that she was going to say it. "In this last year—less than a year actually—you've had too much of everything—fame, money, prizes, adulation, criticism, condemnation, ridicule, love, hate, anger, envy, generosity—everything. In some ways it's a perfect story. Perfectly baroque in its excess. The trouble is that it has, or can have, only one perfect ending." Her eyes were on me, bright with a slanting, probing brilliance. She knew that I knew what she was going to say. She was insane.

She was going to say that nothing that happened to me in the future could ever match the buzz of this. That the whole of the rest of my life was going to be vaguely unsatisfying. And, therefore, the only perfect ending to the story would be death. *My* death.

The thought had occurred to me too. Of course it had. The fact that all this, this global dazzle—these lights in my eyes, the applause, the flowers, the photographers, the journalists feigning a deep interest in my life (yet struggling to get a single fact straight), the men in suits fawning over me, the shiny hotel bathrooms with endless towels—none of it was likely to happen again. Would I miss it? Had I grown to need it? Was I a fame junkie? Would I have withdrawal symptoms?

The more I thought about it, the clearer it became to me that if fame was going to be my permanent condition it would kill me. Club me to death with its good manners and hygiene. I'll admit that I've enjoyed my own five minutes of it immensely, but primarily *because* it was just five minutes. Because I knew (or thought I knew) that I could go home when I was bored and giggle about it. Grow old and irresponsible. Eat mangoes in the moonlight. Maybe write a couple of failed books—worstsellers—to see what it felt like. For a whole year I've cartwheeled across the world, anchored always to thoughts of home and the life I would go back to. Contrary to all the enquiries and predictions about my impending emigration, that was the well I dipped into. That was my sustenance. My strength.

I told my friend there was no such thing as a perfect story. I said in any case hers was an external view of things, this assumption that the trajectory of a person's happiness, or let's say fulfillment, had peaked (and now must trough) because she had accidentally stumbled upon "success." It was premised on the unimaginative belief that wealth and fame were the mandatory stuff of everybody's dreams.

You've lived too long in New York, I told her. There are other worlds. Other kinds of dreams. Dreams in which failure is feasible. Honorable. Sometimes even worth striving for. Worlds in which recognition is not the only barometer of brilliance or human worth. There are plenty of warriors whom I know and love, people far more valuable than myself, who go to war each day, knowing in advance that they will fail. True, they are less "successful" in the most vulgar sense of the word, but by no means less fulfilled.

The only dream worth having, I told her, is to dream that you will live while you're alive and die only when you're dead. (Prescience? Perhaps.)

"Which means exactly what?" (Arched eyebrows, a little annoyed.)

I tried to explain, but didn't do a very good job of it. Sometimes I need to write to think. So I wrote it down for her on a paper napkin. This is what I wrote: *To love. To be loved. To never forget your own insignificance. To never get used to the unspeakable violence and the vulgar disparity of life around you. To seek joy in the saddest places. To pursue beauty to its lair. To never simplify what is complicated or complicate what is simple. To respect strength, never power. Above all, to watch. To try and understand. To never look away. And never, never to forget.*

I've known her for many years, this friend of mine. She's an architect too.

She looked dubious, somewhat unconvinced by my paper-napkin speech. I could tell that structurally, just in terms of the sleek, narrative symmetry of things, and because she loved me, her thrill at my "success" was so keen, so generous, that it weighed in evenly with her (anticipated) horror at the idea of my death. I understood that it was nothing personal. Just a design thing.

Anyhow, two weeks after that conversation, I returned to India. To what I think/thought of as home. Something had died, but it wasn't me. It was infinitely more precious. It was a world that has been ailing for a while, and has finally breathed its last. It's been cremated now. The air is thick with ugliness and there's the unmistakable stench of fascism on the breeze.

Day after day, in newspaper editorials, on the radio, on TV chat shows, on MTV for heaven's sake, people whose instincts one thought one could trust—writers, painters, journalists—make the crossing. The chill seeps into my bones as it becomes painfully apparent from the lessons of everyday life that what you read in history books is true. That fascism is indeed as much about people as about governments. That it begins at home. In drawing rooms. In bedrooms. In beds. "Explosion of Self-Esteem," "Road to Resurgence," "A Moment of Pride," these were headlines in the papers in the days following the nuclear tests. "We have proved that we are not eunuchs any more," said Mr. Thackeray of the Shiv Sena. (Whoever said we were? True, a good number of us are women, but that, as far as I know, isn't the same thing.) Reading the papers, it was often hard to tell when people were referring to Viagra (which was competing for second place on the front pages) and when they were talking about the bomb—"We have superior strength and potency." (This was our Minister for Defence after Pakistan completed its tests.)

"These are not just nuclear tests, they are nationalism tests," we were repeatedly told.

This has been hammered home, over and over again. The bomb is India. India is the bomb. Not just India, Hindu India. Therefore, be warned, any criticism of it is not just antinational, but anti-Hindu. (Of course, in Pakistan the bomb is Islamic. Other than that, politically, the same physics applies.) This is one of the unexpected perks of having a nuclear bomb. Not only can the government use it to threaten the enemy, they can use it to declare war on their own people. Us.

In 1975, one year after India first dipped her toe into the nuclear sea, Mrs. Gandhi declared the Emergency. What will 1999 bring? There's talk of cells being set up to monitor antinational activity. Talk of amending cable laws to ban networks "harming national culture" (*Indian Express*, July 3). Of churches being struck off the list of religious places because "wine is served" (announced and retracted, *Indian Express*, July 3; *Times of India*, July 4). Artists, writers, actors, and singers are being harassed, threatened (and are succumbing to the threats). Not just by goon squads, but by instruments of the government. And in courts of law. There are letters and articles circulating on the Net—creative interpretations of Nostradamus's predictions claiming that a mighty, all-conquering Hindu nation is about to emerge—a resurgent India that will "burst forth upon its former oppressors and destroy them completely." That "the beginning of the terrible revenge (that will wipe out all Moslems) will be in the seventh month of 1999." This may well be the work of some lone nut, or a bunch of arcane god-squadders. The trouble is that having a nuclear bomb makes thoughts like these seem feasible. It *creates* thoughts like these. It bestows on people these utterly misplaced, utterly deadly notions of their own power. It's happening. It's all happening. I wish I could say "slowly but surely"—but I can't. Things are moving at a pretty fair clip.

Why does it all seem so familiar? Is it because, even as you watch, reality dissolves and seamlessly rushes forward into the silent, black-and-white images from old films—scenes of people being hounded out of their lives, rounded up and herded into camps? Of massacre, of mayhem, of endless columns of broken people making their way to nowhere? Why is there no sound track? Why is the hall so quiet? Have I been seeing too many films? Am I mad? Or am I right? Could those images be the inevitable culmination of what we have set into motion? Could our future be rushing forward into our past? I think so. Unless, of course, nuclear war settles it once and for all.

When I told my friends that I was writing this piece, they cautioned me. "Go ahead," they said, "but first make sure you're not vulnerable. Make sure your papers are in order. Make sure your taxes are paid."

My papers are in order. My taxes are paid. But how can one *not* be vulnerable in a climate like this? Everyone is vulnerable. Accidents happen. There's safety only in acquiescence. As I write, I am filled with foreboding. In this country, I have truly known what it means for a writer to feel loved (and, to some degree, hated too). Last year I was one of the items being paraded in the media's end-of-the-year National Pride Parade. Among the others, much to my mortification, were a bomb-maker and an international beauty queen. Each time a beaming person stopped me on the street and said "You have made India proud" (referring to the prize I won, not the book I wrote), I felt a little uneasy. It frightened me then and it terrifies me now, because I know how easily that swell, that tide of emotion, can turn against me. Perhaps the time for that has come. I'm going to step out from under the tiny twinkling lights and say what's on my mind.

It's this:

If protesting against having a nuclear bomb implanted in my brain is anti-Hindu and antinational, then I secede. I hereby declare myself an independent, mobile republic. I am a citizen of the earth. I own no territory. I have no flag. I'm female, but have nothing against eunuchs. My policies are simple. I'm willing to sign any nuclear nonproliferation treaty or nuclear test-ban treaty that's going. Immigrants are welcome. You can help me design our flag.

My world has died. And I write to mourn its passing.

Admittedly it was a flawed world. An unviable world. A scarred and wounded world. It was a world that I myself have criticized unsparingly, but only because I loved it. It didn't deserve to die. It didn't deserve to be dismembered. Forgive me, I realize that sentimentality is uncool—but what shall I do with my desolation?

I loved it simply because it offered humanity a choice. It was a rock out at sea. It was a stubborn chink of light that insisted that there was a different way of living. It was a functioning possibility. A real option. All that's gone now. India's nuclear tests, the manner in which they were conducted, the euphoria with which they have been greeted (by us) is indefensible. To me, it signifies dreadful things. The end of imagination. The end of freedom actually, because, after all, that's what freedom is. Choice.

On August 15 last year we celebrated the fiftieth anniversary of India's independence. In May we can mark our first anniversary in nuclear bondage.

Why did they do it?

Political expediency is the obvious, cynical answer, except that it only raises another, more basic question: Why should it have been politically expedient?

The three Official Reasons given are: China, Pakistan, and Exposing Western Hypocrisy.

Taken at face value, and examined individually, they're somewhat baffling. I'm not for a moment suggesting that these are not real issues. Merely that they aren't new. The only new thing on the old horizon is the Indian government. In his appallingly cavalier letter to the president of the United States (why bother to write at all if you're going to write like this?) our prime minister says India's decision to go ahead with the nuclear tests was due to a "deteriorating security environment." He goes on to mention the war with China in 1962 and the "three aggressions we have suffered in the last fifty years from Pakistan. And for the last ten years we have been the victim of unremitting terrorism and militancy sponsored by it . . . especially in Jammu and Kashmir."

The war with China is thirty-five years old. Unless there's some vital state secret that we don't know about, it certainly seemed as though matters had improved slightly between us. Just a few days before the nuclear tests, General Fu Quanyou, Chief of General Staff of the Chinese People's Liberation Army, was the guest of our Chief of Army Staff. We heard no words of war.

The most recent war with Pakistan was fought twenty-seven years ago. Admittedly Kashmir continues to be a deeply troubled region and no doubt Pakistan is gleefully fanning the flames. But surely there must be flames to fan in the first place? Surely the kindling is crackling and ready to burn? Can the Indian state with even a modicum of honesty absolve itself completely of having a hand in Kashmir's troubles? Kashmir, and for that matter, Assam, Tripura, Nagaland—virtually the whole of the northeast—Jharkhand, Uttarakhand, and all the trouble that's still to come—these are symptoms of a deeper malaise. It cannot and will not be solved by pointing nuclear missiles at Pakistan.

Even Pakistan can't be solved by pointing nuclear missiles at Pakistan. Though we are separate countries, we share skies, we share winds, we share water. Where radioactive fallout will land on any given day depends on the direction of the wind and rain. Lahore and Amritsar are thirty miles apart. If we bomb Lahore, Punjab will burn. If we bomb Karachi, then Gujarat and Rajasthan, perhaps even Bombay, will burn. Any nuclear war with Pakistan will be a war against ourselves.

As for the third Official Reason: exposing Western Hypocrisy—how much more exposed can they be? Which decent human being on earth harbors any illusions about it? These are people whose histories are spongy with the blood of others. Colonialism, apartheid, slavery, ethnic cleansing, germ warfare, chemical weapons—they virtually invented it all. They have plundered nations, snuffed out civilizations, exterminated entire populations. They stand on the world's stage stark naked but entirely unembarrassed, because they know that they have more money, more food, and bigger bombs than anybody else. They know they can wipe us out in the course of an ordinary working day. Personally, I'd say it is more arrogance than hypocrisy.

We have less money, less food, and smaller bombs. However, we have, or had, all kinds of other wealth. Delightful, unquantifiable. What we've done with it is the opposite of what we think we've done. We've pawned it all. We've traded it in. For what? In order to enter into a contract with the very people we claim to despise. In the larger scheme of things, we've agreed to play their game and play it their way. We've accepted their terms and conditions unquestioningly. The Comprehensive Test Ban Treaty ain't nothin' compared to this.

All in all, I think it is fair to say that *we're* the hypocrites. We're the ones who've abandoned what was arguably a moral position, i.e.: *we have the technology, we can make bombs if we want to, but we won't. We don't believe in them.*

We're the ones who have now set up this craven clamoring to be admitted into the club of superpowers. (If we are, we will no doubt gladly slam the door after us, and say to hell with principles about fighting Discriminatory World Orders.) For India to demand the status of a superpower is as ridiculous as demanding to play in the World Cup finals simply because we have a ball. Never mind that we haven't qualified, or that we don't play much soccer and haven't got a team.

Since we've chosen to enter the arena, it might be an idea to begin by learning the rules of the game. Rule number one is Acknowledge the Masters. Who are the best players? The ones with more money, more food, more bombs.

Rule number two is Locate Yourself in Relation to Them, i.e.: make an honest assessment of your position and abilities. The honest assessment of ourselves (in quantifiable terms) reads as follows:

We are a nation of nearly a billion people. In development terms we rank No. 138 out of the 175 countries listed in the UNDP's Human Development Index. More than 400 million of our people are illiterate and live in absolute poverty, over 600 million lack even basic sanitation, and over 200 million have no safe drinking water.

So the three Official Reasons, taken individually, don't hold much water. However, if you link them, a kind of twisted logic reveals itself. It has more to do with us than them.

The key words in our prime minister's letter to the president of the United States were "suffered" and "victim." That's the substance of it. That's our meat and drink. We *need* to feel like victims. We need to feel beleaguered. We need enemies. We have so little sense of ourselves as a nation and therefore constantly cast about for targets to define ourselves against. Prevalent political wisdom suggests that to prevent the state from crumbling, we need a national cause, and other than our currency (and, of course, poverty, illiteracy, and elections), we have none. This is the heart of the matter. This is the road that has led us to the bomb. This search for selfhood. If we are looking for a way out, we need some honest answers to some uncomfortable questions. Once again, it isn't as though these questions haven't been asked before. It's just that we prefer to mumble the answers and hope that no one's heard.

Is there such a thing as an Indian identity?

Do we really need one?

Who is an authentic Indian and who isn't?

Is India Indian?

Does it matter?

Whether or not there has ever been a single civilization that could call itself "Indian Civilization," whether or not India was, is, or ever will become a cohesive cultural entity, depends on whether you dwell on the differences or the similarities in the cultures of the people who have inhabited the subcontinent for centuries. India, as a modern nation-state, was marked out with precise geographical boundaries, in their precise geographical way, by a British Act of Parliament in 1899. Our country, as we know it, was forged on the anvil of the British Empire for the entirely unsentimental reasons of commerce and administration. But even as she was born, she began her struggle against her creators. So is India Indian? It's a tough question. Let's just say that we're an ancient people learning to live in a recent nation.

What is true is that India is an artificial state—a state that was created by a government, not a people. A state created from the top down, not the bottom up. The majority of India's citizens will not (to this day) be able to identify her boundaries on a map, or say which language is spoken where or which god is worshiped in what region. Most are too poor and too uneducated to have even an elementary idea of the extent and complexity of their own country. The impoverished, illiterate agrarian majority have no stake in the state. And indeed, why should they, how can they, when they don't even know what the state is? To them, India is, at best, a noisy slogan that comes around during the elections. Or a montage of people on government TV programs wearing regional costumes and saying "*Mera Bharat Mahaan.*"

The people who have a vital stake (or, more to the point, a business interest) in India's having a single, lucid, cohesive national identity are the politicians who constitute our national political parties. The reason isn't far to seek, it's simply because their struggle, their career goal, is— and must necessarily be—to *become* that identity. To be identified with that identity. If there isn't one, they have to manufacture one and persuade people to vote for it. It isn't their fault. It comes with the territory. It is inherent in the nature of our system of centralized government. A congenital defect in our particular brand of democracy. The greater the numbers of illiterate people, the poorer the country and the more morally bankrupt the politicians, the cruder the ideas of what that identity should be. In a situation like this, illiteracy is not just sad, it's downright dangerous. However, to be fair, cobbling together a viable predigested "National Identity" for India would be a formidable challenge even for the wise and the visionary. Every single Indian citizen could, if he or she wants to, claim to belong to some minority or the other. The fissures, if you look for them, run vertically, horizontally, and are layered, whorled, circular, spiral, inside out, and outside in. Fires when they're lit race along any one of these schisms, and in the process, release tremendous bursts of political energy. Not unlike what happens when you split an atom.

It is this energy that Gandhi sought to harness when he rubbed the magic lamp and invited Ram and Rahim to partake of human politics and India's war of independence against the British. It was a sophisticated, magnificent, imaginative struggle, but its objective was simple and lucid, the target highly visible, easy to identify and succulent with political sin. In the circumstances, the energy found an easy focus. The trouble is that the circumstances are entirely changed now, but the genie is out of its lamp, and won't go back in. (It *could* be sent back, but nobody wants it to go, it's proved itself too useful.) Yes, it won us freedom. But it also won us the carnage of Partition. And now, in the hands of lesser statesmen, it has won us the Hindu Nuclear Bomb.

To be fair to Gandhi and to other leaders of the National Movement, they did not have the benefit of hindsight, and could not possibly have known what the eventual, long-term consequences of their strategy would be. They could not have predicted how quickly the situation would career out of control. They could not have foreseen what would happen when they passed their flaming torches into the hands of their successors, or how venal those hands could be.

It was Indira Gandhi who started the real slide. It is she who made the genie a permanent State Guest. She injected the venom into our political veins. She invented our particularly vile local brand of political expediency. She showed us how to conjure enemies out of thin air, to fire at phantoms that she had carefully fashioned for that very purpose. It was she who discovered the benefits of never burying the dead, but preserving their putrid carcasses and trundling them out to worry old wounds when it suited her. Between herself and her sons she managed to bring the country to its knees. Our new government has just kicked us over and arranged our heads on the chopping block.

The Bharatiya Janata Party (BJP) is, in some senses, a specter that Indira Gandhi and the Congress created. Or, if you want to be less harsh, a specter that fed and reared itself in the political spaces and communal suspicion that the Congress nourished and cultivated. It has put a new complexion on the politics of governance. While Mrs. Gandhi played hidden games with politicians and their parties, she reserved a shrill convent-school rhetoric, replete with tired platitudes, to address the general public. The BJP, on the other hand, has chosen to light its fires directly on the streets and in the homes and hearts of people. It is prepared to do by day what the Congress would do only by night. To legitimize what was previously considered unacceptable (but done anyway). There is perhaps a fragile case to be made here in favor of hypocrisy. Could the hypocrisy of the Congress Party, the fact that it conducts its wretched affairs surreptitiously instead of openly, could that possibly mean there is a tiny glimmer of guilt somewhere? Some small fragment of remembered decency?

Actually, no.

No.

What am I doing? Why am I foraging for scraps of hope?

The way it has worked—in the case of the demolition of the Babri Masjid as well as in the making of the nuclear bomb—is that the Congress sowed the seeds, tended the crop, then the BJP stepped in and reaped the hideous harvest. They waltz together, locked in each other's arms. They're inseparable, despite their professed differences. Between them they have brought us here, to this dreadful, dreadful place.

The jeering, hooting young men who battered down the Babri Masjid are the same ones whose pictures appeared in the papers in the days that followed the nuclear tests. They were on the streets, celebrating India's nuclear bomb and simultaneously "condemning Western Culture" by emptying crates of Coke and Pepsi into public drains. I'm a little baffled by their logic: Coke is Western Culture, but the nuclear bomb is an old Indian tradition?

Yes, I've heard—the bomb is in the Vedas. It might be, but if you look hard enough, you'll find Coke in the Vedas too. That's the great thing about all religious texts. You can find anything you want in them—as long as you know what you're looking for.

But returning to the subject of the non-Vedic 1990s: We storm the heart of whiteness, we embrace the most diabolical creation of Western science and call it our own. But we protest against their music, their food, their clothes, their cinema, and their literature. That's not hypocrisy. That's humor.

It's funny enough to make a skull smile.

We're back on the old ship. The SS *Authenticity & Indianness*.

If there is going to be a pro-authenticity/antinational drive, perhaps the government ought to get its history straight and its facts right. If they're going to do it, they may as well do it properly.

First of all, the original inhabitants of this land were not Hindu. Ancient though it is, there were human beings on earth before there was Hinduism. India's Adivasis have a greater claim to being indigenous to this land than anybody else, and how are they treated by the state and its minions? Oppressed, cheated, robbed of their lands, shunted around like surplus goods. Perhaps the place to start would be to restore to them the dignity that was once theirs. Perhaps the government could make a public undertaking that more dams like the Sardar Sarovar on the Narmada will not be built, that more people will not be displaced.

But, of course, that would be inconceivable, wouldn't it? Why? Because it's impractical. Because Adivasis don't really matter. Their histories, their customs, their deities are dispensable. They must learn to sacrifice these things for the greater good of the nation (that has snatched from them everything they ever had).

Okay, so that's out.

For the rest, I could compile a practical list of things to ban and buildings to break. It'll need some research, but off the top of my head, here are a few suggestions.

They could begin by banning a number of ingredients from our cuisine:

chilies (Mexico), tomatoes (Peru), potatoes (Bolivia), coffee (Morocco), tea, white sugar, cinnamon (China) . . . they could then move into recipes. Tea with milk and sugar, for instance (Britain).

Smoking will be out of the question. Tobacco came from North America.

Cricket, English, and Democracy should be forbidden. Either kabaddi or kho-kho could replace cricket. I don't want to start a riot, so I hesitate to suggest a replacement for English (Italian . . . ? It has found its way to us via a kinder route: marriage, not imperialism). We have already discussed (earlier in this essay) the emerging, apparently acceptable alternative to democracy.

All hospitals in which Western medicine is practiced or prescribed should be shut down. All national newspapers discontinued. The railways dismantled. Airports closed. And what about our newest toy—the mobile phone? Can we live without it, or shall I suggest that they make an exception there? They could put it down in the column marked "universal." (Only essential commodities will be included here. No music, art, or literature.)

Needless to say, sending your children to college in the US and rushing there yourself to have your prostate operated upon will be a cognizable offense.

The building demolition drive could begin with the Rashtrapati Bhavan and gradually spread from cities to the countryside, culminating in the destruction of all monuments (mosques, churches, temples) that were built on what was once Adivasi or forest land.

It will be a long, long list. It would take years of work. I couldn't use a computer because that wouldn't be very authentic of me, would it?

I don't mean to be facetious, merely to point out that this is surely the shortcut to hell. There's no such thing as an Authentic India or a Real Indian. There is no Divine Committee that has the right to sanction one single, authorized version of what India is or should be. There is no one religion or language or caste or region or person or story or book that can claim to be its sole representative. There are, and can only be, visions of India, various ways of seeing it—honest, dishonest, wonderful, absurd, modern, traditional, male, female. They can be argued over, criticized, praised, scorned, but not banned or broken. Not hunted down.

Railing against the past will not heal us. History has *happened*. It's over and done with. All we can do is to change its course by encouraging what we love instead of destroying what we don't. There is beauty yet in this brutal, damaged world of ours. Hidden, fierce, immense. Beauty that is uniquely ours and beauty that we have received with grace from others, enhanced, reinvented, and made our own. We have to seek it out, nurture it, love it. Making bombs will only destroy us. It doesn't *matter* whether or not we use them. They will destroy us either way.

India's nuclear bomb is the final act of betrayal by a ruling class that has failed its people.

However many garlands we heap on our scientists, however many medals we pin to their chests, the truth is that it's far easier to make a bomb than to educate 400 million people.

According to opinion polls, we're expected to believe that there's a national consensus on the issue. It's official now. Everybody loves the bomb. (Therefore the bomb is good.)

Is it possible for a man who cannot write his own name to understand even the basic, elementary facts about the nature of nuclear weapons? Has anybody told him that nuclear war has nothing at all to do with his received notions of war? Nothing to do with honor, nothing to do with pride? Has anybody bothered to explain to him about thermal blasts, radioactive fallout, and the nuclear winter? Are there even words in his language to describe the concepts of enriched uranium, fissile material, and critical mass? Or has his language itself become obsolete? Is he trapped in a time capsule, watching the world pass him by, unable to understand or communicate with it because his language never took into account the horrors that the human race would dream up? Does he not matter at all, this man? Shall we just treat him like some kind of a cretin? If he asks any questions, ply him with iodine pills and parables about how Lord Krishna lifted a hill or how the destruction of Lanka by Hanuman was unavoidable in order to preserve Sita's virtue and Ram's reputation? Use his own beautiful stories as weapons against him? Shall we release him from his capsule only during elections, and once he's voted, shake him by the hand, flatter him with some bullshit about the Wisdom of the Common Man, and send him right back in?

I'm not talking about one man, of course, I'm talking about millions and millions of people who live in this country. This is their land too, you know. They have the right to make an informed decision about its fate and, as far as I can tell, nobody has informed them about anything. The tragedy is that nobody could, even if they wanted to. Truly, literally, there's no language to do it in. This is the real horror of India. The orbits of the powerful and the powerless spinning further and further apart from each other, never intersecting, sharing nothing. Not a language. Not even a country.

Who the hell conducted those opinion polls? Who the hell is the prime minister to decide whose finger will be on the nuclear button that could turn everything we love—our earth, our skies, our mountains, our plains, our rivers, our cities and villages—to ash in an instant? Who the hell is he to reassure us that there will be no accidents? How does he know? Why should we trust him? What has he ever done to make us trust him? What have any of them ever done to make us trust them?

The nuclear bomb is the most antidemocratic, antinational, antihuman, outright evil thing that man has ever made.

If you are religious, then remember that this bomb is Man's challenge to God.

It's worded quite simply: we have the power to destroy everything that You have created.

If you're not (religious), then look at it this way. This world of ours is 4,600 million years old.

It could end in an afternoon.

2. Democracy

Who Is She When She's at Home?

Last night a friend from Baroda called. Weeping. It took her fifteen minutes to tell me what the matter was. It wasn't very complicated. Only that a friend of hers, Sayeeda,[1] had been caught by a mob. Only that her stomach had been ripped open and stuffed with burning rags. Only that after she died someone carved "OM" on her forehead.[2]

Precisely which Hindu scripture preaches this?

Our Prime Minister, A. B. Vajpayee, justified this as part of the retaliation by outraged Hindus against Muslim "terrorists" who burned alive fifty-eight Hindu passengers on the Sabarmati Express in Godhra.[3] Each of those who died that hideous death was someone's brother, someone's mother, someone's child. Of course they were.

Which particular verse in the Koran required that they be roasted alive?

The more the two sides try and call attention to their religious differences by slaughtering each other, the less there is to distinguish them from one another. They worship at the same altar. They're both apostles of the same murderous god, whoever he is. In an atmosphere so vitiated, for anybody, and in particular the Prime Minister, to arbitrarily decree exactly where the cycle started is malevolent and irresponsible.

Originally published in the May 6, 2002, issue of *Outlook* magazine.

Right now we're sipping from a poisoned chalice—a flawed democracy laced with religious fascism. Pure arsenic.

What shall we do? What *can* we do?

We have a ruling party that's hemorrhaging. Its rhetoric against terrorism, the passing of the Prevention of Terrorism Act, the saber-rattling against Pakistan (with the underlying nuclear threat), the massing of almost a million soldiers on the border on hair-trigger alert, and, most dangerous of all, the attempt to communalize and falsify school history textbooks—none of this has prevented it from being humiliated in election after election.[4] Even its old party trick—the revival of the plans to replace the destroyed mosque in Ayodhya with the Ram Mandir—didn't quite work out.[5] Desperate now, it has turned for succor to the state of Gujarat.

Gujarat, the only major state in India to have a Bharatiya Janata Party (BJP) government, has for some years been the petri dish in which Hindu fascism has been fomenting an elaborate political experiment. In March 2002, the initial results were put on public display.

Within hours of the Godhra outrage, a meticulously planned pogrom was unleashed against the Muslim community. It was led from the front by the Hindu nationalist Vishwa Hindu Parishad (VHP) and the Bajrang Dal. Officially the number of dead is eight hundred. Independent reports put the figure as high as two thousand.[6] More than one hundred fifty thousand people, driven from their homes, now live in refugee camps.[7] Women were stripped, gang-raped; parents were bludgeoned to death in front of their children.[8] Two hundred forty dargahs and one hundred eighty masjids were destroyed. In Ahmedabad, the tomb of Wali Gujarati, the founder of the modern Urdu poem, was demolished and paved over in the course of a night.[9] The tomb of the musician Ustad Faiyaz Ali Khan was desecrated and wreathed in burning tires.[10] Arsonists burned and looted shops, homes, hotels, textile mills, buses, and private cars. Tens of thousands have lost their jobs.[11]

A mob surrounded the house of former Congress MP Ehsan Jaffri. His phone calls to the Director General of Police, the Police Commissioner, the Chief Secretary, the Additional Chief Secretary (Home) were ignored. The mobile police vans around his house did not intervene. The mob dragged Ehsan Jaffri out of his house, and dismembered him.[12] Of course it's only a coincidence that Jaffri was a trenchant critic of Gujarat's Chief Minister, Narendra Modi, during his campaign for the Rajkot Assembly by-election in February.

Across Gujarat, thousands of people made up the mobs. They were armed with petrol bombs, guns, knives, swords, and tridents.[13] Apart from the VHP and Bajrang Dal's usual lumpen constituency, there were Dalits and Adivasis who were brought in buses and trucks. Middle-class people participated in the looting. (On one memorable occasion a family arrived in a Mitsubishi Lancer.)[14] There was a deliberate, systematic attempt to destroy the economic base of the Muslim community. The leaders of the mob had computer-generated cadastral lists marking out Muslim homes, shops, businesses, and even partnerships. They had mobile phones to coordinate the action. They had trucks loaded with thousands of gas cylinders, hoarded weeks in advance, which they used to blow up Muslim commercial establishments. They had not just police protection and police connivance but also covering fire.[15]

While Gujarat burned, our Prime Minister was on MTV promoting his new poems.[16] (Reports say cassettes have sold a hundred thousand copies.) It took him more than a month—and two vacations in the hills—to make it to Gujarat.[17] When he did, shadowed by the chilling Modi, he gave a speech at the Shah Alam refugee camp.[18] His mouth moved, he tried to express concern, but no real sound emerged except the mocking of the wind whistling through a burned, bloodied, broken world. Next we knew, he was bobbing around in a golf cart, striking business deals in Singapore.[19]

The killers still stalk Gujarat's streets. For weeks the lynch mob was the arbiter of the routine affairs of daily life: who can live where, who can say what, who can meet whom, and where and when. Its mandate expanded from religious affairs to property disputes, family altercations, the planning and allocation of water resources . . . (which is why Medha Patkar of the Narmada Bachao Andolan was assaulted).[20] Muslim businesses have been shut down. Muslim people are not served in restaurants. Muslim children are not welcome in schools. Muslim students are too terrified to sit for their exams.[21] Muslim parents live in dread that their infants might forget what they've been told and give themselves away by saying "Ammi!" or "Abba!" in public and invite sudden and violent death.

Notice has been given: *this is just the beginning.*

Is this the Hindu Rashtra, the Nation that we've all been asked to look forward to? Once the Muslims have been "shown their place," will milk and Coca-Cola flow across the land? Once the Ram Mandir is built, will there be a shirt on every back and a roti in every belly?[22] Will every tear be wiped from every eye? Can we expect an anniversary celebration next year? Or will there be someone else to hate by then? Alphabetically: Adivasis, Buddhists, Christians, Dalits, Parsis, Sikhs? Those who wear jeans or speak English or those who have thick lips or curly hair? We won't have to wait long. It's started already. Will the established rituals continue? Will people be beheaded, dismembered, and urinated upon? Will fetuses be ripped from their mothers' wombs and slaughtered? (What kind of depraved vision can even *imagine* India without the range and beauty and spectacular anarchy of all these cultures? India would become a tomb and smell like a crematorium.)

No matter who they were, or how they were killed, each person who died in Gujarat in the weeks gone by deserves to be mourned. There have been hundreds of outraged letters to journals and newspapers asking why the "pseudo-secularists" do not condemn the burning of the Sabarmati Express in Godhra with the same degree of outrage with which they condemn the killings in the rest of Gujarat. What they don't seem to understand is that there *is* a fundamental difference between a pogrom such as the one taking place in Gujarat now and the burning of the Sabarmati Express in Godhra. We still don't know who exactly was responsible for the carnage in Godhra.[23] Whoever did it—whatever their political or religious persuasion—committed a terrible crime. But every independent report says the pogrom against the Muslim community in Gujarat—billed by the government as a spontaneous "reaction"—has at best been conducted under the benign gaze of the state and, at worst, with active state collusion.[24] Either way, the state is criminally culpable. And the state acts in the name of its citizens. So, as a citizen, I am forced to acknowledge that I am somehow made complicit in the Gujarat pogrom. It is this that outrages me. And it is this that puts a completely different complexion on the two massacres.

After the Gujarat massacres, at its convention in Bangalore, the Rashtriya Swayamsevak Sangh (RSS), the moral and cultural guild of the BJP, of which the Prime Minister, the Home Minister, and Chief

Minister Modi himself are all members, called upon Muslims to earn the "goodwill" of the majority community.[25] At the meeting of the national executive of the BJP in Goa, Narendra Modi was greeted as a hero. His smirking offer to resign from the Chief Minister's post was unanimously turned down.[26] In a recent public speech he compared the events of the last few weeks in Gujarat to Gandhi's Dandi March—both, according to him, significant moments in the Struggle for Freedom.

While the parallels between contemporary India and pre-war Germany are chilling, they're not surprising. (The founders of the RSS have, in their writings, been frank in their admiration for Hitler and his methods.)[27] One difference is that here in India we don't have a Hitler. We have, instead, a traveling extravaganza, a mobile symphonic orchestra. The hydra-headed, many-armed Sangh Parivar—the "joint family" of Hindu political and cultural organizations—with the BJP, the RSS, the VHP, and the Bajrang Dal, each playing a different instrument. Its utter genius lies in its apparent ability to be all things to all people at all times.

The Parivar has an appropriate head for every occasion. An old versifier with rhetoric for every season. A rabble-rousing hardliner, Lal Krishna Advani, for Home Affairs; a suave one, Jaswant Singh, for Foreign Affairs; a smooth English-speaking lawyer, Arun Jaitley, to handle TV debates; a cold-blooded creature, Narendra Modi, for a Chief Minister; and the Bajrang Dal and the VHP, grassroots workers in charge of the physical labor that goes into the business of genocide. Finally, this many-headed extravaganza has a lizard's tail which drops off when it's in trouble and grows back again: a specious socialist dressed up as Defense Minister, whom it sends on its damage-limitation missions—wars, cyclones, genocides. They trust him to press the right buttons, hit the right note.

The Sangh Parivar speaks in as many tongues as a whole corsage of tridents. It can say several contradictory things simultaneously. While one of its heads (the VHP) exhorts millions of its cadres to prepare for the Final Solution, its titular head (the Prime Minister) assures the nation that all citizens, regardless of their religion, will be treated equally.

It can ban books and films and burn paintings for "insulting Indian culture." Simultaneously, it can mortgage the equivalent of 60 percent of the entire country's rural development budget as profit to Enron.[28] It contains within itself the full spectrum of political opinion, so what would normally be a public fight between two adversarial political parties is now just a family matter. However acrimonious the quarrel, it's *always* conducted in public, always resolved amicably, and the audience always goes away satisfied it's got value for its money—anger, action, revenge, intrigue, remorse, poetry, and plenty of gore. It's our own vernacular version of Full Spectrum Dominance.[29]

But when the chips are down, *really* down, the squabbling heads quiet, and it becomes chillingly apparent that underneath all the clamor and the noise, a single heart beats. And an unforgiving mind with saffron-saturated tunnel vision works overtime.

There have been pogroms in India before, every kind of pogrom—directed at particular castes, tribes, religious faiths. In 1984, following the assassination of Indira Gandhi, the Congress Party presided over the massacre of three thousand Sikhs in Delhi, every bit as macabre as the one in Gujarat.[30] At the time Rajiv Gandhi, never known for an elegant turn of phrase, said, "When a large tree falls, the earth shakes."[31] In 1985 the Congress swept the polls. On a *sympathy* wave! Eighteen years have gone by, and almost no one has been punished.

Take any politically volatile issue—the nuclear tests, the Babri Masjid, the Tehelka scam, the stirring of the communal cauldron for electoral advantage—and you'll see the Congress Party has been there before. In every case, the Congress sowed the seed and the BJP has swept in to reap the hideous harvest. So in the event that we're called upon to vote, *is* there a difference between the two? The answer is a faltering but distinct yes. Here's why: It's true that the Congress Party has sinned, and grievously, and for decades together. But it has done by night what the BJP does by day. It has done covertly, stealthily, hypocritically, shamefacedly what the BJP does with pride. And this is an important difference.

Whipping up communal hatred is part of the mandate of the Sangh Parivar. It has been planned for *years*. It has been injecting a slow-release poison directly into civil society's bloodstream. Hundreds of RSS shakhas and Saraswati shishu mandirs across the country have been indoctrinating thousands of children and young people, stunting their minds with religious hatred and falsified history, including unfactual or wildly exaggerated accounts of the rape and pillaging of Hindu women and Hindu temples by Muslim rulers in the precolonial period. They're no different from, and no less dangerous than, the madrassas all over Pakistan and Afghanistan which spawned the Taliban. In states like Gujarat, the police, the administration, and the political cadres at every level have been systematically penetrated.[32] The whole enterprise has huge popular appeal, which it would be foolish to underestimate or misunderstand. It has a formidable religious, ideological, political, and administrative underpinning. This kind of power, this kind of reach, can only be achieved with state backing.

Some madrassas, the Muslim equivalent of hothouses cultivating religious hatred, try and make up in frenzy and foreign funding what they lack in state support. They provide the perfect foil for Hindu communalists to dance their dance of mass paranoia and hatred. (In fact, they serve that purpose so perfectly they might just as well be working as a team.)

Under this relentless pressure, what will most likely happen is that the majority of the Muslim community will resign itself to living in ghettos as second-class citizens, in constant fear, with no civil rights and no recourse to justice. What will daily life be like for them? Any little thing, an altercation in a cinema queue or a fracas at a traffic light, could turn lethal. So they will learn to keep very quiet, to accept their lot, to creep around the edges of the society in which they live. Their fear will transmit itself to other minorities. Many, particularly the young, will probably turn to militancy. They will do terrible things. Civil society will be called upon to condemn them. Then President Bush's canon will come back to us: "Either you are with us or you are with the terrorists."[33]

Those words hang frozen in time like icicles. For years to come, butchers and genocidists will fit their grisly mouths around them ("lip-sync," filmmakers call it) in order to justify their butchery.

Bal Thackeray of the Shiv Sena, who has lately been feeling a little upstaged by Modi, has the lasting solution. He's called for civil war. Isn't that just perfect? Then Pakistan won't need to bomb us, we can bomb ourselves. Let's turn all of India into Kashmir. Or Bosnia. Or Palestine.

Or Rwanda. Let's all suffer forever. Let's buy expensive guns and explosives to kill each other with. Let the British arms dealers and the American weapons manufacturers grow fat on our spilled blood.[34] We could ask the Carlyle Group—of which the Bush and bin Laden families were both shareholders—for a bulk discount.[35] Maybe if things go really well, we'll become like Afghanistan. (And look at the publicity they've gone and got themselves.) When all our farmlands are mined, our buildings destroyed, our infrastructure reduced to rubble, our children physically maimed and mentally wrecked, when we've nearly wiped ourselves out with self-manufactured hatred, maybe we can appeal to the Americans to help us out. Airdropped airline meals, anyone?

How close we have come to self-destruction! Another step and we'll be in free fall. And yet the government presses on. At the Goa meeting of the BJP's national executive, the Prime Minister of secular, democratic India, A. B. Vajpayee, made history. He became the first Indian Prime Minister to cross the threshold and publicly unveil an unconscionable bigotry against Muslims, which even George Bush and Donald Rumsfeld would be embarrassed to own up to. "Wherever Muslims are," he said, "they do not want to live peacefully."[36]

Shame on him. But if only it were just him: in the immediate aftermath of the Gujarat holocaust, confident of the success of its "experiment," the BJP wants a snap poll. "The *gentlest* of people," my friend from Baroda said to me, "the *gentlest* of people, in the gentlest of voices, says 'Modi is our hero.'"

Some of us nurtured the naive hope that the magnitude of the horror of the last few weeks would make the secular parties, however self-serving, unite in sheer outrage. On its own, the BJP does not have the mandate of the people of India. It does not have the mandate to push through the Hindutva project. We hoped that the twenty-two allies that make up the BJP-led coalition would withdraw their support. We thought, quite stupidly, that they would see that there could be no bigger test of their moral fiber, of their commitment to their avowed principles of secularism.

It's a sign of the times that not a single one of the BJP's allies has withdrawn support. In every shifty eye you see that faraway look of someone doing mental math to calculate which constituencies and portfolios they'll retain and which ones they'll lose if they pull out. Deepak Parekh is one of the only CEOs of India's corporate community to condemn what happened.[37] Farooq Abdullah, Chief Minister of Jammu and Kashmir and the only prominent Muslim politician left in India, is currying favor with the government by supporting Modi because he nurses the dim hope that he might become Vice President of India very soon.[38] And worst of all, Mayawati, leader of the Bahujan Samaj Party (BSP), the People's Socialist Party, the great hope of the lower castes, has forged an alliance with the BJP in Uttar Pradesh.[39]

The Congress and the Left parties have launched a public agitation asking for Modi's resignation.[40] *Resignation*? Have we lost all sense of proportion? Criminals are not meant to *resign*. They're meant to be charged, tried, and convicted. As those who burned the train in Godhra should be. As the mobs and those members of the police force and the administration who planned and participated in the pogrom in the rest of Gujarat should be. As those responsible for raising the pitch of the frenzy to boiling point must be. The Supreme Court has the option of acting against Modi and the Bajrang Dal and the VHP. There are hundreds of testimonies. There are masses of evidence.

But in India if you are a butcher or a genocidist who happens to be a politician, you have every reason to be optimistic. No one even *expects* politicians to be prosecuted. To demand that Modi and his henchmen be arraigned and put away would make other politicians vulnerable to their own unsavory pasts. So instead they disrupt Parliament, shout a lot. Eventually those in power set up commissions of inquiry, ignore the findings, and between themselves makes sure the juggernaut chugs on.

Already the issue has begun to morph. Should elections be allowed or not? Should the Election Commission decide that? Or the Supreme Court? Either way, whether elections are held or deferred, by allowing Modi to walk free, by allowing him to continue with his career as a politician, the fundamental, governing principles of democracy are not just being subverted but deliberately sabotaged. This kind of democracy is the *problem*, not the solution. Our society's greatest strength is being turned into her deadliest enemy. What's the point of us all going on about "deepening democracy," when it's being bent and twisted into something unrecognizable?

What if the BJP *does* win the elections? After all, George Bush had a 60 percent rating in his War Against Terror, and Ariel Sharon has an even stronger mandate for his bestial invasion of Palestine.[41] Does that make everything all right? Why not dispense with the legal system, the constitution, the press—the whole shebang—morality *itself*, why not chuck it and put everything up for a vote? Genocides can become the subject of opinion polls, and massacres can have marketing campaigns.

Fascism's firm footprint has appeared in India. Let's mark the date: Spring 2002. While we can thank the American President and the Coalition Against Terror for creating a congenial international atmosphere for fascism's ghastly debut, we cannot credit them for the years it has been brewing in our public and private lives.

It breezed in after the Pokhran nuclear tests in 1998.[42] From then onward, the massed energy of bloodthirsty patriotism became openly acceptable political currency. The "weapons of peace" trapped India and Pakistan in a spiral of brinkmanship—threat and counter-threat, taunt and counter-taunt.[43] And now, one war and hundreds of dead later,[44] more than a million soldiers from both armies are massed at the border, eyeball to eyeball, locked in a pointless nuclear standoff. The escalating belligerence against Pakistan has ricocheted off the border and entered our own body politic, like a sharp blade slicing through the vestiges of communal harmony and tolerance between the Hindu and Muslim communities. In no time at all, the god-squadders from hell have colonized the public imagination. And we allowed them in. Each time the hostility between India and Pakistan is cranked up, within India there's a corresponding increase in the hostility toward the Muslims. With each battle cry against Pakistan, we inflict a wound on ourselves, on our way of life, on our spectacularly diverse and ancient civilization, on everything that makes India different from Pakistan. Increasingly, Indian nationalism has come to mean Hindu nationalism, which defines itself not through a respect or regard for itself but through a hatred of the Other. And the Other, for the moment, is not just Pakistan, it's Muslims. It's disturbing to see how neatly nationalism dovetails into fascism. While we must not allow the fascists to define what the nation is, or who it belongs to, it's worth keeping in mind that nationalism—in all its many avatars: communist, capitalist, and fascist—has been at the root of almost all the genocide of the twentieth century. On the issue of nationalism, it's wise to proceed with caution.

Can we not find it in ourselves to belong to an ancient civilization instead of to just a recent nation? To love a *land* instead of just patrolling a territory? The Sangh Parivar understands nothing of what civilization means. It seeks to limit, reduce, define, dismember, and desecrate the memory of what we were, our understanding of what we are, and our dreams of who we want to be. What kind of India do they want? A limbless, headless, soulless torso, left bleeding under the butcher's cleaver with a flag driven deep into her mutilated heart? Can we let that happen? Have we let it happen?

The incipient, creeping fascism of the past few years has been groomed by many of our "democratic" institutions. Everyone has flirted with it—Parliament, the press, the police, the administration, the public. Even "secularists" have been guilty of helping to create the right climate. Each time you defend the right of an institution, *any* institution (including the Supreme Court), to exercise unfettered, unaccountable powers that must never be challenged, you move toward fascism. To be fair, perhaps not everyone recognized the early signs for what they were.

The national press has been startlingly courageous in its denunciation of the events of the last few weeks. Many of the BJP's fellow-travelers, who have journeyed with it to the brink, are now looking down the abyss into the hell that was once Gujarat and turning away in genuine dismay. But how hard and for how long will they fight? This is not going to be like a publicity campaign for an upcoming cricket season. And there will not always be spectacular carnage to report on. Fascism is also about the slow, steady infiltration of all the instruments of state power. It's about the slow erosion of civil liberties, about unspectacular day-to-day injustices. Fighting it means fighting to win back the minds and hearts of people. Fighting it does not mean asking for RSS shakhas and the madrassas that are overtly communal to be banned, it means working toward the day when they're voluntarily abandoned as bad ideas. It means keeping an eagle eye on public institutions and demanding accountability. It means putting your ear to the ground and listening to the whispering of the truly powerless. It means giving a forum to the myriad voices from the hundreds of resistance movements across the country which are speaking about *real* things—about bonded labor, marital rape, sexual preferences, women's wages, uranium dumping, unsustainable mining, weavers' woes, farmers' suicides. It means fighting displacement and dispossession and the relentless, everyday violence of abject poverty. Fighting it also means not allowing your newspaper columns and prime-time TV spots to be hijacked by their spurious passions and their staged theatrics, which are designed to divert attention from everything else.

While most people in India have been horrified by what happened in Gujarat, many thousands of the indoctrinated are preparing to journey deeper into the heart of the horror. Look around you and you'll see in little parks, in empty lots, in village commons, the RSS is marching, hoisting its saffron flag. Suddenly they're everywhere, grown men in khaki shorts marching, marching, marching. To *where?* For *what?* Their disregard for history shields them from the knowledge that fascism will thrive for a short while and then self-annihilate because of its inherent stupidity. But unfortunately, like the radioactive fallout of a nuclear strike, it has a half-life that will cripple generations to come.

These levels of rage and hatred cannot be contained, cannot be expected to subside, with public censure and denunciation. Hymns of brotherhood and love are great, but not enough.

Historically, fascist movements have been fueled by feelings of national disillusionment. Fascism has come to India after the dreams that fueled the Freedom Struggle have been frittered away like so much loose change.

Independence itself came to us as what Gandhi famously called a "wooden loaf"—a notional freedom tainted by the blood of the thousands who died during Partition.[45] For more than half a century now, the hatred and mutual distrust has been exacerbated, toyed with, and never allowed to heal by politicians, led from the front by Indira Gandhi. Every political party has tilled the marrow of our secular parliamentary democracy, mining it for electoral advantage. Like termites excavating a mound, they've made tunnels and underground passages, undermining the meaning of "secular," until it has become just an empty shell that's about to implode. Their tilling has weakened the foundations of the structure that connects the constitution, Parliament, and the courts of law—the configuration of checks and balances that forms the backbone of a parliamentary democracy. Under the circumstances, it's futile to go on blaming politicians and demanding from them a morality of which they're incapable. There's something pitiable about a people that constantly bemoans its leaders. If they've let us down, it's only because we've allowed them to. It could be argued that civil society has failed its leaders as much as leaders have failed civil society. We have to accept that there is a dangerous, systemic flaw in our parliamentary democracy that politicians *will* exploit. And that's what results in the kind of conflagration that we have witnessed in Gujarat. There's fire in the ducts. We have to address this issue and come up with a *systemic* solution.

But politicians' exploitation of communal divides is by no means the only reason that fascism has arrived on our shores.

Over the past fifty years, ordinary citizens' modest hopes for lives of dignity, security, and relief from abject poverty have been systematically snuffed out. Every "democratic" institution in this country has shown itself to be unaccountable, inaccessible to the ordinary citizen, and either unwilling or incapable of acting in the interests of genuine social justice. *Every* strategy for real social change—land reform, education, public health, the equitable distribution of natural resources, the implementation of positive discrimination—has been cleverly, cunningly, and consistently scuttled and rendered ineffectual by those castes and that class of people which have a stranglehold on the political process. And now corporate globalization is being relentlessly and arbitrarily imposed on an essentially feudal society, tearing through its complex, tiered social fabric, ripping it apart culturally and economically.

There is very real grievance here. And the fascists didn't create it. But they have seized upon it, upturned it, and forged from it a hideous, bogus sense of pride. They have mobilized human beings using the lowest common denominator—religion. People who have lost control over their lives, people who have been uprooted from their homes and communities, who have lost their culture and their language, are being made to feel proud of *something*. Not something they have striven for and achieved, not something they can count as a personal accomplishment, but something they just happen to be. Or, more accurately, something they happen *not* to be. And the falseness, the emptiness, of that pride is fueling a gladiatorial anger that is then directed toward a simulated target that has been wheeled into the amphitheater.

How else can you explain the project of trying to disenfranchise, drive out, or exterminate the second-poorest community in this country, using as your foot soldiers the very poorest (Dalits and Adivasis)? How else can you explain why Dalits in Gujarat, who have been despised, oppressed, and treated worse than refuse by the upper castes for thousands of years, have joined hands with their oppressors to turn on those who are only marginally less unfortunate than they themselves? Are they just wage slaves, mercenaries for hire? Is it all right to patronize them and absolve them of responsibility for their own actions? Or am I being obtuse? Perhaps it's common practice for the unfortunate to vent their rage and hatred on the *next* most unfortunate, because their *real* adversaries are inaccessible, seemingly invincible, and completely out of range. Because their own leaders have cut loose and are feasting at the high table, leaving them to wander rudderless in the wilderness, spouting nonsense about returning to the Hindu fold. (The first step, presumably, toward founding a global Hindu empire, as realistic a goal as fascism's previously failed projects—the restoration of Roman glory, the purification of the German race, or the establishment of an Islamic sultanate.)

One hundred thirty million Muslims live in India.[46] Hindu fascists regard them as legitimate prey. Do people like Modi and Bal Thackeray think that the world will stand by and watch while they're liquidated in a "civil war"? Press reports say that the European Union and several other countries have condemned what happened in Gujarat and likened it to Nazi rule.[47] The Indian government's portentous response is that foreigners should not use the Indian media to comment on what is an "internal matter" (like the chilling goings-on in Kashmir?).[48] What next? Censorship? Closing down the Internet? Blocking international calls? Killing the wrong "terrorists" and fudging the DNA samples? There is no terrorism like state terrorism.

But who will take them on? Their fascist cant can perhaps be dented by some blood and thunder from the Opposition. So far only Laloo Yadav, head of the Rashtriya Janata Dal (RJD), the National People's Party, in Bihar, has shown himself to be truly passionate: "*Kaun mai ka lal kehtha hai ki yeh Hindu Rashtra hai? Usko yahan bhej do, chhaahti phad doonga!*" (Which mother's son says this is a Hindu Nation? Send him here, I'll tear his chest open).[49]

Unfortunately, there's no quick fix. Fascism itself can only be turned away if all those who are outraged by it show a commitment to social justice that equals the intensity of their indignation.

Are we ready to get off our starting blocks? Are we ready, many millions of us, to rally, not just on the streets but at work and in schools and in our homes, in every decision we take, and every choice we make?

Or not just yet . . . ?

If not, then years from now, when the rest of the world has shunned us (as it should), we too will learn, like the ordinary citizens of Hitler's Germany, to recognize revulsion in the gaze of our fellow human beings. We too will find ourselves unable to look our own children in the eye, for the shame of what we did and didn't do. For the shame of what we allowed to happen.

This is *us*. In *India*. Heaven help us make it through the night.

3. When the Saints Go Marching Out

The Strange Fate of Martin, Mohandas, and Mandela

We're coming up to the fortieth anniversary of the March on Washington, when Martin Luther King Jr. gave his famous "I Have a Dream" speech. Perhaps it's time to reflect—again—on what has become of that dream.

It's interesting how icons, when their time has passed, are commodified and appropriated (some voluntarily, others involuntarily) to promote the prejudice, bigotry, and inequity they battled against. But then in an age when everything's up for sale, why not icons? In an era when all of humanity, when every creature of God's earth, is trapped between the IMF checkbook and the American cruise missile, can icons stage a getaway?

Martin Luther King is part of a trinity. So it's hard to think of him without two others elbowing their way into the picture: Mohandas Gandhi and Nelson Mandela. The three high priests of nonviolent resistance. Together they represent (to a greater or lesser extent) the twentieth century's nonviolent liberation struggles (or should we say "negotiated settlements"?): of colonized against colonizer, former slave against slave owner.

Today the elites of the very societies and peoples in whose name the battles for freedom were waged use them as mascots to entice new masters.

Expanded version of essay originally broadcast by BBC Radio 4, August 25, 2003.

Mohandas, Mandela, Martin.

India, South Africa, the United States.

Broken dreams, betrayal, nightmares.

A quick snapshot of the supposedly "Free World" today.

Last March in India, in Gujarat—Gandhi's Gujarat—right-wing Hindu mobs murdered two thousand Muslims in a chillingly efficient orgy of violence. Women were gang-raped and burned alive. Muslim tombs and shrines were razed to the ground. More than a hundred fifty thousand Muslims have been driven from their homes. The economic base of the community has been destroyed. Eyewitness accounts and several fact-finding commissions have accused the state government and the police of collusion in the violence.[1] I was present at a meeting where a group of victims kept wailing, "Please save us from the police! That's all we ask ..."

In December 2002, the same state government was voted back to office. Narendra Modi, who was widely accused of having orchestrated the riots, has embarked on his second term as Chief Minister of Gujarat. On August 15, 2003, Independence Day, he hoisted the Indian flag before thousands of cheering people. In a gesture of menacing symbolism, he wore the black RSS cap—which proclaims him as a member of the Hindu nationalist guild that has not been shy of admiring Hitler and his methods.[2]

One hundred thirty million Muslims—not to mention the other minorities, Dalits, Christians, Sikhs, Adivasis—live in India under the shadow of Hindu nationalism.

As his confidence in his political future brimmed over, Narendra Modi, master of seizing the political moment, invited Nelson Mandela to Gujarat to be the chief guest at the celebration of Gandhi's birth anniversary on October 2, 2002.[3] Fortunately the invitation was turned down.[4]

And what of Mandela's South Africa? Otherwise known as the Small Miracle, the Rainbow Nation of God? South Africans say that the only miracle they know of is how quickly the rainbow has been privatized, sectioned off, and auctioned to the highest bidders. In its rush to replace Argentina as neoliberalism's poster child, it has instituted a massive program of privatization and structural adjustment. The government's promise to redistribute agricultural land to 26 million landless people has remained in the realm of dark humor.[5] While more than 50 percent of the population remains landless, almost all agricultural land is owned by sixty thousand white farmers.[6] (Small wonder that George Bush on his recent visit to South Africa referred to Thabo Mbeki as his "point man" on the Zimbabwe issue.)

Post-apartheid, the income of the poorest 40 percent of Black families has diminished by about 20 percent.[7] Two million have been evicted from their homes.[8] Six hundred die of AIDS every day. Forty percent of the population is unemployed, and that number is rising sharply.[9] The corporatization of basic services has meant that millions have been disconnected from water and electricity.[10]

A fortnight ago, I visited the home of Teresa Naidoo in Chatsworth, Durban. Her husband had died the previous day of AIDS. She had no money for a coffin. She and her two small children are HIV-positive. The government disconnected her water supply because she was unable to pay her water bills and her rent arrears for her tiny council flat. The government dismisses her troubles and those of millions like her as a "culture of non-payment."[11]

In what ought to be an international scandal, this same government has officially asked the judge in a US court case to rule against forcing companies to pay reparations for the role they played during apartheid.[12] Its reasoning is that reparations—in other words, justice—will discourage foreign investment.[13] So South Africa's poorest must pay apartheid's debts, so that those who amassed profit by exploiting Black people during apartheid can profit even more from the goodwill generated by Nelson Mandela's Rainbow Nation of God. President Thabo Mbeki is still called "comrade" by his colleagues in government. In South Africa, Orwellian parody goes under the genre of Real Life.

What's left to say about Martin Luther King's America? Perhaps it's worth asking a simple question: Had he been alive today, would he have chosen to stay warm in his undisputed place in the pantheon of Great Americans? Or would he have stepped off his pedestal, shrugged off the empty hosannas, and walked out on to the streets to rally his people once more?

On April 4, 1967, one year before he was assassinated, Martin Luther King spoke at the Riverside Church in New York City. That evening he said: "I could never again raise my voice against the violence of the oppressed in the ghettos without having first spoken clearly to the greatest purveyor of violence in the world today—my own government."[14]

Has anything happened in the thirty-six years between 1967 and 2003 that would have made him change his mind? Or would he be doubly confirmed in his opinion after the overt and covert wars and acts of mass killing that successive governments of his country, both Republican and Democrat, have engaged in since then?

Let's not forget that Martin Luther King Jr. didn't start out as a militant. He began as a Persuader, a Believer. In 1964 he won the Nobel Peace Prize. He was held up by the media as an exemplary Black leader, unlike, say, the more militant Malcolm X. It was only three years later that Martin Luther King publicly connected the US government's racist war in Vietnam with its racist policies at home.

In 1967, in an uncompromising, militant speech, he denounced the American invasion of Vietnam. He said:

> We have been repeatedly faced with the cruel irony of watching Negro and white boys on TV screens as they kill and die together for a nation that has been unable to seat them together in the same schools. So we watch them in brutal solidarity burning the huts of a poor village, but we realize that they would never live on the same block in Detroit.[15]

The *New York Times* had some wonderful counter-logic to offer the growing anti-war sentiment among Black Americans: "In Vietnam," it said, "the Negro for the first time has been given the chance to do his share of fighting for his country."[16]

It omitted to mention Martin Luther King Jr.'s remark that "there are twice as many Negroes dying in Vietnam as whites in proportion to their size in the population."[17] It omitted to mention that when the body bags came home, some of the Black soldiers were buried in segregated graves in the Deep South.

What would Martin Luther King Jr. say today about the fact that federal statistics show that African Americans, who account for 12 percent of America's population, make up 21 percent of the total armed forces and 29 percent of the US Army?[18]

Perhaps he would take a positive view and look at this as affirmative action at its most effective?

What would he say about the fact that having fought so hard to win the right to vote, today 1.4 million African Americans, which means 13 percent of all voting-age Black people, have been disenfranchised because of felony convictions?[19]

To Black soldiers fighting in Vietnam, Martin Luther King Jr. said, "As we counsel young men concerning military service we must clarify for them our nation's role in Vietnam and challenge them with the alternative of conscientious objection."[20]

In April 1967, at a massive anti-war demonstration in Manhattan, Stokely Carmichael described the draft as "white people sending Black people to make war on yellow people in order to defend land they stole from red people."[21]

What's changed? Except of course the compulsory draft has become a poverty draft—a different kind of compulsion. Would Martin Luther King Jr. say today that the invasion and occupation of Iraq and Afghanistan are in any way morally different from the US government's invasion of Vietnam? Would he say that it was just and moral to participate in these wars? Would he say that it was right for the US government to have supported a dictator like Saddam Hussein politically and financially for years while he committed his worst excesses against Kurds, Iranians, and Iraqis—in the 1980s when he was an ally against Iran? And that when that dictator began to chafe at the bit, as Saddam Hussein did, would he say it was right to go to war against Iraq, to fire several hundred tons of depleted uranium into its fields, to degrade its water supply systems, to institute a regime of economic sanctions that resulted in the death of half a million children, to use UN weapons inspectors to force it to disarm, to mislead the public about an arsenal of weapons of mass destruction that could be deployed in a matter of minutes, and then, when the country was on its knees, to send in an invading army to conquer it, occupy it, humiliate its people, take control of its natural resources and infrastructure, and award contracts worth hundreds of millions of dollars to American corporations like Bechtel?

When he spoke out against the Vietnam War, Martin Luther King Jr. drew some connections that many these days shy away from making. He said, "The problem of racism, the problem of economic exploitation, and the problem of war are all tied together. These are the triple evils that are interrelated."[22] Would he tell people today that it is right for the US government to export its cruelties—its racism, its economic bullying, and its war machine—to poorer countries?

Would he say that Black Americans must fight for their fair share of the American pie and the bigger the pie, the better their share—never mind the terrible price that the people of Africa, Asia, the Middle East, and Latin America are paying for the American Way of Life? Would he support the grafting of the Great American Dream onto his own dream, which was a very different, very beautiful sort of dream? Or would he see that as a desecration of his memory and everything that he stood for?

The Black American struggle for civil rights gave us some of the most magnificent political fighters, thinkers, public speakers, and writers of our times. Martin Luther King Jr., Malcolm X, Fannie Lou Hamer, Ella Baker, James Baldwin, and of course the marvelous, magical, mythical Muhammad Ali.

Who has inherited their mantle?

Could it be the likes of Colin Powell? Condoleezza Rice? Michael Powell?

They're the exact opposite of icons or role models. They *appear* to be the embodiment of Black people's dreams of material success, but in actual fact they represent the Great Betrayal. They are the liveried doormen guarding the portals of the glittering ballroom against the press and swirl of the darker races. Their role and purpose is to be trotted out by the Bush administration looking for brownie points in its racist wars and African safaris.

If these are Black America's new icons, then the old ones must be dispensed with because they do not belong in the same pantheon. If these are Black America's new icons, then perhaps the haunting image that Mike Marqusee describes in his beautiful book *Redemption Song*— an old Muhammad Ali, afflicted with Parkinson's disease, advertising a retirement pension—symbolizes what has happened to Black Power, not just in the United States but the world over.[23]

If Black America genuinely wishes to pay homage to its real heroes, and to all those unsung people who fought by their side, if the world wishes to pay homage, then it's time to march on Washington. Again. Keeping hope alive—for all of us.

4. In Memory of Shankar Guha Niyogi

We are gathered here today exactly twelve years after the murder of your beloved leader Shankar Guha Niyogi. All these years have gone by, and we are still waiting for those who murdered him to be brought to justice.

I'm a writer, but in this time of urgent, necessary battle, it is important for everybody, even for writers, not usually given to public speaking, to stand before thousands of people and share their thoughts.

I am here on this very important day to say that I support and respect the spectacular struggle of the Chhattisgarh Mukti Morcha.

Yesterday I visited the settlement around the iron-ore mines of Dalli Rajhara where the Chhattisgarh Mukti Morcha's battle began. Now it has spread across the whole of Chhattisgarh. I was deeply moved by what I saw and the people I met. What inspired me most of all was the fact that yours is and always has been a struggle not just for workers' rights and farmers' rights, not just about wages and bonuses and jobs, but a struggle that has dared to dream about what it means to be human. Whenever people's rights have been assaulted, whether they are women or children, whether they are Sikhs or Muslims during communal killings, whether they are workers or farmers who were denied irrigation, you have always stood by them.

This sharp, compelling sense of humanity will have to be our weapon

Talk delivered in Raipur, India, September 28, 2003.

in times to come, when everything—our homes, our fields, our jobs, our rivers, our electricity, our right to protest, and our dignity—is being taken from us.

This is happening not just in India but in poor countries all over the world, and in response to this the poor are rising in revolt across the world.

The culmination of the process of corporate globalization is taking place in Iraq.

Imagine if you can what we would feel if thousands of armed American soldiers were patrolling the streets of India, of Chhattisgarh, deciding where we may go, who we may meet, what we must think.

It is of utmost importance that we understand that the American occupation of Iraq and the snatching away of our fields, homes, rivers, jobs, infrastructure, and resources are products of the very same process. For this reason, any struggle against corporate globalization, any struggle for the rights and dignity of human beings must support the Iraqi people who are resisting the American occupation.

After India won independence from British rule in 1947, perhaps many of your lives did not undergo radical material change for the better. Even so, we cannot deny that it was a kind of victory, it was a kind of freedom. But today, fifty years on, even this is being jeopardized. The process of selling this country back into slavery began in the mid-1980s. The Chhattisgarh Mukti Morcha was one of the first people's resistance movements to recognize this, and so today you are an example, a beacon of light, a ray of hope for the rest of the country—and perhaps the rest of the world.

Exactly at the time when the government of India was busy undermining labor laws and dismantling the formal structures that protected workers' rights, the Chhattisgarh Mukti Morcha intensified its struggle for the rights of all workers—formal, informal, and contract laborers. For this Shankar Guha Niyogi and at least sixteen others lost their lives, killed by assassins and police bullets.[1]

When the government of India made it clear that it is not concerned with public health, the Chhattisgarh Mukti Morcha, with contributions from workers, built the wonderful Shaheed Hospital and drew attention to the urgent necessity of providing health care to the poor.

When the state made it clear that it was more than happy to keep the poor of India illiterate and vulnerable, the Chhattisgarh Mukti Morcha started schools for the children of workers. These schools don't just educate children but inculcate in them revolutionary thought and create new generations of activists. Today these children led our rally, tomorrow they'll lead the resistance. It is of immense significance that this movement is led by the workers and farmers of Chhattisgarh.

To belong to a people's movement that recognized and struggled against the project of neo-imperialism as early as the Chhattisgarh Mukti Morcha did is to shoulder a great responsibility.

But you have shown, with your courage, your wisdom, and your perseverance, that you are more than equal to this task. You know better than me that the road ahead is long and hard.

As a writer, as a human being, I salute you. Lal Johar.

5. How Deep Shall We Dig?

Recently a young Kashmiri friend was talking to me about life in Kashmir. Of the morass of political venality and opportunism, the callous brutality of the security forces, of the osmotic, inchoate edges of a society saturated in violence, where militants, police, intelligence officers, government servants, businessmen, and even journalists encounter each other and gradually, over time, *become* each other. He spoke of having to live with the endless killing, the mounting "disappearances," the whispering, the fear, the unresolved rumors, the insane disconnection between what is actually happening, what Kashmiris know is happening, and what the rest of us are told is happening in Kashmir. He said, "Kashmir used to be a business. Now it's a mental asylum."

The more I think about that remark, the more apposite a description it seems for all of India. Admittedly, Kashmir and the Northeast are separate wings that house the more perilous wards in the asylum. But in the heartland, too, the schism between knowledge and information, between what we know and what we're told, between what is unknown and what is asserted, between what is concealed and what is revealed, between fact and conjecture, between the "real" world and the virtual world, has become a place of endless speculation and potential insanity. It's a poisonous brew which is stirred and simmered and put to the most ugly, destructive, political purpose.

Full text of the first I. G. Khan Memorial Lecture, delivered at Aligarh Muslim University, in Aligarh, India, on April 6, 2004.

Each time there is a so-called terrorist strike, the government rushes in, eager to assign culpability with little or no investigation. The burning of the Sabarmati Express in Godhra, the December 13, 2001, attack on the Parliament building, and the massacre of Sikhs by so-called terrorists in Chittisinghpura in March 2000 are only a few high-profile examples. (The so-called terrorists who were later killed by security forces turned out to be innocent villagers. The state government subsequently admitted that fake blood samples were submitted for DNA testing.)[1] In each of these cases, the evidence that eventually surfaced raised very disturbing questions and so was immediately put into cold storage. Take the case of Godhra: as soon as it happened the Home Minister announced it was an Inter Services Intelligence plot. The VHP says it was the work of a Muslim mob throwing petrol bombs.[2] Serious questions remain unanswered. There is endless conjecture. Everybody believes what they want to believe, but the incident is used to cynically and systematically whip up communal frenzy.

The US government used the lies and disinformation generated around the September 11 attacks to invade not just one country but two—and heaven knows what else is in store.

The Indian government uses the same strategy, not with other countries but against its own people.

Over the last decade, the number of people who have been killed by the police and security forces runs into the thousands. Recently several Bombay policemen spoke openly to the press about how many "gangsters" they had eliminated on "orders" from their senior officers.[3] Andhra Pradesh chalks up an average of about two hundred "extremists" in "encounter" deaths a year.[4] In Kashmir, in a situation that almost amounts to war, an estimated eighty thousand people have been killed since 1989. Thousands have simply "disappeared."[5] According to the records of the Association of Parents of Disappeared People (APDP), more than 3,000 people were killed in 2003, of whom 463 were soldiers.[6] Since the Mufti Mohammed Sayeed government came to power in October 2002 on the promise of bringing a "healing touch," the APDP says, there have been fifty-four custodial deaths.[7] In this age of hypernationalism, as long as the people who are killed are labeled gangsters, terrorists, insurgents, or extremists, their killers can strut around as crusaders in the national interest and are answerable to no one. Even if it were true (which it most certainly isn't) that every person who has been killed was in fact a gangster, terrorist, insurgent, or extremist, it only tells us there is something terribly wrong with a society that drives so many people to take such desperate measures.

The Indian state's proclivity to harass and terrorize people has been institutionalized, consecrated, by the enactment of the Prevention of Terrorism Act (POTA), which has been promulgated in ten states. A cursory reading of POTA will tell you that it is draconian and ubiquitous. It's a versatile, hold-all law that could apply to anyone—from an Al-Qaeda operative caught with a cache of explosives to an Adivasi playing his flute under a neem tree, to you or me. The genius of POTA is that it can be anything the government wants it to be. We live on the sufferance of those who govern us. In Tamil Nadu it has been used to stifle criticism of the state government.[8] In Jharkhand thirty-two hundred people, mostly poor Adivasis accused of being Maoists, have been indicted under POTA.[9] In eastern Uttar Pradesh the act is used to clamp down on those who dare to protest about the alienation of their land and livelihood rights.[10] In Gujarat and Mumbai, it is used almost exclusively against Muslims.[11] In Gujarat after the 2002 state-assisted pogrom in which an estimated 2,000 Muslims were killed and 150,000 driven from their homes, 287 people have been accused under POTA. Of these, 286 are Muslim and one is a Sikh![12] POTA allows confessions extracted in police custody to be admitted as judicial evidence. In effect, under the POTA regime, police torture tends to replace police investigation. It's quicker, cheaper, and ensures results. Talk of cutting back on public spending.

In March 2004 I was a member of a people's tribunal on POTA. Over a period of two days we listened to harrowing testimonies of what goes on in our wonderful democracy. Let me assure you that in our police stations it's everything: from people being forced to drink urine to being stripped, humiliated, given electric shocks, burned with cigarette butts, having iron rods put up their anuses to being beaten and kicked to death.

Across the country hundreds of people, including some very young children charged under POTA, have been imprisoned and are being held without bail, awaiting trial in special POTA courts that are not open to public scrutiny. A majority of those booked under POTA are guilty of one of two crimes. Either they're poor—for the most part Dalit and Adivasi—or they're Muslim. POTA inverts the accepted dictum of criminal law: that a person is innocent until proven guilty. Under POTA you cannot get bail unless you can prove you are innocent—of a crime that you have not been formally charged with. Essentially, you have to prove you're innocent even if you're unaware of the crime you are supposed to have committed. And that applies to all of us. Technically, we are a nation waiting to be accused.

It would be naive to imagine that POTA is being "misused." On the contrary. It is being used for precisely the reasons it was enacted. Of course, if the recommendations of the Malimath Committee are implemented, POTA will soon become redundant. The Malimath Committee recommends that in certain respects normal criminal law should be brought in line with the provisions of POTA.[13] There'll be no more criminals then. Only terrorists. It's kind of neat.

Today in Jammu and Kashmir and many northeastern states of India, the Armed Forces Special Powers Act allows not just officers but even junior commissioned officers and noncommissioned officers of the army to use force against (and even kill) any person on suspicion of disturbing public order or carrying a weapon.[14] On *suspicion of*! Nobody who lives in India can harbor any illusions about what that leads to. The documentation of instances of torture, disappearances, custodial deaths, rape, and gang-rape (by security forces) is enough to make your blood run cold. The fact that, despite all this, India retains its reputation as a legitimate democracy in the international community and among its own middle class is a triumph.

The Armed Forces Special Powers Act is a harsher version of the ordinance that Lord Linlithgow passed in August 15, 1942, to handle the Quit India Movement. In 1958 it was clamped on parts of Manipur, which were declared "disturbed areas." In 1965 the whole of Mizoram, then still part of Assam was declared "disturbed." In 1972 the act was extended to Tripura. By 1980, the whole of Manipur had been declared "disturbed."[15] What more evidence does anybody need to realize that repressive measures are counterproductive and only exacerbate the problem?

Juxtaposed against this unseemly eagerness to repress and eliminate people is the Indian state's barely hidden reluctance to investigate and bring to trial cases in which there is plenty of evidence: the massacre of three thousand Sikhs in Delhi in 1984 and the massacres of Muslims in Bombay in 1993 and in Gujarat in 2002 (not one conviction to date); the murder a few years ago of Chandrashekhar Prasad, former president of the Jawaharlal Nehru University student union; and the murder twelve years ago of Shankar Guha Niyogi of the Chhattisgarh Mukti Morcha are just a few examples.[16] Eyewitness accounts and masses of incriminating evidence are not enough when all of the state machinery is stacked against you.

Meanwhile, economists cheering from the pages of corporate newspapers inform us that the GDP growth rate is phenomenal, unprecedented. Shops are overflowing with consumer goods. Government storehouses are overflowing with food grain. Outside this circle of light, farmers steeped in debt are committing suicide in the hundreds. Reports of starvation and malnutrition come in from across the country. Yet the government allowed 63 million tons of grain to rot in its granaries.[17] Twelve million tons were exported and sold at a subsidized price the Indian government was not willing to offer the Indian poor.[18] Utsa Patnaik, the well-known agricultural economist, has calculated food grain availability and food grain absorption in India for nearly a century, based on official statistics. She calculates that in the period between the early 1990s and 2001, food grain absorption has dropped to levels lower than during the World War II years, including during the Bengal Famine, in which 3 million people died of starvation.[19] As we know from the work of Professor Amartya Sen, democracies don't take kindly to starvation deaths. They attract too much adverse publicity from the "free press."[20] So dangerous levels of malnutrition and permanent hunger are the preferred model these days. Forty-seven percent of India's children below three suffer from malnutrition, 46 percent are stunted.[21] Utsa Patnaik's study reveals that about 40 percent of the rural population in India has the same food grain absorption level as sub-Saharan Africa.[22] Today, an average rural family eats about 100 kilograms less food in a year than it did in the early 1990s.[23]

But in urban India, wherever you go—shops, restaurants, railway stations, airports, gymnasiums, hospitals—you have TV monitors in which election promises have already come true. India's Shining, Feeling Good. You only have to close your ears to the sickening crunch of the policeman's boot on someone's ribs, you only have to raise your eyes from the squalor, the slums, the ragged broken people on the streets and seek a friendly TV monitor and you will be in that other beautiful world. The singing-dancing world of Bollywood's permanent pelvic thrusts, of permanently privileged, permanently happy Indians waving the tricolor flag and Feeling Good. It's becoming harder and harder to tell which one's the real world and which one's virtual. Laws like POTA are like buttons on a TV. You can use it to switch off the poor, the troublesome, the unwanted.

There is a new kind of secessionist movement taking place in India. Shall we call it New Secessionism? It's an inversion of Old Secessionism. It's when people who are actually part of a whole different economy, a whole different country, a whole different *planet*, pretend they're part of this one. It is the kind of secession in which a relatively small section of people become immensely wealthy by appropriating everything—land, rivers, water, freedom, security, dignity, fundamental rights, including the right to protest—from a large group of people. It's a vertical secession, not a horizontal, territorial one. It's the real Structural Adjustment—the kind that separates India Shining from India. India Pvt. Ltd. from India the Public Enterprise.

It's the kind of secession in which public infrastructure, productive public assets—water, electricity, transport, telecommunications, health services, education, natural resources—assets that the Indian state is supposed to hold in trust for the people it represents, assets that have been built and maintained with public money over decades, are sold by the state to private corporations. In India 70 percent of the population—70 million people—live in rural areas.[24] Their livelihoods depend on access to natural resources. To snatch these away and sell them as stock to private companies is beginning to result in dispossession and impoverishment on a barbaric scale.

India Pvt. Ltd. is on its way to being owned by a few corporations and major multinationals. The CEOs of these companies will control this country, its infrastructure and its resources, its media and its journalists, but will owe nothing to its people. They are completely unaccountable—legally, socially, morally, politically. Those who say that in India a few of these CEOs are more powerful than the Prime Minister know exactly what they're talking about.

Quite apart from the economic implications of all this, even if it were all that it is cracked up to be (which it isn't)—miraculous, efficient, amazing—is the *politics* of it acceptable to us? If the Indian state chooses to mortgage its responsibilities to a handful of corporations, does it mean that the theater of electoral democracy is entirely meaningless? Or does it still have a role to play?

The Free Market (which is actually far from free) needs the State, and needs it badly. As the disparity between the rich and poor grows in poor countries, states have their work cut out for them. Corporations on the prowl for "sweetheart deals" that yield enormous profits cannot push through those deals and administer those projects in developing countries without the active connivance of state machinery. Today corporate globalization needs an international confederation of loyal, corrupt, preferably authoritarian governments in poorer countries, to push through unpopular reforms and quell the mutinies. It's called "Creating a Good Investment Climate."

When we vote, we choose which political party we would like to invest the coercive, repressive powers of the state in.

Right now in India we have to negotiate the dangerous crosscurrents of neoliberal capitalism and communal neo-fascism. While the word *capitalism* hasn't completely lost its sheen yet, using the word *fascism* often causes offense. So we must ask ourselves, are we using the word loosely? Are we exaggerating our situation, does what we are experiencing on a daily basis qualify as fascism?

When a government more or less openly supports a pogrom against members of a minority community in which up to two thousand people are brutally killed, is it fascism? When women of that community are publicly raped and burned alive, is it fascism? When authorities collude to see to it that nobody is punished for these crimes, is it fascism? When one hundred fifty thousand people are driven from their homes, ghettoized, and economically and socially boycotted, is it fascism? When the cultural guild that runs hate camps across the country commands the respect and admiration of the Prime Minister, the Home Minister, the

Law Minister, the Disinvestment Minister, is it fascism? When painters, writers, scholars, and filmmakers who protest are abused, threatened, and have their work burned, banned, and destroyed, is it fascism? When a government issues an edict requiring the arbitrary alteration of school history textbooks, is it fascism? When mobs attack and burn archives of ancient historical documents, when every minor politician masquerades as a professional medieval historian and archaeologist, when painstaking scholarship is rubbished using baseless populist assertion, is it fascism? When murder, rape, arson, and mob justice are condoned by the party in power and its stable of stock intellectuals as an appropriate response to a real or perceived historical wrong committed centuries ago, is it fascism? When the middle-class and the well-heeled pause a moment, tut-tut, and then go on with their lives, is it fascism? When the Prime Minister who presides over all of this is hailed as a statesman and visionary, are we not laying the foundations for full-blown fascism?

That the history of oppressed and vanquished people remains for the most part unchronicled is a truism that does not apply only to Savarna Hindus. If the politics of avenging historical wrong is our chosen path, then surely the Dalits and Adivasis of India have the right to murder, arson, and wanton destruction?

In Russia, they say the past is unpredictable. In India, from our recent experience with school history textbooks, we know how true that is. Now all "pseudo-secularists" have been reduced to hoping that archaeologists digging under the Babri Masjid wouldn't find the ruins of a Ram temple. But even if it were true that there is a Hindu temple under every mosque in India, what was under the temple? Perhaps another Hindu temple to another god. Perhaps a Buddhist stupa. Most likely an Adivasi shrine. History didn't begin with Savarna Hinduism, did it? How deep shall we dig? How much should we overturn? And why is it that while Muslims—who are socially, culturally, and economically an unalienable part of India—are called outsiders and invaders and are cruelly targeted, the government is busy signing corporate deals and contracts for development aid with a government that colonized us for centuries? Between 1876 and 1892, during the great famines, millions of Indians died of starvation while the British government continued to export food and raw materials to England. Historical records put the figure between 12 and 29 million people.[25] That should figure somewhere in the politics of revenge, should it not? Or is vengeance only fun when its victims are vulnerable and easy to target?

Successful fascism takes hard work. And so does Creating a Good Investment Climate. Do the two work well together? Historically, corporations have not been shy of fascists. Corporations such as Siemens, I. G. Farben, Bayer, IBM, and Ford did business with the Nazis.[26] We have the more recent example of our own Confederation of Indian Industry abasing itself to the Gujarat government after the pogrom in 2002.[27] As long as our markets are open, a little homegrown fascism won't come in the way of a good business deal.

It's interesting that just around the time Manmohan Singh, then the finance minister, was preparing India's markets for neoliberalism, L. K. Advani was making his first Rath Yatra, fueling communal passion and preparing us for neo-fascism. In December 1992, rampaging mobs destroyed the Babri Masjid. In 1993 the Congress government of Maharashtra signed a power purchase agreement with Enron. It was the first private power project in India. The Enron contract, disastrous as it has turned out, kick-started the era of privatization in India. Now, as the Congress whines from the sidelines, the Bharatiya Janata Party (BJP) has wrested the baton from its hands.[28] The government is conducting an extraordinary dual orchestra. While one arm is busy selling off the nation's assets in chunks, the other, to divert attention, is arranging a baying, howling, deranged chorus of cultural nationalism. The inexorable ruthlessness of one process feeds directly into the insanity of the other.

Economically, too, the dual orchestra is a viable model. Part of the enormous profits generated by the process of indiscriminate privatization (and the accruals of "India Shining") goes into financing Hindutva's vast army—the RSS, the VHP, the Bajrang Dal, and the myriad other charities and trusts that run schools, hospitals, and social services. Between them they have tens of thousands of shakhas across the country. The hatred they preach, combined with the unmanageable frustration generated by the relentless impoverishment and dispossession of the corporate globalization project, fuels the violence of poor on poor—the perfect smoke screen to keep the structures of power intact and unchallenged.

However, directing people's frustrations into violence is not always enough. In order to Create a Good Investment Climate, the State often needs to intervene directly.

In recent years, the police has repeatedly opened fire on unarmed people, mostly Adivasis, at peaceful demonstrations. In Nagarnar, Jharkhand; in Mehndi Kheda, Madhya Pradesh; in Umergaon, Gujarat; in Rayagara and Chilika, Orissa; in Muthanga, Kerala. People are killed for encroaching on forest land, as well as when they're trying to protect forest land from dams, mining operations, steel plants.

The repression goes on and on. Jambudweep, Kashipur, Maikanj. In almost every instance of police firing, those who have been fired upon are immediately called militants.

When victims refuse to be victims, they are called terrorists and are dealt with as such. POTA is the broad-spectrum antibiotic for the disease of dissent. There are other, more specific steps that are being taken— court judgments that in effect curtail free speech, the right to strike, the right to life and livelihood.

This year, 181 countries voted in the United Nations for increased protection of human rights in the era of the War on Terror. Even the United States voted in favor of the resolution. India abstained.[29] The stage is being set for a full-scale assault on human rights.

So how can ordinary people counter the assault of an increasingly violent state?

The space for nonviolent civil disobedience has atrophied. After struggling for several years, several nonviolent people's resistance movements have come up against a wall and feel, quite rightly, they have to now change direction. Views about what that direction should be are deeply polarized. There are some who believe that an armed struggle is the only avenue left. Leaving aside Kashmir and the Northeast, huge swathes of territory, whole districts in Jharkhand, Bihar, Uttar Pradesh, and Madhya Pradesh, are controlled by those who hold that view. Others increasingly are beginning to feel they must participate in electoral politics—enter the system, negotiate from within. (Similar, is it not, to the choices people faced in Kashmir?) The thing to remember is that while their methods differ radically, both sides share the belief that, to put it crudely, Enough Is Enough. *Ya Basta.*

There is no debate taking place in India that is more crucial than this one. Its outcome will, for better or for worse, change the quality of life in this country. For everyone. Rich, poor, rural, urban.

Armed struggle provokes a massive escalation of violence from the State. We have seen the morass it has led to in Kashmir and across the Northeast.

So then, should we do what our Prime Minister suggests we do? Renounce dissent and enter the fray of electoral politics? Join the road show? Participate in the shrill exchange of meaningless insults which serve only to hide what is otherwise an almost absolute consensus? Let's not forget that on every major issue—nuclear bombs, Big Dams, the Babri Masjid controversy, and privatization—the Congress sowed the seeds and the BJP swept in to reap the hideous harvest.

This does not mean that the Parliament is of no consequence and elections should be ignored. Of course there is a difference between an overtly communal party with fascist leanings and an opportunistically communal party. Of course there is a difference between a politics that openly, proudly preaches hatred and a politics that slyly pits people against each other.

But the legacy of one has led us to the horror of the other. Between them, they have eroded any real choice that parliamentary democracy is supposed to provide. The frenzy, the fairground atmosphere created around elections, takes center stage in the media because everybody is secure in the knowledge that regardless of who wins, the status quo will essentially remain unchallenged. (After the impassioned speeches in Parliament, repealing POTA doesn't seem to be a priority in any party's election campaign. They all know they need it, in one form or another.) Whatever they say during elections or when they're in the opposition, no state or national government and no political party—right, left, center, or sideways—has managed to stay the hand of neoliberalism. There will be no radical change "from within."

Personally, I don't believe that entering the electoral fray is a path to alternative politics. Not because of that middle-class squeamishness—"politics is dirty" or "all politicians are corrupt"—but because I believe that strategically battles must be waged from positions of strength, not weakness.

The targets of the dual assault of neoliberalism and communal fascism are the poor and the minority communities. As neoliberalism drives its wedge between the rich and the poor, between India Shining and India, it becomes increasingly absurd for any mainstream political party to pretend to represent the interests of both the rich and the poor, because the interests of one can only be represented at the *cost* of the other. My "interests" as a wealthy Indian (were I to pursue them) would hardly coincide with the interests of a poor farmer in Andhra Pradesh.

A political party that represents the poor will be a poor party. A party with very meager funds. Today it isn't possible to fight an election without funds. Putting a couple of well-known social activists into Parliament is interesting but not really politically meaningful. Not a process worth channeling all our energies into. Individual charisma, personality politics, cannot effect radical change.

However, being poor is not the same as being weak. The strength of the poor is not indoors in office buildings and courtrooms. It's outdoors, in the fields, the mountains, the river valleys, the city streets, and university campuses of this country. That's where negotiations must be held. That's where the battle must be waged.

Right now, those spaces have been ceded to the Hindu Right. Whatever anyone might think of their politics, it cannot be denied that they're out there, working extremely hard. As the State abrogates its responsibilities and withdraws funds from health, education, and essential public services, the foot soldiers of the Sangh Parivar have moved in. Alongside their tens of thousands of shakhas disseminating deadly propaganda, they run schools, hospitals, clinics, ambulance services, disaster management cells. They understand powerlessness. They also understand that people, and particularly powerless people, have needs and desires that are not only practical, humdrum day-to-day needs but emotional, spiritual, recreational. They have fashioned a hideous crucible into which the anger, the frustration, the indignity of daily life—and dreams of a different future—can be decanted and directed to deadly purpose. Meanwhile, the traditional, mainstream Left still dreams of "seizing power" but remains strangely unbending, unwilling to address the times. It has laid siege to itself and retreated into an inaccessible intellectual space, where ancient arguments are proffered in an archaic language that few can understand.

The only ones who present some semblance of a challenge to the onslaught of the Sangh Parivar are the grassroots resistance movements scattered across the country, fighting the dispossession and violation of fundamental rights caused by our current model of "development." Most of these movements are isolated and, despite the relentless accusation that they are "foreign-funded agents," work with almost no money or resources at all. They're magnificent firefighters. They have their backs to the wall. But they have their ears to the ground, and they are in touch with grim reality. If they got together, if they were supported and strengthened, they could grow into a force to reckon with. Their battle, when it is fought, will have to be an idealistic one—not a rigidly ideological one.

At a time when opportunism is everything, when hope seems lost, when everything boils down to a cynical business deal, we must find the courage to dream. To reclaim romance. The romance of believing in justice, in freedom, and in dignity. For everybody. We have to make common cause, and to do this we need to understand how this big old machine works—who it works for and who it works against. Who pays, who profits.

Many nonviolent resistance movements fighting isolated, single-issue battles across the country have realized that their kind of special interest politics, which had its time and place, is no longer enough. That they feel cornered and ineffectual is not good enough reason to abandon nonviolent resistance as a strategy. It is, however, good enough reason to do some serious introspection. We need vision. We need to make sure that those of us who say we want to reclaim democracy are egalitarian and democratic in our own methods of functioning. If our struggle is to be an idealistic one, we cannot really make caveats for the internal injustices that we perpetrate on one another, on women, on children. For example, those fighting communalism cannot turn a blind eye to economic injustices. Those fighting dams or development projects cannot elide issues of communalism or caste politics in their spheres of influence—even at the cost of short-term success in their immediate campaign. If opportunism and expediency come at the cost of our beliefs, then there is nothing to separate us from mainstream politicians. If it is justice that we want, it must be justice and equal rights for all—not only for special interest groups with special interest prejudices. That is nonnegotiable.

We have allowed nonviolent resistance to atrophy into feel-good political theater, which at its most successful is a photo opportunity for the media, and at its least successful is simply ignored.

We need to look up and urgently discuss strategies of resistance, wage real battles, and inflict real damage. We must remember that the Dandi March was not just fine political theater. It was a strike at the economic underpinning of the British Empire.

We need to redefine the meaning of politics. The "NGO-ization" of civil society initiatives is taking us in exactly the opposite direction. It's depoliticizing us. Making us dependent on aid and handouts. We need to reimagine the meaning of civil disobedience.

Perhaps we need an elected shadow parliament *outside* the Lok Sabha, without whose support and affirmation Parliament cannot easily function. A shadow parliament that keeps up an underground drumbeat, that shares intelligence and information (all of which is increasingly unavailable in the mainstream media). Fearlessly, but nonviolently, we must disable the working parts of this machine that is consuming us.

We're running out of time. Even as we speak, the circle of violence is closing in. Either way, change will come. It could be bloody, or it could be beautiful. It depends on us.

Part II

6. The Greater Common Good

If you are to suffer, you should suffer in the interest of the country . . .
—Jawaharlal Nehru, speaking to villagers who were to be
displaced by the Hirakud dam, 1948[1]

I stood on a hill and laughed out loud.

I had crossed the Narmada by boat from Jalsindhi and climbed the headland on the opposite bank, from where I could see, ranged across the crowns of low bald hills, the Adivasi hamlets of Sikka, Surung, Neemgavan, and Domkhedi. I could see their airy, fragile homes. I could see their fields and the forests behind them. I could see little children with littler goats scuttling across the landscape like motorized peanuts. I knew I was looking at a civilization older than Hinduism, slated—*sanctioned* (by the highest court in the land)—to be drowned this monsoon [1999], when the waters of the Sardar Sarovar reservoir will rise to submerge it.

Why did I laugh?

Because I suddenly remembered the tender concern with which the Supreme Court judges in Delhi (before vacating the legal stay on further construction of the Sardar Sarovar dam) had inquired whether Adivasi children in the resettlement colonies would have children's

First published in *Outlook* and *Frontline*, June 4, 1999.

parks to play in. The lawyers representing the government had hastened to assure them that indeed they would, and what's more, that there were seesaws and slides and swings in every park. I looked up at the endless sky and down at the river rushing past, and for a brief, brief moment the absurdity of it all reversed my rage and I laughed. I meant no disrespect.

Let me say at the outset that I'm not a city-basher. I've done my time in a village. I've had firsthand experience of the isolation, the inequity, and the potential savagery of it. I'm not an antidevelopment junkie, nor a proselytizer for the eternal upholding of custom and tradition. What I *am*, however, is curious. Curiosity took me to the Narmada valley. Instinct told me that this was the big one. The one in which the battle lines were clearly drawn, the warring armies massed along them. The one in which it would be possible to wade through the congealed morass of hope, anger, information, disinformation, political artifice, engineering ambition, disingenuous socialism, radical activism, bureaucratic subterfuge, misinformed emotionalism, and, of course, the pervasive, invariably dubious, politics of International Aid.

Instinct led me to set aside Joyce and Nabokov, to postpone reading Don DeLillo's big book and substitute for it reports on drainage and irrigation, with journals and books and documentary films about dams and why they're built and what they do.

My first tentative questions revealed that few people know what is really going on in the Narmada valley. Those who know, know a lot. Most know nothing at all. And yet almost everyone has a passionate opinion. Nobody's neutral. I realized very quickly that I was straying into mined territory.

In India over the last ten years the fight against the Sardar Sarovar dam has come to represent far more than the fight for one river. This has been its strength as well as its weakness. Some years ago it became a debate that captured the popular imagination. That's what raised the stakes and changed the complexion of the battle. From being a fight over the fate of a river valley it began to raise doubts about an entire political system. What is at issue now is the very nature of our democracy. Who owns this land? Who owns its rivers? Its forests? Its fish? These are huge questions. They are being taken hugely seriously by the State. They are being answered in one voice by every institution at its command—the army, the police, the bureaucracy, the courts. And not just answered, but answered unambiguously, in bitter, brutal ways.

For the people of the valley, the fact that the stakes were raised to this degree has meant that their most effective weapon—*specific* facts about *specific* issues in this *specific* valley—has been blunted by the debate on the big issues. The basic premise of the argument has been inflated until it has burst into bits that have, over time, bobbed away. Occasionally a disconnected piece of the puzzle floats by—an emotionally charged account of the government's callous treatment of displaced people; an outburst at how the Narmada Bachao Andolan (NBA), "a handful of activists," is holding the nation to ransom; a legal correspondent reporting on the progress of the NBA's writ petition in the Supreme Court.

Though there has been a fair amount of writing on the subject, most of it is for a "special interest" readership. News reports tend to be about isolated aspects of the project. Government documents are classified as secret. I think it's fair to say that public perception of the issue is pretty crude and is divided crudely, into two categories.

On the one hand, it is seen as a war between modern, rational, progressive forces of "Development" v. a sort of neo-Luddite impulse—an irrational, emotional "Anti-development" resistance, fueled by an arcadian, preindustrial dream.

On the other, as a Nehru v. Gandhi contest. This lifts the whole sorry business out of the bog of deceit, lies, false promises, and increasingly successful propaganda (which is what it's *really* about) and confers on it a false legitimacy. It makes out that both sides have the Greater Good of the Nation in mind—but merely disagree about the means by which to achieve it.

Both interpretations put a tired spin on the dispute. Both stir up emotions that cloud the particular facts of this particular story. Both are indications of how urgently we need new heroes—new *kinds* of heroes—and how we've overused our old ones (like we overbowl our bowlers).

The Nehru v. Gandhi argument pushes this very contemporary issue back into an old bottle. Nehru and Gandhi were generous men. Their paradigms for development are based on assumptions of inherent morality.

Nehru's on the paternal, protective morality of the Soviet-style centralized State. Gandhi's on the nurturing, maternal morality of romanticized village republics. Both would probably work, if only we were better human beings. If we all wore homespun khadi and suppressed our base urges. Fifty years down the line, it's safe to say that we haven't made the grade. We haven't even come close. We need an updated insurance plan against our own basic natures.

It's possible that as a nation we've exhausted our quota of heroes for this century, but while we wait for shiny new ones to come along, we have to limit the damage. We have to support our small heroes. (Of these we have many. Many.) We have to fight specific wars in specific ways. Who knows, perhaps that's what the twenty-first century has in store for us. The dismantling of the Big. Big bombs, big dams, big ideologies, big contradictions, big countries, big wars, big heroes, big mistakes. Perhaps it will be the Century of the Small. Perhaps right now, this very minute, there's a small god up in heaven readying herself for us. Could it be? Could *it possibly* be? It sounds finger-licking good to me.

I was drawn to the valley because I sensed that the fight for the Narmada had entered a newer, sadder phase. I went because writers are drawn to stories the way vultures are drawn to kills. My motive was not compassion. It was sheer greed. I was right. I found a story there.

And what a story it is . . .

People say that the Sardar Sarovar dam is an expensive project. But it is bringing drinking water to millions. This is our lifeline. Can you put a price on this? Does the air we breathe have a price? We will live. We will drink. We will bring glory to the state of Gujarat.
    —**Urmilaben Patel, wife of Gujarat Chief Minister Chiman-bhai Patel, speaking at a public rally in Delhi in 1993**

We will request you to move from your houses after the dam comes up. If you move, it will be good. Otherwise we shall release the waters and drown you all.
    —**Morarji Desai, speaking at a public meeting in the submergence zone of the Pong dam in 1961**[2]

Why didn't they just poison us? Then we wouldn't have to live in this shithole and the government could have survived alone with its precious dam all to itself.

—Ram Bai, whose village was submerged when the Bargi dam was built on the Narmada; she now lives in a slum in Jabalpur[3]

In the fifty years since Independence, after Nehru's famous "Dams Are the Temples of Modern India" speech (one that he grew to regret in his own lifetime),[4] his foot soldiers threw themselves into the business of building dams with unnatural fervor. Dam-building grew to be equated with nation-building. Their enthusiasm alone should have been reason enough to make one suspicious. Not only did they build new dams and new irrigation systems, they took control of small traditional systems that had been managed by village communities for thousands of years, and allowed them to atrophy.[5] To compensate the loss, the government built more and more dams. Big ones, little ones, tall ones, short ones. The result of its exertions is that India now boasts of being the world's third largest dam-builder. According to the Central Water Commission, we have 3,600 dams that qualify as Big Dams, 3,300 of them built after Independence. One thousand more are under construction.[6] Yet one-fifth of our population—200 million people—does not have safe drinking water, and two-thirds—600 million—lack basic sanitation.[7]

Big Dams started well but have ended badly. There was a time when everybody loved them, everybody had them—the Communists, Capitalists, Christians, Muslims, Hindus, Buddhists. There was a time when Big Dams moved men to poetry. Not any longer. All over the world there is a movement growing against Big Dams.

In the first world they're being decommissioned, blown up.[8] The fact that they do more harm than good is no longer just conjecture. Big Dams are obsolete. They're uncool. They're undemocratic. They're a government's way of accumulating authority (deciding who will get how much water and who will grow what where). They're a guaranteed way of taking a farmer's wisdom away from him. They're a brazen means of taking water, land, and irrigation away from the poor and gifting it to the rich. Their reservoirs displace huge populations of people, leaving them homeless and destitute.

Ecologically, too, they're in the doghouse.[9] They lay the earth to waste. They cause floods, waterlogging, salinity, they spread disease. There is mounting evidence that links Big Dams to earthquakes.

Big Dams haven't really lived up to their role as the monuments of Modern Civilization, emblems of Man's ascendancy over Nature. Monuments are supposed to be timeless, but dams have an all too finite lifetime. They last only as long as it takes Nature to fill them with silt.[10] It's common knowledge now that Big Dams do the opposite of what their Publicity People say they do—the Local Pain for National Gain myth has been blown wide open.

For all these reasons, the dam-building industry in the first world is in trouble and out of work. So it's exported to the third world in the name of Development Aid, along with their other waste, like old weapons, superannuated aircraft carriers, and banned pesticides.[11]

On the one hand the Indian government, *every* Indian government, rails self-righteously against the first world, and on the other, it actually *pays* to receive their gift-wrapped garbage. Aid is just another praetorian business enterprise. Like colonialism was. It has destroyed most of Africa. Bangladesh is reeling from its ministrations. We *know* all this, in numbing detail. Yet in India our leaders welcome it with slavish smiles (and make nuclear bombs to shore up their flagging self-esteem).

Over the last fifty years India has spent Rs 87,000 crore[12] on the irrigation sector alone.[13] Yet there are more drought-prone areas and more flood-prone areas today than there were in 1947. Despite the disturbing evidence of irrigation disasters, dam-induced floods, and rapid disenchantment with the Green Revolution[14] (declining yields, degraded land), the government has not commissioned a post-project evaluation of a *single one* of its 3,600 dams to gauge whether or not it has achieved what it set out to achieve, whether or not the (always phenomenal) costs were justified, or even what the costs actually were.

The government of India has detailed figures for how many million tons of food grain or edible oils the country produces and how much more we produce now than we did in 1947. It can tell you how much bauxite is mined in a year or what the total surface area of the national highways adds up to. It's possible to access minute-by-minute information about the stock exchange or the value of the rupee in the world market. We know how many cricket matches we've lost on a Friday in Sharjah. It's not hard to find out how many graduates India produces, or how many men had vasectomies in any given year. But the government of India does not have a figure for the number of people who have been displaced by dams or sacrificed in other ways at the altars of "national progress." Isn't this *astounding*? How can you measure progress if you don't know what it costs and who has paid for it? How can the "market" put a price on things—food, clothes, electricity, running water—when it doesn't take into account the *real* cost of production?

According to a detailed study of fifty-four Big Dams done by the Indian Institute of Public Administration,[15] the *average* number of people displaced by a Big Dam in India is 44,182. Admittedly, 54 dams out of 3,300 is not a big enough sample. But since it's all we have, let's try and do some rough arithmetic. A first draft.

To err on the side of caution, let's halve the number of people. Or let's err on the side of *abundant* caution and take an average of just 10,000 people per Big Dam. It's an improbably low figure, I know, but . . . never mind. Whip out your calculators. 3,300 × 10,000 = 33,000,000.

That's what it works out to. Thirty-three *million* people. Displaced by Big Dams *alone* in the last fifty years. What about those who have been displaced by the thousands of other Development projects? In a private lecture N. C. Saxena, Secretary to the Planning Commission, said he thought the number was in the region of 50 million (of whom 40 million were displaced by dams).[16] We daren't say so, because it isn't official. It isn't official because we daren't say so. You have to murmur it, for fear of being accused of hyperbole. You have to whisper it to yourself, because it really does sound unbelievable. It *can't be*, I've been telling myself. I must have got the zeroes muddled. *It can't be true.* I barely have the courage to say it aloud. To run the risk of sounding like a sixties hippie dropping acid ("It's the System, man!"), or a paranoid schizophrenic with a persecution complex. But it *is* the System, man. What else can it be?

Fifty million people.

Go on, government, quibble. Bargain. Beat it down. Say *something*.

I feel like someone who's just stumbled on a mass grave.

Fifty million is more than the population of Gujarat. Almost three times the population of Australia. More than three times the number of refugees that Partition created in India. Ten times the number of Palestinian refugees. The Western world today is convulsed over the future of one million people who have fled from Kosovo.

A huge percentage of the displaced are Adivasis (57.6 percent in the case of the Sardar Sarovar dam).[17] Include Dalits and the figure becomes obscene. According to the Commissioner for Scheduled Castes and Tribes, it's about 60 percent.[18] If you consider that Adivasis account for only 8 percent, and Dalits another 15 percent, of India's population, it opens up a whole other dimension to the story. The ethnic "otherness" of their victims takes some of the pressure off the nation-builders. It's like having an expense account. Someone else pays the bills. People from another country. Another world. India's poorest people are subsidizing the lifestyles of her richest.

Did I hear someone say something about the world's biggest democracy?

What has happened to all these millions of people? Where are they now? How do they earn a living? Nobody really knows. (Recently the *Indian Express* had an account of how Adivasis displaced from the Nagarjunasagar Dam Project are selling their babies to foreign adoption agencies.[19] The government intervened and put the babies in two public hospitals, where six infants died of neglect.) When it comes to rehabilitation, the government's priorities are clear. India does not *have* a national rehabilitation policy. According to the Land Acquisition Act of 1894 (amended in 1984) the government is not legally bound to provide a displaced person anything but a cash compensation. Imagine that. A cash compensation, to be paid by an Indian government official to an illiterate male Adivasi (the women get nothing) in a land where even the postman demands a tip for a delivery! Most Adivasis have no formal title to their land and therefore cannot claim compensation anyway. Most Adivasis—or let's say most small farmers—have as much use for money as a Supreme Court judge has for a bag of fertilizer.

The millions of displaced people don't exist anymore. When history is written they won't be in it. Not even as statistics. Some of them have subsequently been displaced three and four times—a dam, an artillery-proof range, another dam, a uranium mine, a power project. Once they start rolling there's no resting place. The great majority is eventually absorbed into slums on the periphery of our great cities, where it coalesces into an immense pool of cheap construction labor (that builds more projects that displace more people). True, they're not being annihilated or taken to gas chambers, but I can warrant that the quality of their accommodation is worse than in any concentration camp of the Third Reich. They're not captive, but they redefine the meaning of liberty.

And still the nightmare doesn't end. They continue to be uprooted even from their hellish hovels by government bulldozers that fan out on cleanup missions whenever elections are comfortingly far away and the urban rich get twitchy about hygiene. In cities like Delhi, they run the risk of being shot by the police for shitting in public places—like three slum dwellers were not more than two years ago.

In the French-Canadian wars of the 1770s, Lord Amherst exterminated most of Canada's Native Indians by offering them blankets infested with the smallpox virus. Two centuries on, we of the Real India have found less obvious ways of achieving similar ends.

The millions of displaced people in India are nothing but refugees of an unacknowledged war. And we, like the citizens of White America and French Canada and Hitler's Germany, are condoning it by looking away. Why? Because we're told that it's being done for the sake of the Greater Common Good. That it's being done in the name of Progress, in the name of the National Interest (which, of course, is paramount). Therefore gladly, unquestioningly, almost gratefully, we believe what we're told. We believe what it benefits us to believe.

Allow me to shake your faith. Put your hand in mine and let me lead you through the maze. Do this because it's important that you understand. If you find reason to disagree, by all means take the other side. But please don't ignore it, don't look away. It isn't an easy tale to tell. It's full of numbers and explanations. Numbers used to make my eyes glaze over. Not anymore. Not since I began to follow the direction in which they point.

Trust me. There's a story here.

It's true that India has progressed. It's true that in 1947, when colonialism formally ended, India was food-deficient. In 1950 we produced 51 million tons of food grain. Today we produce close to 200 million tons.[20]

It's true that in 1995 the state granaries were overflowing with 30 million tons of unsold grain. It's also true that at the same time, 40 percent of India's population—more than 350 million people—were living below the poverty line.[21] That's more than the country's population in 1947.

Indians are too poor to buy the food their country produces. Indians are being forced to grow the kinds of food they can't afford to eat themselves. Look at what happened in Kalahandi District in western Orissa, best known for its starvation deaths. In the drought of 1996, people died of starvation (sixteen according to the state, over one hundred according to the press).[22] Yet that same year rice production in Kalahandi was higher than the national average! Rice was exported from Kalahandi District to the center.

Certainly India has progressed, but most of its people haven't. Our leaders say that we must have nuclear missiles to protect us from the threat of China and Pakistan. But who will protect us from ourselves?

What kind of country is this? Who owns it? Who runs it? What's going on?

It's time to spill a few state secrets. To puncture the myth about the inefficient, bumbling, corrupt, but ultimately genial, essentially democratic Indian State. Carelessness cannot account for 50 million disappeared people. Nor can Karma. Let's not delude ourselves. There is method here, precise, relentless, and 100 percent man-made.

The Indian State is not a state that has failed. It is a state that has succeeded impressively in what it set out to do. It has been ruthlessly efficient in the way it has appropriated India's resources—its land, its water, its forests, its fish, its meat, its eggs, its air—and redistributed them to a favored few (in return, no doubt, for a few favors). It is superbly accomplished in the art of protecting its cadres of paid-up elite, consummate in its methods of pulverizing those who inconvenience its intentions. But its finest feat of all is the way it achieves all this and emerges smelling sweet. The way it manages to keep its secrets, to contain information—that vitally concerns the daily lives of one billion people—in government files, accessible only to the keepers of the flame: ministers, bureaucrats, state engineers, defense strategists. Of course we make it easy for them, we its beneficiaries. We take care not to dig too deep. We don't really *want* to know the grisly details.

Thanks to us, Independence came (and went), elections come and go, but there has been no shuffling of the deck. On the contrary, the old order has been consecrated, the rift fortified. We, the rulers, won't pause to look up from our groaning table. We don't seem to know that the resources we're feasting on are finite and rapidly depleting. There's cash in the bank, but soon there'll be nothing left to buy with it. The food's running out in the kitchen. And the servants haven't eaten yet. Actually, the servants stopped eating a long time ago.

India lives in her villages, we're told, in every other sanctimonious public speech. That's bullshit. It's just another fig leaf from the government's bulging wardrobe. India doesn't live in her villages. India *dies* in her villages. India gets kicked around in her villages. India lives in her cities. India's villages live only to serve her cities. Her villagers are her citizens' vassals and for that reason must be controlled and kept alive, but only just.

This impression we have of an overstretched State, struggling to cope with the sheer weight and scale of its problems, is a dangerous one. The fact is that it's *creating* the problems. It's a giant poverty-producing machine, masterful in its methods of pitting the poor against the very poor, of flinging crumbs to the wretched so that they dissipate their energies fighting each other, while peace (and advertising) reigns in the Master's Lodgings.

Until this process is recognized for what it is, until it is addressed and attacked, elections—however fiercely they're contested—will continue to be mock battles that serve only to further entrench unspeakable inequity. Democracy (our version of it) will continue to be the benevolent mask behind which a pestilence flourishes unchallenged. On a scale that will make old wars and past misfortunes look like controlled laboratory experiments. Already 50 million people have been fed into the Development mill and have emerged as air conditioners and popcorn and rayon suits *subsidized* air conditioners and popcorn and rayon suits. If we must have these nice things—and they *are* nice—at least we should be made to pay for them.

There's a hole in the flag that needs mending.

It's a sad thing to have to say, but as long as we have faith, we have no hope. To hope, we have to *break* the faith. We have to fight specific wars in specific ways and we have to fight to win. Listen, then, to the story of the Narmada valley. Understand it. And, if you wish, enlist. Who knows, it may lead to magic.

The Narmada wells up on the plateau of Amarkantak in the Shahdol District of Madhya Pradesh, then winds its way through 1,300 kilometers of beautiful, broad-leaved forest and perhaps the most fertile agricultural land in India. Twenty-five million people live in the river valley, linked to the ecosystem and to each other by an ancient intricate web of interdependence (and, no doubt, exploitation).

Though the Narmada has been targeted for "water resource development" for more than fifty years now, the reason it has, until recently, evaded being captured and dismembered is that it flows through three states—Madhya Pradesh, Maharashtra, and Gujarat.

Ninety percent of the river flows through Madhya Pradesh; it merely skirts the northern border of Maharashtra, then flows through Gujarat for about 180 kilometers before emptying into the Arabian Sea at Bharuch.

As early as 1946, plans had been afoot to dam the river at Gora in Gujarat. In 1961 Nehru laid the foundation stone for a 49.8-meter-high dam—the midget progenitor of the Sardar Sarovar.

Around the same time, the Survey of India drew up new topographical maps of the river basin. The dam planners in Gujarat studied the new maps and decided that it would be more profitable to build a much bigger dam. But this meant hammering out an agreement with neighboring states.

For years the three states bickered and balked but failed to agree on a water-sharing formula. Eventually, in 1969, the central government set up the Narmada Water Disputes Tribunal. It took the tribunal another ten years to announce its award.

The people whose lives were going to be devastated were neither informed nor consulted nor heard.

To apportion shares in the waters, the first, most basic thing the tribunal had to do was to find out how much water there was in the river. Usually this can only be reliably estimated if there is at least forty years of recorded data on the volume of actual flow in the river. Since this was not available, they decided to extrapolate from rainfall data. They arrived at a figure of 27.22 million acre feet (MAF).[23]

This figure is the statistical bedrock of the Narmada Valley Projects. We are still living with its legacy. It more or less determines the overall design of the projects—the height, location, and number of dams. By inference, it determines the cost of the projects, how much area will be submerged, how many people will be displaced, and what the benefits will be.

In 1992 actual observed flow data for the Narmada—which was now available for forty-five years (from 1948 to 1992)—showed that the yield from the river was only 22.69 MAF—18 percent less![24] The Central Water Commission admits that there is less water in the Narmada than had previously been assumed.[25] The government of India says: "It may be noted that clause II [of the decision of the tribunal] relating to determination of dependable flow as 28 MAF is nonreviewable"![26]

Never mind the data—the Narmada is legally bound by human decree to produce as much water as the government of India commands.

Its proponents boast that the Narmada Valley Projects are the most ambitious river valley development scheme ever conceived in human history. They plan to build 3,200 dams that will reconstitute the Narmada and her forty-one tributaries into a series of step reservoirs—an immense staircase of amenable water. Of these, 30 will be major dams, 135 medium, and the rest small. Two of the major dams will be multipurpose megadams. The Sardar Sarovar in Gujarat and the Narmada Sagar in Madhya Pradesh will, between them, hold more water than any other reservoir on the Indian subcontinent.

Whichever way you look at it, the Narmada Valley Development Projects are Big. They will alter the ecology of the entire river basin of one of India's biggest rivers. For better or for worse, they will affect the lives of 25 million people who live in the valley. They will submerge and destroy 4,000 square kilometers of natural deciduous forest.[27] Yet even before the Ministry of Environment cleared the projects, the World Bank offered to finance the linchpin of the project—the Sardar Sarovar dam, whose reservoir displaces people in Madhya Pradesh and Maharashtra but whose benefits go to Gujarat. The Bank was ready with its checkbook *before* any costs were computed, *before* any studies had been done, *before* anybody had any idea of what the human cost or the environmental impact of the dam would be!

The $450 million loan for the Sardar Sarovar Projects was sanctioned and in place in 1985. The Ministry of Environment clearance for the project came only in 1987! Talk about enthusiasm. It fairly borders on evangelism. Can anybody care so much?

Why were they so keen?

Between 1947 and 1994 the World Bank's management had submitted six thousand projects to the executive board. The board hadn't turned down a single one. *Not a single one.* Terms like "moving money" and "meeting loan targets" suddenly begin to make sense.

India is in a situation today where it pays back more money to the Bank in interest and repayment installments than it receives from it. We are forced to incur new debts in order to be able to repay our old ones. According to the World Bank Annual Report, last year (1998), after the arithmetic, India paid the Bank $478 million more than it borrowed. Over the last five years (1993 to 1998) India paid the Bank $1.475 billion more than it received.[28]

The relationship between us is exactly like the relationship between a landless laborer steeped in debt and the village moneylender—it is an affectionate relationship, the poor man loves his moneylender because he's always there when he's needed. It's not for nothing that we call the world a global village. The only difference between the landless laborer and the government of India is that one uses the money to survive; the other just funnels it into the private coffers of its officers and agents, pushing the country into an economic bondage that it may never overcome.

The international dam industry is worth $20 billion a year.[29] If you follow the trails of Big Dams the world over, wherever you go—China, Japan, Malaysia, Thailand, Brazil, Guatemala—you'll rub up against the same story, encounter the same actors: the Iron Triangle (dam jargon for the nexus comprising politicians, bureaucrats, and dam-construction companies), the racketeers who call themselves International Environmental Consultants (who are usually directly employed by dam-builders or their subsidiaries), and, more often than not, the friendly neighborhood World Bank. You'll grow to recognize the same inflated rhetoric, the same noble "Peoples' Dam" slogans, the same swift, brutal repression that follows the first sign of civil insubordination. (Of late, especially after its experience in the Narmada valley, the Bank is more cautious about choosing the countries in which it finances projects that involve mass displacement. At present China is its most favored client. It's the great irony of our times—American citizens protest the massacre in Tiananmen Square, but the Bank has used their money to fund studies for the Three Gorges dam in China, which is going to displace 1.3 million people. The Bank is today the biggest foreign financier of large dams in China.)[30]

It's a skillful circus, and the acrobats know each other well. Occasionally they'll swap parts—a bureaucrat will join the Bank, a banker will surface as a project consultant. At the end of play, a huge percentage of what's called "Development Aid" is rechanneled back to the countries it came from, masquerading as equipment cost or consultants' fees or salaries to the agencies' own staff. Often aid is openly "tied" (as in the case of the Japanese loan for the Sardar Sarovar dam—to a contract for purchasing turbines from the Sumitomo Corporation).[31] Sometimes the connections are more murky. In 1993 Britain financed the Pergau dam in Malaysia with a subsidized loan of £234 million, despite an Overseas Development Administration report that said that the dam would be a "bad buy" for Malaysia. It later emerged that the loan was offered to "encourage"Malaysia to sign a £1.3 *billion* contract to buy British arms.[32]

In 1994 British consultants earned $2.5 billion on overseas contracts.[33] The second biggest sector of the market after Project Management was writing what are called EIAs (Environmental Impact Assessments). In the Development racket, the rules are pretty simple. If you get invited by a government to write an EIA for a big dam project and you point out a problem (say, you quibble about the amount of water available in a river, or, God forbid, you suggest that the human costs are perhaps too high), then you're history. You're an OOWC. An Out-of-Work Consultant. And oops! There goes your Range Rover. There goes your holiday in Tuscany. There goes your children's private boarding school. There's good money in poverty. Plus perks.

In keeping with Big Dam tradition, concurrent with the construction of the 138.68-meter-high Sardar Sarovar dam began the elaborate government pantomime of conducting studies to estimate the actual project costs and the impact it would have on people and the environment. The World Bank participated wholeheartedly in the charade—occasionally it beetled its brows and raised feeble requests for more information on issues like the resettlement and rehabilitation of what it calls PAPs—Project-Affected Persons. (They help, these acronyms, they manage to mutate muscle and blood into cold statistics. PAPs soon cease to be people.)

The merest crumbs of information satisfied the Bank, and it proceeded with the project. The implicit, unwritten, but fairly obvious understanding between the concerned agencies was that whatever the costs—economic, environmental, or human—the project would go ahead. They would justify it as they went along. They knew full well that eventually, in a courtroom or to a committee, no argument works as well as a Fait Accompli.

Milord, the country is losing two crore a day due to the delay.

The government refers to the Sardar Sarovar Projects as the "most studied project in India," yet the game goes something like this: when the Tribunal first announced its award and the Gujarat government announced its plan of how it was going to use its share of water, *there was no mention of drinking water for villages in Kutch and Saurashtra*, the arid areas of Gujarat. When the project ran into political trouble, the government suddenly discovered the emotive power of thirst. Suddenly, quenching the thirst of parched throats in Kutch and Saurashtra became the whole *point* of the Sardar Sarovar Projects. (Never mind that water from two rivers—the Sabarmati and the Mahi, both of which are *miles* closer to Kutch and Saurashtra than the Narmada—have been dammed and diverted to Ahmedabad, Mehsana, and Kheda. Neither Kutch nor Saurashtra has seen a drop of it.) Officially, the number of people who will be provided drinking water by the Sardar Sarovar canal fluctuates from 28 million (1983) to 32.5 million (1989)—nice touch, the decimal point!—to 40 million (1992) and down to 25 million (1993).[34]

In 1979 the number of villages that would receive drinking water was zero. In the early 1980s it was 4,719. In 1990 it was 7,234. In 1991 it was 8,215.[35] When pressed, the government admitted that the figures for 1991 included 236 *uninhabited* villages![36]

Every aspect of the project is approached in this almost playful manner, as if it's a family board game. Even when it concerns the lives and futures of vast numbers of people.

In 1979 the number of families that would be displaced by the Sardar Sarovar reservoir was estimated to be a little over 6,000. In 1987 it grew to 12,000. In 1991 it surged to 27,000. In 1992 the government acknowledged that 40,000 families would be affected. Today, the official figure hovers between 40,000 and 41,500.[37] (Of course even this is an absurd figure, because the reservoir isn't the *only* thing that displaces people. According to the NBA the actual figure is about 85,000 families—that's *half a million* people.)

The estimated cost of the project bounced up from under Rs 5,000 crore[38] to Rs 20,000 crore (officially). The NBA says that it will cost Rs 44,000 crore.[39]

The government claims the Sardar Sarovar Projects will produce 1,450 megawatts of power.[40] The thing about multipurpose dams like the Sardar Sarovar is that their "purposes" (irrigation, power production, and flood control) conflict with one another. Irrigation uses up the water you need to produce power. Flood control requires you to keep the reservoir empty during the monsoon months to deal with an anticipated surfeit of water. And if there's no surfeit, you're left with an empty dam. And this defeats the purpose of irrigation, which is to *store* the monsoon water. It's like the conundrum of trying to ford a river with a fox, a chicken, and a bag of grain. The result of these mutually conflicting aims, studies say, is that when the Sardar Sarovar Projects are completed and the scheme is fully functional, it will end up producing only 3 percent of the power that its planners say it will. About fifty megawatts. And if you take into account the power needed to pump water through its vast network of canals, the Sardar Sarovar Projects will end up *consuming* more electricity than they produce![41]

In an old war, everybody has an ax to grind. So how do you pick your way through these claims and counterclaims? How do you decide whose estimate is more reliable? One way is to take a look at the track record of Indian dams.

The Bargi dam near Jabalpur was the first dam on the Narmada to be completed (in 1990). It cost ten times more than was budgeted and submerged three times more land than the engineers said it would. About seventy thousand people from 101 villages were supposed to be displaced, but when they filled the reservoir (without warning anybody), 162 villages were submerged. Some of the resettlement sites built by the government were submerged as well. People were flushed out like rats from the land they had lived on for centuries. They salvaged what they could and watched their houses being washed away. One hundred four-teen thousand people were displaced.[42] There was no rehabilitation policy. Some were given meager cash compensation. Many got absolutely nothing. A few were moved to government rehabilitation sites. The site at Gorakhpur is, according to government publicity, an "ideal village."

Between 1990 and 1992, five people died of starvation there. The rest either returned to live illegally in the forests near the reservoir or moved to slums in Jabalpur.

The Bargi dam irrigates only as much land as it submerged in the first place—*and only 5 percent of the area that its planners claimed it would irrigate.*[43] Even that is waterlogged.

Time and again, it's the same story. The Andhra Pradesh Irrigation II scheme claimed it would displace 63,000 people. When completed, it displaced 150,000 people.[44] The Gujarat Medium Irrigation II scheme displaced 140,000 people instead of 63,600.[45] The revised estimate of the number of people to be displaced by the Upper Krishna irrigation project in Karnataka is 240,000, against its initial claims of displacing only 20,000.[46]

These are World Bank figures. Not the NBA's. Imagine what this does to our conservative estimate of 33 million.

Construction work on the Sardar Sarovar dam site, which had continued sporadically since 1961, began in earnest in 1988. At the time, nobody, not the government, nor the World Bank, was aware that a woman called Medha Patkar had been wandering through the villages slated to be submerged, asking people whether they had any idea of the plans that the government had in store for them. When she arrived in the valley all those years ago, opposing the construction of the dam was the farthest thing from her mind. Her chief concern was that displaced villagers should be resettled in an equitable, humane way. It gradually became clear to her that the government's intentions toward them were far from honorable. By 1986 word had spread, and each state had a people's organization that questioned the promises about resettlement and rehabilitation that were being bandied about by government officials. It was only some years later that the full extent of the horror—the impact that the dams would have, both on the people who were to be displaced and the people who were supposed to benefit—began to surface. The Narmada Valley Development Projects came to be known as India's Greatest Planned Environmental Disaster. The various people's organizations massed into a single organization, and the Narmada Bachao Andolan—the extraordinary NBA—was born.

In 1988 the NBA formally called for all work on the Narmada Valley Development Projects to be stopped. People declared that they would drown if they had to but would not move from their homes. Within two years the struggle had burgeoned and had support from other resistance movements. In September 1989, more than fifty thousand people gathered in the valley from all over India to pledge to fight "destructive development." The dam site and its adjacent areas, already under the Indian Official Secrets Act, were clamped under Section 144, which prohibits the gathering of groups of more than five people. The whole area was turned into a police camp. Despite the barricades, one year later, on September 28, 1990, thousands of villagers made their way on foot and by boat to a little town called Badwani, in Madhya Pradesh, to reiterate their pledge to drown rather than agree to move from their homes.

News of the people's opposition to the projects spread to other countries. The Japanese arm of Friends of the Earth mounted a campaign in Japan that succeeded in getting the government of Japan to withdraw its ¥27 billion loan to finance the Sardar Sarovar Projects. (The contract for the turbines still holds.) Once the Japanese withdrew, international pressure from various environmental activist groups who supported the struggle began to mount on the World Bank.

This, of course, led to an escalation of repression in the valley. Government policy, described by a particularly articulate minister, was to "flood the valley with khaki."

On Christmas Day 1990, six thousand men and women walked more than a hundred kilometers, carrying their provisions and their bedding, accompanying a seven-member sacrificial squad that had resolved to lay down its lives for the river. They were stopped at Ferkuwa on the Gujarat border by battalions of armed police and crowds of people from the city of Baroda, many of whom were hired, some of whom perhaps genuinely believed that the Sardar Sarovar was "Gujarat's lifeline." It was a telling confrontation. Middle-class urban India versus a rural, predominantly Adivasi army. The marching people demanded they be allowed to cross the border and walk to the dam site. The police refused them passage. To stress their commitment to nonviolence, each villager had his or her hands bound together. One by one, they defied the battalions of police. They were beaten, arrested, and dragged into waiting trucks in which they were driven off and dumped some miles away, in the wilderness. They just walked back and began all over again.

The faceoff continued for almost two weeks. Finally, on January 7, 1991, the seven members of the sacrificial squad announced that they were going on an indefinite hunger strike. Tension rose to dangerous levels. The Indian and international press, TV camera crews, and documentary filmmakers were present in force. Reports appeared in the papers almost every day. Environmental activists stepped up the pressure in Washington. Eventually, acutely embarrassed by the glare of unfavorable media, the World Bank announced that it would commission an independent review of the Sardar Sarovar Projects—unprecedented in the history of Bank behavior. When the news reached the valley, it was received with distrust and uncertainty. The people had no reason to trust the World Bank. But still, it was a victory of sorts. The villagers, understandably upset by the frightening deterioration in the condition of their comrades, who had not eaten for twenty-two days, pleaded with them to call off the fast. On January 28 the fast at Ferkuwa was called off and the brave, ragged army returned to their homes shouting "*Hamara gaon mein hamara raj!*" (Our rule in our villages).

There has been no army quite like this one anywhere else in the world. In other countries—China (Chairman Mao got a Big Dam for his seventy-seventh birthday), Malaysia, Guatemala, Paraguay—every sign of revolt has been snuffed out almost before it began. Here in India, it goes on and on. Of course, the State would like to take credit for this too. It would like us to be grateful to it for not crushing the movement completely, for *allowing* it to exist. After all, what *is* all this, if not a sign of a healthy, functioning democracy in which the State has to intervene when its people have differences of opinion?

I suppose that's one way of looking at it. (Is this my cue to cringe and say "Thank you, thank you, for allowing me to write the things I write"?)

We don't need to be grateful to the State for permitting us to protest. We can thank ourselves for that. It is we who have insisted on these rights. It is we who have refused to surrender them. If we have anything to be truly proud of as a people, it is this.

The struggle in the Narmada valley lives, *despite* the State.

The Indian State makes war in devious ways. Apart from its apparent benevolence, its other big weapon is its ability to wait. To roll with the punches. To wear out the opposition. The State never tires, never ages, never needs a rest. It runs an endless relay.

But fighting people tire. They fall ill, they grow old. Even the young age prematurely. For twenty years now, since the Tribunal's award, the ragged army in the valley has lived with the fear of eviction. For twenty years, in most areas there has been no sign of "development"—no roads, no schools, no wells, no medical help. For twenty years, it has borne the stigma "slated for submergence"—so it's isolated from the rest of society (no marriage proposals, no land transactions). They're a bit like the Hibakusha in Japan (the victims and their descendants of the bombing in Hiroshima and Nagasaki). The "fruits of modern development," when they finally came, brought only horror. Roads brought surveyors. Surveyors brought trucks. Trucks brought policemen. Policemen brought bullets and beatings and rape and arrest, and in one case murder. The only genuine "fruit" of modern development that reached them, reached them inadvertently—the right to raise their voices, the right to be heard. But they have fought for twenty years now. How much longer will they last?

The struggle in the valley is tiring. It's no longer as fashionable as it used to be. The international camera crews and the radical reporters have moved (like the World Bank) to newer pastures. The documentary films have been screened and appreciated. Everybody's sympathy is all used up. But the dam goes on. It's getting higher and higher . . .

Now, more than ever before, the ragged army needs reinforcements. If we let it die, if we allow the struggle to be crushed, if we allow the people to be brutalized, we will lose the most precious thing we have: our spirit, or what's left of it.

"India will go on," they'll tell you, the sage philosophers who don't want to be troubled by piddling current affairs. As though "India" is somehow more valuable than her people.

Old Nazis probably soothe themselves in similar ways.

It's too late, some people say. Too much time and money has gone into the project to revoke it now.

So far, the Sardar Sarovar reservoir has submerged only a fourth of the area that it will when (if) the dam reaches its full height. If we stop it now, we would save 325,000 people from certain destitution. As for the economics of it—it's true that the government has already spent Rs 7,500 crore, but continuing with the project would mean throwing good money after bad. We would save something like Rs 35,000 crore of public money, probably enough to fund local water-harvesting projects in every village in all of Gujarat. What could possibly be a more worthwhile war?

The war for the Narmada valley is not just some exotic tribal war, or a remote rural war or even an exclusively Indian war. It's a war for the rivers and the mountains and the forests of the world. All sorts of warriors from all over the world, anyone who wishes to enlist, will be honored and welcomed. Every kind of warrior will be needed. Doctors, lawyers, teachers, judges, journalists, students, sportsmen, painters, actors, singers, lovers . . . The borders are open, folks! Come on in.

Anyway, back to the story.

In June 1991 the World Bank appointed Bradford Morse, a former head of the United Nations Development Program, as chairman of the Independent Review. His brief was to make a thorough assessment of the Sardar Sarovar Projects. He was guaranteed free access to all secret World Bank documents relating to the projects.

Morse and his team arrived in India in September 1991. The NBA, convinced that this was yet another setup, at first refused to meet them. The Gujarat government welcomed the team with a red carpet (and a nod and a wink) as covert allies.

A year later, in June 1992, the historic Independent Review (known also as the Morse Report) was published.

The Independent Review unpeels the project delicately, layer by layer, like an onion. Nothing was too big and nothing too small for the members of the Morse Committee to inquire into. They met ministers and bureaucrats, they met NGOs working in the area, went from village to village, from resettlement site to resettlement site. They visited the good ones. The bad ones. The temporary ones, the permanent ones. They spoke to hundreds of people. They traveled extensively in the submergence area and the command area. They went to Kutch and other drought-hit areas in Gujarat. They commissioned their own studies. They examined every aspect of the project: hydrology and water management, the upstream environment, sedimentation, catchment-area treatment, the downstream environment, the anticipation of likely problems in the command area— water logging, salinity, drainage, health, the impact on wildlife.

What the Independent Review reveals, in temperate, measured tones (which I admire but cannot achieve), is scandalous. It is the most balanced, unbiased, yet damning indictment of the relationship between the Indian State and the World Bank. Without appearing to, perhaps even without intending to, the report cuts through to the cozy core, to the space where they live together and love each other (somewhere between what they say and what they do).

The core recommendation of the 357-page Independent Review was unequivocal and wholly unexpected:

> We think the Sardar Sarovar Projects as they stand are flawed, that resettlement and rehabilitation of all those displaced by the Projects is not possible under prevailing circumstances, and that environmental impacts of the Projects have not been properly considered or adequately addressed. Moreover we believe that the Bank shares responsibility with the borrower for the situation that has developed. . . . It seems clear that engineering and economic imperatives have driven the Projects to the exclusion of human and environmental concerns. . . . India and the states involved . . . have spent a great deal of money. No one wants to see this money wasted. But we caution that it may be more wasteful to proceed without full knowledge of the human and environmental costs. . . . As a result, we think that the wisest course would be for the Bank to step back from the Projects and consider them afresh . . .[47]

Four committed, knowledgeable, truly independent men—they do a lot to make up for the faith eroded by hundreds of other venal ones who are paid to do similar jobs.

The World Bank, however, was still not prepared to give up. It continued to fund the project. Two months after the Independent Review, it sent out the Pamela Cox Committee, which did exactly what the Morse Review had cautioned against ("it would be irresponsible for us to patch together a series of recommendations on implementation when the flaws in the Projects are as obvious as they seem to us")[48] and suggested a sort of patchwork remedy to try and salvage the operation. In October 1992, on the recommendation of the Pamela Cox Committee, the Bank asked the Indian government to meet some minimum primary conditions within a period of six months.[49] Even that much the government couldn't do. Finally, on March 30, 1993, the World Bank pulled out of the Sardar Sarovar Projects. (Actually, technically, on March 29, one day *before* the deadline, the government of India asked the World Bank to withdraw.)[50] Details. Details.

No one has ever managed to make the World Bank step back from a project before. Least of all a ragtag army of the poorest people in one of the world's poorest countries. A group of people whom Lewis Preston, then president of the Bank, never managed to fit into his busy schedule when he visited India.[51] Sacking the Bank was and is a huge moral victory for the people in the valley.

The euphoria didn't last. The government of Gujarat announced that it was going to raise the $200 million shortfall on its own and push ahead with the project.

During the period of the Independent Review and after it was published, confrontation between people and the authorities continued unabated in the valley—humiliation, arrests, baton charges. Indefinite fasts terminated by temporary promises and permanent betrayals. People who had agreed to leave the valley and be resettled had begun returning to their villages from their resettlement sites. In Manibeli, a village in Maharashtra and one of the nerve centers of the resistance, hundreds of villagers participated in a Monsoon Satyagraha. In 1993, families in Manibeli remained in their homes as the waters rose. They clung to wooden posts with their children in their arms and refused to move. Eventually policemen prized them loose and dragged them away. The NBA declared that if the government did not agree to review the project, on August 6, 1993, a band of activists would drown themselves in the rising waters of the reservoir. On August 5 the Union government constituted yet another committee called the Five Member Group (FMG) to review the Sardar Sarovar Projects.

The government of Gujarat refused it entry into Gujarat.[52]

The FMG report[53] (a "desk report") was submitted the following year. It tacitly endorsed the grave concerns of the Independent Review. But it made no difference. Nothing changed. This is another of the State's tested strategies. It kills you with committees.

In February 1994 the government of Gujarat ordered the permanent closure of the sluice gates of the dam.

In May 1994 the NBA filed a writ petition in the Supreme Court questioning the whole basis of the Sardar Sarovar dam and seeking a stay on its construction.[54]

During the monsoon of that year, when the level in the reservoir rose and water smashed down on the other side of the dam, 65,000 cubic meters of concrete and 35,000 cubic meters of rock were torn out of a stilling basin, leaving a crater 65 meters wide. The riverbed powerhouse was flooded. The damage was kept secret for months.[55] Reports started appearing about it in the press only in January 1995.

In early 1995, on the grounds that the rehabilitation of displaced people had not been adequate, the Supreme Court ordered work on the dam to be suspended until further notice.[56] The height of the dam was 80 meters above mean sea level.

Meanwhile, work had begun on two more dams in Madhya Pradesh—the massive Narmada Sagar (without which the Sardar Sarovar loses 17 to 30 percent of its efficiency)[57] and the Maheshwar dam. The Maheshwar dam is next in line, upstream from the Sardar Sarovar. The government of Madhya Pradesh has signed a power purchase contract with a private company—S. Kumars, one of India's leading textile magnates.

Tension in the Sardar Sarovar area abated temporarily, and the battle moved upstream, to Maheshwar, in the fertile plains of Nimad.

The case pending in the Supreme Court led to a palpable easing of repression in the valley. Construction work had stopped on the dam, but the rehabilitation charade continued. Forests (slated for submergence) continued to be cut and carted away in trucks, forcing people who depended on them for a livelihood to move out.

Even though the dam is nowhere near its eventual projected height, its impact on the environment and the people living along the river is already severe.

Around the dam site and the nearby villages, the number of cases of malaria has increased sixfold.[58]

Several kilometers upstream from the Sardar Sarovar dam, huge deposits of silt, hip deep and over 200 meters wide, have cut off access to the river. Women carrying water pots now have to walk miles, literally *miles*, to find a negotiable entry point. Cows and goats get stranded in the mud and die. The little single-log boats that the Adivasis use have become unsafe on the irrational circular currents caused by the barricade downstream.

Farther upstream, where the silt deposits have not yet become a problem, there's another tragedy. Landless people (predominantly Adivasis and

Dalits) have traditionally cultivated rice, melons, cucumbers, and gourds on the rich, shallow silt banks the river leaves when it recedes in the dry months. Every now and then, the engineers manning the Bargi dam (way upstream, near Jabalpur) release water from the reservoir without warning. Downstream, the water level in the river suddenly rises. Hundreds of families have had their crops washed away several times, leaving them with no livelihood.

Suddenly they can't trust their river anymore. It's like a loved one who has developed symptoms of psychosis. Anyone who has loved a river can tell you that the loss of a river is a terrible, aching thing. But I'll be rapped on the knuckles if I continue in this vein. When we're discussing the Greater Common Good there's no place for sentiment. One must stick to facts. Forgive me for letting my heart wander.

The state governments of Madhya Pradesh and Maharashtra continue to be completely cavalier in their dealings with displaced people. The government of Gujarat has a rehabilitation policy (on paper) that makes the other two states look medieval. It boasts of having the best rehabilitation package in the world.[59] The program offers land for land to displaced people from Maharashtra and Madhya Pradesh and recognizes the claims of "encroachers" (usually Adivasis with no papers). The deception, however, lies in its definition of who qualifies as "Project-Affected."

In point of fact, the government of Gujarat hasn't even managed to rehabilitate people from its own 19 villages slated for submergence, let alone the rest of the 226 villages in the other two states. The inhabitants of these 19 villages have been scattered to 175 separate rehabilitation sites. Social links have been smashed, communities broken up.

In practice, the resettlement story (with a few "ideal village" exceptions) continues to be one of callousness and broken promises. Some people have been given land, others haven't. Some have land that is stony and uncultivable. Some have land that is irredeemably waterlogged. Some have been driven out by landowners who had sold their land to the government but hadn't been paid.[60]

Some who were resettled on the periphery of other villages have ·been robbed, beaten, and chased away by their host villagers. There have been instances when displaced people from two different dam projects have been allotted contiguous lands. In one case, displaced people from *three* dams—the Ukai dam, the Sardar Sarovar dam, and the Karjan dam—were resettled in the *same* area.[61] In addition to fighting among themselves for resources—water, grazing land, jobs—they had to fight a group of landless laborers who had been sharecropping the land for absentee landlords who had subsequently sold it to the government.

There's another category of displaced people—people whose lands have been acquired by the government for resettlement sites. There's a pecking order even among the wretched—Sardar Sarovar "oustees" are more glamorous than other "oustees" because they're occasionally in the news and have a case in court. (In other development projects where there's no press, no NBA, no court case, there are no records. The displaced leave no trail at all.)

In several resettlement sites, people have been dumped in rows of corrugated tin sheds that are furnaces in summer and fridges in winter. Some of them are located in dry riverbeds that during the monsoon turn into fast-flowing drifts. I've been to some of these "sites." I've seen film footage[62] of others: shivering children, perched like birds on the edges of cots, while swirling waters enter their tin homes. Frightened, fevered eyes watch pots and pans carried through the doorway by the current, floating out into the flooded fields, thin fathers swimming after them to retrieve what they can.

When the waters recede they leave ruin. Malaria, diarrhea, sick cattle stranded in the slush. The ancient teak beams dismantled from their previous homes, carefully stacked away like postponed dreams, now spongy, rotten, and unusable.

Forty households were moved from Manibeli to a resettlement site in Gujarat. In the first year, thirty-eight children died.[63] In today's paper (*Indian Express*, April 26, 1999) there's a report about nine deaths in a single rehabilitation site in Gujarat. In the course of a single week. That's 1.2875 PAPs a day, if you're counting.

Many of those who have been resettled are people who have lived all their lives deep in the forest with virtually no contact with money and the modern world. Suddenly they find themselves left with the option of starving to death or walking several kilometers to the nearest town, sitting in the marketplace (both men and women), offering themselves as wage laborers like goods on sale.

Instead of a forest from which they gathered everything they needed—food, fuel, fodder, rope, gum, tobacco, tooth powder, medicinal herbs, housing materials—they earn between ten and twenty rupees a day with which to feed and keep their families. Instead of a river, they have a hand pump. In their old villages they had no money, but they were insured. If the rains failed, they had the forests to turn to. The river to fish in. Their livestock was their fixed deposit. Without all this, they're a heartbeat away from destitution.

In Vadaj, a resettlement site I visited near Baroda, the man who was talking to me rocked his sick baby in his arms, clumps of flies gathered on its sleeping eyelids. Children collected around us, taking care not to burn their bare skin on the scorching tin walls of the shed they call a home. The man's mind was far away from the troubles of his sick baby. He was making me a list of the fruits he used to pick in the forest. He counted forty-eight kinds. He told me that he didn't think he or his children would ever be able to afford to eat any fruit again. Not unless he stole it. I asked him what was wrong with his baby. He said it would be better for the baby to die than live like this. I asked what the baby's mother thought about that. She didn't reply. She just stared.

For the people who've been resettled, everything has to be relearned. Every little thing, every big thing: from shitting and pissing (where d'you do it when there's no jungle to hide you?) to buying a bus ticket, to learning a new language, to understanding money. And worst of all, learning to be supplicants. Learning to take orders. Learning to have masters. Learning to answer only when you're addressed.

In addition to all this, they have to learn how to make written representations (in triplicate) to the Grievance Redressal Committee or the Sardar Sarovar Narmada Nigam for any particular problems they might have. Recently 3,000 people came to Delhi to protest their situation—traveling overnight by train, living on the blazing streets.[64] The president wouldn't meet them because he had an eye infection. Maneka Gandhi, the Minister for Social Justice and Empowerment, wouldn't meet them but asked for a written representation (*Dear Maneka, Please don't build the dam, Love, The People*). When the representation was handed to her, she scolded the little delegation for not having written it in English.

From being self-sufficient and free to being impoverished and yoked to the whims of a world you know nothing, *nothing* about—what d'you suppose it must feel like? Would you like to trade your beach house in Goa for a hovel in Paharganj? No? Not even for the sake of the nation?

Truly, it is just not possible for a state administration, *any* state administration, to carry out the rehabilitation of a people as fragile as this, on such an immense scale. It's like using a pair of hedge clippers to trim an infant's fingernails. You can't do it without clipping its fingers off.

Land for land sounds like a reasonable swap, but how do you implement it? How do you uproot 200,000 people (the official blinkered estimate)—of whom 117,000 are Adivasi—and relocate them in a humane fashion? How do you keep their communities intact in a country where every inch of land is fought over, where almost all litigation pending in courts has to do with land disputes?

Where is all this fine, unoccupied, but arable land that is waiting to receive these intact communities?

The simple answer is that there isn't any. Not even for the "officially" displaced of this one dam.

What about the rest of the 3,199 dams?

What about the remaining thousands of PAPs earmarked for annihilation? Shall we just put the Star of David on their doors and get it over with?

The reservoir of the Maheshwar dam will wholly or partially submerge sixty villages in the Nimad plains of Madhya Pradesh. A significant section of the population in these villages—roughly a third—are Kevats and Kahars, ancient communities of ferrymen, fisherfolk, sand quarriers, and cultivators of the riverbank when the waters recede in the dry season. Most of them own no land, but the river sustains them and means more to them than to anyone else. When the dam is built, thousands of Kevats and Kahars will lose their only source of livelihood. Yet simply because they are landless, they do not qualify as project-affected and will not be eligible for rehabilitation.

Jalud is the first of sixty villages that will be submerged by the reservoir of the Maheshwar dam. Jalud is not an Adivasi village and is therefore riven with the shameful caste divisions that are the scourge of every ordinary Hindu village. A majority of the landowning farmers (the ones who qualify as PAPs) are Rajputs. They farm some of the most fertile soil in India. Their houses are piled with sacks of wheat and lentils and rice. They boast so much about the things they grow on their land that if it weren't so tragic, it could get on your nerves. Their houses have already begun to crack with the impact of the dynamiting on the dam site.

Twelve families who had small holdings in the vicinity of the dam site had their land acquired. They told me how, when they objected, cement was poured into their water pipes, their standing crops were bulldozed, and the police occupied the land by force. All twelve families are now landless and work as wage laborers.

The area that the Rajputs of Jalud are going to be moved to is a few kilometers inland, away from the river, adjoining a predominantly Dalit and Adivasi precinct in a village called Samraj. I saw the huge tract of land that had been marked off for them. It was a hard, stony hillock with stubbly grass and scrub, on which truckloads of silt were being unloaded and spread out in a thin layer to make it look like rich black humus.

The story goes like this: on behalf of the S. Kumars (textile tycoons turned nation-builders) the district magistrate acquired the hillock, which was actually village common grazing land that belonged to the people of Samraj. In addition to this, the land of eighty-four Dalit and Adivasi villagers was acquired. No compensation was paid.

The villagers, whose main source of income was their livestock, had to sell their goats and buffalo because they no longer had anywhere to graze them. Their only remaining source of income lies (lay) on the banks of a small lake on the edge of the village. In summer, when the water level recedes, it leaves a shallow ring of rich silt on which the villagers grow (grew) rice and melons and cucumber.

The S. Kumars have excavated this silt to cosmetically cover the stony grazing ground (which the Rajputs of Jalud don't want). The banks of the lake are now steep and uncultivable.

The already impoverished people of Samraj have been left to starve, while this photo opportunity is being readied for German and Swiss funders, Indian courts, and anybody else who cares to pass that way.

This is how India works. This is the genesis of the Maheshwar dam. The story of the first village. What will happen to the other fifty-nine? May bad luck pursue this dam. May bulldozers turn upon the textile tycoons.

Nothing can justify this kind of behavior.

In circumstances like these, to even entertain a debate about rehabilitation is to take the first step toward setting aside the principles of
justice. Resettling 200,000 people in order to take (or pretend to take)
drinking water to 40 million—there's something very wrong with the
scale of operations here. This is fascist math. It strangles stories. Blud-
geons detail. And manages to blind perfectly reasonable people with its
spurious, shining vision.

When I arrived on the banks of the Narmada in late March 1999,
it was a month after the Supreme Court had suddenly vacated the stay
on construction work of the Sardar Sarovar dam. I had read pretty much
everything I could lay my hands on (all those "secret" government documents). I had a clear idea of the lay of the land—of what had happened
where and when and to whom. The story played itself out before my
eyes like a tragic film whose actors I'd already met. Had I not known its
history, nothing would have made sense. Because in the valley there are
stories within stories, and it's easy to lose the clarity of rage in the sludge
of other people's sorrow.

I ended my journey in Kevadia Colony, where it all began.

Thirty-eight years ago, this is where the government of Gujarat decided to locate the infrastructure it would need for starting work on the
dam: guesthouses, office blocks, accommodation for engineers and their
staff, roads leading to the dam site, warehouses for construction material.

It is located on the cusp of what is now the Sardar Sarovar reservoir
and the Wonder Canal, Gujarat's "lifeline," that is going to quench the
thirst of millions.

Nobody knows this, but Kevadia Colony is the key to the world. Go
there, and secrets will be revealed to you.

In the winter of 1961, a government officer arrived in a village called
Kothie and told the villagers that some of their land would be needed
to construct a helipad because someone terribly important was going
to come visiting. In a few days a bulldozer arrived and flattened standing crops. The villagers were made to sign papers and were paid a sum
of money, which they assumed was payment for their destroyed crops.
When the helipad was ready, a helicopter landed on it, and out came
Prime Minister Nehru. Most of the villagers couldn't see him because he

was surrounded by policemen. Nehru made a speech. Then he pressed a button and there was an explosion on the other side of the river. After the explosion he flew away.[65] That was the genesis of what was to become the Sardar Sarovar dam.

Could Nehru have known when he pressed that button that he had unleashed an incubus?

After Nehru left, the government of Gujarat arrived in strength. It acquired 1,600 acres of land from 950 families from six villages.[66] The people were Tadvi Adivasis who, because of their proximity to the city of Baroda, were not entirely unversed in the ways of a market economy. They were sent notices and told that they would be paid cash compensation and given jobs on the dam site. Then the nightmare began.

Trucks and bulldozers rolled in. Forests were felled, standing crops destroyed. Everything turned into a whirl of jeeps and engineers and cement and steel. Mohan Bai Tadvi watched eight acres of his land with standing crops of sorghum, lentils, and cotton being leveled. Overnight he became a landless laborer. *Three years later* he received his cash compensation of Rs 250 an acre in three separate installments.

Dersukh Bhai Vesa Bhai's father was given Rs 3,500 for his house and five acres of land with its standing crops and all the trees on it. He remembers walking all the way to Rajpipla (the district headquarters) as a little boy, holding his father's hand.

He remembers how terrified they were when they were called in to the Tehsildar's office. They were made to surrender their compensation notices and sign a receipt. They were illiterate, so they didn't know how much the receipt was made out for.

Everybody had to go to Rajpipla, but they were always summoned on different days, one by one. So they couldn't exchange information or compare stories.

Gradually, out of the dust and bulldozers, an offensive, diffuse configuration emerged. Kevadia Colony. Row upon row of ugly cement flats, offices, guesthouses, roads. All the graceless infrastructure of Big Dam construction. The villagers' houses were dismantled and the villagers moved to the periphery of the colony where they remain today, squatters on their own land. Those that caused trouble were intimidated by the police and the construction company. The villagers told me that in the contractor's headquarters they have a "lockup" like a police lockup, where recalcitrant villagers are incarcerated and beaten.

The people who were evicted to build Kevadia Colony do not qualify as "Project-Affected" in Gujarat's rehabilitation package.

Some of them work as servants in the officers' bungalows and waiters in the guesthouse built on the land where their own houses once stood. Can there be anything more poignant?

Those who had some land left tried to cultivate it, but Kevadia municipality introduced a scheme in which they brought in pigs to eat uncollected refuse on the streets. The pigs stray into the villagers' fields and destroy their crops.

In 1992, thirty years later, each family has been offered a sum of Rs 12,000 per acre, up to a maximum of Rs 36,000, *provided* they agree to leave their homes and go away! Yet 40 percent of the land that was acquired is lying unused. The government refuses to return it. Eleven acres acquired from Deviben, who is a widow now, has been given over to the Swami Narayan Trust (a big religious sect). On a small portion of it, the trust runs a little school. The rest it cultivates, while Deviben watches through the barbed-wire fence. On two hundred acres acquired in the village of Gora, villagers were evicted and blocks of flats were built. They lay empty for years. Eventually the government rented them for a nominal fee to Jai Prakash Associates, the dam contractors, who, the villagers say, sublet them privately for Rs 32,000 a month. (Jai Prakash Associates, the biggest dam contractors in the country, the *real* nation-builders, owns the Siddharth Continental and the Vasant Continental Hotels in Delhi.)

On an area of about thirty acres there is an absurd cement Public Works Department replica of the ancient Shoolpaneshwar temple that was submerged in the reservoir. The same political formation that plunged a whole nation into a bloody, medieval nightmare because it insisted on destroying an old mosque to dig up a nonexistent temple thinks nothing of submerging a hallowed pilgrimage route and hundreds of temples that have been worshiped in for centuries.

It thinks nothing of destroying the sacred hills and groves, the places of worship, the ancient homes of the gods and demons of the Adivasis.

It thinks nothing of submerging a valley that has yielded fossils, microliths, and rock paintings, the only valley in India, according to archaeologists, that contains an uninterrupted record of human occupation from the Old Stone Age.

What can one say?

In Kevadia Colony, the most barbaric joke of all is the wildlife museum. The Shoolpaneshwar Sanctuary Interpretation Center gives you quick, comprehensive evidence of the government's sincere commitment to conservation.

The Sardar Sarovar reservoir, when the dam reaches its full height, is going to submerge about 13,000 hectares of prime forest land. (In anticipation of submergence, the forest began to be felled many greedy years ago.) Between the Narmada Sagar dam and the Sardar Sarovar dam, 50,000 hectares of old-growth, broad-leaved forest will be submerged. Madhya Pradesh has the highest rate of forest-cover loss in the whole of India. This is partly responsible for the reduced flow in the Narmada and the increase in siltation. Have engineers made the connection between forest, rivers, and rain? Unlikely. It isn't part of their brief. Environmentalists and conservationists were quite rightly alarmed at the extent of loss of biodiversity and wildlife habitat that the submergence would cause. To mitigate this loss, the government decided to expand the Shoolpaneshwar Wildlife Sanctuary near the dam, south of the river. There is a harebrained scheme that envisages drowning animals from the submerged forests swimming their way to "wildlife corridors" that will be created for them, and setting up home in the New! Improved! Shoolpaneshwar Sanctuary.

Presumably wildlife and biodiversity can be protected and maintained only if human activity is restricted and traditional rights to use forest resources curtailed. Forty thousand Adivasis from 101 villages within the boundaries of the Shoolpaneshwar Sanctuary depend on the forest for a livelihood. They will be "persuaded" to leave.

They are not included in the definition of "Project-Affected."

Where will they go? I imagine you know by now.

Whatever their troubles in the real world, in the Shoolpaneshwar Sanctuary Interpretation Center (where an old stuffed leopard and a moldy sloth bear have to make do with a shared corner) the Adivasis have a whole room to themselves. On the walls there are clumsy wooden carvings, government-approved Adivasi art, with signs that say TRIBAL

ART. In the center there is a life-sized thatched hut with the door open. The pot's on the fire, the dog is asleep on the floor, and all's well with the world. Outside, to welcome you, are Mr. and Mrs. Adivasi. A lumpy papier-mâché couple, smiling.

Smiling. They're not even permitted the grace of rage. That's what I can't get over.

Oh, but have I got it wrong? What if they're smiling with national pride? Brimming with the joy of having sacrificed their lives to bring drinking water to thirsty millions in Gujarat?

For twenty years now, the people of Gujarat have waited for the water they believe the Wonder Canal will bring them. For years the government of Gujarat has invested 85 percent of the state's irrigation budget into the Sardar Sarovar Projects. Every smaller, quicker, local, more feasible scheme has been set aside for the sake of this. Election after election has been contested and won on the "water ticket." Everyone's hopes are pinned to the Wonder Canal. Will she fulfill Gujarat's dreams?

From the Sardar Sarovar dam, the Narmada flows through 180 kilometers of rich lowland into the Arabian Sea in Bharuch. What the Wonder Canal does, more or less, is to reroute most of the river, bending it almost 90 degrees northward. It's a pretty drastic thing to do to a river. The Narmada estuary in Bharuch is one of the last-known breeding places of the hilsa, probably the hottest contender for India's favorite fish.

The Stanley dam wiped out hilsa from the Cauvery River in south India, and Pakistan's Ghulam Mohammed dam destroyed its spawning area on the Indus. Hilsa, like the salmon, is an anadromous fish—born in freshwater, migrating to the ocean as a smolt, and returning to the river to spawn. The drastic reduction in water flow, the change in the chemistry of the water because of all the sediment trapped *behind* the dam, will radically alter the ecology of the estuary and modify the delicate balance of freshwater and seawater, which is bound to affect the spawning. At present, the Narmada estuary produces 13,000 metric tons of hilsa and freshwater prawn (which also breeds in brackish water). Ten thousand fisher families depend on it for a living.[67]

The Morse Committee was appalled to discover that no studies had been done of the downstream environment[68]—no documentation of the riverine ecosystem, its seasonal changes, its biological species, or the pattern of how its resources are used. The dam-builders had no idea what the impact of the dam would be on the people and the environment downstream, let alone any ideas on what steps to take to mitigate it.

The government simply says that it will alleviate the loss of hilsa fisheries by stocking the reservoir with hatchery-bred fish. (Who'll control the reservoir? Who'll grant the commercial fishing to its favorite paying customers?) The only hitch is that, so far, scientists have not managed to breed hilsa artificially. The rearing of hilsa depends on getting spawn from wild adults, which will in all likelihood be eliminated by the dam. Dams have either eliminated or endangered one-fifth of the world's freshwater fish.[69]

So! Quiz question—where will the 40,000 fisherfolk go? E-mail your answers to The Government That Cares dot com.

At the risk of losing readers—I've been warned several times, "How can you write about *irrigation*? Who the *hell* is interested?"—let me tell you what the Wonder Canal is and what she's meant to achieve. *Be* interested, if you want to snatch your future back from the sweaty palms of the Iron Triangle.

Most rivers in India are monsoon-fed. Eighty to eighty-five percent of the flow takes place during the rainy months—usually between June and September. The purpose of a dam, an irrigation dam, is to store monsoon water in its reservoir and then use it judiciously for the rest of the year, distributing it across dry land through a system of canals. The area of land irrigated by the canal network is called the "command area."

How will the command area, accustomed only to seasonal irrigation, its entire ecology designed for that single pulse of monsoon rain, react to being irrigated the whole year round? Perennial irrigation does to soil roughly what anabolic steroids do to the human body. Steroids can turn an ordinary athlete into an Olympic medal–winner; perennial irrigation can convert soil that produced only a single crop a year into soil that yields *several* crops a year. Land on which farmers traditionally grew crops that don't need a great deal of water (maize, millet, barley, and a whole range of pulses) suddenly yield water-guzzling cash crops—cotton, rice, soybeans, and the biggest guzzler of all (like those finned fifties cars), sugarcane. This completely alters traditional crop patterns in the command area. People stop growing things that they can afford to *eat* and start growing things that they can only afford to *sell*. By linking themselves to the "market" they lose control over their lives.

Ecologically too this is a poisonous payoff. Even if the markets hold out, the soil doesn't. Over time it becomes too poor to support the extra demands made on it. Gradually, in the way a steroid-using athlete becomes an invalid, the soil becomes depleted and degraded, and agricultural yields begin to decrease.[70]

In India, land irrigated by well water is today almost twice as productive as land irrigated by canals.[71] Certain kinds of soil are less suitable for perennial irrigation than others. Perennial canal irrigation raises the level of the water table. As the water moves up through the soil, it absorbs salts. Saline water is drawn to the surface by capillary action, and the land becomes waterlogged. The "logged" water (to coin a phrase) is then breathed into the atmosphere by plants, causing an even greater concentration of salts in the soil. When the concentration of salts in the soil reaches 1 percent, that soil becomes toxic to plant life. This is what's called salinization.

A study[72] by the Center for Resource and Environmental Studies at the Australian National University says that one-fifth of the world's irrigated land is salt-affected.

By the mid-1980s, 25 million of the 37 million hectares under irrigation in Pakistan were estimated to be either salinized or waterlogged or both.[73] In India the estimates vary between 6 and 10 million hectares.[74] According to "secret" government studies,[75] more than 52 percent of the Sardar Sarovar command area is prone to waterlogging and salinization.

And that's not the end of the bad news.

The 460-kilometer-long, concrete-lined Sardar Sarovar Wonder Canal and its 75,000-kilometer network of branch canals and sub-branch canals is designed to irrigate a total of 2 million hectares of land spread over twelve districts. The districts of Kutch and Saurashtra (the billboards of Gujarat's thirst campaign) are at the very tail end of this network.

The system of canals superimposes an arbitrary concrete grid on the existing pattern of natural drainage in the command area. It's a little like reorganizing the pattern of reticulate veins on the surface of a leaf. When a canal cuts across the path of a natural drain, it blocks the flow of the natural, seasonal water and leads to waterlogging. The engineering solution to this is to map the pattern of natural drainage in the area and replace it with an alternate artificial drainage system that is built in conjunction with the canals. The problem, as you can imagine, is that doing this is enormously expensive. The cost of drainage is not included as part of the Sardar Sarovar Projects. It usually isn't, in most irrigation projects.

David Hopper, the World Bank's vice president for South Asia, has admitted[76] that the Bank does not usually include the cost of drainage in its irrigation projects in South Asia because irrigation projects *with* adequate drainage are just too expensive. *It costs five times as much to provide adequate drainage as it does to irrigate the same amount of land.* It makes the cost of a complete project appear unviable.

The Bank's solution to the problem is to put in the irrigation system and wait—for salinity and waterlogging to set in. When all the money's spent and the land is devastated and the people are in despair, who should pop by? Why, the friendly neighborhood banker! And what's that bulge in his pocket? Could it be a loan for a drainage project?

In Pakistan, the World Bank financed the Tarbela (1977) and Mangla dam (1967) projects on the Indus. The command areas are waterlogged.[77] Now the Bank has given Pakistan a $785 million loan for a drainage project. In India, in Punjab and in Haryana, it's doing the same.

Irrigation without drainage is like having a system of arteries and no veins. Pretty damn pointless.

Since the World Bank stepped back from the Sardar Sarovar Projects, it's a little unclear where the money for the drainage is going to come from. This hasn't deterred the government from going ahead with the canal work. The result is that even before the dam is ready, before the Wonder Canal has been commissioned, before a single drop of irrigation water has been delivered, waterlogging has set in. Among the worst-affected areas are the resettlement colonies.

There is a difference between the planners of the Sardar Sarovar irrigation scheme and the planners of previous projects. At least they acknowledge that water-logging and salinization are *real* problems and need to be addressed.

Their solutions, however, are corny enough to send a Hoolock gibbon to a hooting hospital.

They plan to have a series of electronic groundwater sensors placed in every 100 square kilometers of the command area. (That works out to about 1,800 ground sensors.) These will be linked to a central computer that will analyze the data and send out commands to the canal heads to stop water flowing into areas that show signs of waterlogging. A network of "Only irrigation," "Only drainage," and "Irrigation cum drainage" tube-wells will be sunk, and electronically synchronized by the central computer. The saline water will be pumped out, mixed with mathematically computed quantities of freshwater, and then recirculated into a network of surface and subsurface drains (for which more land will be acquired).[78]

To achieve the irrigation efficiency that they claim they'll achieve, according to a study done by Dr. Rahul Ram for Kalpavriksh,[79] 82 percent of the water that goes into the Wonder Canal network will have to be pumped out again!

They've never implemented an electronic irrigation scheme before, not even as a pilot project. It hasn't occurred to them to experiment with some already degraded land, just to see if it works. No, they'll use our money to install it over the whole of the 2 million hectares and *then* see if it works.

What if it doesn't? If it doesn't, it won't matter to the planners. They'll still draw the same salaries. They'll still get their pensions and their bonuses and whatever else you get when you retire from a career of inflicting mayhem on a people.

How can it possibly work? It's like sending in a rocket scientist to milk a troublesome cow. How can they manage a gigantic electronic irrigation system when they can't even line the walls of the canals without having them collapse and cause untold damage to crops and people?

When they can't even prevent the Big Dam itself from breaking off in bits when it rains?

To quote from one of their own studies: "The design, the implementation and management of the integration of groundwater and surface water in the above circumstance is complex."[80]

Agreed. To say the least.

Their recommendation of how to deal with the complexity: "It will only be possible to implement such a system if all groundwater and surface water supplies are managed by a single authority."[81]

Aha!

It's beginning to make sense now. Who will own the water? The Single Authority.

Who will sell the water? The Single Authority.

Who will profit from the sales? The Single Authority.

The Single Authority has a scheme whereby it will sell water by the liter, not to individuals but to farmers' cooperatives (which don't exist just yet, but no doubt the Single Authority can create cooperatives and force farmers to cooperate).

Computer water, unlike ordinary river water, is expensive. Only those who can afford it will get it. Gradually, small farmers will get edged out by big farmers, and the whole cycle of uprootment will begin all over again.

The Single Authority, because it owns the computer water, will also decide who will grow what. It says that farmers getting computer water will not be allowed to grow sugarcane because they'll use up the share of the thirsty millions who live at the tail end of the canal. But the Single Authority has *already* given licenses to ten large sugar mills right near the head of the canal.[82] The chief promoter of one of them is Sanat Mehta, who was chairman of the Sardar Sarovar Narmada Nigam for several years. The chief promoter of another sugar mill was Chimanbhai Patel, former chief minister of Gujarat. He (along with his wife) was the most vocal, ardent proponent of the Sardar Sarovar dam. When he died, his ashes were scattered over the dam site.

In Maharashtra, thanks to a different branch of the Single Authority, the politically powerful sugar lobby that occupies one-tenth of the state's irrigated land uses *half* the state's irrigation water.

In addition to the sugar growers, the Single Authority has recently announced a scheme[83] that envisages a series of five-star hotels, golf courses, and water parks that will come up along the Wonder Canal. What earthly reason could possibly justify this?

The Single Authority says it's the only way to raise money to complete the project!

I really worry about those millions of good people in Kutch and Saurashtra.

Will the water *ever* reach them?

First of all, we know that there's a lot less water in the river than the Single Authority claims there is.

Second of all, in the absence of the Narmada Sagar dam, the irrigation benefits of the Sardar Sarovar drop by a further 17 to 30 percent.

Third of all, the irrigation efficiency of the Wonder Canal (the actual amount of water delivered by the system) has been arbitrarily fixed at 60 percent. The *highest* irrigation efficiency in India, taking into account system leaks and surface evaporation, is 35 percent.[84] This means it's likely that only half of the command area will be irrigated.

Which half? The first half.

Fourth, to get to Kutch and Saurashtra, the Wonder Canal has to negotiate its way past the ten sugar mills, the golf courses, the five-star hotels, the water parks, and the cash-crop-growing, politically powerful, Patel-rich districts of Baroda, Kheda, Ahmedabad, Gandhinagar, and Mehsana. (Already, in complete contravention of its own directives, the Single Authority has allotted the city of Baroda a sizable quantity of water.[85] When Baroda gets it, can Ahmedabad be left behind? The political clout of powerful urban centers in Gujarat will ensure that they secure their share.)

Fifth, even in the (100 percent) unlikely event that water gets there, it has to be piped and distributed to those eight thousand waiting villages.

It's worth knowing that of the one billion people in the world who have no access to safe drinking water, 855 million live in rural areas.[86] This is because the cost of installing an energy-intensive network of thousands of kilometers of pipelines, aqueducts, pumps, and treatment plants that would be needed to provide drinking water to scattered rural populations is prohibitive. *Nobody* builds Big Dams to provide drinking water to rural people. Nobody can *afford* to.

When the Morse Committee first arrived in Gujarat, it was impressed by the Gujarat government's commitment to taking drinking water to such distant rural districts.[87] The members of the committee asked to see the detailed drinking-water plans. There weren't any. (There still aren't any.)

They asked if any costs had been worked out. "A few thousand crores" was the breezy answer.[88] A billion dollars is an expert's calculated guess. It's not included as part of the project cost. So where is the money going to come from?

Never mind. Jus' askin'.

It's interesting that the Farakka Barrage that diverts water from the Ganga to Calcutta Port has reduced the drinking water availability for 40 million people who live downstream in Bangladesh.[89]

At times there's something so precise and mathematically chilling about nationalism.

Build a dam to take water *away* from 40 million people. Build a dam to pretend to *bring* water to 40 million people.

Who are these gods that govern us? Is there no limit to their powers?

The last person I met in the valley was Bhaiji Bhai. He is a Tadvi Adivasi from Undava, one of the first villages where the government began to acquire land for the Wonder Canal and its 75,000-kilometer network. Bhaiji Bhai lost seventeen of his nineteen acres to the Wonder Canal. It crashes through his land, 700 feet wide including its walkways and steep, sloping embankments, like a velodrome for giant bicyclists.

The canal network affects more than 200,000 families. People have lost wells and trees, people have had their houses separated from their farms by the canal, forcing them to walk two or three kilometers to the nearest bridge and then two or three kilometers back along the other side. Twenty-three thousand families, let's say 100,000 people, will be, like Bhaiji Bhai, seriously affected. They don't count as "Project-Affected" and are not entitled to rehabilitation.

Like his neighbors in Kevadia Colony, Bhaiji Bhai became a pauper overnight.

Bhaiji Bhai and his people, forced to smile for photographs on government calendars. Bhaiji Bhai and his people, denied the grace of rage. Bhaiji Bhai and his people, squashed like bugs by this country they're supposed to call their own.

It was late evening when I arrived at his house. We sat down on the floor and drank oversweet tea in the dying light. As he spoke, a memory stirred in me, a sense of déjà vu. I couldn't imagine why. I knew I hadn't met him before. Then I realized what it was. I didn't recognize him, but I remembered his story. I'd seen him in an old documentary film, shot more than ten years ago in the valley. He was frailer now, his beard softened with age. But his story hadn't aged. It was still young and full of passion. It broke my heart, the patience with which he told it. I could tell he had told it over and over and over again, hoping, praying, that one day, one of the strangers passing through Undava would turn out to be Good Luck. Or God.

Bhaiji Bhai, Bhaiji Bhai, when will you get angry? When will you stop waiting? When will you say "That's enough!" and reach for your weapons, whatever they may be? When will you show us the whole of your resonant, terrifying, invincible strength? When will you break the faith? *Will* you break the faith? Or will you let it break you?

To slow a beast, you break its limbs. To slow a nation, you break its people. You rob them of volition. You demonstrate your absolute command over their destiny. You make it clear that ultimately it falls to you to decide who lives, who dies, who prospers, who doesn't. To exhibit your capability you show off all that you can do, and how easily you can do it. How easily you could press a button and annihilate the earth. How you can start a war or sue for peace. How you can snatch a river away from one and gift it to another. How you can green a desert, or fell a forest and plant one somewhere else. You use caprice to fracture a people's faith in ancient things—earth, forest, water, air.

Once that's done, what do they have left? Only you. They will turn to you because you're all they have. They will love you even while they despise you. They will trust you even though they know you well. They will vote for you even as you squeeze the very breath from their bodies. They will drink what you give them to drink. They will breathe what you give them to breathe. They will live where you dump their belongings. They have to. What else can they do? There's no higher court of redress. You are their mother and their father. You are the judge and the jury. You are the World. You are God.

Power is fortified not just by what it destroys but also by what it creates. Not just by what it takes but also by what it gives. And powerlessness reaffirmed not just by the helplessness of those who have lost but also by the gratitude of those who have (or *think* they have) gained.

This cold contemporary cast of power is couched between the lines of noble-sounding clauses in democratic-sounding constitutions. It's wielded by the elected representatives of an ostensibly free people. Yet no monarch, no despot, no dictator in any other century in the history of human civilization has had access to weapons like these.

Day by day, river by river, forest by forest, mountain by mountain, missile by missile, bomb by bomb—almost without our knowing it—we are being broken.

Big Dams are to a nation's "development" what nuclear bombs are to its military arsenal. They're both weapons of mass destruction. They're both weapons governments use to control their own people. Both twentieth-century emblems that mark a point in time when human intelligence has outstripped its own instinct for survival. They're both malignant indications of a civilization turning upon itself. They represent the severing of the link, not just the link—the *understanding*—between human beings and the planet they live on. They scramble the intelligence that connects eggs to hens, milk to cows, food to forests, water to rivers, air to life, and the earth to human existence.

Can we unscramble it?

Maybe. Inch by inch. Bomb by bomb. Dam by dam. Maybe by fighting specific wars in specific ways. We could begin in the Narmada valley.

This July will bring the last monsoon of the twentieth century. The ragged army in the Narmada valley has declared that it will not move when the waters of the Sardar Sarovar reservoir rise to claim its lands and homes. Whether you love the dam or hate it, whether you want it or you don't, it is in the fitness of things that you understand the price that's being paid for it. That you have the courage to watch while the dues are cleared and the books are squared.

Our dues. Our books. Not theirs.

Be there.

7. Power Politics

The Reincarnation of Rumpelstiltskin

Remember him? The gnome who could turn straw into gold? Well, he's back now, but you wouldn't recognize him. To begin with, he's not an individual gnome anymore. I'm not sure how best to describe him. Let's just say he's metamorphosed into an accretion, a cabal, an assemblage, a malevolent, incorporeal, transnational multi-gnome. Rumpelstiltskin is a notion (gnotion), a piece of deviant, insidious white logic that will eventually self-annihilate. But for now, he's more than okay. He's cock of the walk. King of All That Really Counts (Cash). He's decimated the competition, killed all the other kings, the other kinds of kings. He's persuaded us that he's all we have left. Our only salvation.

What kind of potentate is Rumpelstiltskin? Powerful, pitiless, and armed to the teeth. He's a kind of king the world has never known before. His realm is raw capital, his conquests emerging markets, his prayers profits, his borders limitless, his weapons nuclear. To even try and imagine him, to hold the whole of him in your field of vision, is to situate yourself at the very edge of sanity, to offer yourself up for ridicule. King Rumpel reveals only part of himself at a time. He has a bank account heart. He has television eyes and a newspaper nose in which you see

First published in *Outlook*, November 27, 2000.

only what he wants you to see and read only what he wants you to read. (See what I mean about the edge of sanity?) There's more: a Surround Sound stereo mouth that amplifies his voice and filters out the sound of the rest of the world, so that you can't hear it even when it's shouting (or starving, or dying), and King Rumpel is only whispering, rolling his *r*'s in his North American way.

Listen carefully. This is most of the rest of his story. (It hasn't ended yet, but it will. It must.) It ranges across seas and continents, sometimes majestic and universal, sometimes confining and local. Now and then I'll peg it down with disparate bits of history and geography that could mar the gentle art of storytelling. So please bear with me.

In March this year (AD 2000), the President of the United States (H.E., the most exalted plenipotentiary of Rumpeldom) visited India. He brought his own bed, the feather pillow he hugs at night, and a merry band of businessmen. He was courted and fawned over by the genuflecting representatives of this ancient civilization with a fervor that can only be described as indecent. Whole cities were superficially spruced up. The poor were herded away, hidden from the presidential gaze. Streets were soaped and scrubbed and festooned with balloons and welcome banners. In Delhi's dirty sky, vindicated nuclear hawks banked and whistled: *Dekho ji dekho!* Bill is here because we have the Bomb.

Those Indian citizens with even a modicum of self-respect were so ashamed they stayed in bed for days. Some of us had puzzled furrows on our brows. Since everybody behaved like a craven, happy slave when Master visited, we wondered why we hadn't gone the whole distance. Why hadn't we just crawled under Master's nuclear umbrella in the first place? Then we could spend our pocket money on other things (instead of bombs) and still be all safe and slavey. No?

Just before The Visit, the Government of India lifted import restrictions on fourteen hundred commodities, including milk, grain, sugar, and cotton (even though there was a glut of sugar and cotton in the market, even though 42 million tons of grain were rotting in government storehouses). During The Visit, contracts worth about three (some say four) billion US dollars were signed.[1]

For reasons of my own, I was particularly interested in a Memorandum of Intent signed by the Ogden Energy Group, a company that specializes in operating garbage incinerators in the United States, and S. Kumars, an Indian textile company that manufactures what it calls "suiting blends."[2]

Now what might garbage incineration and suiting blends possibly have in common? Suit-incineration? Guess again. Garbage-blends? Nope. A big hydroelectric dam on the River Narmada in central India. Neither Ogden nor S. Kumars has ever built or operated a large dam before.

The four-hundred-megawatt Shri Maheshwar Hydel Project being promoted by S. Kumars is part of the Narmada Valley Development Project, which boasts of being the most ambitious river valley project in the world. It envisages building 3,200 dams (30 big dams, 135 medium dams, and the rest small) that will reconstitute the Narmada and her forty-one tributaries into a series of step reservoirs. It will alter the ecology of an entire river basin, affect the lives of about 25 million people who live in the valley, and submerge four thousand square kilometers of old-growth deciduous forest and hundreds of temples, as well as archaeological sites dating back to the Lower Paleolithic Age.[3]

The dams that have been built on the river so far are all government projects. The Maheshwar dam is slated to be India's first major private hydel power project.

What is interesting about this is not only that it's part of the most bitterly opposed river valley project in India, but also that it is a strand in the skein of a mammoth global enterprise. Understanding what is happening in Maheshwar, decoding the nature of the deals that are being struck between two of the world's great democracies, will go a long way toward gaining a rudimentary grasp of what is being done to us, while we, poor fools, stand by and clap and cheer and hasten things along. (When I say "us," I mean people, human beings. Not countries, not governments.)

Personally, I took the first step toward arriving at this understanding when, over a few days in March this year (AD 2000), I lived through a writer's bad dream. I witnessed the ritualistic slaughter of language as I know and understand it. Let me explain.

On the very days that President Clinton was in India, in faraway Holland the World Water Forum was convened.[4] Four thousand five hundred bankers, businessmen, government ministers, policy writers, engineers, economists—and, in order to pretend that the "other side" was also represented, a handful of activists, indigenous dance troupes, impoverished street theater groups, and half a dozen young girls dressed as inflatable silver faucets—gathered at The Hague to discuss the future of the world's water. Every speech was generously peppered with phrases like "women's empowerment," "people's participation," and "deepening democracy." Yet it turned out that the whole purpose of the forum was to press for the privatization of the world's water. There was pious talk of having access to drinking water declared a Basic Human Right. How would this be implemented, you might ask. Simple. By putting a market value on water. By selling it at its "true price." (It's common knowledge that water is becoming a scarce resource. One billion people in the world have no access to safe drinking water.)[5] The "market" decrees that the scarcer something is, the more expensive it becomes. But there is a difference between valuing water and putting a market value on water. No one values water more than a village woman who has to walk miles to fetch it. No one values it less than urban folk who pay for it to flow endlessly at the turn of a tap.

So the talk of connecting human rights to a "true price" was more than a little baffling. At first I didn't quite get their drift. Did they believe in human rights for the rich, that only the rich are human, or that all humans are rich? But I see it now. A shiny, climate-controlled human rights supermarket with a clearance sale on Christmas Day.

One marrowy American panelist put it rather nicely: "God gave us the rivers," he drawled, "but he didn't put in the delivery systems. That's why we need private enterprise." No doubt with a little Structural Adjustment to the rest of the things God gave us, we could all live in a simpler world. (If all the seas were one sea, what a big sea it would be . . . Evian could own the water, Rand the earth, Enron the air. Old Rumpelstiltskin could be the handsomely paid supreme CEO.)

When all the rivers and valleys and forests and hills of the world have been priced, packaged, bar-coded, and stacked in the local supermarket, when all the hay and coal and earth and wood and water have been turned to gold, what then shall we do with all the gold? Make nuclear bombs to obliterate what's left of the ravaged landscapes and the notional nations in our ruined world?

As a writer, one spends a lifetime journeying into the heart of language, trying to minimize, if not eliminate, the distance between language and thought. "Language is the skin on my thought," I remember saying to someone who once asked what language meant to me. At The Hague I stumbled on a denomination, a sub-world, whose life's endeavor was entirely the opposite of mine. For them the whole purpose of language is to mask intent. They earn their abundant livings by converting bar graphs that plot their companies' profits into consummately written, politically exemplary, socially just policy documents that are impossible to implement and designed to remain forever on paper, secret even (especially) from the people they're written for. They breed and prosper in the space that lies between what they say and what they sell. What they're lobbying for is not simply the privatization of natural resources and essential infrastructure, but the privatization of policy making itself. Dam builders want to control public water policies. Power utility companies want to draft power policies, and financial institutions want to supervise government disinvestment.

Let's begin at the beginning. What does privatization really mean? Essentially, it is the transfer of productive public assets from the state to private companies. Productive assets include natural resources. Earth, forest, water, air. These are assets that the state holds in trust for the people it represents. In a country like India, 70 percent of the population lives in rural areas.[6] That's 700 million people. Their lives depend directly on access to natural resources. To snatch these away and sell them as stock to private companies is a process of barbaric dispossession on a scale that has no parallel in history.

What happens when you "privatize" something as essential to human survival as water? What happens when you commodify water and say that only those who can come up with the cash to pay the "market price" can have it?

In 1999, the government of Bolivia privatized the public water supply system in the city of Cochabamba and signed a forty-year lease with a consortium headed by Bechtel, a giant US engineering firm. The first thing Bechtel did was to raise the price of water. Hundreds of thousands of people simply couldn't afford it anymore. Citizens came out on the streets to protest. A transport strike brought the entire city to a standstill. Hugo Banzer, the former Bolivian dictator (then the president), ordered the police to confront the crowds. One person was killed, and many more were injured. The protest continued because people had no options—what's the option to thirst? In April 2000, Banzer declared martial law. The protest continued. Eventually Bechtel was forced to flee its offices. Many people expect Bechtel will try to extort a $12 million exit payment from the Bolivian government for loss of future profits.[7]

Cochabamba has a population of six hundred thousand people. Think of what would happen in an Indian city. Even a small one.

Rumpelstiltskin thinks big. Today he's stalking mega-game: dams, mines, armaments, power plants, public water supply, telecommunications, the management and dissemination of knowledge, biodiversity, seeds (he wants to own life and the very process of reproduction), and the industrial infrastructure that supports all this. His minions arrive in third world countries masquerading as missionaries come to redeem the wretched. They have a completely different dossier in their briefcases. To understand what they're really saying (selling), you have to teach yourself to unscramble their vernacular.

Recently Jack Welch, the CEO of General Electric (GE), was on TV in India. "I beg and pray to the Indian government to improve infrastructure," he said, and added touchingly, "Don't do it for GE's sake, do it for yourselves." He went on to say that privatizing the power sector was the only way to bring India's one billion people into the digital network. "You can talk about information and intellectual capital, but without the power to drive it, you will miss the next revolution."[8]

What he meant, of course, was "You are a market of one billion customers. If you don't buy our equipment, *we* will miss the next revolution."

Will someone please tell Jack Welch that of his one billion "customers," 300 million are illiterate and live without even one square meal a day, and 200 million have no access to safe drinking water?[9] Being brought into the "digital framework" is hardly what's uppermost on their minds.

The story behind the story is as follows: There are four corporations that dominate the production of power-generation equipment in the world. GE is one of them. Together, each year they manufacture (and therefore need to sell) equipment that can generate at least twenty thousand megawatts of power.[10] For a variety of reasons, there is little (read: almost zero) additional demand for power equipment in the first world. This leaves these mammoth multinationals with a redundant capacity that they desperately need to offload. India and China are their big target markets because, between these two countries, the demand for power-generating equipment is ten thousand megawatts per year.[11]

The first world needs to sell, the third world needs to buy—it ought to be a reasonable business proposition. But it isn't. For many years, India has been more or less self-sufficient in power equipment. The Indian public sector company Bharat Heavy Electricals (BHEL) manufactured and even exported world-class power equipment. All that's changed now. Over the years, our own government has starved it of orders, cut off funds for research and development, and more or less edged it out of a dignified existence. Today BHEL is no more than a sweatshop. It is being forced into "joint ventures" (one with GE and one with Siemens) in which its only role is to provide cheap, unskilled labor while they—Siemens and GE—provide the equipment and the technology.[12]

Why? Why does more expensive imported equipment suit our bureaucrats and politicians better? We all know why. Because graft is factored into the deal. Buying equipment from your local store is just not the same thing. It's not surprising that almost half the officials named in the major corruption scandal that came to be known as the Jain Hawala case were officials from the power sector involved with the selection and purchase of power equipment.[13]

The privatization of power (felicitous phrase!) is at the top of the Indian government's agenda. The United States is the single largest foreign investor in the power sector (which, to some extent, explains The Visit).[14] The argument being advanced (both by the government and by the private sector) in favor of privatization is that over the last fifty years the government has bungled its brief. It has failed to deliver. The State Electricity Boards (SEBs) are insolvent. Inefficiency, corruption, theft, and heavy subsidies have run them into the ground.

In the push for privatization, the customary depiction of the corrupt, oily third world government official selling his country's interests for personal profit fits perfectly into the scheme of things. The private sector bristles accusingly. The government coyly acknowledges the accusation and pleads its inability to reform itself. In fact, it goes out of its way to exaggerate its own inefficiencies. This is meant to come across as refreshing candor.

In a speech he made just before he died, Minister for Power P. R. Kumaramangalam said that the overall figure of loss and deficit in the power sector was 7.86 billion US dollars. He went on to say that India's transmission and distribution (T&D) losses are between 35 and 40 percent. Of the remaining 60 percent, according to the minister, billing is restricted to only 40 percent. His conclusion: that only about a quarter of the electricity that is produced in India is metered.[15] Official sources say that this is a somewhat exaggerated account. The situation is bad enough. It doesn't need to be exaggerated. According to figures put out by the Power Ministry, the national average T&D losses are 23 percent. In 1947 they were 14.39 percent. Even without the minister's hyperbole, this puts India in the same league as countries with the worst T&D losses in the world, like the Dominican Republic, Myanmar, and Bangladesh.[16]

The solution to this malaise, we discover, is not to improve our housekeeping skills, not to try and minimize our losses, not to force the state to be more accountable, but to permit it to abdicate its responsibility altogether and privatize the power sector. Then magic will happen. Economic viability and Swiss-style efficiency will kick in like clockwork.

But there's a subplot missing in this narrative. Over the years, the SEBs have been bankrupted by massive power thefts. Who's stealing the power? Some of it no doubt is stolen by the poor—slum dwellers, people who live in unauthorized colonies on the fringes of big cities. But they don't have the electrical gadgetry to consume the quantum of electricity we're talking about. The big stuff, the megawatt thievery, is orchestrated by the industrial sector in connivance with politicians and government officers.

Consider as an example the state of Madhya Pradesh, in which the Maheshwar dam is being built. Seven years ago it was a power surplus state. Today it finds itself in an intriguing situation. Industrial demand has declined by 30 percent. Power production has increased from 3,813 megawatts to 4,025 megawatts. And the State Electricity Board is showing a loss of $255 million. An inspection drive solved the puzzle. It found that 70 percent of the industrialists in the state steal electricity![17] The theft adds up to a loss of nearly $106 million. That's 41 percent of the total deficit. Madhya Pradesh is by no means an unusual example. States like Orissa, Andhra Pradesh, and Delhi have T&D losses of between 30 and 50 percent (way over the national average), which indicates massive power theft.[18]

No one talks very much about this. It's so much nicer to blame the poor. The average economist, planner, or drawing-room intellectual will tell you that the SEBs have gone belly up for two reasons: (a) because "political compulsions" ensure that domestic power tariffs are kept unviably low, and (b) because subsidies given to the farm sector result in enormous hidden losses.

The first step that a "reformed" privatized power sector is expected to take is to cut agricultural subsidies and put a "realistic" tariff (market value) on power.

What are political compulsions? Why are they considered such a bad thing? Basically, it seems to me, *political compulsions* is a phrase that describes the fancy footwork that governments have to perform in order to strike a balance between redeeming a sinking economy and serving an impoverished electorate. Striking a balance between what the market demands and what people can afford is—or certainly ought to be—the primary, fundamental responsibility of any democratic government. Privatization seeks to disengage politics from the market. To do that would be to blunt the very last weapon that India's poor still have—their vote. Once that's gone, elections will become even more of a charade than they already are, and democracy will just become the name of a new rock band. The poor will be absent from the negotiating table. They will simply cease to matter.

But the cry has already gone up. The demand to cut subsidies has almost become a blood sport. It's a small world. Bolivia is only a short walk down the road from here.

When it recommends privatizing the power sector, does the government mean that it is going to permit just anybody who wishes to generate power to come in and compete in a free market? Of course not. There's nothing free about the market in the power sector. Reforming the power sector in India means that the concerned state government underwrites preposterously one-sided Power Purchase Agreements with select companies, preferably huge multinationals. Essentially, it is the transfer of assets and infrastructure from bribe-taker to bribe-giver, which involves more bribery than ever. Once the agreements are signed, the companies are free to produce power at exorbitant rates that no one can afford. Not even, ironically enough, the Indian industrialists who have been rooting for them all along. They, poor chaps, end up like vultures on a carcass that get chased off by a visiting hyena.

The fishbowl of the drive to privatize power, its truly star turn, is the story of Enron, the Houston-based natural gas company.[19] The Enron project was the first private power project in India. The Power Purchase Agreement between Enron and the Congress Party–ruled State Government of Maharashtra for a 695-megawatt power plant was signed in 1993. The opposition parties, the Hindu nationalist Bharatiya Janata Party (BJP) and the Shiv Sena, set up a howl of *swadeshi* (nationalist) protest and filed legal proceedings against Enron and the state government. They alleged malfeasance and corruption at the highest level. A year later, when state elections were announced, it was the only campaign issue of the BJP–Shiv Sena alliance.

In February 1995, this combo won the elections. True to their word, they "scrapped" the project. In a savage, fiery statement, the opposition leader L. K. Advani attacked the phenomenon he called "loot-through-liberalization."[20] He more or less directly accused the Congress Party government of having taken a $13 million bribe from Enron. Enron had made no secret of the fact that, in order to secure the deal, it had paid out millions of dollars to "educate" the politicians and bureaucrats involved in the deal.[21]

Following the annulment of the contract, the US government began to pressure the Maharashtra government. US Ambassador Frank Wisner made several statements deploring the cancelation. (Soon after he completed his term as ambassador, he joined Enron as a director.)[22] In November 1995, the BJP–Shiv Sena government in Maharashtra announced a "renegotiation" committee. In May 1996, a minority federal government headed by the BJP was sworn in at New Delhi. It lasted for exactly thirteen days and then resigned before facing a vote of no confidence in Parliament. On its last day in office, even as the motion of no confidence was in progress, the cabinet met for a hurried "lunch" and reratified the national government's counter-guarantee (which had become void because of the earlier "canceled" contract with Enron). In August 1996, the government of Maharashtra signed a fresh contract with Enron on terms that would astound the most hardboiled cynic.[23]

The impugned contract had involved annual payments to Enron of

$430 million for Phase I (695 megawatts) of the project, with Phase II (2,015 megawatts) being optional. The "renegotiated" Power Purchase Agreement makes Phase II of the project mandatory and legally binds the Maharashtra State Electricity Board (MSEB) to pay Enron a sum of $30 billion! It constitutes the largest contract ever signed in the history of India.

In India, experts who have studied the project have called it the most massive fraud in the country's history. The project's gross profits work out to between $12 and $14 billion. The official return on equity is more than 30 percent.[24] That's almost double what Indian law and statutes permit in power projects. In effect, for an increase in installed capacity of 18 percent, the MSEB has to set aside 70 percent of its revenue to be able to pay Enron. There is, of course, no record of what mathematical formula was used to "reeducate" the new government. Nor any trace of how much trickled up or down or sideways and to whom.

But there's more: in one of the most extraordinary decisions in its not entirely pristine history, in May 1997 the Supreme Court of India refused to entertain an appeal against Enron.[25]

Today, four years later, everything that critics of the project predicted has come true with an eerie vengeance. The power that the Enron plant produces is twice as expensive as that of its nearest competitor and seven times as expensive as the cheapest electricity available in Maharashtra.[26] In May 2000, the Maharashtra Electricity Regulatory Committee (MERC) ruled that temporarily, until as long as was absolutely necessary, no power should be bought from Enron.[27] It was based on a calculation that it would be cheaper to just pay Enron the mandatory fixed charges for the maintenance and administration of the plant that they are contractually obliged to pay than to actually buy any of its exorbitant power. The fixed charges alone work out to around $220 million a year for Phase I of the project. Phase II will be nearly twice the size.

Two hundred and twenty million dollars a year for the next twenty years.

Meanwhile, industrialists in Maharashtra have begun to generate their own power at a much cheaper rate, with private generators. The demand for power from the industrial sector has begun to decline rapidly. The SEB, strapped for cash, with Enron hanging like an albatross around its neck, will now have no choice but to make private generators illegal. That's the only way that industrialists can be coerced into buying Enron's exorbitantly priced electricity.

According to the MSEB's calculations, from January 2002 onward, even if it were to buy 90 percent of Enron's output, its losses will amount to $1.2 billion a year.

That's more than 60 percent of India's annual rural development budget.[28]

In contravention of the MERC ruling, the MSEB is cutting back production from its own cheaper plants in order to buy electricity from Enron. Hundreds of small industrial units have closed down because they cannot afford such expensive electricity.

In January 2001, the Maharashtra government (the Congress Party is back in power with a new Chief Minister) announced that it did not have the money to pay Enron's bills. On January 31, only five days after the earthquake in the neighboring state of Gujarat, at a time when the country was still reeling from the disaster, the newspapers announced that Enron had decided to invoke the counter-guarantee and that if the government did not come up with the cash, it would have to auction the government properties named as collateral security in the contract.[29]

At the time that this book [*Power Politics*] is going to press, Enron and the government of Maharashtra are locked in a legal battle in the High Court of the State of Maharashtra. But Enron has friends in high places.[30] It was one of the biggest corporate contributors to President George W. Bush's election campaign. President Bush has helped Enron with its global business from as far back as 1998. So the old circus has started up all over again. The former US Ambassador (Richard Celeste this time) publicly chastised the Maharashtra Chief Minister for reneging on payments.[31] US government officials have warned India about vitiating the "investment climate" and running the risk of frightening away future investors. In other words: Allow us to rob you blind, or else we'll go away.

The pressure is on for re-re-negotiation. Who knows, perhaps Phase III is on the anvil.

In business circles, the Enron contract is called "the sweetheart deal." A euphemism for rape without redress. There are plenty of Enron clones in the pipeline. Indian citizens have a lot to look forward to.

Here's to the "free" market.

Having said all this, there's no doubt that there *is* a power-shortage crisis in India. But there's another, more serious crisis on hand.

Planners in India boast that India consumes twenty times more electricity today than it did fifty years ago. They use it as an index of progress. They omit to mention that 70 percent of rural households still have no electricity.[32] In the poorest states, Bihar, Uttar Pradesh, and Orissa, more than 85 percent of the poorest people, mostly Dalit and Adivasi households, have no electricity. What a shameful, shocking record for the world's biggest democracy.

Unless this crisis is acknowledged and honestly addressed, generating "lots and lots of power" (as Mr. Welch put it) will only mean that it will be siphoned off by the rich with their endless appetites. It will require a very imaginative, very radical form of "structural adjustment" to right this.

"Privatization" is presented as being the only alternative to an inefficient, corrupt state. In fact, it's not a choice at all. It's only made to look like one. Essentially, privatization is a mutually profitable business contract between the private (preferably foreign) company or financial institution and the ruling elite of the third world. (One of the fallouts is that even corruption becomes an elitist affair. Your average small-fry government official is in grave danger of losing his or her bit on the side.)

India's politicians have virtually mortgaged their country to the World Bank. Today, India pays back more money in interest and repayment installments than it receives. It is forced to incur new debts in order to repay old ones.[33] In other words, it's exporting capital. Of late, however, institutions like the World Bank and the International Monetary Fund, which have bled the third world all these years, look like benevolent saints compared to the new mutants in the market. These are known as ECAs—export credit agencies. If the World Bank is a colonizing army hamstrung by red tape and bureaucracy, the ECAs are freewheeling, marauding mercenaries.

Basically, ECAs insure private companies operating in foreign countries against commercial and political risks. The device is called an export credit guarantee. It's quite simple, really. No first world private company wants to export capital or goods or services to a politically and/or economically unstable country without insuring itself against unforeseen contingencies. So the private company covers itself with an export credit guarantee. The ECA, in turn, has an agreement with the government of its own country. The government of its own country has an agreement with the government of the importing country. The upshot of this fine imbrication is that if a situation does arise in which the ECA has to pay its client, its own government pays the ECA and recovers its money by adding it to the bilateral debt owed by the importing country. (So the real guarantors are actually, once again, the poorest people in the poorest countries.) Complicated, but cool. And foolproof.

The quadrangular private company–ECA–government–government formation neatly circumvents political accountability. Though they're all actually business associates, flak from noisy, tiresome nongovernmental organizations and activist groups can be diverted and funneled to the ECA, where, like noxious industrial effluent, it lies in cooling ponds before being disposed of. The attraction of the ECAs (for both governments and private companies) is that they are secretive and don't bother with tedious details like human rights violations and environmental guidelines. (The rare ones that do, like the US Export-Import Bank, are under pressure to change.) It short-circuits lumbering World Bank–style bureaucracy. It makes projects like Big Dams (which involve the displacement and impoverishment of large numbers of people, which in turn is politically risky) that much easier to finance. With an ECA guarantee, "developers" can go ahead and dig and quarry and mine and dam the hell out of people's lives without having to even address, never mind answer, embarrassing questions.

Now, coming back to Maheshwar . . .

In order to place India's first private Big Dam in perspective, I need to briefly set out the short, vulgar history of Big Dams in India in general and on the Narmada in particular.

The international dam industry alone is worth $32–46 billion a year.[34] In the first world, dams are being decommissioned, blown up. That leaves us with another industry threatened with redundancy desperately in search of dumping grounds. Fortunately (for the industry) most third world countries, India especially, are deeply committed to Big Dams.

India has the third largest number of Big Dams in the world. Three thousand six hundred Indian dams qualify as Big Dams under the ICOLD (International Commission on Large Dams) definition. Six hundred and ninety-five more are under construction. This means that 40 percent of all the Big Dams being built in the world are being built in India.[35] For reasons more cynical than honorable, politicians and planners have successfully portrayed Big Dams to an unquestioning public as symbols of nationalism—huge, wet cement flags. Jawaharlal Nehru's famous speech about Big Dams being "the temples of modern India" has made its way into primary school textbooks in every Indian language.[36] Every schoolchild is taught that Big Dams will deliver the people of India from hunger and poverty.

Will they? Have they?

To merely ask these questions is to invite accusations of sedition, of being anti-national, of being a spy, and, most ludicrous of all, of receiving "foreign funds." The distinguished Home Minister Mr. Advani, while speaking at the inauguration of construction at the Sardar Sarovar dam site on October 31, 2000, said that the three greatest achievements of his government were the nuclear tests in 1998, the war with Pakistan in 1999, and the Supreme Court verdict in favor of the construction of the Sardar Sarovar dam in 2000. He called it a victory for "developmental nationalism" (a twisted variation of cultural nationalism). For the Home Minister to call a Supreme Court verdict a victory for his government doesn't say much for the Supreme Court.

I have no quarrel with Mr. Advani clubbing together nuclear bombs, Big Dams, and wars. However, calling them "achievements" is sinister. Mr. Advani then went on to make farcical allegations about how those of us who were against the dam were "working at the behest of . . . outsiders" and "those who do not wish to see India becoming strong in security and socio-economic development."[37] Unfortunately, this is not imbecilic paranoia. It's a deliberate, dangerous attempt to suppress outrageous facts by whipping up mindless mob frenzy. He did it in the run-up to the destruction of the Babri Masjid. He's doing it again. He has given notice that he will stop at nothing. Those who come in his way will be dealt with by any methods he deems necessary.

Nevertheless, there is too much at stake to remain silent. After all, we don't want to be like good middle-class Germans in the 1930s, who drove their children to piano classes and never noticed the concentration camps springing up around them—or do we?

There are questions that must be asked. And answered. There is space here for no more than a brief summary of the costs and benefits of Big Dams. A brief summary is all we need.

Ninety percent of the Big Dams in India are irrigation dams.[38] They are the key, according to planners, to India's "food security."

So how much food do Big Dams produce?

The extraordinary thing is that there is no official government figure for this.

The India Country Study section in the World Commission on Dams Report was prepared by a team of experts—the former secretary of Water Resources, the former director of the Madras Institute of Development Studies, a former secretary of the Central Water Commission, and two members of the faculty of the Indian Institute of Public Administration.[39] One of the chapters in the study deduces that the contribution of large dams to India's food grain produce is less than 10 percent.[40] *Less than 10 percent!*

Ten percent of the total produce currently works out to 20 million tons. This year, more than double that amount is rotting in government storehouses while at the same time 350 million Indian citizens live below the poverty line.[41] The Ministry of Food and Civil Supplies says that 10 percent of India's total food grain produce every year is spoiled or eaten by rats.[42] India must be the only country in the world that builds dams, uproots millions of people, and submerges thousands of acres of forest in order to feed rats.

It's hard to believe that things can go so grievously, so perilously wrong. But they have. It's understandable that those who are responsible find it hard to own up to their mistakes, because Big Dams did not start out as a cynical enterprise. They began as a dream. They have ended as grisly nightmare. It's time to wake up.

So much for the benefits of India's Big Dams. Let's take a look at the costs. How many people have been displaced by Big Dams?

Once again, there is no official record.

In fact, there's no record at all. This is unpardonable on the part of the Indian state. And unpardonable on the part of planners, economists, funding agencies, and the rest of the urban intellectual community who are so quick to rise up in defense of Big Dams.

Last year, just in order to do a sanity check, I extrapolated an average from a study of fifty-four dams done by the Indian Institute of Public Administration. After quartering the average they arrived at, my very conservative estimate of the number of people displaced by Big Dams in India over the last fifty years was 33 million people. This was jeered at by some economists and planners as being a preposterously exaggerated figure. India's secretary for rural development put the figure at 40 million.

Today, a chapter in the India Country Study says the figure could be as high as 56 million people.[43]

That's almost twice the population of Canada. More than three times the population of Australia.

Think about it: 56 million people displaced by Big Dams in the last fifty years. And India still does not have a national rehabilitation policy.

When the history of India's miraculous leap to the forefront of the Information Revolution is written, let it be said that 56 million Indians (and their children and their children's children) paid for it with everything they ever had. Their homes, their lands, their languages, their histories.

You can see them from your car window when you drive home every night. Try not to look away. Try to meet their eyes. Fifty-six million displaced, impoverished, pulverized people. Almost half of them are Dalit and Adivasi.[44] (There is devastating meaning couched in this figure.)

There's a saying in the villages of the Narmada valley: "You can wake someone who's sleeping. But you can't wake someone who's pretending to be asleep." When it comes to the politics of forced, involuntary displacement, there's a deafening silence in this country. People's eyes glaze over. They behave as though it's just a blip in the democratic process.

The nicer ones say, "Oh, but it's such a pity. People must be resettled." (Where? I want to scream. Where's the land? Has someone invented a Land-Manufacturing Machine?)

The nasties say, "Someone has to pay the price for National Development."

The point is that 56 million is more than a blip, folks. It's civil war.

Quite apart from the human costs of Big Dams, there are the staggering environmental costs. More than 3 million acres of submerged forest, ravaged ecosystems, destroyed rivers, defunct, silted-up reservoirs, endangered wildlife, disappearing biodiversity, and 24 million acres of agricultural land that is now waterlogged and saline. Today there are more drought-prone and flood-prone areas in India than there were in 1947. Not a single river in the plains has potable water. Remember, 200 million Indians have no access to safe drinking water.[45]

Planners, when confronted with past mistakes, say sagely, "Yes, it's true that mistakes have been made. But we're on a learning curve." The lives and livelihoods of 56 million people and all this environmental mayhem serve only to extend the majestic arc of their learning curve.

Will they ever get off the curve and actually *learn*?

The evidence against Big Dams is mounting alarmingly. None of it appears on the balance sheet. There *is* no balance sheet. There has not been an official audit, a comprehensive post-project evaluation, of a single Big Dam in India to see whether or not it has achieved what it set out to achieve.

This is what is hardest to believe. That the Indian government's unshakable faith in Big Dams is based on nothing. No studies. No system of checks and balances. Nothing at all. And of course, those of us who question it are spies.

Is it unreasonable to call for a moratorium on the construction of Big Dams until past mistakes have been rectified and the millions of uprooted people have been truly recompensed and rehabilitated? It is the only way an industry that has so far been based on lies and false promises can redeem itself.

Of the series of thirty Big Dams proposed on the main stem of the Narmada River, four are megadams. Of these, only one—the Bargi dam—has been completed. Three are under construction.

The Bargi dam was completed in 1990. It cost ten times more than was budgeted and submerged three times more land than engineers said it would.[46] To save the cost and effort of doing a detailed survey, in order to mark the Full Reservoir Level, the government closed the sluice gates one monsoon and filled the reservoir without warning. Water entered villagers' homes at night. They had to take their children, their cattle, their pots and pans, and flee up the hillside. The Narmada Control Authority had estimated that 70,000 people from 101 villages would be displaced. Instead, when they filled the reservoir, 114,000 people from 162 villages were displaced. In addition, 26 government "resettlement colonies" (which consisted of house plots but no agricultural land) were submerged.[47] Eventually there was no rehabilitation. Some "oustees" got a meager cash compensation. Most got nothing. Some died of starvation. Others moved to slums in Jabalpur, where they now work as rickshaw pullers and construction labor.

Today, ten years after it was completed, the Bargi dam irrigates only as much land as it submerged. Only 5 percent of the land its planners claimed it would irrigate. The government says it has no money to make the canals. Yet work has begun downstream, on the mammoth Narmada Sagar dam, which will submerge 251 villages, on the Maheshwar dam, and, of course, on the most controversial dam in history, the Sardar Sarovar.[48]

The Sardar Sarovar dam is currently 90 meters high. Its final projected height is 138 meters. It is located in Gujarat, but most of the villages that will be submerged by its gigantic reservoir are in Maharashtra and Madhya Pradesh. The Sardar Sarovar dam has become the showcase of India's Violation of Human Rights Initiative. It has ripped away the genial mask of Dams-as-Development and revealed its brutish innards.

I have written about Sardar Sarovar extensively in a previous essay ("The Greater Common Good"), so I'll be brief. The Sardar Sarovar dam will displace close to half a million people. More than half of them do not officially qualify as "project-affected" and are not entitled to rehabilitation. It will submerge thirty-two thousand acres of deciduous forest.[49]

In 1985, before a single study had been done, before anyone had any idea what the human cost or environmental impact of the dam would be, the World Bank sanctioned a $450 million loan for the dam. The Ministry of Environment's conditional clearance (without any studies being done) came in 1987! At no point in the decision-making process were the people to be affected consulted or even informed about the project. In 1993, after a spectacular struggle by the NBA, the people of the valley forced the Bank to withdraw from the project.[50] The Gujarat government decided to go ahead with the project.

In 1994 the NBA filed a petition in the Supreme Court. For six years, the court put a legal injunction on further construction of the dam. On October 18, 2000, in a shocking 2–1 majority judgment, the Supreme

Court lifted the injunction.[51] After having seen fit to hold up the construction for six years, the court chastised (using unseemly, insulting language) the people of the Narmada valley for approaching it too late and said that on these grounds alone their petition should be dismissed. It permitted construction to continue according to the guidelines laid down by the Narmada Water Disputes Tribunal.

It did this despite the fact that it was aware that the tribunal guidelines have been consistently violated for thirteen years. Despite the fact that none of the conditions of the environment ministry's clearance have been met. Despite the fact that thirteen years have passed and the government hasn't even produced a resettlement plan. Despite the fact that not a single village has been resettled according to the directives of the tribunal. Despite the fact that the Madhya Pradesh government has stated on oath that it has no land on which to resettle "oustees" (80 percent of them live in Madhya Pradesh).[52] Despite the fact that since construction began, the Madhya Pradesh government has not given a single acre of agricultural land to displaced families. Despite the fact that the court was fully aware that even families displaced by the dam at its current height have not been rehabilitated.

In other words, the Supreme Court has actually ordered and sanctioned the violation of the Narmada Water Disputes Tribunal Award.

"But this is the problem with the government," Mr. and Mrs. Well-Meaning say. "It's so inefficient. These things wouldn't happen with a private company. Things like resettlement and rehabilitation of poor people will be so much better managed."

The Maheshwar experience teaches you otherwise.

In a private project, the only things that are better managed are the corruption, the lies, and the swiftness and brutality of repression. And, of course, the escalating costs.

In 1994, the project cost of the Maheshwar dam was estimated at $99 million. In 1996, following the contract with S. Kumars, it rose to $333 million. Today it stands at $467 million.[53] Initially, 80 percent of this money was to be raised from foreign investors. There has been a procession of them—Pacgen of the United States and Bayernwerk, VEW, Siemens, and the HypoVereinsbank of Germany. And now, the latest in the line of ardent suitors, Ogden of the United States.

According to the NBA's calculations, the cost of the electricity at the factory gate will be 13.9 cents per kilowatt hour, which is twenty-six times more expensive than existing hydel power in the state, five and a half times more expensive than thermal power, and four times more expensive than power from the central grid. (It's worth mentioning here that Madhya Pradesh today generates 1,500 megawatts more power than it can transmit and distribute.)

Though the installed capacity of the Maheshwar project is supposed to be 400 megawatts, studies using twenty-eight years of actual river flow data show that 80 percent of the electricity will be generated only during the monsoon months, when the river is full. What this means is that most of the supply will be generated when it's least needed.[54]

S. Kumars has no worries on this count. They have Enron as a precedent. They have an escrow clause in their contract, which guarantees them first call on government funds. This means that however much (or however little) electricity they produce, whether anybody buys it or not, for the next thirty-five years they are guaranteed a minimum payment from the government of approximately $127 million a year. This money will be paid to them even before employees of the bankrupt State Electricity Board get their salaries.

What did S. Kumars do to deserve this largesse? It isn't hard to guess. So who's actually paying for this dam that nobody needs?

According to government surveys, the reservoir of the Maheshwar dam will submerge sixty-one villages. Thirteen will be wholly submerged; the rest will lose their farmlands.[55] As usual, none of the villagers were informed about the dam or their impending eviction. (Of course, if they go to court now they'll be told it's too late, since construction has already begun.)

The first surveys were done under a ruse that a railway line was being constructed. It was only in 1997, when blasting began at the dam site, that realization dawned on people and the NBA became active in Maheshwar. The agency in charge of the survey is the same one that was in charge of the surveys for the Bargi reservoir. We know what happened there.

People in the submergence zone of the Maheshwar dam say that the surveys are completely wrong. Some villages marked for submergence are at a higher level than villages that are not counted as project-affected. Since the Maheshwar dam is located in the broad plains of Nimad, even a small miscalculation in the surveys will lead to huge discrepancies between what is marked for submergence and what is actually submerged. The consequences of these errors will be far worse than what happened at Bargi.

There are other egregious assumptions in the "survey." Annexure Six of the resettlement plan states that there are 176 trees and 38 wells in all the affected 61 villages combined. The villagers point out that in just a single village—Pathrad—there are 40 wells and more than 4,000 trees.

As with trees and wells, so with people.

There is no accurate estimate of how many people will be affected by the dam. Even the project authorities admit that new surveys must be done. So far they've managed to survey only one out of the sixty-one villages. The number of affected households rose from 190 (in the preliminary survey) to 300 (in the new one).

In circumstances such as these, it's impossible for even the NBA to have an accurate idea of the number of project-affected people. Their rough guess is about fifty thousand. More than half of them are Dalits, Kevats, and Kahars—ancient communities of ferrymen, fisherfolk, sand quarriers, and cultivators of the riverbed. Most of them own no land, but the river sustains them and means more to them than to anyone else. If the dam is built, thousands of them will lose their only source of livelihood. Yet simply because they are landless, they do not qualify as project-affected and will not be eligible for rehabilitation.

Jalud is the first of the sixty-one villages slated for submergence in the reservoir of the dam.[56] As early as 1985, twelve families, mostly Dalit, who had small holdings near the dam site had their land acquired. When they protested, cement was poured into their water pipes, their standing crops were bulldozed, and the police occupied the land by force. All twelve families are now landless and work as wage laborers. The new "private" initiative has made no effort to help them.

According to the environmental clearance from the central government, the people affected by the project ought to have been resettled in 1997. To date, S. Kumars hasn't even managed to produce a list of project-affected people, let alone land on which they are to be resettled. Yet construction continues. S. Kumars is so well entrenched with the state government that they don't even need to pretend to cover their tracks.

This is how India works.

This is the genesis of the Maheshwar dam. This is the legacy that the Ogden Energy Group of the United States was so keen to inherit. What they don't realize is that the fight is on. Over the last three years, the struggle against the Maheshwar dam has grown into a veritable civil disobedience movement, though you wouldn't know it if you read the papers. The mainstream media is hugely dependent on revenue from advertising. S. Kumars sponsors massive advertisements for their blended suitings. After their James Bond campaign with Pierce Brosnan, they've signed India's biggest film star—Hrithik Roshan—as their star campaigner.[57] It's extraordinary how much silent admiration and support a hunk in a blended suit can evoke.

Over the last two years, tens of thousands of villagers have captured the dam site several times and halted construction work.[58] Protests in the region forced two companies, Bayernwerk and VEW of Germany, to withdraw from the project.[59] The German company Siemens remained in the fray (angling for an export credit guarantee from Hermes, the German ECA).

In the summer of 2000, the German Ministry of Economic Cooperation and Development sent in a team of experts headed by Richard Bissell (former chairman of the Inspection Panel of the World Bank) to undertake an independent review of the resettlement and rehabilitation aspects of the project.[60] The report, published on June 15, 2000, was unambiguous that resettlement and rehabilitation of people displaced by the Maheshwar dam was simply not possible.

At the end of August, Siemens withdrew its application for a Hermes guarantee.[61]

The people of the valley don't get much time to recover between bouts of fighting. In September, S. Kumars was part of the Indian Prime Minister's business entourage when he visited the United States.[62] Desperate to replace Siemens, they were hoping to convert their Memorandum of Understanding with Ogden into a final contract. That, fortunately, didn't happen, and now Ogden has withdrawn from the Maheshwar project.[63]

The only time I have ever felt anything close to what most people would describe as national pride was when I walked one night with four thousand people toward the Maheshwar dam site, where we knew hundreds of armed policemen were waiting for us. Since the previous evening, people from all over the valley had begun to gather in a village called Sulgaon. They came in tractors, in bullock carts, and on foot. They came prepared to be beaten, humiliated, and taken to prison.

We set out at three in the morning. We walked for three hours—farmers, fisherfolk, sand quarriers, writers, painters, filmmakers, lawyers, journalists. All of India was represented. Urban, rural, touchable, untouchable. This alliance is what gives the movement its raw power, its intellectual rigor, and its phenomenal tenacity. As we crossed fields and forded streams, I remember thinking: "This is my land, this is the dream to which the whole of me belongs, this is worth more to me than anything else in the world." We were not just fighting against a dam. We were fighting for a philosophy. For a worldview.

We walked in utter silence. Not a throat was cleared. Not a *beedi* lit. We arrived at the dam site at dawn. Though the police were expecting us, they didn't know exactly where we would come from. We captured the dam site. People were beaten, humiliated, and arrested.

I was arrested and pushed into a private car that belonged to S. Kumars. I remember feeling a hot stab of shame—as quick and sharp as my earlier sense of pride. This was my land, too. My feudal land. Where even the police have been privatized. (On the way to the police station, they complained that S. Kumars had given them nothing to eat all day.) That evening there were so many arrests, the jail could not contain the people. The administration broke down and abandoned the jail. The people locked themselves in and demanded answers to their questions. So far, none have been forthcoming.

A Dutch documentary filmmaker recently asked me a very simple question: What can India teach the world?

A documentary filmmaker needs to see to understand. I thought of three places I could take him to.

First, to a "Call Center College" in Gurgaon, on the outskirts of Delhi. I thought it would be interesting for a filmmaker to see how easily an ancient civilization can be made to abase itself completely. In a Call Center College, hundreds of young English-speaking Indians are being groomed to staff the backroom operations of giant transnational companies.[64] They are trained to answer telephone queries from the United States and the United Kingdom (on subjects ranging from a credit card inquiry to advice about a malfunctioning washing machine or the availability of cinema tickets). On no account must the caller know that his or her inquiry is being attended to by an Indian sitting at a desk on the outskirts of Delhi. The Call Center Colleges train their students to speak in American and British accents. They have to read foreign papers so they can chitchat about the news or the weather. On duty they have to change their given names. Sushma becomes Susie, Govind becomes Jerry, Advani becomes Andy. (Hi! I'm Andy. Gee, hot day, innit? Shoot, how can I help ya?) Actually it's worse: Sushma becomes Mary. Govind becomes David. Perhaps Advani becomes Ulysses.

Call center workers are paid one-tenth of the salaries of their counterparts abroad. From all accounts, call centers are billed to become a multibillion-dollar industry.[65] Recently the giant Tata industrial group announced its plans to redeploy twenty thousand of its retrenched workers in call centers after a brief "period of training" for the business, such as "picking up [the] American accent and slang."[66] The news report said that the older employees may find it difficult to work at night, a requirement for US-based companies, given the time difference between India and the United States.

The second place I thought I'd take the filmmaker was another kind of training center, a Rashtriya Swayamsevak Sangh (RSS) *shakha*, where the terrible backlash to this enforced abasement is being nurtured and groomed. Where ordinary people march around in khaki shorts and learn that amassing nuclear weapons, religious bigotry, misogyny, homophobia, book burning, and outright hatred are the ways in which to retrieve a nation's lost dignity. Here he might see for himself how the two arms of government work in synergy. How they have evolved and pretty near perfected an extraordinary pincer action—while one arm is busy selling the nation off in chunks, the other, to divert attention, is orchestrating a baying, howling, deranged chorus of cultural nationalism. It would be fascinating to actually see how the inexorable ruthlessness of one process results in the naked, vulgar terrorism perpetrated by the other. They're Siamese twins—Advani and Andy. They share organs. They have the ability to say two entirely contradictory things simultaneously, to hold all positions at all times. There's no separating them.

The third place I thought I'd take him was the Narmada valley. To witness the ferocious, magical, magnificent, tenacious, and above all nonviolent resistance that has grown on the banks of that beautiful river.

What is happening to our world is almost too colossal for human comprehension to contain. But it is a terrible, terrible thing. To contemplate its girth and circumference, to attempt to define it, to try and fight it all at once, is impossible. The only way to combat it is by fighting specific wars in specific ways. A good place to begin would be the Narmada valley.

The borders are open. Come on in. Let's bury Rumpelstiltskin.

8. The Ladies Have Feelings, So . . .

Shall We Leave It to the Experts?

India lives in several centuries at the same time. Somehow we manage to progress and regress simultaneously. As a nation we age by pushing outward from the middle—adding a few centuries on to either end of our extraordinary c.v. We greaten like the maturing head of a hammerhead shark with eyes looking in diametrically opposite directions. I have no doubt that even here in North America you have heard that Germany is considering changing its immigration laws in order to import Indian software engineers.[1] I have even less doubt that you've heard of the Naga Sadhu at the Kumbh Mela who towed the District Commissioner's car with his penis while the Commissioner sat in it solemnly with his wife and children.[2]

As Indian citizens we subsist on a regular diet of caste massacres and nuclear tests, mosque break-ins and fashion shows, church burnings and expanding cell phone networks, bonded labor and the digital revolution, female infanticide and the Nasdaq crash, husbands who continue to burn their wives for dowry and our delectable stockpile of Miss Worlds. I don't mean to put a simplistic value judgment on this peculiar form of "progress" by suggesting that Modern is Good and Traditional is

Based on a talk given as the Third Annual Eqbal Ahmad Lecture, Amherst, Massachusetts, February 15, 2001.

Bad—or vice versa. What's hard to reconcile oneself to, both personally and politically, is the schizophrenic nature of it. That applies not just to the ancient/modern conundrum, but to the utter illogic of what appears to be the current national enterprise. In the lane behind my house, every night I walk past road gangs of emaciated laborers digging a trench to lay fiber-optic cables to speed up our digital revolution. In the bitter winter cold, they work by the light of a few candles.

It's as though the people of India have been rounded up and loaded onto two convoys of trucks (a huge big one and a tiny little one) that have set off resolutely in opposite directions. The tiny convoy is on its way to a glittering destination somewhere near the top of the world. The other convoy just melts into the darkness and disappears. A cursory survey that tallies the caste, class, and religion of who gets to be on which convoy would make a good Lazy Person's Concise Guide to the History of India. For some of us, life in India is like being suspended between two of the trucks, one in each convoy, and being neatly dismembered as they move apart, not bodily, but emotionally and intellectually.

Of *course* India is a microcosm of the world. Of *course* versions of what happens there happen everywhere. Of *course*, if you're willing to look, the parallels are easy to find. The difference in India is only in the scale, the magnitude, and the sheer proximity of the disparity. In India your face is slammed right up against it. To address it, to deal with it, to not deal with it, to try and understand it, to insist on not understanding it, to simply survive it—on a daily, hourly basis—is a fine art in itself. Either an art or a form of insular, inward-looking insanity. Or both.

To be a writer—a supposedly "famous" writer—in a country where 300 million people are illiterate is a dubious honor.[3] To be a writer in a country that gave the world Mahatma Gandhi, that invented the concept of nonviolent resistance, and then, half a century later, followed that up with nuclear tests, is a ferocious burden. (Though no more ferocious a burden, it has to be said, than being a writer in a country that has enough nuclear weapons to destroy the earth several times over.) To be a writer in a country where something akin to an undeclared civil war is being waged on its subjects in the name of "development" is an onerous responsibility. When it comes to writers and writing, I use words like *onerous* and *responsibility* with a heavy heart and not a small degree of sadness.

This is what I'm here to talk to you, to think aloud with you, about. What is the role of writers and artists in society? Do they have a definable role? Can it be fixed, described, characterized in any definite way? Should it be?

Personally, I can think of few things more terrifying than if writers and artists were charged with an immutable charter of duties and responsibilities that they had to live and work by. Imagine if there was this little black book—a sort of Approved Guide to Good Writing—that said: All writers shall be politically conscious and sexually moral, or: All writers should believe in God, globalization, and the joys of family life . . .

Rule One for a writer, as far as I'm concerned, is There Are No Rules. And Rule Two (since Rule One was made to be broken) is There Are No Excuses for Bad Art. Painters, writers, singers, actors, dancers, filmmakers, musicians are meant to fly, to push at the frontiers, to worry the edges of the human imagination, to conjure beauty from the most unexpected things, to find magic in places where others never thought to look. If you limit the trajectory of their flight, if you weight their wings with society's existing notions of morality and responsibility, if you truss them up with preconceived values, you subvert their endeavor.

A good or great writer may refuse to accept any responsibility or morality that society wishes to impose on her. Yet the best and greatest of them know that if they abuse this hard-won freedom, it can only lead to bad art. There is an intricate web of morality, rigor, and responsibility that art, that writing itself, imposes on a writer. It's singular, it's individual, but nevertheless it's there. At its best, it's an exquisite bond between the artist and the medium. At its acceptable end, it's a sort of sensible cooperation. At its worst, it's a relationship of disrespect and exploitation.

The absence of external rules complicates things. There's a very thin line that separates the strong, true, bright bird of the imagination from the synthetic, noisy bauble. Where is that line? How do you recognize it? How do you know you've crossed it? At the risk of sounding esoteric and arcane, I'm tempted to say that you just know. The fact is that nobody—no reader, no reviewer, agent, publisher, colleague, friend, or enemy—can tell for sure. A writer just has to ask herself that question and answer it as honestly as possible. The thing about this "line" is that once you learn to recognize it, once you see it, it's impossible to ignore. You have no choice but to live with it, to follow it through. You have to bear with all its complexities, contradictions, and demands. And that's not always easy. It doesn't always lead to compliments and standing ovations. It can lead you to the strangest, wildest places. In the midst of a bloody military coup, for instance, you could find yourself fascinated by the mating rituals of a purple sunbird, or the secret life of captive goldfish, or an old aunt's descent into madness. And nobody can say that there isn't truth and art and beauty in that. Or, on the contrary, in the midst of putative peace, you could, like me, be unfortunate enough to stumble on a silent war. The trouble is that once you see it, you can't unsee it. And once you've seen it, keeping quiet, saying nothing, becomes as political an act as speaking out. There's no innocence. Either way, you're accountable.

Today, perhaps more so than in any other era in history, the writer's right to free speech is guarded and defended by the civil societies and state establishments of the most powerful countries in the world. Any overt attempt to silence or muffle a voice is met with furious opposition. The writer is embraced and protected. This is a wonderful thing. The writer, the actor, the musician, the filmmaker—they have become radiant jewels in the crown of modern civilization. The artist, I imagine, is finally as free as he or she will ever be. Never before have so many writers had their books published. (And now, of course, we have the Internet.) Never before have we been more commercially viable. We live and prosper in the heart of the marketplace. True, for every so-called success there are hundreds who "fail." True, there are myriad art forms, both folk and classical, myriad languages, myriad cultural and artistic traditions that are being crushed and cast aside in the stampede to the big bumper sale in Wonderland. Still, there have never been more writers, singers, actors, or painters who have become influential, wealthy superstars. And they, the successful ones, spawn a million imitators, they become the torchbearers, their work becomes the benchmark for what art is, or ought to be.

Nowadays in India the scene is almost farcical. Following the recent commercial success of some Indian authors, Western publishers are desperately prospecting for the next big Indo-Anglian work of fiction. They're doing everything short of interviewing English-speaking Indians for the post of "writer." Ambitious middle-class parents who, a few years ago, would only settle for a future in Engineering, Medicine, or

Management for their children, now hopefully send them to creative writing schools. People like myself are constantly petitioned by computer companies, watch manufacturers, even media magnates to endorse their products. A boutique owner in Bombay once asked me if he could "display" my book *The God of Small Things* (as if it were an accessory, a bracelet or a pair of earrings) while he filmed me shopping for clothes! Jhumpa Lahiri, the American writer of Indian origin who won the Pulitzer Prize, came to India recently to have a traditional Bengali wedding. The wedding was reported on the front page of national newspapers.

Now where does all this lead us? Is it just harmless nonsense that's best ignored? How does all this ardent wooing affect our art? What kind of lenses does it put in our spectacles? How far does it remove us from the world around us?

There is very real danger that this neoteric seduction can shut us up far more effectively than violence and repression ever could. We have free speech. Maybe. But do we have Really Free Speech? If what we have to say doesn't "sell," will we still say it? Can we? Or is everybody looking for Things That Sell to say? Could writers end up playing the role of palace entertainers? Or the subtle twenty-first-century version of court eunuchs attending to the pleasures of our incumbent CEOs? You know—naughty, but nice. Risqué perhaps, but not risky.

It has been nearly four years now since my first, and so far only, novel, *The God of Small Things*, was published. In the early days, I used to be described—introduced—as the author of an almost freakishly "successful" (if I may use so vulgar a term) first book. Nowadays I'm introduced as something of a freak myself. I am, apparently, what is known in twenty-first century vernacular as a "writer-activist." (Like a sofa-bed.)

Why am I called a "writer-activist" and why—even when it's used approvingly, admiringly—does that term make me flinch? I'm called a writer-activist because after writing *The God of Small Things* I wrote three political essays: "The End of Imagination," about India's nuclear tests, "The Greater Common Good," about Big Dams and the "development" debate, and "Power Politics: The Reincarnation of Rumpelstiltskin," about the privatization and corporatization of essential infrastructure like water and electricity. Apart from the building of the temple in Ayodhya, these currently also happen to be the top priorities of the Indian government.[4]

Now, I've been wondering why it should be that the person who wrote *The God of Small Things* is called a writer, and the person who wrote the political essays is called an activist. True, *The God of Small Things* is a work of fiction, but it's no less political than any of my essays. True, the essays are works of nonfiction, but since when did writers forgo the right to write nonfiction?

My thesis—my humble theory, as we say in India—is that I've been saddled with this double-barreled appellation, this awful professional label, not because my work is political but because in my essays, which are about very contentious issues, I take sides. I take a position. I have a point of view. What's worse, I make it clear that I think it's right and moral to take that position, and what's even worse, I use everything in my power to flagrantly solicit support for that position. Now, for a writer of the twenty-first century, that's considered a pretty uncool, unsophisticated thing to do. It skates uncomfortably close to the territory occupied by political party ideologues—a breed of people that the world has learned (quite rightly) to mistrust. I'm aware of this. I'm all for being circumspect. I'm all for discretion, prudence, tentativeness, subtlety, ambiguity, complexity. I love the unanswered question, the unresolved story, the unclimbed mountain, the tender shard of an incomplete dream. Most of the time.

But is it mandatory for a writer to be ambiguous about everything? Isn't it true that there have been fearful episodes in human history when prudence and discretion would have just been euphemisms for pusillanimity? When caution was actually cowardice? When sophistication was disguised decadence? When circumspection was really a kind of espousal?

Isn't it true, or at least theoretically possible, that there are times in the life of a people or a nation when the political climate demands that we—even the most sophisticated of us—overtly take sides? I believe that such times are upon us. And I believe that in the coming years intellectuals and artists in India will be called upon to take sides.

And this time, unlike the struggle for Independence, we won't have the luxury of fighting a colonizing "enemy." We'll be fighting ourselves.

We will be forced to ask ourselves some very uncomfortable questions about our values and traditions, our vision for the future, our responsibilities as citizens, the legitimacy of our "democratic institutions," the role of the state, the police, the army, the judiciary, and the intellectual community.

Fifty years after Independence, India is still struggling with the legacy of colonialism, still flinching from the "cultural insult." As citizens we're still caught up in the business of "disproving" the white world's definition of us. Intellectually and emotionally, we have just begun to grapple with communal and caste politics that threaten to tear our society apart. But in the meanwhile, something new looms on our horizon.

It's not war, it's not genocide, it's not ethnic cleansing, it's not a famine or an epidemic. On the face of it, it's just ordinary, day-to-day business. It lacks the drama, the large-format, epic magnificence, of war or genocide or famine. It's dull in comparison. It makes bad TV. It has to do with boring things like jobs, money, water supply, electricity, irrigation. But it also has to do with a process of barbaric dispossession on a scale that has few parallels in history. You may have guessed by now that I'm talking about the modern version of globalization.

What is globalization? Who is it for? What is it going to do to a country like India, in which social inequality has been institutionalized in the caste system for centuries? A country in which seven hundred million people live in rural areas.[5] In which 80 percent of the landholdings are small farms. In which 300 million people are illiterate.

Is the corporatization and globalization of agriculture, water supply, electricity, and essential commodities going to pull India out of the stagnant morass of poverty, illiteracy, and religious bigotry? Is the dismantling and auctioning off of elaborate public sector infrastructure, developed with public money over the last fifty years, really the way forward? Is globalization going to close the gap between the privileged and the underprivileged, between the upper castes and the lower castes, between the educated and the illiterate? Or is it going to give those who already have a centuries-old head start a friendly helping hand?

Is globalization about "eradication of world poverty," or is it a mutant variety of colonialism, remote controlled and digitally operated? These are huge, contentious questions. The answers vary depending on whether they come from the villages and fields of rural India, from the slums and shantytowns of urban India, from the living rooms of the burgeoning middle class, or from the boardrooms of the big business houses.

Today India produces more milk, more sugar, more food grain than ever before. This year government warehouses are overflowing with 42 million tons of food grain.[6] That's almost a quarter of the total annual food grain produce. Farmers with too much grain on their hands were driven to despair. In regions that wielded enough political clout, the government went on a buying spree, purchasing more grain than it could possibly store or use. While the grain rots in government warehouses, three hundred fifty million Indian citizens live below the poverty line and do not have the means to eat a square meal a day.[7] And yet in March 2000, just before President Clinton's visit to India, the Indian government lifted import restrictions on one thousand four hundred commodities, including milk, grain, sugar, cotton, tea, coffee, and palm oil.[8] This despite the fact that there was a glut of these products in the market.

From April 1—April Fool's Day—2001, according to the terms of its agreement with the World Trade Organization (WTO), the Indian government will have to drop its quantitative import restrictions. The Indian market is already flooded with cheap imports. Though India is technically free to export its agricultural produce, in practice most of it cannot be exported because it doesn't meet the first world's "environmental standards." (You don't eat bruised mangoes, or bananas with mosquito bites, or rice with a few weevils in it. Whereas we don't mind the odd mosquito and the occasional weevil.)

Developed countries like the United States, whose hugely subsidized farm industry engages only 2–3 percent of its total population, are using the WTO to pressure countries like India to drop agricultural subsidies in order to make the market "competitive." Huge, mechanized corporate enterprises working thousands of acres of farmland want to compete with impoverished subsistence farmers who own a couple of acres of land.

In effect, India's rural economy, which supports 700 million people, is being garroted. Farmers who produce too much are in distress, farmers who produce too little are in distress, and landless agricultural laborers are out of work as big estates and farms lay off their workers. They're all flocking to the cities in search of employment.

"Trade Not Aid" is the rallying cry of the headmen of the new Global Village headquartered in the shining offices of the WTO. Our

British colonizers stepped onto our shores a few centuries ago disguised as traders. We all remember the East India Company. This time around, the colonizer doesn't even need a token white presence in the colonies. The CEOs and their men don't need to go to the trouble of tramping through the tropics, risking malaria, diarrhea, sunstroke, and an early death. They don't have to maintain an army or a police force, or worry about insurrections and mutinies. They can have their colonies and an easy conscience. "Creating a good investment climate" is the new euphemism for third world repression. Besides, the responsibility for implementation rests with the local administration.

In India, in order to clear the way for "development projects," the government is in the process of amending the present Land Acquisition Act (which, ironically, was drafted by the British in the nineteenth century) and making it more draconian than it already is.[9] State governments are preparing to ratify "anti-terrorist" laws so that those who oppose development projects (in Madhya Pradesh, for example) will be counted as terrorists. They can be held without trial for three years. They can have their lands and cattle seized.

Recently, globalization has come in for some criticism. The protests in Seattle and Prague will go down in history. Each time the WTO or the World Economic Forum wants to have a meeting, ministers have to barricade themselves with thousands of heavily armed police. Still, all its admirers, from Bill Clinton, Kofi Annan, and A. B. Vajpayee (the Indian prime minister) to the cheering brokers in the stalls, continue to say the same lofty things. If we have the right institutions of governance in place—effective courts, good laws, honest politicians, participatory democracy, a transparent administration that respects human rights and gives people a say in decisions that affect their lives—then the globalization project will work for the poor as well. They call this "globalization with a human face."

The point is, if all this were in place, almost *anything* would succeed: socialism, capitalism, you name it. Everything works in Paradise, a Communist State as well as a Military Dictatorship. But in an imperfect world, is it globalization that's going to bring us all this bounty? Is that what's happening in India now that it's on the fast track to the free market? Does any one thing on that lofty list apply to life in India today?

Are state institutions transparent? Have people had a say, have they even been informed—let alone consulted—about decisions that vitally affect their lives? And are Mr. Clinton (or now Mr. Bush) and Prime Minister Vajpayee doing everything in their power to see that the "right institutions of governance" are in place? Or are they involved in exactly the opposite enterprise? Do they mean something else altogether when they talk of the "right institutions of governance"?

On October 18, 2000, in one of the most extraordinary legal decisions in post-Independence India, the Supreme Court permitted the construction of the Sardar Sarovar dam on the Narmada River to proceed.[10] The court did this despite indisputable evidence placed before it that the Sardar Sarovar Projects did not have the mandatory environmental clearance from the central government. Despite the fact that no comprehensive studies have ever been done on the social and ecological impact of the dam. Despite the fact that in the last fifteen years not one single village has been resettled according to the project's own guidelines, and that there was no possibility of rehabilitating the four hundred thousand people who would be displaced by the project.[11] In effect, the Supreme Court has virtually endorsed the violation of human rights to life and livelihood.

Big Dams in India have displaced not hundreds, not thousands, but millions—more than 30 million people in the last fifty years.[12] Almost half of them are Dalit and Adivasi, the poorest of the poor.[13] Yet India is the only country in the world that refused permission to the World Commission on Dams to hold a public hearing. The government in Gujarat, the state in which the Sardar Sarovar dam is being built, threatened members of the commission with arrest.[14] The World Commission on Dams report was released by Nelson Mandela in November 2000.[15] In February 2001, the Indian government formally rejected the report. Does this sound like a transparent, accountable, participatory democracy?

Recently the Supreme Court ordered the closure of seventy-seven thousand "polluting and nonconforming" industrial units in Delhi. The order could put five hundred thousand people out of work. What are these "industrial units"? Who are these people? They're the millions who have migrated from their villages, some voluntarily, others involuntarily, in search of work. They're the people who aren't supposed to exist, the "noncitizens" who survive in the folds and wrinkles, the cracks and fissures, of the "official" city. They exist just outside the net of the "official" urban infrastructure.

Close to 40 percent of Delhi's population of 12 million—about 5 million people—live in slums and unauthorized colonies.[16] Most of them are not serviced by municipal services—no electricity, no water, no sewage systems. About fifty thousand people are homeless and sleep on the streets. The "noncitizens" are employed in what economists rather stuffily call the "informal sector," the fragile but vibrant parallel economy. That both shocks and delights the imagination. They work as hawkers, rickshaw pullers, garbage recyclers, car battery rechargers, street tailors, transistor knob makers, buttonhole stitchers, paper bag makers, dyers, printers, barbers. These are the "industrial units" that have been targeted as nonconforming by the Supreme Court. (Fortunately I haven't heard *that* knock on my door yet, though I'm as nonconforming a unit as the rest of them.)

The trains that leave Delhi these days carry thousands of people who simply cannot survive in the city. They're returning to the villages they fled in the first place. Millions of others, because they're "illegal," have become easy meat for the rapacious, bribe-seeking police and predatory government officials. They haven't yet been driven out of the city but now must live in perpetual fear and anticipation of that happening.

In India the times are full of talk of the "free market," reforms, deregulation, and the dismantling of the "license raj"—all in the name of encouraging entrepreneurship and discouraging corruption. Yet when the state, supported by the judiciary, curbs freedom and obliterates a flourishing market, when it breaks the backs of numerous imaginative, resourceful, small-scale entrepreneurs and delivers millions of others as fodder to the doorstep of the corruption industry, few comment on the irony.

No doubt it's true that the informal sector is polluting and, according to a colonial understanding of urban land use, "nonconforming." But then we don't live in a clean, perfect world. What about the fact that 67 percent of Delhi's pollution comes from motor vehicles?[17] Is it conceivable that the Supreme Court will come up with an act that bans private cars? The courts and the government have shown no great enthusiasm for closing down big factories run by major industrialists that have polluted rivers, denuded forests, depleted and poisoned groundwater, and destroyed the livelihoods of hundreds of thousands of people who depend on these resources for a living. The Grasim factory in Kerala, the Orient Paper Mill in Madhya Pradesh, the "sunrise belt" industries in Gujarat. The uranium mines in Jadugoda, the aluminum plants in Orissa. And hundreds of others.

This is our in-house version of first world bullying in the global warming debate: i.e., we pollute, you pay.

In circumstances like these, the term *writer-activist* as a professional description of what I do makes me flinch doubly. First, because it is strategically positioned to diminish both writers and activists. It seeks to reduce the scope, the range, the sweep of what a writer is and can be. It suggests somehow that the writer by definition is too effete a being to come up with the clarity, the explicitness, the reasoning, the passion, the grit, the audacity, and, if necessary, the vulgarity to publicly take a political position. And, conversely, it suggests that the activist occupies the coarser, cruder end of the intellectual spectrum. That the activist is by profession a "position-taker" and therefore lacks complexity and intellectual sophistication, and is instead fueled by a crude, simple-minded, one-sided understanding of things. But the more fundamental problem I have with the term is that professionalizing the whole business of protest, putting a label on it, has the effect of containing the problem and suggesting that it's up to the professionals—activists and writer-activists—to deal with.

The fact is that what's happening in India today is not a *problem*, and the issues that some of us are raising are not *causes*. They are huge political and social upheavals that are convulsing the nation. One is not involved by virtue of being a writer or activist. One is involved because one is a human being. Writing about it just happens to be the most effective thing I can do. I think it's vital to deprofessionalize the public debate on matters that vitally affect the lives of ordinary people. It's time to snatch our futures back from the "experts." Time to ask, in ordinary language, the public question and to demand, in ordinary language, the public answer.

Frankly, however trenchantly, however angrily, however combatively one puts forward one's case, at the end of the day I'm only a citizen, one of many, who is demanding public information, asking for a public explanation. I have no ax to grind. I have no professional stakes to protect.

I'm prepared to be persuaded. I'm prepared to change my mind. But instead of an argument, or an explanation, or a disputing of facts, one gets insults, invective, legal threats, and the Expert's Anthem: "You're too emotional. You don't understand, and it's too complicated to explain." The subtext, of course, is: Don't worry your little head about it. Go and play with your toys. Leave the real world to us.

It's the old Brahminical instinct. Colonize knowledge, build four walls around it, and use it to your advantage. The Manusmriti, the Vedic Hindu code of conduct, says that if a Dalit overhears a *shloka* or any part of a sacred text, he must have molten lead poured into his ear. It isn't a coincidence that while India is poised to take its place at the forefront of the Information Revolution, 300 million of its citizens are illiterate. (It would be interesting, as an exercise, to find out how many "experts"— scholars, professionals, consultants—in India are actually Brahmins and upper castes.)

If you're one of the lucky people with a berth booked on the small convoy, then Leaving it to the Experts is, or can be, a mutually beneficial proposition for both the expert and yourself. It's a convenient way of shrugging off your own role in the circuitry. And it creates a huge professional market for all kinds of "expertise." There's a whole ugly universe waiting to be explored there. This is not at all to suggest that all consultants are racketeers or that expertise is unnecessary, but you've heard the saying—there's a lot of money in poverty. There are plenty of ethical questions to be asked of those who make a professional living off their expertise in poverty and despair.

For instance, at what point does a scholar stop being a scholar and become a parasite who feeds off despair and dispossession? Does the source of your funding compromise your scholarship? We know, after all, that World Bank studies are among the most quoted studies in the world. Is the World Bank a dispassionate observer of the global situation? Are the studies it funds entirely devoid of self-interest?

Take, for example, the international dam industry. It's worth US $32 billion to $46 billion a year.[18] It's bursting with experts and consultants. Given the number of studies, reports, books, PhDs, grants, loans, consultancies, EIAs, it's odd, wouldn't you say, that there is no really reliable estimate of how many people have been displaced by Big Dams in India?

That there is no estimate for exactly what the contribution of Big Dams has been to overall food production in India? That there hasn't been an official audit, a comprehensive, honest, thoughtful, post-project evaluation of a single Big Dam to see whether or not it has achieved what it set out to achieve? Whether or not the costs were justified, or even what the costs actually were?

What *are* the experts up to?

If you manage to ignore the invective, shut out the din of the Expert's Anthem, and keep your eye on the ball, you'll find that a lot of dubious politics lurks inside the stables of "expertise." Probe further, and it all precipitates in a bilious rush of abuse, intimidation, and blind anger. The intellectual equivalent of a police baton charge. The advantage of provoking this kind of unconstrained, spontaneous rage is that it allows you to get a good look at the instincts of some of these normally cautious, supposedly "neutral" people, the pillars of democracy—judges, planners, academics. It becomes very clear that it's not really a question of experts versus laypersons or of knowledge versus ignorance. It's the pitting of one value system against another, one kind of political instinct against another. It's interesting to watch so many supposedly "rational" people turn into irrational, instinctive political beings. To see how they find reasons to support their views, and how, if those reasons are argued away, they continue to cling to their views anyway. Perhaps for this alone, provocation is important. In a crisis, it helps to clarify who's on which side.

A wonderful illustration of this is the Supreme Court's reaction to my essay "The Greater Common Good," which was published in May 1999. In July and August of that year, the monsoon waters rose in the Narmada and submerged villages. While villagers stood in their homes for days together in chest-deep water to protest against the dam, while their crops were submerged, and while the NBA—Narmada Bachao Andolan, the people's movement in the Narmada valley—pointed out (citing specific instances) that government officials had committed perjury by signing false affidavits claiming that resettlement had been carried out when it hadn't, the three-judge bench in the Supreme Court met over three sessions. The only subject they discussed was whether or not the dignity of the court had been undermined. To assist them in their deliberations, they appointed what is called an *amicus curiae* (friend of the court) to advise them about whether or not they should initiate criminal proceedings against the NBA and me for contempt of court. The thing to keep in mind is that while the NBA was the petitioner, I was (and hopefully still am) an independent citizen. I wasn't present in court, but I was told that the three-judge bench ranted and raved and referred to me as "that woman." (I began to think of myself as the hooker who won the Booker.)

On October 15, 1999, they issued an elaborate order.[19] Here's an extract:

> Judicial process and institution cannot be permitted to be scandalised or subjected to contumacious violation in such a blatant manner in which it has been done by her [Arundhati Roy] . . . vicious stultification and vulgar debunking cannot be permitted to pollute the stream of justice . . . we are unhappy at the way in which the leaders of NBA and Ms. Arundhati Roy have attempted to undermine the dignity of the Court. We expected better behaviour from them . . . After giving this matter thoughtful consideration . . . we are not inclined to initiate contempt proceedings against the petitioners, its leaders or Arundhati Roy . . . after the 22nd of July 1999 . . . nothing has come to our notice which may show that Ms. Arundhati Roy has continued with the objectionable writings insofar as the judiciary is concerned. She may have by now realised her mistake . . .

What's dissent without a few good insults?

Anyway, eventually, as you can see, they let me off. And I continued with my Objectionable Writings. I hope in the course of this lecture I've managed to inspire at least some of the students in this audience to embark on careers as Vicious Stultificators and Vulgar Debunkers. We could do with a few more of those.

On the whole, in India, the prognosis is—to put it mildly—Not Good. And yet one cannot help but marvel at the fantastic range and depth and wisdom of the hundreds of people's resistance movements all over the country. They're being beaten down, but they simply refuse to lie down and die.

Their political ideologies and battle strategies span the range. We have the maverick Malayali professor who petitions the president every day against the communalization of history texts; Sunderlal Bahugana, who risks his life on indefinite hunger strikes protesting the Tehri dam; the Adivasis in Jadugoda protesting uranium mining on their lands; the Koel Karo Sanghathan resisting a megadam project in Jharkhand; the awe-inspiring Chattisgarh Mukti Morcha; the relentlessly dogged Mazdoor Kisan Shakti Sangathan; the Beej Bachao Andolan in Tehri-Garhwal fighting to save biodiversity of seeds; and of course, the Narmada Bachao Andolan, the people's movement in the Narmada valley.

India's redemption lies in the inherent anarchy and factiousness of its people, and in the legendary inefficiency of the Indian State. Even our heel-clicking, boot-stamping Hindu fascists are undisciplined to the point of being chaotic. They can't bring themselves to agree with each other for more than five minutes at a time. Corporatizing India is like trying to impose an iron grid on a heaving ocean and forcing it to behave.

My guess is that India will not behave. It cannot. It's too old and too clever to be made to jump through the hoops all over again. It's too diverse, too grand, too feral, and—eventually, I hope—too democratic to be lobotomized into believing in one single idea, which is, ultimately, what globalization really is: Life Is Profit.

What is happening to the world lies, at the moment, just outside the realm of common human understanding. It is the writers, the poets, the artists, the singers, the filmmakers who can make the connections, who can find ways of bringing it into the realm of common understanding. Who can translate cash-flow charts and scintillating boardroom speeches into real stories about real people with real lives. Stories about what it's like to lose your home, your land, your job, your dignity, your past, and your future to an invisible force. To someone or something you can't see. You can't hate. You can't even imagine.

It's a new space that's been offered to us today. A new kind of challenge. It offers opportunities for a new kind of art. An art which can make the impalpable palpable, make the intangible tangible, and the invisible visible. An art which can draw out the incorporeal adversary and make it real. Bring it to book.

Cynics say that real life is a choice between the failed revolution and the shabby deal. I don't know—maybe they're right. But even they should know that there's no limit to just how shabby that shabby deal can be. What we need to search for and find, what we need to hone and perfect into a magnificent, shining thing, is a new kind of politics. Not the politics of governance, but the politics of resistance. The politics of opposition. The politics of forcing accountability. The politics of slowing things down. The politics of joining hands across the world and preventing certain destruction. In the present circumstances, I'd say that the only thing worth globalizing is dissent. It's India's best export.

9. On Citizens' Rights to Express Dissent

In February 2001, a criminal petition filed by five advocates was listed before the Supreme Court of India. The petition accused Medha Patkar (leader of the Narmada Bachao Andolan), Prashant Bhushan (legal counsel for the NBA), and Arundhati Roy of committing criminal contempt of court by organizing and participating in a demonstration outside the gates of the Supreme Court to protest the court judgment on the Sardar Sarovar dam on the Narmada River. Based on the petition, the Supreme Court sent notices to the three accused, ordering them to appear personally in court on April 23, 2001.

The case is still pending in court. The maximum punishment for committing contempt of court in India is six months' imprisonment.

Arundhati Roy did not have a lawyer at her trial. Reproduced here is the text of her affidavit in reply to the criminal charges.

IN THE SUPREME COURT OF INDIA
ORIGINAL JURISDICTION
CONTEMPT PETITION (CR) NO: 2/2001
IN THE MATTER OF:
J.R. PARASHAR & ORS

Court affadavit filed April 23, 2001. First published in Arundhati Roy, *Power Politics*, 2nd ed. (Cambridge, MA: South End Press, 2001).

VERSUS
PRASHANT BHUSHAN & ORS
AFFIDAVIT IN REPLY FILED BY RESPONDENT NO: 3

The gravamen of the charges in the petition against me are contained in the FIR [First Information Report] that the petitioners say they lodged in the Tilak Marg police station on the 14th of December 2000. The FIR is annexed to the main petition and is reproduced verbatim below.

First Information Report dated December 14, 2000

I, Jagdish Prasar, with colleagues Shri Umed Singh and Rajender were going out from Supreme Court at 7.00 p.m and saw that Gate No. C was closed.

We came out from the Supreme Court premises from other path and inquired why the gate is close. The were [we were] surrounded by Prasant Bhusan, Medha Patekar and Arundhanti Roy alongwith their companion and they told Supreme Court your father's property. On this we told them they could not sit on Dharna by closing the gate. The proper place of Dharna is Parliament. In the mean time Prastant Bhusan said, "You Jagdish Prasar are the tout of judiciary." Again medha said *"sale ko jaan se maar do"* [kill him]. Arundhanti Roy commanded the crow that Supreme Court of India is the thief and all these are this touts. Kill them, Prasant Bhushan "pulled" by having "caught" my "haired [*sic*] and said that if you would be seen in the Supreme Court again he would get them killed." But they were shouting inspite of the presence of S.H.O and ACP Bhaskar Tilak marg. We ran away with great with great hardship otherwise their goonda might have done some mischief because of their drunken state. Therefore, it is requested to you that proper action may be taken after registering our complaint in order to save on lives and property. We complainants will be highly obliged.

Sd. Complainants.

The main petition is as shoddily drafted as the FIR. The lies, the looseness, the ludicrousness of the charges displays more contempt for the

Apex Court than any of the offenses allegedly committed by Prashant Bhushan, Medha Patkar, and myself. Its contents are patently false and malicious. The police station in Tilak Marg, where the FIR was lodged, has not registered a case. No policeman ever contacted me, there was no police investigation, no attempt to verify the charges, to find out whether the people named in the petition were present at the *dharna*, and whether indeed the incident described in the FIR (on which the entire contempt petition is based) occurred at all.

Under the circumstances, it is distressing that the Supreme Court has thought it fit to entertain this petition and issue notice directing me and the other respondents to appear personally in court on the 23rd of April 2001, and to "continue to attend the Court on all the days thereafter to which the case against you stands and until final orders are passed on the charges against you. WHEREIN FAIL NOT."

For the ordinary working citizen, these enforced court appearances mean that in effect, the punishment for the uncommitted crime has already begun.

The facts relating to the petition are as follows:

Contrary to everything the petition says, insinuates and implies—I am not a leader of the Narmada Bachao Andolan. I am a writer, an independent citizen with independent views who supports and admires the cause of the Andolan. I was not a petitioner in the Public Interest Litigation petition in the case of the Sardar Sarovar Project. I am not an "interested party." Prashant Bhushan is not my lawyer and has never represented me.

Furthermore in all humility I aver that I do not know who the petitioners are. That I never tried to murder anybody, or incite anybody to murder anybody, in broad daylight outside the gates of the Supreme Court in full view of the Delhi police. That I did not raise any slogans against the court. That I did not see Prashant Bhushan "pulled" anyone by having "caught" their "haired" [*sic*] and said that "if you would be seen in the Supreme Court again he would get them killed." That I did not see Medha Patkar, leader of India's most prominent nonviolent resistance movement, metamorphose into a mediocre film actor and say *"sale ko jaan se maar do."* (Kill the bastard.) That I did not notice the presence of any *"goondas"* in a "drunken state." And finally, that my name is spelled wrong.

On the morning of the 13th of December 2000, I learned that people from the Narmada valley had gathered outside the gates of the Supreme Court. When I arrived at the Supreme Court at about 11.30 a.m., gate No. C was already closed. Four to five hundred people were standing outside. Most of them were Adivasi people who, as a consequence of the recent Supreme Court judgment that allowed the construction of the Sardar Sarovar dam to proceed, will lose their lands and homes this monsoon to the rising waters of the reservoir. They have not been rehabilitated. In a few months they will be destitute and have nowhere to go. These people had traveled all the way from the Narmada valley to personally convey their despair and anguish to the court. To tell the court that, in contravention of its order, no land has been offered to them for rehabilitation and that the reality of the situation in the Narmada valley is very different from the one portrayed in the Supreme Court judgment. They asked the Registrar of the Court for a meeting with the Chief Justice.

A number of representatives of peoples' movements in Delhi, and other supporters of the Andolan like myself, were also there to express their solidarity. I would like to stress that I did not see Prashant Bhushan, the main accused in the petition, at the *dharna*. Medha Patkar, who was there, asked me to speak to the people for five minutes.

My exact words were: "*Mujhe paanch minute bhi nahi chahiye aapke saamne apni baat rakhne ke liye. Mein aapke saath hoon.*" (I do not even need five minutes to tell you why I'm here. I'm here because I support you.) This is easy to verify as there were several film and television crews shooting the event. The villagers had cloth labels hung around their necks that said, "Project-Affected at 90 Meters" (the current height of the dam). As time went by and it became clear that the request for a meeting with the Chief Justice was not going to be granted, people grew disheartened. Several people (who I don't know or recognize) made speeches critical of the Court, its inaccessibility to common people, and its process. Others spoke about corruption in the judiciary, about the judges and how far removed they are from ground realities. I admit that I made absolutely no attempt to intervene. I am not a policeman or a public official. As a writer I am deeply interested in peoples' perceptions of the functioning of one of the most important institutions in this country.

However, I would like to clarify that I have never, either in my writing or in any public forum, cast aspersions on the character or integrity of the judges. I believe that the reflexive instinct of the powerful to protect the powerful is sufficient explanation for the kind of iniquitous judgment as in the case of the Sardar Sarovar Project. I did not raise slogans against the court. I did not, as the petition claims, say "Supreme Court *bika hua hai.*" (The Supreme Court has sold out.) I certainly did not "command the crow that Supreme Court of India is the thief and all these are this touts." (Perhaps the petitioners meant "crowd"?)

I went to the *dharna* because I have been deeply distressed and angered by the Supreme Court's majority—and therefore operative—verdict on the Sardar Sarovar Project. The verdict allowed the project to proceed even though the court was well aware that the Narmada Water Disputes Tribunal had been consistently violated for thirteen years. That not a single village had been resettled according to the directives of the tribunal, and that the Madhya Pradesh government (which is responsible for eighty percent of the oustees) had given a written affidavit in court stating that it has no land to resettle them. In effect, the Supreme Court ordered the violation of the fundamental rights to life and livelihood of hundreds of thousands of Indian citizens, most of them Dalit and Adivasi.

As a consequence of the Supreme Court judgment, it is these unfortunate citizens who stand to lose their homes, their livelihoods, their gods and their histories. When they came calling on the Supreme Court on the morning of December 13, 2000, they were asking the court to restore their dignity. To accuse them of lowering the dignity of the court suggests that the dignity of the court and the dignity of Indian citizens are incompatible, oppositional, adversarial things. That the dignity of one can only exist at the cost of the other. If this is so, it is a sad and shameful proposition. In his Republic Day speech, President K. R. Narayanan called upon the nation, and specifically the judiciary, to take special care of these fragile communities. He said, "The developmental path we have adopted is hurting them, the marginalized, the Scheduled Castes and Scheduled Tribes, and threatening their very existence."

I believe that the people of the Narmada valley have the constitutional right to protest peacefully against what they consider an unjust and unfair judgment. As for myself, I have every right to participate in any peaceful protest meeting that I choose to. Even outside the gates of the Supreme Court. As a writer I am fully entitled to put forward my views, my reasons and arguments for why I believe that the judgment in the Sardar Sarovar case is flawed and unjust and violates the human rights of Indian citizens. I have the right to use all my skills and abilities, such as they are, and all the facts and figures at my disposal, to persuade people to my point of view.

The petition is a pathetic attempt to target what the petitioners perceive to be the three main fronts of the resistance movement in the Narmada valley. The activist Medha Patkar, leader of the Narmada Bachao Andolan and representative of the people in the valley; the lawyer, Prashant Bhushan, legal counsel for the Narmada Bachao Andolan; and the writer (me), who is seen as one of those who carries the voice of the Andolan to the world outside. It is significant that this is the third time that I, as a writer, have had to face legal harassment connected with my writing.

In July 1999, the three-judge bench in the Supreme Court hearing the public interest petition on the Sardar Sarovar Project took offense at my essay "The Greater Common Good," published in *Outlook* and *Frontline* magazines. While the waters rose in the Narmada, while villagers stood in their homes in chest-deep water for days on end, protesting the court's interim order, the Supreme Court held three hearings in which the main topic they discussed was whether or not the dignity of the court had been violated by my essay. On the 15th of October 1999, without giving me an opportunity to be heard, the court passed an insulting order. Here is an extract:

> Judicial process and institution cannot be permitted to be scandalised or subjected to contumacious violation in such a blatant manner in which it has been done by her [Arundhati Roy] . . . vicious stultification and vulgar debunking cannot be permitted to pollute the stream of justice . . . we are unhappy at the way in which the leaders of NBA and Ms. Arundhati Roy have attempted to undermine the dignity of the Court. We expected better behaviour from them . . .

The order contained a veiled warning to me not to continue with my "objectionable writings."

In 1997, a criminal case for Corrupting Public Morality was filed against me in a district magistrate's court in Kerala for my book *The God of Small Things*. It has been pending for the last four years. I have had to hire criminal lawyers, draft affidavits, and travel all the way to Kerala to appear in court.

And now I have to defend myself on this third, ludicrous charge.

As a writer I wish to state as emphatically as I can that this is a dangerous trend. If the court uses the Contempt of Court law, and allows citizens to abuse its process to intimidate and harass writers, it will have the chilling effect of interfering with a writer's imagination and the creative act itself. This fear of harassment will create a situation in which even before a writer puts pen to paper, she will have to anticipate what the court might think of her work. It will induce a sort of enforced, fearful self-censorship. It would be bad for law, worse for literature and sad for the world of art and beauty.

I have written and published several essays and articles on the Narmada issue and the Supreme Court judgment. None of them was intended to show contempt to the court. However, I have every right to disagree with the Court's views on the subject and to express my disagreement in any publication or forum that I choose to. Regardless of everything the operative Supreme Court judgment on the Sardar Sarovar says, I continue to be opposed to Big Dams. I continue to believe that they are economically unviable, ecologically destructive, and deeply undemocratic. I continue to believe that the judgment disregarded the evidence placed before the court. I continue to write what I believe. Not to do so would undermine the dignity of writers, their art, their very purpose. I need hardly add that I also believe that those who hold the opposite point of view to mine, those who wish to disagree with my views, criticize them, or denounce them, have the same rights to free speech and expression as I do.

I left the *dharna* at about 6 p.m. Until then, contrary to the lurid scenario described in the petitioners' FIR, I can state on oath that no blood was spilled, no mob was drunk, no hair was pulled, no murder attempted. A little *khichdi* was cooked and consumed. No litter was left. There were over a hundred police constables and some senior police officers present. Though I would very much like to, I cannot say in good conscience that I have never set eyes on the petitioners because I don't know who they are or what they look like. They could have been any one of the hundreds of people who were milling around on that day.

But whoever they are, and whatever their motives, for the petitioners to attempt to misuse the Contempt of Court Act and the good offices of the Supreme Court to stifle criticism and stamp out dissent strikes at the very roots of the notion of democracy.

In recent months this court has issued judgments on several major public issues. For instance, the closure of polluting industries in Delhi, the conversion of public transport buses from diesel to CNG [compressed natural gas], and the judgment permitting the construction of the Sardar Sarovar dam to proceed. All of these have had far-reaching and often unanticipated impacts. They have materially affected, for better or for worse, the lives and livelihoods of millions of Indian citizens. Whatever the justice or injustice of these judgments, whatever their finer legal points, for the court to become intolerant of criticism or expressions of dissent would mark the beginning of the end of democracy.

An "activist" judiciary that intervenes in public matters to provide a corrective to a corrupt, dysfunctional executive surely has to be more, not less accountable. To a society that is already convulsed by political bankruptcy, economic distress, and religious and cultural intolerance, any form of judicial intolerance will come as a crippling blow. If the judiciary removes itself from public scrutiny and accountability, and severs its links with the society that it was set up to serve in the first place, it would mean that yet another pillar of Indian democracy will crumble. A judicial dictatorship is as fearsome a prospect as a military dictatorship or any other form of totalitarian rule.

The Tehelka tapes broadcast recently on a national television network show the repulsive sight of the Presidents of the Bhartiya Janata Party and the Samata Party (both part of the ruling coalition) accepting bribes from spurious arms dealers.[1] Though this ought to have been considered *prima facie* evidence of corruption, the Delhi High Court declined to entertain a petition seeking an enquiry into the defense deals that were referred to in the tapes. The bench took strong exception to the petitioner approaching the court without substantial evidence and even warned the petitioner's counsel that if he failed to substantiate its allegations, the court would impose costs on the petitioner.

On the grounds that judges of the Supreme Court were too busy, the Chief Justice of India refused to allow a sitting judge to head the judicial enquiry into the Tehelka scandal, even though it involves matters of national security and corruption in the highest places.[2]

Yet, when it comes to an absurd, despicable, entirely unsubstantiated petition in which all the three respondents happen to be people who have publicly—though in markedly different ways—questioned the policies of the government and severely criticized a recent judgment of the Supreme Court, the Court displays a disturbing willingness to issue notice.

It indicates a disquieting inclination on the part of the court to silence criticism and muzzle dissent, to harass and intimidate those who disagree with it. By entertaining a petition based on an FIR that even a local police station does not see fit to act upon, the Supreme Court is doing its own reputation and credibility considerable harm.

In conclusion, I wish to reaffirm that as a writer I have the right to state my opinions and beliefs. As a free citizen of India, I have the right to be part of any peaceful *dharna*, demonstration, or protest march. I have the right to criticize any judgment of any court that I believe to be unjust. I have the right to make common cause with those I agree with. I hope that each time I exercise these rights I will not be dragged to court on false charges and forced to explain my actions.

The petitioners have committed civil and criminal defamation. They ought to be investigated and prosecuted for perjury. They ought to be made to pay damages for the time they have wasted of this Apex Court by filing these false charges. Above all they ought to be made to apologize to all those citizens who are patiently awaiting the attention of the Supreme Court in more important matters.

10. Ahimsa

(Nonviolent Resistance)

While the rest of us are mesmerized by talk of war and terrorism and wars against terror, in the state of Madhya Pradesh in central India, a little life raft has set sail into the wind. On a pavement in Bhopal, in an area called Tin Shed, a small group of people has embarked on a journey of faith and hope. There's nothing new in what they're doing. What's new is the climate in which they're doing it.

Today is the twenty-ninth day of the indefinite hunger strike by four activists of the Narmada Bachao Andolan (NBA), the Save the Narmada Movement.[1] They have fasted two days longer than Gandhi did on any of his fasts during the freedom struggle. Their demands are more modest than his ever were. They are protesting against the Madhya Pradesh government's forcible eviction of more than one thousand Adivasi (indigenous) families to make way for the Maan dam. All they're asking is that the government of Madhya Pradesh implement its own policy of providing land to those being displaced by the Maan dam.

There's no controversy here. The dam has been built. The displaced people must be resettled before the reservoir fills up in the monsoon and submerges their villages. The four activists on fast are Vinod Patwa,

Based on an article published in the *Christian Science Monitor*, July 5, 2002.

who was one of the 114,000 people displaced in 1990 by the Bargi dam (which now, twelve years later, irrigates less land than it submerged); Mangat Verma, who will be displaced by the Maheshwar dam if it is ever completed; Chittaroopa Palit, who has worked with the NBA for almost fifteen years; and twenty-two-year-old Ram Kunwar, the youngest and frailest of the activists. Hers is the first village that will be submerged when the waters rise in the Maan reservoir. In the weeks since she began her fast, Ram Kunwar has lost twenty pounds—almost one-fourth of her original body weight.

Unlike the other large dams such as the Sardar Sarovar, Maheshwar, and Indira Sagar, where the resettlement of hundreds of thousands of displaced people is simply not possible (except on paper, in court documents), in the case of Maan the total number of displaced people is about six thousand. People have even identified land that is available and could be bought and allotted to them by the government. And yet the government refuses.

Instead it's busy distributing paltry cash compensation, which is illegal and violates its own policy. It says quite openly that if it were to give in to the demands of the Maan "oustees" (that is, if it implemented its own policy), it would set a precedent for the hundreds of thousands of people, most of them Dalits (Untouchables) and Adivasis, who are slated to be submerged (without rehabilitation) by the twenty-nine other big dams planned in the Narmada valley. And the state government's commitment to these projects remains absolute, regardless of the social and environmental costs.

As Vinod, Mangat, Chittaroopa, and Ram Kunwar gradually weaken, as their systems close down and the risk of irreversible organ failure and sudden death sets in, no government official has bothered to even pay them a visit.

Let me tell you a secret—it's not all unwavering resolve and steely determination on the burning pavement under the pitiless sun at Tin Shed. The jokes about slimming and weight loss are becoming a little poignant now. There are tears of anger and frustration. There is trepidation and real fear. But underneath all that, there's pure grit.

What will happen to them? Will they just go down in the ledgers as "the price of progress"? That phrase cleverly frames the whole argument as one between those who are pro-development versus those who are anti-development—and suggests the inevitability of the choice you have to make: pro-development, what else? It slyly suggests that movements like the NBA are antiquated and absurdly anti-electricity or anti-irrigation. This of course is nonsense.

The NBA believes that Big Dams are obsolete. It believes there are more democratic, more local, more economically viable and environmentally sustainable ways of generating electricity and managing water systems. It is demanding *more* modernity, not less. It is demanding *more* democracy, not less. And look at what's happening instead.

Even at the height of the war rhetoric, even as India and Pakistan threatened each other with nuclear annihilation, the question of reneging on the Indus Waters Treaty between the two countries did not arise. Yet in Madhya Pradesh, the police and administration entered Adivasi villages with bulldozers. They sealed hand pumps, demolished school buildings, and clear-felled trees in order to force people from their homes. They *sealed* hand pumps. And so the indefinite hunger strike.

Any government's condemnation of terrorism is only credible if it shows itself to be responsive to persistent, reasonable, closely argued, nonviolent dissent. And yet what's happening is just the opposite. The world over, nonviolent resistance movements are being crushed and broken. If we do not respect and honor them, by default we privilege those who turn to violent means.

Across the world, when governments and the media lavish all their time, attention, funds, research, space, sophistication, and seriousness on war talk and terrorism, then the message that goes out is disturbing and dangerous: if you seek to air and redress a public grievance, violence is more effective than nonviolence. Unfortunately, if peaceful change is not given a chance, then violent change becomes inevitable. That violence will be (and already is) random, ugly, and unpredictable. What's happening in Kashmir, the northeastern states of India, and Andhra Pradesh is all part of this process.

Right now the NBA is not just fighting big dams. It's fighting for the survival of India's greatest gift to the world: nonviolent resistance. You could call it the Ahimsa Bachao Andolan (*ahimsa* means "nonviolent resistance"), or the Save Nonviolence Movement.

Over the years our government has shown nothing but contempt for the people of the Narmada valley. Contempt for their argument. Contempt for their movement.

In the twenty-first century the connection between religious fundamentalism, nuclear nationalism, and the pauperization of whole populations because of corporate globalization is becoming impossible to ignore. While the Madhya Pradesh government has categorically said it has no land for the rehabilitation of displaced people, reports say that it is preparing the ground (pardon the pun) to make huge tracts of land available for corporate agriculture. This in turn will set off another cycle of displacement and impoverishment.

Can we prevail on Digvijay Singh—the secular "green" chief minister of Madhya Pradesh—to substitute some of his public relations with a *real* change in policy? If he did, he would go down in history as a man of vision and true political courage.

If the Congress Party wishes to be taken seriously as an alternative to the destructive right-wing religious fundamentalists who have brought us to the threshold of ruin, it will have to do more than condemn communalism and participate in empty nationalist rhetoric. It will have to do some real work and some real listening to the people it claims to represent.

As for the rest of us, concerned citizens, peace activists, and the like—it's not enough to sing songs about giving peace a chance. Doing everything we can to support movements like the Narmada Bachao Andolan is *how* we give peace a chance. *This* is the real war against terror.

Go to Bhopal. Just ask for Tin Shed.[2]

Part III

11. The Algebra of Infinite Justice

In the aftermath of the unconscionable September 11 suicide attacks on the Pentagon and the World Trade Center, an American newscaster said: "Good and Evil rarely manifest themselves as clearly as they did last Tuesday. People who we don't know massacred people who we do. And they did so with contemptuous glee." Then he broke down and wept.[1]

Here's the rub: America is at war against people it doesn't know (because they don't appear much on TV). Before it has properly identified or even begun to comprehend the nature of its enemy, the US government has, in a rush of publicity and embarrassing rhetoric, cobbled together an "International Coalition Against Terror," mobilized its army, its air force, its navy, and its media, and committed them to battle.

The trouble is that once America goes off to war, it can't very well return without having fought one. If it doesn't find its enemy, for the sake of the enraged folks back home it will have to manufacture one. Once war begins, it will develop a momentum, a logic, and a justification of its own, and we'll lose sight of why it's being fought in the first place.

What we're witnessing here is the spectacle of the world's most powerful country reaching reflexively, angrily, for an old instinct to fight a new kind of war. Suddenly, when it comes to defending itself, America's streamlined warships, its cruise missiles, and its F-16 jets look like obsolete,

First published in the *Guardian*, September 29, 2001, and *Outlook*, October 8, 2001.

lumbering things. As deterrence, its arsenal of nuclear bombs is no longer worth its weight in scrap. Box cutters, penknives, and cold anger are the weapons with which the wars of the new century will be waged. Anger is the lock pick. It slips through customs unnoticed. Doesn't show up in baggage checks.

Who is America fighting? On September 20, the FBI said that it had doubts about the identities of some of the hijackers. On the same day, President George Bush said he knew exactly who the terrorists were and which governments were supporting them.[2] It sounds as though the President knows something that the FBI and the American public don't.

In his September 20 address to the US Congress, President George Bush called the enemies of America "enemies of freedom." "Americans are asking, 'Why do they hate us?'" he said. "They hate our freedoms—our freedom of religion, our freedom of speech, our freedom to vote and assemble and disagree with each other."[3] People are being asked to make two leaps of faith here. First, to assume that The Enemy is who the US government says it is, even though it has no substantial evidence to support that claim. And second, to assume that The Enemy's motives are what the US government says they are, and there's nothing to support that either.

For strategic, military, and economic reasons, it is vital for the US government to persuade the American public that America's commitment to freedom and democracy and the American Way of Life are under attack. In the current atmosphere of grief, outrage, and anger, it's an easy notion to peddle. However, if that were true, it's reasonable to wonder why the symbols of America's economic and military dominance—the World Trade Center and the Pentagon—were chosen as the targets of the attacks. Why not the Statue of Liberty? Could it be that the stygian anger that led to the attacks has its taproot not in American freedom and democracy, but in the US government's record of commitment to and support for exactly the opposite things—military and economic terrorism, insurgency, military dictatorship, religious bigotry, and unimaginable genocide (outside America)?

It must be hard for ordinary Americans so recently bereaved to look up at the world with their eyes full of tears and encounter what might appear to them to be indifference. It isn't indifference. It's just augury. An absence of surprise. The tired wisdom of knowing that what goes around eventually comes around. American people ought to know that it is not them but their government's policies that are so hated. All of us have been moved by the courage and grace shown by America's firefighters, rescue workers, and ordinary office-goers in the days that followed the attacks. American people can't possibly doubt that they themselves, their extraordinary musicians, their writers, their actors, their spectacular athletes, and their cinema, are universally welcomed.

America's grief at what happened has been immense and immensely public. It would be grotesque to expect it to calibrate or modulate its anguish. However, it will be a pity if, instead of using this as an opportunity to try and understand why September 11 happened, Americans use it as an opportunity to usurp the whole world's sorrow to mourn and avenge only their own. Because then it falls to the rest of us to ask the hard questions and say the harsh things. And for our pains, for our bad timing, we will be disliked, ignored, and perhaps eventually silenced.

The world will probably never know what motivated those particular hijackers who flew planes into those particular American buildings. They were not glory boys. They left no suicide notes, no political messages. No organization has claimed credit for the attacks. All we know is that their belief in what they were doing outstripped the natural human instinct for survival or any desire to be remembered. It's almost as though they could not scale down the enormity of their rage to anything smaller than their deeds. And what they did has blown a hole in the world as we knew it.

In the absence of information, politicians, political commentators, and writers (like myself) will invest the act with their own politics, with their own interpretations. This speculation, this analysis of the political climate in which the attacks took place, can only be a good thing.

But war is looming large. Whatever remains to be said must be said quickly.

Before America places itself at the helm of the International Coalition Against Terror, before it invites (and coerces) countries to actively participate in its almost godlike mission—called Operation Infinite Justice until it was pointed out that this could be seen as an insult to Muslims, who believe that only Allah can mete out infinite justice, and was renamed Operation Enduring Freedom—it would help if some small clarifications are made. For example, Infinite Justice / Enduring Freedom for whom?

Is this America's War Against Terror in America or against terror in general? What exactly is being avenged here? Is it the tragic loss of almost seven thousand lives, the gutting of 15 million square feet of office space in Manhattan, the destruction of a section of the Pentagon, the loss of several hundreds of thousands of jobs, the potential bankruptcy of some airline companies, and the crash of the New York Stock Exchange?[4] Or is it more than that?

In 1996, Madeleine Albright, then the US Ambassador to the United Nations, was asked on national television what she felt about the fact that five hundred thousand Iraqi children had died as a result of US-led economic sanctions. She replied that it was "a very hard choice" but that, all things considered, "we think the price is worth it."[5] Albright never lost her job for saying this. She continued to travel the world representing the views and aspirations of the US government. More pertinently, the sanctions against Iraq remain in place. Children continue to die.

So here we have it. The equivocating distinction between civilization and savagery, between the "massacre of innocent people," or, if you like, "a clash of civilizations," and "collateral damage." The sophistry and fastidious algebra of Infinite Justice. How many dead Iraqis will it take to make the world a better place? How many dead Afghans for every dead American? How many dead children for every dead man? How many dead mujahideen for each dead investment banker?

As we watch, mesmerized, Operation Enduring Freedom unfolds on television monitors across the world. A coalition of the world's superpowers is closing in on Afghanistan, one of the poorest, most ravaged, war-torn countries in the world, whose ruling Taliban government is sheltering Osama bin Laden, the man being held responsible for the September 11 attacks. The only thing in Afghanistan that could possibly count as collateral value is its citizenry. (Among them, half a million maimed orphans.[6] There are accounts of hobbling stampedes that occur when artificial limbs are airdropped into remote, inaccessible villages.)

Afghanistan's economy is in a shambles. In fact, the problem for an invading army is that Afghanistan has no conventional coordinates or signposts to plot on a map—no military bases, no industrial complexes, no water treatment plants. Farms have been turned into mass graves. The countryside is littered with land mines—10 million is the most recent estimate.[7] The American army would first have to clear the mines and build roads in order to take its soldiers in.

Fearing an attack from America, one million citizens have fled from their homes and arrived at the border between Pakistan and Afghanistan. The United Nations estimates that there are 7.5 million Afghan citizens who will need emergency aid.[8] As supplies run out—food and aid agencies have been evacuated—the BBC reports that one of the worst humanitarian disasters of recent times has begun to unfold.[9] Witness the Infinite Justice of the new century. Civilians starving to death while they're waiting to be killed.

In America there has been rough talk of "bombing Afghanistan back to the stone age."[10] Someone please break the news that Afghanistan is already there. And if it's any consolation, America played no small part in helping it on its way. The American people may be a little fuzzy about where exactly Afghanistan is (we hear reports that there's a run on maps of the country), but the US government and Afghanistan are old friends.[11]

In 1979, after the Soviet invasion of Afghanistan, the CIA and Pakistan's ISI (Inter Services Intelligence) launched the CIA's largest covert operation since the Vietnam War.[12] Their purpose was to harness the energy of Afghan resistance to the Soviets and expand it into a holy war, an Islamic jihad, which would turn Muslim countries within the Soviet Union against the Communist regime and eventually destabilize it. When it began, it was meant to be the Soviet Union's Vietnam. It turned out to be much more than that. Over the years, through the ISI, the CIA funded and recruited tens of thousands of radical mujahideen from forty Islamic countries as soldiers for America's proxy war.[13] The rank and file of the mujahideen were unaware that their jihad was actually being fought on behalf of Uncle Sam. (The irony is that America was equally unaware that it was financing a future war against itself.)

In 1989, after being bloodied by ten years of relentless conflict, the Russians withdrew, leaving behind a civilization reduced to rubble. Civil war in Afghanistan raged on. The jihad spread to Chechnya, Kosovo, and eventually Kashmir. The CIA continued to pour in money and military equipment, but the overheads had become immense, and more money was needed. The mujahideen ordered farmers to plant opium as a "revolutionary tax."[14] Under the protection of the ISI, hundreds of heroin-processing laboratories were set up across Afghanistan. Within two years of the CIA's arrival, the Pakistan–Afghanistan borderland had become the biggest producer of heroin in the world, and the single biggest source on American streets. The annual profits, said to be between one hundred and two hundred billion dollars, were plowed back into training and arming militants.[15]

In 1996 the Taliban—then a marginal sect of dangerous hardline fundamentalists—fought its way to power in Afghanistan. It was funded by the ISI, that old cohort of the CIA, and supported by many political parties in Pakistan.[16] The Taliban unleashed a regime of terror. Its first victims were its own people, particularly women. It closed down girls' schools, dismissed women from government jobs, and enforced Sharia laws under which women deemed to be "immoral" are stoned to death and widows guilty of being adulterous are buried alive.[17] Given the Taliban government's human rights track record, it seems unlikely that it will in any way be intimidated or swerved from its purpose by the prospect of war or the threat to the lives of its civilians.

After all that has happened, can there be anything more ironic than Russia and America joining hands to re-destroy Afghanistan? The question is, can you destroy destruction? Dropping more bombs on Afghanistan will only shuffle the rubble, scramble some old graves, and disturb the dead.

The desolate landscape of Afghanistan was the burial ground of Soviet Communism and the springboard of a unipolar world dominated by America. It made the space for neocapitalism and corporate globalization, again dominated by America. And now Afghanistan is poised to become the graveyard for the unlikely soldiers who fought and won this war for America.

And what of America's trusted ally? Pakistan, too, has suffered enormously. The US government has not been shy to support military dictators who have blocked the idea of democracy from taking root in the country. Before the CIA arrived, there was a small rural market for opium in Pakistan. Between 1979 and 1985, the number of heroin addicts grew from next to nothing to a massive number.[18] Even before September 11, there were millions of Afghan refugees living in tented camps along the border.

Pakistan's economy is crumbling.[19] Sectarian violence, globalization's Structural Adjustment Programs, and drug lords are tearing the country to pieces. Set up to fight the Soviets, the terrorist training centers and madrassas, sown like dragon's teeth across the country, produced fundamentalists with tremendous popular appeal within Pakistan itself. The Taliban, which the Pakistan government has supported, funded, and propped up for years, has material and strategic alliances with Pakistan's own political parties.[20] Now the US government is asking (asking?) Pakistan to garrote the pet it has hand-reared in its backyard for so many years. President Pervez Musharraf, having pledged his support to the US, could well find he has something resembling civil war on his hands.[21]

India, thanks in part to its geography and in part to the vision of its former leaders, has so far been fortunate enough to be left out of this Great Game. Had it been drawn in, it's more than likely that our democracy, such as it is, would not have survived. Today, as some of us watch in horror, the Indian government is furiously gyrating its hips, begging the US to set up its base in India rather than Pakistan.[22]

Having had this ringside view of Pakistan's sordid fate, it isn't just odd, it's unthinkable, that India should want to do this. Any third world country with a fragile economy and a complex social base should know by now that to invite a superpower such as America in (whether it says it's staying or just passing through) would be like inviting a brick to drop through your windshield.

In the media blitz that followed September 11, mainstream television stations largely ignored the story of America's involvement with Afghanistan. So to those unfamiliar with the story, the coverage of the attacks could have been moving, disturbing, and, perhaps to cynics, self-indulgent. However, to those of us who are familiar with Afghanistan's recent history, American TV coverage and the rhetoric of the International Coalition Against Terror is just plain insulting. America's "free press," like its "free market," has a lot to account for.

Operation Enduring Freedom is ostensibly being fought to uphold the American Way of Life. It'll probably end up undermining it completely. It will spawn more anger and more terror across the world. For ordinary people in America, it will mean lives lived in a climate of sickening uncertainty: Will my child be safe in school? Will there be nerve gas in the subway? A bomb in the cinema hall? Will my love come home tonight? There have been warnings about the possibility of biological warfare—smallpox, bubonic plague, anthrax—the deadly payload of an innocuous crop duster.[23] Being picked off a few at a time may end up being worse than being annihilated all at once by a nuclear bomb.

The US government, and no doubt governments all over the world, will use the climate of war as an excuse to curtail civil liberties, deny free speech, lay off workers, harass ethnic and religious minorities, cut back on public spending, and divert huge amounts of money to the defense industry.

To what purpose? President George Bush can no more "rid the world of evildoers" than he can stock it with saints.[24] It's absurd for the US government to even toy with the notion that it can stamp out terrorism with more violence and oppression. Terrorism is the symptom, not the disease. Terrorism has no country. It's transnational, as global an enterprise as Coke or Pepsi or Nike. At the first sign of trouble, terrorists can pull up stakes and move their "factories" from country to country in search of a better deal. Just like the multinationals.

Terrorism as a phenomenon may never go away. But if it is to be contained, the first step is for America to at least acknowledge that it shares the planet with other nations, with other human beings who, even if they are not on TV, have loves and griefs and stories and songs and sorrows and, for heaven's sake, rights. Instead, when Donald Rumsfeld, the US Defense Secretary, was asked what he would call a victory in America's new war, he said that if he could convince the world that Americans must be allowed to continue with their way of life, he would consider it a victory.[25]

The September 11 attacks were a monstrous calling card from a world gone horribly wrong. The message may have been written by bin Laden (who knows?) and delivered by his couriers, but it could well have been signed by the ghosts of the victims of America's old wars.

The millions killed in Korea, Vietnam, and Cambodia, the seventeen thousand killed when Israel—backed by the United States—invaded Lebanon in 1982, the tens of thousands of Iraqis killed in Operation Desert Storm, the thousands of Palestinians who have died fighting Israel's occupation of the West Bank. And the millions who died, in Yugoslavia,

Somalia, Haiti, Chile, Nicaragua, El Salvador, the Dominican Republic, Panama, at the hands of all the terrorists, dictators, and genocidists whom the American government supported, trained, bankrolled, and supplied with arms. [26] And this is far from being a comprehensive list.

For a country involved in so much warfare and conflict, the American people have been extremely fortunate. The strikes on September 11 were only the second on American soil in more than a century. The first was Pearl Harbor. The reprisal for this took a long route but ended with Hiroshima and Nagasaki. This time the world waits with bated breath for the horrors to come.

Someone recently said that if Osama bin Laden didn't exist, America would have had to invent him.[27] But in a way, America did invent him. He was among the jihadists who moved to Afghanistan after 1979, when the CIA commenced its operations there. Bin Laden has the distinction of being created by the CIA and wanted by the FBI. In the course of a fortnight he has been promoted from Suspect to Prime Suspect, and then, despite the lack of any real evidence, straight up the charts to being "wanted dead or alive."

From all accounts, it will be impossible to produce evidence (of the sort that would stand up to scrutiny in a court of law) to link bin Laden to the September 11 attacks.[28] So far, it appears that the most incriminating piece of evidence against him is the fact that he has not condemned them. From what is known about the location of bin Laden and the living conditions where he operates, it's entirely possible that he did not personally plan and carry out the attacks—that he is the inspirational figure, "the CEO of the holding company."[29]

The Taliban's response to US demands for the extradition of bin Laden has been uncharacteristically reasonable: produce the evidence, then we'll hand him over. President Bush's response is that the demand is "nonnegotiable."[30]

(While talks are on for the extradition of CEOs—can India put in a side request for the extradition of Warren Anderson of the USA? He was the chairman of Union Carbide, responsible for the 1984 Bhopal gas leak, which killed sixteen thousand people.[31] We have collated the necessary evidence. It's all in the files. Could we have him, please?)

But who is Osama bin Laden really?

Let me rephrase that. What is Osama bin Laden?

He's America's family secret. He is the American President's dark doppelganger. The savage twin of all that purports to be beautiful and civilized. He has been sculpted from the spare rib of a world laid to waste by America's foreign policy: its gunboat diplomacy, its nuclear arsenal, its vulgarly stated policy of "full spectrum dominance," its chilling disregard for non-American lives, its barbarous military interventions, its support for despotic and dictatorial regimes, its merciless economic agenda that has munched through the economies of poor countries like a cloud of locusts.[32] Its marauding multinationals, which are taking over the air we breathe, the ground we stand on, the water we drink, the thoughts we think.

Now that the family secret has been spilled, the twins are blurring into one another and gradually becoming interchangeable. Their guns, bombs, money, and drugs have been going around in the loop for a while. (The Stinger missiles that will greet US helicopters were supplied by the CIA. The heroin used by America's drug addicts comes from Afghanistan. The Bush administration recently gave Afghanistan a $43 million subsidy to its "war on drugs.")[33]

Now they've even begun to borrow each other's rhetoric. Each refers to the other as "the head of the snake." Both invoke God and use the loose millenarian currency of Good and Evil as their terms of reference. Both are engaged in unequivocal political crimes.

Both are dangerously armed—one with the nuclear arsenal of the obscenely powerful, the other with the incandescent, destructive power of the utterly hopeless.

The fireball and the ice pick. The bludgeon and the ax. The important thing to keep in mind is that neither is an acceptable alternative to the other.

President Bush's ultimatum to the people of the world—"either you are with us or you are with the terrorists"[34]—is a piece of presumptuous arrogance.

It's not a choice that people want to, need to, or should have to make.

12. War Is Peace

As darkness deepened over Afghanistan on Sunday, October 7, 2001, the US government, backed by the International Coalition Against Terror (the new, amenable surrogate for the United Nations), launched air strikes against Afghanistan. TV channels lingered on computer-animated images of cruise missiles, stealth bombers, Tomahawks, "bunker-busting" missiles, and Mark 82 high drag bombs.[1] All over the world, little boys watched goggle-eyed and stopped clamoring for new video games.

The UN, reduced now to an ineffective acronym, wasn't even asked to mandate the air strikes. (As Madeleine Albright once said, "We will behave multilaterally when we can and unilaterally when we must.")[2]

The "evidence" against the terrorists was shared among friends in the International Coalition. After conferring, they announced that it didn't matter whether or not the "evidence" would stand up in a court of law.[3] Thus in an instant were centuries of jurisprudence carelessly trashed.

Nothing can excuse or justify an act of terrorism, whether it is committed by religious fundamentalists, private militias, people's resistance movements—or whether it's dressed up as a war of retribution by a recognized government. The bombing of Afghanistan is not revenge for New York and Washington. It is yet another act of terror against the people of the world. Each innocent person that is killed must be added

First published in *Outlook*, October 29, 2001.

to, not set off against, the grisly toll of civilians who died in New York and Washington.

People rarely win wars; governments rarely lose them. People get killed. Governments molt and regroup, hydra-headed. They first use flags to shrink-wrap people's minds and smother real thought, and then as ceremonial shrouds to bury the willing dead. On both sides, in Afghanistan as well as America, civilians are now hostage to the actions of their own governments. Unknowingly, ordinary people in both countries share a common bond—they have to live with the phenomenon of blind, unpredictable terror. Each batch of bombs that is dropped on Afghanistan is matched by a corresponding escalation of mass hysteria in America about anthrax, more hijackings, and other terrorist acts.

There is no easy way out of the spiraling morass of terror and brutality that confronts the world today. It is time now for the human race to hold still, to delve into its wells of collective wisdom, both ancient and modern. What happened on September 11 changed the world forever. Freedom, progress, wealth, technology, war—these words have taken on new meaning. Governments have to acknowledge this transformation and approach their new tasks with a modicum of honesty and humility. Unfortunately, up to now, there has been no sign of any introspection from the leaders of the International Coalition. Or the Taliban.

When he announced the air strikes, President George Bush said, "We're a peaceful nation."[4] America's favorite ambassador, Tony Blair (who also holds the portfolio of Prime Minister of the UK), echoed him: "We're a peaceful people."

So now we know. Pigs are horses. Girls are boys. War is peace.

Speaking at the FBI's headquarters a few days later, President Bush said, "This is the calling of the United States of America, the most free nation in the world, a nation built on fundamental values; that rejects hate, rejects violence, rejects murderers, rejects evil. And we will not tire."[5]

Here is a list of the countries that America has been at war with—and bombed—since World War II: China (1945–46, 1950–53), Korea (1950–53), Guatemala (1954, 1967–69), Indonesia (1958), Cuba (1959–60), the Belgian Congo (1964), Peru (1965), Laos (1964–73), Vietnam (1961–73), Cambodia (1969–70), Grenada (1983), Libya (1986), El Salvador (1980s), Nicaragua (1980s), Panama (1989), Iraq (1991–2001),

Bosnia (1995), Sudan (1998), Yugoslavia (1999). And now Afghanistan.

Certainly it does not tire—this, the Most Free Nation in the world. What freedoms does it uphold? Within its borders, the freedoms of speech, religion, thought; of artistic expression, food habits, sexual preferences (well, to some extent), and many other exemplary, wonderful things. Outside its borders, the freedom to dominate, humiliate, and subjugate—usually in the service of America's real religion, the "free market." So when the US government christens a war Operation Infinite Justice, or Operation Enduring Freedom, we in the third world feel more than a tremor of fear. Because we know that Infinite Justice for some means Infinite Injustice for others. And Enduring Freedom for some means Enduring Subjugation for others.

The International Coalition Against Terror is largely a cabal of the richest countries in the world. Between them, they manufacture and sell almost all of the world's weapons. They possess the largest stockpile of weapons of mass destruction—chemical, biological, and nuclear. They have fought the most wars, account for most of the genocide, subjection, ethnic cleansing, and human rights violations in modern history, and have sponsored, armed, and financed untold numbers of dictators and despots. Between them, they have worshiped, almost deified, the cult of violence and war. For all its appalling sins, the Taliban just isn't in the same league.

The Taliban was compounded in the crumbling crucible of rubble, heroin, and land mines in the backwash of the Cold War. Its oldest leaders are in their early forties. Many of them are disfigured and handicapped, missing an eye, an arm, or a leg. They grew up in a society scarred and devastated by war. Between the Soviet Union and America, over twenty years, about $45 billion worth of arms and ammunition was poured into Afghanistan.[6]

The latest weaponry was the only shard of modernity to intrude upon a thoroughly medieval society. Young boys—many of them orphans—who grew up in those times had guns for toys, never knew the security and comfort of family life, never experienced the company of women. Now, as adults and rulers, the Taliban beat, stone, rape, and brutalize women. They don't seem to know what else to do with them. Years of war has stripped them of gentleness, inured them to kindness and human compassion. They dance to the percussive rhythms of bombs raining down around them. Now they've turned their monstrosity on their own people.

With all due respect to President Bush, the people of the world do not have to choose between the Taliban and the US government. All the beauty of human civilization—our art, our music, our literature—lies beyond these two fundamentalist ideological poles. There is as little chance that the people of the world can all become middle-class consumers as there is that they will all embrace any one particular religion.

The issue is not about Good versus Evil or Islam versus Christianity as much as it is about space. About how to accommodate diversity, how to contain the impulse toward hegemony—every kind of hegemony: economic, military, linguistic, religious, and cultural. Any ecologist will tell you how dangerous and fragile a monoculture is. A hegemonic world is like having a government without a healthy opposition. It becomes a kind of dictatorship. It's like putting a plastic bag over the world and preventing it from breathing. Eventually, it will be torn open.

One and a half million Afghan people lost their lives in the twenty years of conflict that preceded this new war.[7]

Afghanistan was reduced to rubble, and now the rubble is being pounded into finer dust. By the second day of the air strikes, US pilots were returning to their bases without dropping their assigned payload of bombs.[8]

As one senior official put it, Afghanistan is "not a target-rich environment."[9] At a press briefing at the Pentagon, US Defense Secretary Donald Rumsfeld was asked if America had run out of targets. "First we're going to re-hit targets," he said, "and second, we're not running out of targets, Afghanistan is . . ." This was greeted with gales of laughter in the briefing room.[10]

By the third day of the strikes, the US Defense Department boasted that it had "achieved air supremacy over Afghanistan."[11] (Did it mean that it had destroyed both, or maybe all sixteen, of Afghanistan's planes?)

On the ground in Afghanistan, the Northern Alliance—the Taliban's old enemy, and therefore the International Coalition's newest friend—is making headway in its push to capture Kabul. (For the archives, let it be said that the Northern Alliance's track record is not very different from the Taliban's. But for now, because it's inconvenient, that little detail is being glossed over.)[12]

The visible, moderate, "acceptable" leader of the Alliance, Ahmed Shah Massoud, was killed in a suicide-bomb attack early in September 2001.[13] The rest of the Northern Alliance is a brittle confederation of brutal warlords, ex-Communists, and unbending clerics. It is a disparate group divided along ethnic lines, some of whom have tasted power in Afghanistan in the past.

Until the US air strikes, the Northern Alliance controlled about 5 percent of the geographical area of Afghanistan. Now, with the International Coalition's help and "air cover," it is poised to topple the Taliban.[14] Meanwhile, Taliban soldiers, sensing imminent defeat, have begun to defect to the Alliance. So the fighting forces are busy switching sides and changing uniforms. But in an enterprise as cynical as this one, it seems to matter hardly at all. Love is hate, north is south, peace is war.

Among the global powers, there is talk of "putting in a representative government." Or, on the other hand, of "restoring" the kingdom to Afghanistan's eighty-six-year-old former king, Muhammad Zahir Shah, who has lived in exile in Rome since 1973.[15] That's the way the game goes—support Saddam Hussein, then "take him out"; finance the mujahideen, then bomb them to smithereens; put in Zahir Shah and see if he's going to be a good boy. (Is it possible to "put in" a representative government? Can you place an order for Democracy—with extra cheese and jalapeño peppers?)

Reports have begun to trickle in about civilian casualties, about cities emptying out as Afghan civilians flock to the borders, which have been closed.[16] Main arterial roads have been blown up or sealed off. Those who have experience of working in Afghanistan say that by early November, food convoys will not be able to reach the millions of Afghans (7.5 million according to the UN) who run the very real risk of starving to death during the course of this winter.[17] They say that in the days that are left before winter sets in, there can be either a war or an attempt to reach food to the hungry. Not both.

As a gesture of humanitarian support, the US government airdropped thirty-seven thousand packets of emergency rations into Afghanistan. It says it plans to drop more than five hundred thousand packets. That will still only add up to a single meal for half a million people out of the several million in dire need of food. Aid workers have condemned this as a cynical, dangerous public relations exercise. They say that airdropping food packets is worse than futile. First, because the food will never get to those who really need it. More dangerously, because those who run out to retrieve the packets risk being blown up by land mines.[18] A tragic alms race.

Nevertheless, the food packets had a photo-op all to themselves. Their contents were listed in major newspapers. They were vegetarian, we're told, as per Muslim Dietary Law (!). Each yellow packet, decorated with the American flag, contained rice, peanut butter, bean salad, strawberry jam, crackers, raisins, flat bread, an apple fruit bar, seasoning, matches, a set of plastic cutlery, a napkin, and illustrated user instructions.[19]

After three years of unremitting drought, an airdropped airline meal in Jalalabad! The level of cultural ineptitude, the failure to understand what months of relentless hunger and grinding poverty really mean, the US government's attempt to use even this abject misery to boost its self-image, beggars description.

Reverse the scenario for a moment. Imagine if the Taliban government were to bomb New York City, saying all the while that its real target was the US government and its policies. And suppose, during breaks between the bombing, the Taliban dropped a few thousand packets containing nan and kababs impaled on an Afghan flag. Would the good people of New York ever find it in themselves to forgive the Afghan government? Even if they were hungry, even if they needed the food, even if they ate it, how would they ever forget the insult, the condescension? Rudy Giuliani, Mayor of New York City, returned a gift of $10 million from a Saudi prince because it came with a few words of friendly advice about American policy in the Middle East.[20] Is pride a luxury that only the rich are entitled to?

Far from stamping it out, igniting this kind of rage is what creates terrorism. Hate and retribution don't go back into the box once you've let them out. For every "terrorist" or his "supporter" who is killed, hundreds of innocent people are being killed, too. And for every hundred innocent people killed, there is a good chance that several future terrorists will be created.

Where will it all lead?

Setting aside the rhetoric for a moment, consider the fact that the world has not yet found an acceptable definition of what "terrorism" is. One country's terrorist is too often another's freedom fighter. At the heart of the matter lies the world's deep-seated ambivalence toward violence. Once violence is accepted as a legitimate political instrument, then the morality and political acceptability of terrorists (insurgents or freedom fighters) become contentious, bumpy terrain.

The US government itself has funded, armed, and sheltered plenty of rebels and insurgents around the world. The CIA and Pakistan's ISI trained and armed the mujahideen who, in the 1980s, were seen as terrorists by the government in Soviet-occupied Afghanistan, while President Reagan praised them as freedom fighters.[21]

Today, Pakistan—America's ally in this new war—sponsors insurgents who cross the border into Kashmir in India. Pakistan lauds them as freedom fighters, India calls them terrorists. India, for its part, denounces countries that sponsor and abet terrorism, but the Indian army has in the past trained separatist Tamil rebels asking for a homeland in Sri Lanka—the LTTE, responsible for countless acts of bloody terrorism.

(Just as the CIA abandoned the mujahideen after they had served its purpose, India abruptly turned its back on the LTTE for a host of political reasons. It was an enraged LTTE suicide bomber who assassinated former Indian Prime Minister Rajiv Gandhi in 1991.)

It is important for governments and politicians to understand that manipulating these huge, raging human feelings for their own narrow purposes may yield instant results, but eventually and inexorably, they have disastrous consequences. Igniting and exploiting religious sentiments for reasons of political expediency is the most dangerous legacy that governments or politicians can bequeath to any people—including their own. People who live in societies ravaged by religious or communal bigotry know that every religious text, from the Bible to the Bhagavad Gita, can be mined and misinterpreted to justify anything from nuclear war to genocide to corporate globalization.

This is not to suggest that the terrorists who perpetrated the outrage on September 11 should not be hunted down and brought to book. They must be. But is war the best way to track them down? Will burning the haystack find you the needle? Or will it escalate the anger and make the world a living hell for all of us?

At the end of the day, how many people can you spy on, how many bank accounts can you freeze, how many conversations can you eavesdrop on, how many e-mails can you intercept, how many letters can you open, how many phones can you tap? Even before September 11, the CIA had accumulated more information than is humanly possible to process. (Sometimes too much data can actually hinder intelligence—small wonder the US spy satellites completely missed the preparation that preceded India's nuclear tests in 1998.)

The sheer scale of the surveillance will become a logistical, ethical, and civil rights nightmare. It will drive everybody clean crazy. And freedom—that precious, precious thing—will be the first casualty. It's already hurt and hemorrhaging dangerously.

Governments across the world are cynically using the prevailing paranoia to promote their own interests. All kinds of unpredictable political forces are being unleashed. In India, for instance, members of the All India People's Resistance Forum who were distributing antiwar and anti-US pamphlets in Delhi have been jailed. Even the printer of the leaflets was arrested.[22] The right-wing government (while it shelters Hindu extremist groups like the Vishwa Hindu Parishad and the Bajrang Dal) has banned the Students' Islamic Movement of India and is trying to revive an antiterrorist act that had been withdrawn after the Human Rights Commission reported that it had been more abused than used.[23] Millions of Indian citizens are Muslim. Can anything be gained by alienating them?

Every day that the war goes on, raging emotions are being let loose into the world. The international press has little or no independent access to the war zone. In any case, the mainstream media, particularly in the United States, has more or less rolled over, allowing itself to be tickled on the stomach with press handouts from military men and government officials. Afghan radio stations have been destroyed by the bombing. The Taliban has always been deeply suspicious of the press. In the propaganda war, there is no accurate estimate of how many people have been killed, or how much destruction has taken place. In the absence of reliable information, wild rumors spread.

Put your ear to the ground in this part of the world, and you can hear the thrumming, the deadly drumbeat of burgeoning anger. Please. Please, stop the war now. Enough people have died. The smart missiles are just not smart enough. They're blowing up whole warehouses of suppressed fury.

President George Bush recently boasted, "When I take action, I'm not going to fire a two million dollar missile at a ten dollar empty tent and hit a camel in the butt. It's going to be decisive."[24] President Bush should know that there are no targets in Afghanistan that will give his missiles their money's worth. Perhaps, if only to balance his books, he should develop some cheaper missiles to use on cheaper targets and cheaper lives in the poor countries of the world. But then, that may not make good business sense to the International Coalition's weapons manufacturers.

It wouldn't make any sense at all, for example, to the Carlyle Group—described by the *Industry Standard* as "one of the world's largest private investment funds," with $13 billion under management.[25] Carlyle invests in the defense sector and makes its money from military conflicts and weapons spending.

Carlyle is run by men with impeccable credentials. Former US Defense Secretary Frank Carlucci is its chairman and managing director (he was a college roommate of Donald Rumsfeld's). Carlyle's other partners include former US Secretary of State James A. Baker III, George Soros, and Fred Malek (George Bush Sr.'s campaign manager).

An American paper—the *Baltimore Chronicle and Sentinel*—says that former President Bush is reported to be seeking investments for the Carlyle Group from Asian markets. He is reportedly paid not inconsiderable sums of money to make "presentations" to potential government clients.[26]

Ho Hum. As the tired saying goes, it's all in the family.

Then there's that other branch of traditional family business—oil. Remember, President George Bush (Jr.) and Vice President Dick Cheney both made their fortunes working in the US oil industry.

Turkmenistan, which borders the northwest of Afghanistan, holds the world's third-largest gas reserves and an estimated 6 billion barrels of oil reserves. Enough, experts say, to meet American energy needs for the next thirty years (or a developing country's energy requirements for a couple of centuries).[27]

America has always viewed oil as a security consideration and protected it by any means it deems necessary. Few of us doubt that its military presence in the Gulf has little to do with its concern for human rights and almost entirely to do with its strategic interest in oil.

Oil and gas from the Caspian region currently move northward to European markets. Geographically and politically, Iran and Russia are major impediments to American interests.

In 1998 Dick Cheney—then CEO of Halliburton, a major player in the oil industry—said, "I can't think of a time when we've had a region emerge as suddenly to become as strategically significant as the Caspian. It's almost as if the opportunities have arisen overnight."[28] True enough.

For some years now, an American oil giant called Unocal has been negotiating with the Taliban for permission to construct an oil pipeline through Afghanistan to Pakistan and out to the Arabian Sea. From here, Unocal hopes to access the lucrative "emerging markets" in South and Southeast Asia. In December 1997 a delegation of Taliban mullahs traveled to America and even met US State Department officials and Unocal executives in Houston.[29]

At that time the Taliban's taste for public executions and its treatment of Afghan women were not made out to be the crimes against humanity that they are now. Over the next six months, pressure from hundreds of outraged American feminist groups was brought to bear on the Clinton administration. Fortunately, they managed to scuttle the deal. And now comes the US oil industry's big chance.

In America, the arms industry, the oil industry, the major media networks, and, indeed, US foreign policy are all controlled by the same business combines. Therefore it would be foolish to expect this talk of guns and oil and defense deals to get any real play in the media.

In any case, to a distraught, confused people whose pride has just been wounded, whose loved ones have been tragically killed, whose anger is fresh and sharp, the inanities about the "clash of civilizations" and the "good versus evil" home in unerringly. They are cynically doled out by government spokesmen like a daily dose of vitamins or antidepressants. Regular medication ensures that mainland America continues to remain the enigma it has always been—a curiously insular people administered by a pathologically meddlesome, promiscuous government.

And what of the rest of us, the numb recipients of this onslaught of what we know to be preposterous propaganda? The daily consumers of the lies and brutality smeared in peanut butter and strawberry jam being airdropped into our minds just like those yellow food packets. Shall we look away and eat because we're hungry, or shall we stare unblinking at the grim theater unfolding in Afghanistan until we retch collectively and say, in one voice, that we have had enough?

As the first year of the new millennium rushes to a close, one wonders: Have we forfeited our right to dream? Will we ever be able to re-imagine beauty? Will it be possible ever again to watch the slow, amazed blink of a newborn gecko in the sun, or whisper back to the marmot who has just whispered in one's ear, without thinking of the World Trade Center and Afghanistan?

13. War Talk

Summer Games with Nuclear Bombs

When India and Pakistan conducted their nuclear tests in 1998, even those of us who condemned them balked at the hypocrisy of Western nuclear powers. Implicit in their denunciation of the tests was the notion that Blacks cannot be trusted with the Bomb. Now we are presented with the spectacle of our governments competing to confirm that belief.

As diplomats' families and tourists disappear from the subcontinent, Western journalists arrive in Delhi in droves. Many call me. "Why haven't you left the city?" they ask. "Isn't nuclear war a real possibility? Isn't Delhi a prime target?"

If nuclear weapons exist, then nuclear war is a real possibility. And Delhi is a prime target. It is.

But where shall we go? Is it possible to go out and buy another life because this one's not panning out?

If I go away, and everything and everyone—every friend, every tree, every home, every dog, squirrel, and bird that I have known and loved—is incinerated, how shall I live on? Whom shall I love? And who will love me back? Which society will welcome me and allow me to be the hooligan that I am here, at home?

Originally published in *Frontline* (India) 19, no. 12 (June 8–21, 2002).

So we're all staying. We huddle together. We realize how much we love each other. And we think, what a shame it would be to die now. Life's normal only because the macabre has become normal. While we wait for rain, for football, for justice, the old generals and eager boy-anchors on TV talk of first-strike and second-strike capabilities as though they're discussing a family board game.

My friends and I discuss *Prophecy*, the documentary about the bombing of Hiroshima and Nagasaki.[1] The fireball. The dead bodies choking the river. The living stripped of skin and hair. The singed, bald children, still alive, their clothes burned into their bodies. The thick, black, toxic water. The scorched, burning air. The cancers, implanted genetically, a malignant letter to the unborn. We remember especially the man who just melted into the steps of a building. We imagine ourselves like that. As stains on staircases. I imagine future generations of hushed school-children pointing at my stain . . . That was a writer. Not she or he. *That.*

I'm sorry if my thoughts are stray and disconnected, not always worthy. Often ridiculous.

I think of a little mixed-breed dog I know. Each of his toes is a different color. Will he become a radioactive stain on a staircase too? My husband's writing a book on trees. He has a section on how figs are pollinated. Each fig only by its own specialized fig wasp. There are nearly a thousand different species of fig wasps, each a precise, exquisite synchrony, the product of millions of years of evolution.

All the fig wasps will be nuked. Zzzz. Ash. And my husband. And his book.

A dear friend, who's an activist in the anti-dam movement in the Narmada valley, is on indefinite hunger strike. Today is the fourteenth day of her fast. She and the others fasting with her are weakening quickly. They're protesting because the Madhya Pradesh government is bulldozing schools, clear-felling forests, uprooting hand pumps, forcing people from their villages to make way for the Maan dam. The people have nowhere to go. And so the hunger strike.[2]

What an act of faith and hope! How brave it is to believe that in today's world, reasoned, nonviolent protest will register, will matter. But will it? To governments that are comfortable with the notion of a wasted world, what's a wasted valley?

The threshold of horror has been ratcheted up so high that nothing short of genocide or the prospect of nuclear war merits mention. Peaceful resistance is treated with contempt. Terrorism's the real thing. The underlying principle of the War Against Terror, the very notion that war is an acceptable solution to terrorism, has ensured that terrorists in the subcontinent now have the power to trigger a nuclear war.

Displacement, dispossession, starvation, poverty, disease—these are now just the funnies, the comic-strip items. Our Home Minister says that Nobel laureate Amartya Sen has it all wrong—the key to India's development is not education and health but defense (and don't forget the kickbacks, O Best Beloved).[3]

Perhaps what he really meant was that war is the key to distracting the world's attention from fascism and genocide. To avoid dealing with any single issue of real governance that urgently needs to be addressed.

For the governments of India and Pakistan, Kashmir is not a *problem*, it's their perennial and spectacularly successful *solution*. Kashmir is the rabbit they pull out of their hats every time they need a rabbit. Unfortunately, it's a radioactive rabbit now, and it's careening out of control.

No doubt there is Pakistan-sponsored cross-border terrorism in Kashmir. But there are other kinds of terror in the valley. There's the inchoate nexus between jihadist militants, ex-militants, foreign mercenaries, local mercenaries, underworld mafiosi, security forces, arms dealers, and criminalized politicians and officials on both sides of the border. There are also rigged elections, daily humiliation, "disappearances," and staged "encounters."[4]

And now the cry has gone up in the heartland: India is a Hindu country. Muslims can be murdered under the benign gaze of the state. Mass murderers will not be brought to justice. Indeed, they will stand for elections. Is India to be a Hindu nation in the heartland and a secular one around the edges?

Meanwhile the International Coalition Against Terror makes war and preaches restraint. While India and Pakistan bay for each other's blood, the coalition is quietly laying gas pipelines, selling us weapons, and pushing through their business deals. (Buy now, pay later.) Britain, for example, is busy arming both sides.[5] Tony Blair's "peace" mission a few months ago was actually a business trip to discuss a billion-pound deal (and don't forget the kickbacks, O Best Beloved) to sell sixty-six Hawk fighter-bombers to India.[6] Roughly, for the price of a *single* Hawk bomber, the government could provide 1.5 million people with clean drinking water for life.[7]

"Why isn't there a peace movement?" Western journalists ask me ingenuously. How can there be a peace movement when, for most people in India, peace means a daily battle: for food, for water, for shelter, for dignity? War, on the other hand, is something professional soldiers fight far away on the border. And nuclear war—well, that's completely outside the realm of most people's comprehension. No one knows what a nuclear bomb is. No one cares to explain. As the Home Minister said, education is not a pressing priority.

The last question every visiting journalist always asks me is: Are you writing another book? That question mocks me. Another book? Right *now*? This talk of nuclear war displays such contempt for music, art, literature, and everything else that defines civilization. So what kind of book should I write?

It's not just the one million soldiers on the border who are living on hair-trigger alert. It's all of us. That's what nuclear bombs do. Whether they're used or not, they violate everything that is humane. They alter the meaning of life itself.

Why do we tolerate them? Why do we tolerate the men who use nuclear weapons to blackmail the entire human race?

14. Come September

Writers imagine that they cull stories from the world. I'm beginning to believe that vanity makes them think so. That it's actually the other way around. Stories cull writers from the world. Stories reveal themselves to us. The public narrative, the private narrative—they colonize us. They commission us. They insist on being told. Fiction and nonfiction are only different techniques of storytelling. For reasons I do not fully understand, fiction dances out of me. Nonfiction is wrenched out by the aching, broken world I wake up to every morning.

The theme of much of what I write, fiction as well as nonfiction, is the relationship between power and powerlessness and the endless, circular conflict they're engaged in. John Berger, that most wonderful writer, once wrote: "Never again will a single story be told as though it's the only one."[1]

There can never be a single story. There are only ways of seeing. So when I tell a story, I tell it not as an ideologue who wants to pit one absolutist ideology against another but as a storyteller who wants to share her way of seeing. Though it might appear otherwise, my writing is not really about nations and histories, it's about power. About the paranoia and ruthlessness of power. About the physics of power. I believe that the accumulation of vast unfettered power by a state or a country, a corporation

First delivered as a lecture in Santa Fe, New Mexico, September 18, 2002.

or an institution—or even an individual, a spouse, friend, or sibling—regardless of ideology, results in excesses such as the ones I will recount here.

Living as I do, as millions of us do, in the shadow of the nuclear holocaust that the governments of India and Pakistan keep promising their brainwashed citizenry, and in the global neighborhood of the War Against Terror (what President Bush rather biblically calls "the task that does not end"), I find myself thinking a great deal about the relationship between citizens and the state.[2]

In India, those of us who have expressed views on nuclear bombs, Big Dams, corporate globalization, and the rising threat of communal Hindu fascism—views that are at variance with the Indian government's—are branded "anti-national." While this accusation does not fill me with indignation, it's not an accurate description of what I do or how I think. An anti-national is a person who is against her own nation and, by inference, is pro some other one. But it isn't necessary to be anti-national to be deeply suspicious of all nationalism, to be anti-national*ism*. Nationalism of one kind or another was the cause of most of the genocide of the twentieth century. Flags are bits of colored cloth that governments use first to shrink-wrap people's minds and then as ceremonial shrouds to bury the dead. When independent, thinking people (and here I do not include the corporate media) begin to rally under flags, when writers, painters, musicians, filmmakers suspend their judgment and blindly yoke their art to the service of the nation, it's time for all of us to sit up and worry. In India we saw it happen soon after the nuclear tests in 1998 and during the Kargil War against Pakistan in 1999.

In the US we saw it during the Gulf War and we see it now, during the War Against Terror. That blizzard of made-in-China American flags.[3]

Recently those who have criticized the actions of the US government (myself included) have been called "anti-American." Anti-Americanism is in the process of being consecrated into an ideology.

The term *anti-American* is usually used by the American establishment to discredit and—not falsely, but shall we say inaccurately—define its critics. Once someone is branded anti-American, the chances are that he or she will be judged before they're heard and the argument will be lost in the welter of bruised national pride.

What does the term *anti-American mean*? Does it mean you're anti-jazz? Or that you're opposed to free speech? That you don't delight in Toni Morrison or John Updike? That you have a quarrel with giant sequoias? Does it mean you don't admire the hundreds of thousands of American citizens who marched against nuclear weapons, or the thousands of war resisters who forced their government to withdraw from Vietnam? Does it mean that you hate all Americans?

This sly conflation of America's culture, music, literature, the breathtaking physical beauty of the land, the ordinary pleasures of ordinary people, with criticism of the US government's foreign policy (about which, thanks to America's "free press," sadly, most Americans know very little) is a deliberate and extremely effective strategy. It's like a retreating army taking cover in a heavily populated city, hoping that the prospect of hitting civilian targets will deter enemy fire.

There are many Americans who would be mortified to be associated with their government's policies. The most scholarly, scathing, incisive, hilarious critiques of the hypocrisy and the contradictions in US government policy come from American citizens. When the rest of the world wants to know what the US government is up to, we turn to Noam Chomsky, Edward Said, Howard Zinn, Ed Herman, Amy Goodman, Michael Albert, Chalmers Johnson, William Blum, and Anthony Arnove to tell us what's really going on.

Similarly, in India, not hundreds but millions of us would be ashamed and offended if we were in any way implicated with the present Indian government's fascist policies, which, apart from the perpetration of state terrorism in the valley of Kashmir (in the name of fighting terrorism), have also turned a blind eye to the recent state-supervised pogrom against Muslims in Gujarat.[4] It would be absurd to think that those who criticize the Indian government are "anti-Indian"—although the government itself never hesitates to take that line. It is dangerous to cede to the Indian government or the American government, or *anyone* for that matter, the right to define what "India" or "America" is or ought to be.

To call someone anti-American, indeed, to *be* anti-American (or for that matter anti-Indian, or anti-Timbuktuan), is not just racist, it's a failure of the imagination. An inability to see the world in terms other than those that the establishment has set out for you: If you're not a Bushie, you're a Taliban. If you don't love us, you hate us. If you're not Good, you're Evil. If you're not with us, you're with the terrorists.

Last year, like many others, I too made the mistake of scoffing at this post–September 11th rhetoric, dismissing it as foolish and arrogant. I've realized that it's not foolish at all. It's actually a canny recruitment drive for a misconceived, dangerous war. Every day I'm taken aback at how many people believe that opposing the war in Afghanistan amounts to supporting terrorism or voting for the Taliban. Now that the initial aim of the war—capturing Osama bin Laden (dead or alive)—seems to have run into bad weather, the goalposts have been moved.[5] It's being made out that the whole point of the war was to topple the Taliban regime and liberate Afghan women from their burqas. We're being asked to believe that the US marines are actually on a feminist mission. (If so, will their next stop be America's military ally Saudi Arabia?) Think of it this way: In India there are some pretty reprehensible social practices, against "Untouchables," against Christians and Muslims, against women. Pakistan and Bangladesh have even worse ways of dealing with minority communities and women. Should they be bombed? Should Delhi, Islamabad, and Dhaka be destroyed? Is it possible to bomb bigotry out of India? Can we bomb our way to a feminist paradise? Is that how women won the vote in the United States? Or how slavery was abolished? Can we win redress for the genocide of the millions of Native Americans, upon whose corpses the United States was founded, by bombing Santa Fe?

None of us need anniversaries to remind us of what we cannot forget. So it is no more than coincidence that I happen to be here, on American soil, in September—this month of dreadful anniversaries. Uppermost on everybody's mind of course, particularly here in America, is the horror of what has come to be known as "9/11." Three thousand civilians lost their lives in that lethal terrorist strike.[6] The grief is still deep. The rage still sharp. The tears have not dried. And a strange, deadly war is raging around the world. Yet each person who has lost a loved one surely knows secretly, deeply, that no war, no act of revenge, no daisy-cutters dropped on someone else's loved ones or someone else's children will blunt the edges of their pain or bring their own loved ones back. War cannot avenge those who have died. War is only a brutal desecration of their memory.

To fuel yet another war—this time against Iraq—by cynically manipulating people's grief, by packaging it for TV specials sponsored by corporations selling detergent or running shoes, is to cheapen and devalue grief, to drain it of meaning. What we are seeing now is a vulgar display of the *business* of grief, the commerce of grief, the pillaging of even the most private human feelings for political purpose. It is a terrible, violent thing for a state to do to its people.

It's not a clever enough subject to speak of from a public platform, but what I would really love to talk to you about is loss. Loss and losing. Grief, failure, brokenness, numbness, uncertainty, fear, the death of feeling, the death of dreaming. The absolute, relentless, endless, habitual unfairness of the world. What does loss mean to individuals? What does it mean to whole cultures, whole peoples who have learned to live with it as a constant companion?

Since it is September 11th that we're talking about, perhaps it's in the fitness of things that we remember what that date means, not only to those who lost their loved ones in America last year but to those in other parts of the world to whom that date has long held significance. This historical dredging is not offered as an accusation or a provocation. But just to share the grief of history. To thin the mist a little. To say to the citizens of America, in the gentlest, most human way: Welcome to the World.

Twenty-nine years ago, in Chile, on the 11th of September 1973, General Pinochet overthrew the democratically elected government of Salvador Allende in a CIA-backed coup. "I don't see why we need to stand by and watch a country go Communist due to the irresponsibility of its own people," said Henry Kissinger, Nobel Peace Laureate, then President Nixon's National Security Adviser.[7]

After the coup President Allende was found dead inside the presidential palace. Whether he was killed or whether he killed himself, we'll never know. In the regime of terror that ensued, thousands of people were killed. Many more simply "disappeared." Firing squads conducted public executions. Concentration camps and torture chambers were opened across the country. The dead were buried in mine shafts and unmarked graves. For more than sixteen years the people of Chile lived in dread of the midnight knock, of routine disappearances, of sudden arrest and torture.[8]

In 2000, following the 1998 arrest of General Pinochet in Britain, thousands of secret documents were declassified by the US government.[9] They contain unequivocal evidence of the CIA's involvement in the coup as well as the fact that the US government had detailed information about the situation in Chile during General Pinochet's reign. Yet Kissinger assured the general of his support: "In the United States, as you know, we are sympathetic with what you are trying to do," he said. "We wish your government well."[10]

Those of us who have only ever known life in a democracy, however flawed, would find it hard to imagine what living in a dictatorship and enduring the absolute loss of freedom really means. It isn't just those who Pinochet murdered, but the lives he stole from the living that must be accounted for too.

Sadly, Chile was not the only country in South America to be singled out for the US government's attentions. Guatemala, Costa Rica, Ecuador, Brazil, Peru, the Dominican Republic, Bolivia, Nicaragua, Honduras, Panama, El Salvador, Peru, Mexico, and Colombia—they've all been the playground for covert—and overt—operations by the CIA.[11] Hundreds of thousands of Latin Americans have been killed, tortured, or have simply disappeared under the despotic regimes and tin-pot dictators, drug runners, and arms dealers that were propped up in their countries. (Many of them learned their craft in the infamous US government–funded School of the Americas in Fort Benning, Georgia, which has produced sixty thousand graduates.)[12] If this were not humiliation enough, the people of South America have had to bear the cross of being branded as a people who are incapable of democracy—as if coups and massacres are somehow encrypted in their genes.

This list does not of course include countries in Africa or Asia that suffered US military interventions—Somalia, Vietnam, Korea, Indonesia, Laos, and Cambodia.[13] For how many Septembers for decades together have millions of Asian people been bombed, burned, and slaughtered? How many Septembers have gone by since August 1945, when hundreds of thousands of ordinary Japanese people were obliterated by the nuclear strikes in Hiroshima and Nagasaki? For how many Septembers have the thousands who had the misfortune of surviving those strikes endured the living hell that was visited on them, their unborn children, their children's children, on the earth, the sky, the wind, the water, and all the creatures that swim and walk and crawl and fly? Not far from here, in Albuquerque, is the National Atomic Museum, where Fat Man and Little Boy (the affectionate nicknames for the bombs that were dropped on Hiroshima and Nagasaki) were available as souvenir earrings. Funky young people wore them. A massacre dangling in each ear. But I am straying from my theme. It's September that we're talking about, not August.

September 11th has a tragic resonance in the Middle East too. On the 11th of September 1922, ignoring Arab outrage, the British government proclaimed a mandate in Palestine, a follow-up to the 1917 Balfour Declaration, which imperial Britain issued, with its army massed outside the gates of the city of Gaza.[14] The Balfour Declaration promised European Zionists "a national home for Jewish people."[15] (At the time, the empire on which the sun never set was free to snatch and bequeath national homes like the school bully distributes marbles.) Two years after the declaration, Lord Arthur James Balfour, the British foreign secretary said, "In Palestine we do not propose even to go through the form of consulting the wishes of the present inhabitants of the country. . . . Zionism, be it right or wrong, good or bad, is rooted in age-long tradition, in present needs, in future hopes, of far profounder import than the desires and prejudices of the 700,000 Arabs who now inhabit that ancient land."[16]

How carelessly imperial power decreed whose needs were profound and whose were not. How carelessly it vivisected ancient civilizations. Palestine and Kashmir are imperial Britain's festering, blood-drenched gifts to the modern world. Both are fault lines in the raging international conflicts of today.

In 1937 Winston Churchill said of the Palestinians:

> I do not agree that the dog in a manger has the final right to the manger, even though he may have lain there for a very long time. I do not admit that right. I do not admit, for instance, that a great wrong has been done to the Red Indians of America, or the black people of Australia. I do not admit that a wrong has been done to these people by the fact that a stronger race, a higher grade race, a more worldly-wise race, to put it that way, has come in and taken their place.[17]

That set the trend for the Israeli state's attitude toward Palestinians. In 1969 Israeli Prime Minister Golda Meir said, "Palestinians do not exist." Her successor, Prime Minister Levi Eshkol, said, "Where are Palestinians? When I came here [to Palestine] there were 250,000 non-Jews, mainly Arabs and Bedouins. It was desert, more than underdeveloped. Nothing." Prime Minister Menachem Begin called Palestinians "two-legged beasts." Prime Minister Yitzhak Shamir called them "'grasshoppers' who could be crushed."[18] This is the language of heads of state, not the words of ordinary people. In 1947 the UN formally partitioned Palestine and allotted 55 percent of Palestine's land to the Zionists. Within a year they had captured more than 76 percent.[19] On May 14, 1948, the State of Israel was declared. Minutes after the declaration, the United States recognized Israel. The West Bank was annexed by Jordan. The Gaza Strip came under the military control of Egypt.[20] Formally, Palestine ceased to exist except in the minds and hearts of the hundreds of thousands of Palestinian people who became refugees.

In the summer of 1967, Israel occupied the West Bank and the Gaza Strip. Settlers were offered state subsidies and development aid to move into the occupied territories. Almost every day more Palestinian families are forced off their lands and driven into refugee camps. Palestinians who continue to live in Israel do not have the same rights as Israelis and live as second-class citizens in their former homeland.[21]

Over the decades there have been uprisings, wars, intifadas. Thousands have lost their lives.[22] Accords and treaties have been signed. Ceasefires declared and violated. But the bloodshed doesn't end. Palestine still remains illegally occupied. Its people live in inhuman conditions, in virtual Bantustans, where they are subjected to collective punishments and twenty-four-hour curfews, where they are humiliated and brutalized on a daily basis. They never know when their homes will be demolished, when their children will be shot, when their precious trees will be cut, when their roads will be closed, when they will be allowed to walk down to the market to buy food and medicine. And when they will not. They live with no semblance of dignity. With not much hope in sight. They have no control over their lands, their security, their movement, their communication, their water supply. So when accords are signed and words like *autonomy* and even *statehood* are bandied about, it's always worth asking: What sort of autonomy? What sort of state? What sort of rights will its citizens have?

Young Palestinians who cannot contain their anger turn themselves into human bombs and haunt Israel's streets and public places, blowing themselves up, killing ordinary people, injecting terror into daily life, and eventually hardening both societies' suspicion and mutual hatred of each other. Each bombing invites merciless reprisals and even more hardship on Palestinian people. But then suicide bombing is an act of individual despair, not a revolutionary tactic. Although Palestinian attacks strike terror into Israeli civilians, they provide the perfect cover for the Israeli government's daily incursions into Palestinian territory, the perfect excuse for old-fashioned nineteenth-century colonialism, dressed up as a new-fashioned twenty-first-century war.

Israel's staunchest political and military ally is and always has been the US government. The US government has blocked, along with Israel, almost every UN resolution that sought a peaceful, equitable solution to the conflict.[23] It has supported almost every war that Israel has fought. When Israel attacks Palestine, it is American missiles that smash through Palestinian homes. And every year Israel receives several billion dollars from the United States.[24]

What lessons should we draw from this tragic conflict? Is it really impossible for Jewish people who suffered so cruelly themselves—more cruelly perhaps than any other people in history—to understand the vulnerability and the yearning of those whom they have displaced? Does extreme suffering always kindle cruelty? What hope does this leave the human race with? What will happen to the Palestinian people in the event of a victory? When a nation without a state eventually proclaims a state, what kind of state will it be? What horrors will be perpetrated under its flag? Is it a separate state that we should be fighting for, or the rights to a life of liberty and dignity for everyone regardless of their ethnicity or religion?

Palestine was once a secular bulwark in the Middle East. But now the weak, undemocratic, by all accounts corrupt, but avowedly nonsectarian Palestinian Liberation Organization (PLO) is losing ground to Hamas, which espouses an overtly sectarian ideology and fights in the name of Islam. To quote from its manifesto: "We will be its soldiers and the firewood of its fire, which will burn the enemies."[25]

The world is called upon to condemn suicide bombers. But can we ignore the long road they have journeyed on before they arrived at this destination? September 11th, 1922, to September 11th, 2002—eighty years is a long, long time to have been waging war. Is there some advice the world can give the people of Palestine? Some scrap of hope we can hold out? Should they just settle for the crumbs that are thrown their way and behave like the grasshoppers or two-legged beasts they've been described as? Should they just take Golda Meir's suggestion and make a real effort to not exist?

In another part of the Middle East, September 11th strikes a more recent chord. It was on the 11th of September 1990 that George W. Bush Sr., then President of the United States, made a speech to a joint session of Congress announcing his government's decision to go to war against Iraq.[26]

The US government says that Saddam Hussein is a war criminal, a cruel military despot who has committed genocide against his own people. That's a fairly accurate description of the man. In 1988 he razed hundreds of villages in northern Iraq and used chemical weapons and machine guns to kill thousands of Kurdish people. Today we know that that same year the US government provided him with $500 million in subsidies to buy American agricultural products. The next year, after he had successfully completed his genocidal campaign, the US government doubled its subsidy to $1 billion.[27] It also provided him with high-quality germ seed for anthrax, as well as helicopters and dual-use material that could be used to manufacture chemical and biological weapons.[28]

So it turns out that while Saddam Hussein was carrying out his worst atrocities, the US and the UK governments were his close allies. Even today the government of Turkey, which has one of the most appalling human rights records in the world, is one of the US government's closest allies. The fact that the Turkish government has oppressed and murdered Kurdish people for years has not prevented the US government from plying Turkey with weapons and development aid.[29] Clearly it was not concern for the Kurdish people that provoked President Bush's speech to Congress.

What changed? In August 1990, Saddam Hussein invaded Kuwait. His sin was not so much that he had committed an act of war but that he acted independently, without orders from his masters. This display of independence was enough to upset the power equation in the Gulf. So it was decided that Saddam Hussein should be exterminated, like a pet that has outlived its owner's affection.

The first Allied attack on Iraq took place in January 1991. The world watched the primetime war as it was played out on TV. (In India those days, you had to go to a five-star hotel lobby to watch CNN.) Tens of thousands of people were killed in a month of devastating bombing.[30] What many do not know is that the war did not end then. The initial fury simmered down into the longest sustained air attack on a country since the Vietnam War. Over the last decade, American and British forces have fired thousands of missiles and bombs on Iraq. Iraq's fields and farmlands have been shelled with three hundred tons of depleted uranium.[31] In their bombing sorties, the Allies targeted and destroyed water treatment plants, aware of the fact that they could not be repaired without foreign assistance.[32] In southern Iraq there has been a fourfold increase in cancer among children. In the decade of economic sanctions that followed the war, Iraqi civilians have been denied food, medicine, hospital equipment, ambulances, clean water—the basic essentials.[33]

About half a million Iraqi children have died as a result of the sanctions. Of them, Madeleine Albright, then US Ambassador to the United Nations, famously said, "I think this is a very hard choice, but the price—we think the price is worth it."[34] "Moral equivalence" was the term that was used to denounce those who criticized the war on Afghanistan. Madeleine Albright cannot be accused of moral equivalence. What she said was just straightforward algebra.

A decade of bombing has not managed to dislodge Saddam Hussein, the "Beast of Baghdad." Now, almost twelve years on, President George Bush Jr. has ratcheted up the rhetoric once again. He's proposing an all-out war whose goal is nothing short of a "regime change." The *New York Times* says that the Bush administration is "following a meticulously planned strategy to persuade the public, the Congress and the allies of the need to confront the threat of Saddam Hussein." Andrew Card, the White House Chief of Staff, described how the administration was stepping up its war plans for the fall: "From a marketing point of view," he said, "you don't introduce new products in August."[35] This time the catchphrase for

Washington's "new product" is not the plight of Kuwaiti people but the assertion that Iraq has weapons of mass destruction. Forget "the feckless moralising of 'peace' lobbies," wrote Richard Perle, chairman of the Defense Policy Board; the United States will "act alone if necessary" and use a "pre-emptive strike" if it determines it's in US interests.[36]

Weapons inspectors have conflicting reports about the status of Iraq's "weapons of mass destruction," and many have said clearly that its arsenal has been dismantled and that it does not have the capacity to build one.[37] However, there is no confusion over the extent and range of America's arsenal of nuclear and chemical weapons. Would the US government welcome weapons inspectors? Would the UK? Or Israel?

What if Iraq *does* have a nuclear weapon, does that justify a preemptive US strike? The United States has the largest arsenal of nuclear weapons in the world. It's the only country in the world to have actually used them on civilian populations. If the United States is justified in launching a preemptive attack on Iraq, why then any nuclear power is justified in carrying out a preemptive attack on any other. India could attack Pakistan, or the other way around. If the US government develops a distaste for the Indian Prime Minister, can it just "take him out" with a preemptive strike?

Recently the United States played an important part in forcing India and Pakistan back from the brink of war. Is it so hard for it to take its own advice? Who is guilty of feckless moralizing? Of preaching peace while it wages war? The United States, which George Bush calls "a peaceful nation," has been at war with one country or another every year for the last fifty years.[38]

Wars are never fought for altruistic reasons. They're usually fought for hegemony, for business. And then of course, there's the business of war. Protecting its control of the world's oil is fundamental to US foreign policy. The US government's recent military interventions in the Balkans and Central Asia have to do with oil. Hamid Karzai, the puppet president of Afghanistan installed by the United States, is said to be a former employee of Unocal, the American-based oil company.[39] The US government's paranoid patrolling of the Middle East is because it has two-thirds of the world's oil reserves.[40] Oil keeps America's engines purring sweetly. Oil keeps the free market rolling. Whoever controls the world's oil controls the world's markets.

And how do you control the oil? Nobody puts it more elegantly than the *New York Times* columnist Thomas Friedman. In an article called "Craziness Pays," he says "the U.S. has to make clear to Iraq and U.S. allies that . . . America will use force, without negotiation, hesitation, or UN approval."[41] His advice was well taken. In the wars against Iraq and Afghanistan, as well as in the almost daily humiliation the US government heaps on the UN. In his book on globalization, *The Lexus and the Olive Tree,* Friedman says, "The hidden hand of the market will never work without a hidden fist. McDonald's cannot flourish without McDonnell Douglas. . . . And the hidden fist that keeps the world safe for Silicon Valley's technologies to flourish is called the U.S. Army, Air Force, Navy, and Marine Corps."[42]

Perhaps this was written in a moment of vulnerability, but it's certainly the most succinct, accurate description of the project of corporate globalization that I have read.

After September 11th, 2001, and the War Against Terror, the hidden hand and fist have had their cover blown, and we have a clear view now of America's other weapon—the free market—bearing down on the developing world, with a clenched unsmiling smile. The Task That Does Not End is America's perfect war, the perfect vehicle for the endless expansion of American imperialism. In Urdu, the word for profit is *fayda.* *Al-Qaeda* means The Word, The Word of God, The Law. So in India some of us call the War Against Terror *Al-Qaeda versus Al Fayda*—The Word versus The Profit (no pun intended). For the moment it looks as though *Al Fayda* will carry the day. But then you never know . . . In the last ten years of unbridled corporate globalization, the world's total income has increased by an average of 2.5 percent a year. And yet the number of the poor in the world has increased by 100 million. Of the top hundred biggest economies, fifty-one are corporations, not countries. The top 1 percent of the world has the same combined income as the bottom 57 percent, and the disparity is growing.[43] Now, under the spreading canopy of the War Against Terror, this process is being hustled along. The men in suits are in an unseemly hurry. While bombs rain down on us and cruise missiles skid across the skies, while nuclear weapons are stockpiled to make the world a safer place, contracts are being signed, patents are being registered, oil pipelines are being laid, natural resources are being plundered, water is being privatized, and democracies are being undermined.

In a country like India, the "structural adjustment" end of the corporate globalization project is ripping through people's lives. "Development" projects, massive privatization, and labor "reforms" are pushing people off their lands and out of their jobs, resulting in a kind of barbaric dispossession that has few parallels in history. Across the world as the free market brazenly protects Western markets and forces developing countries to lift their trade barriers, the poor are getting poorer and the rich richer. Civil unrest has begun to erupt in the global village. In countries like Argentina, Brazil, Mexico, Bolivia, and India, the resistance movements against corporate globalization are growing. To contain them, governments are tightening their control. Protesters are being labeled "terrorists" and then being dealt with as such. But civil unrest does not only mean marches and demonstrations and protests against globalization. Unfortunately, it also means a desperate downward spiral into crime and chaos and all kinds of despair and disillusionment, which, as we know from history (and from what we see unspooling before our eyes), gradually becomes a fertile breeding ground for terrible things—cultural nationalism, religious bigotry, fascism, and of course terrorism.

All these march arm in arm with corporate globalization.

There is a notion gaining credence that the free market breaks down national barriers and that corporate globalization's ultimate destination is a hippie paradise where the heart is the only passport and we all live together happily inside a John Lennon song (*Imagine there's no countries . . .*). This is a canard.

What the free market undermines is not national sovereignty but *democracy*. As the disparity between the rich and poor grows, the hidden fist has its work cut out for it. Multinational corporations on the prowl for sweetheart deals that yield enormous profits cannot push through those deals and administer those projects in developing countries without the active connivance of state machinery—the police, the courts, sometimes even the army. Today corporate globalization needs an international confederation of loyal, corrupt, authoritarian governments in poorer countries to push through unpopular reforms and quell the mutinies. It needs a press that pretends to be free. It needs courts that pretend to dispense justice.

It needs nuclear bombs, standing armies, sterner immigration laws, and watchful coastal patrols to make sure that it's only money, goods, patents, and services that are globalized—not the free movement of people, not a respect for human rights, not international treaties on racial discrimination, or chemical and nuclear weapons, or greenhouse gas emissions, climate change, or, god forbid, justice.[44] It's as though even a *gesture* toward international accountability would wreck the whole enterprise.

Close to one year after the War Against Terror was officially flagged off in the ruins of Afghanistan, freedoms are being curtailed in country after country in the name of protecting freedom, civil liberties are being suspended in the name of protecting democracy.[45] All kinds of dissent is being defined as "terrorism." All kinds of laws are being passed to deal with it. Osama bin Laden seems to have vanished into thin air. Mullah Omar is said to have made his escape on a motorbike.[46] (They could have sent Tin-Tin after him.) The Taliban may have disappeared, but their spirit, and their system of summary justice, is surfacing in the unlikeliest of places. In India, in Pakistan, in Nigeria, in America, in all the Central Asian republics run by all manner of despots, and of course in Afghanistan under the US-backed Northern Alliance.[47]

Meanwhile down at the mall there's a midseason sale. Everything's discounted—oceans, rivers, oil, gene pools, fig wasps, flowers, childhoods, aluminum factories, phone companies, wisdom, wilderness, civil rights, ecosystems, air—all 4.6 billion years of evolution. It's packed, sealed, tagged, valued, and available off the rack (no returns). As for justice—I'm told it's on offer too. You can get the best that money can buy.

Donald Rumsfeld said that his mission in the War Against Terror was to persuade the world that Americans must be allowed to continue their way of life.[48] When the maddened king stamps his foot, slaves tremble in their quarters. So, standing here today, it's hard for me to say this, but The American Way of Life is simply not sustainable. Because it doesn't acknowledge that there is a world beyond America.

Fortunately power has a shelf life. When the time comes, maybe this mighty empire will, like others before it, overreach itself and implode from within. It looks as though structural cracks have already appeared. As the War Against Terror casts its net wider and wider, America's corporate heart is hemorrhaging. For all the endless empty chatter about democracy, today the world is run by three of the most secretive institutions in the world: the International Monetary Fund, the World Bank, and the World Trade Organization, all three of which, in turn, are dominated by the United States. Their decisions are made in secret. The people who head them are appointed behind closed doors. Nobody really knows anything about them, their politics, their beliefs, their intentions. Nobody elected them. Nobody said they could make decisions on our behalf. A world run by a handful of greedy bankers and CEOs who nobody elected can't possibly last.

Soviet-style communism failed, not because it was intrinsically evil, but because it was flawed. It allowed too few people to usurp too much power. Twenty-first-century market capitalism, American style, will fail for the same reasons. Both are edifices constructed by human intelligence, undone by human nature.

The time has come, the Walrus said. Perhaps things will get worse and then better. Perhaps there's a small god up in heaven readying herself for us. Another world is not only possible, she's on her way. Maybe many of us won't be here to greet her, but on a quiet day, if I listen very carefully, I can hear her breathing.

15. An Ordinary Person's Guide
to Empire

Mesopotamia. Babylon. The Tigris and Euphrates. How many children in how many classrooms, over how many centuries, have hang-glided through the past, transported on the wings of these words?

And now the bombs are falling, incinerating, and humiliating that ancient civilization.

On the steel torsos of their missiles, adolescent American soldiers scrawl colorful messages in childish handwriting: "For Saddam, from the Fat Boy Posse."[1] A building goes down. A marketplace. A home. A girl who loves a boy. A child who only ever wanted to play with his older brother's marbles.

On March 21, the day after American and British troops began their illegal invasion and occupation of Iraq, an "embedded" CNN correspondent interviewed an American soldier. "I wanna get in there and get my nose dirty," Private AJ said. "I wanna take revenge for 9/11."[2]

To be fair to the correspondent, even though he was "embedded," he did sort of weakly suggest that so far there was no real evidence that linked the Iraqi government to the September 11 attacks. Private AJ stuck his teenage tongue out all the way down to the end of his chin. "Yeah, well, that stuff's way over my head," he said.[3]

The original version of this essay was published in the *Guardian* (London), April 2, 2003.

According to a *New York Times* / CBS News survey, 42 percent of the American public believes that Saddam Hussein is directly responsible for the September 11 attacks on the World Trade Center and the Pentagon.[4] And an ABC News poll says that 55 percent of Americans believe that Saddam Hussein directly supports Al-Qaeda.[5] What percentage of America's armed forces believes these fabrications is anybody's guess.

It is unlikely that British and American troops fighting in Iraq are aware that their governments supported Saddam Hussein both politically and financially through his worst excesses.

But why should poor AJ and his fellow soldiers be burdened with these details? It doesn't matter anymore, does it? Hundreds of thousands of men, tanks, ships, choppers, bombs, ammunition, gas masks, high-protein food, whole aircrafts ferrying toilet paper, insect repellent, vitamins, and bottled mineral water are on the move. The phenomenal logistics of Operation Iraqi Freedom make it a universe unto itself. It doesn't need to justify its existence any more. It exists. It *is*.

President George W. Bush, commander in chief of the US Army, Navy, Air Force, and Marines, has issued clear instructions: "Iraq. Will. Be. Liberated."[6] (Perhaps he means that even if Iraqi people's bodies are killed, their souls will be liberated.) American and British citizens owe it to the Supreme Commander to forsake thought and rally behind their troops. Their countries are at war.

And what a war it is.

After using the "good offices" of UN diplomacy (economic sanctions and weapons inspections) to ensure that Iraq was brought to its knees, its people starved, half a million of its children killed, its infrastructure severely damaged, after making sure that most of its weapons have been destroyed, in an act of cowardice that must surely be unrivaled in history, the "Allies" / "Coalition of the Willing" (better known as the Coalition of the Bullied and Bought) sent in an invading army!

Operation Iraqi Freedom? I don't think so. It's more like Operation Let's Run a Race, but First Let Me Break Your Knees.

So far the Iraqi army, with its hungry, ill-equipped soldiers, its old guns and aging tanks, has somehow managed to temporarily confound and occasionally even outmaneuver the "Allies." Faced with the richest, best-equipped, most powerful armed forces the world has ever seen, Iraq has shown spectacular courage and has even managed to put up what actually amounts to a defense. A defense which the Bush/Blair Pair have immediately denounced as deceitful and cowardly. (But then deceit is an old tradition with us natives. When we're invaded/colonized/occupied and stripped of all dignity, we turn to guile and opportunism.)

Even allowing for the fact that Iraq and the "Allies" are at war, the extent to which the "Allies" and their media cohorts are prepared to go is astounding to the point of being counterproductive to their own objectives.

When Saddam Hussein appeared on national TV to address the Iraqi people following the failure of the most elaborate assassination attempt in history—Operation Decapitation—we had Geoff Hoon, British defense secretary, deriding him for not having the courage to stand up and be killed, calling him a coward who hides in trenches.[7] We then had a flurry of coalition speculation: Was it really Saddam Hussein, was it his double? Or was it Osama with a shave? Was it prerecorded? Was it a speech? Was it black magic? Will it turn into a pumpkin if we really, really want it to?

After dropping not hundreds but thousands of bombs on Baghdad, when a marketplace was mistakenly blown up and civilians killed, a US army spokesman implied that the Iraqis were blowing themselves up! "They're also using very old stocks . . . and those stocks are not reliable, and [their] missiles are going up and coming down."[8]

If so, may we ask how this squares with the accusation that the Iraqi regime is a paid-up member of the Axis of Evil and a threat to world peace?

When the Arab TV station Al-Jazeera shows civilian casualties, it's denounced as "emotive" Arab propaganda aimed at orchestrating hostility toward the "Allies," as though Iraqis are dying only in order to make the "Allies" look bad. Even French television has come in for some stick for similar reasons. But the awed, breathless footage of aircraft carriers, stealth bombers, and cruise missiles arcing across the desert sky on American and British TV is described as the "terrible beauty" of war.[9]

When invading American soldiers (from the army "that's only here to help") are taken prisoner and shown on Iraqi TV, George Bush says it violates the Geneva Convention and exposes "the Iraqi regime and the evil at its heart."[10] But it is entirely acceptable for US television stations to show the hundreds of prisoners being held by the US government in

Guantánamo Bay, kneeling on the ground with their hands tied behind their backs, blinded with opaque goggles and with earphones clamped on their ears, to ensure complete visual and aural deprivation.[11] When questioned about the treatment of prisoners in Guantánamo Bay, US government officials don't deny that they're being ill-treated. They deny that they're prisoners of war! They call them "unlawful combatants,"[12] implying that their ill-treatment is legitimate! (So what's the party line on the massacre of prisoners in Mazar-e-Sharif, Afghanistan?[13] Forgive and forget? And what of the prisoner tortured to death by the Special Forces at the Bagram Air Force Base? Doctors have formally called it homicide.[14])

When the "Allies" bombed the Iraqi television station (also, incidentally, a contravention of the Geneva Convention), there was vulgar jubilation in the American media. In fact, Fox TV had been lobbying for the attack for a while.[15] It was seen as a righteous blow against Arab propaganda. But mainstream American and British TV continue to advertise themselves as "balanced" when their propaganda has achieved hallucinatory levels.

Why should propaganda be the exclusive preserve of the Western media? Just because they do it better?

Western journalists "embedded" with troops are given the status of heroes reporting from the front lines of war. Non-"embedded" journalists (like the BBC's Rageh Omaar, reporting from besieged and bombed Baghdad, witnessing, and clearly affected by, the sight of bodies of burned children and wounded people)[16] are undermined even before they begin their reportage: "We have to tell you that he is being monitored by the Iraqi authorities."

Increasingly, on British and American TV, Iraqi soldiers are being referred to as "militia" (i.e., rabble). One BBC correspondent portentously referred to them as "quasi-terrorists." Iraqi defense is "resistance" or, worse still, "pockets of resistance," Iraqi military strategy is deceit. (The US government bugging the phone lines of UN Security Council delegates, reported by the London *Observer*, is hardheaded pragmatism.)[17] Clearly for the "Allies" the only morally acceptable strategy the Iraqi army can pursue is to march out into the desert and be bombed by B-52s or be mowed down by machine-gun fire. Anything short of that is cheating.

And now we have the siege of Basra. About a million and a half people, 40 percent of them children.[18] Without clean water, and with very little food. We're still waiting for the legendary Shia "uprising," for the happy hordes to stream out of the city and rain roses and hosannas on the "liberating" army. Where are the hordes? Don't they know that television productions work to tight schedules? (It may well be that if the Saddam Hussein regime falls there will be dancing on the streets the world over.)

After days of enforcing hunger and thirst on the citizens of Basra, the "Allies" have brought in a few trucks of food and water and positioned them tantalizingly on the outskirts of the city. Desperate people flock to the trucks and fight each other for food. (The water, we hear, is being sold.[19] To revitalize the dying economy, you understand.) On top of the trucks, desperate photographers fought each other to get pictures of desperate people fighting each other for food. Those pictures will go out through photo agencies to newspapers and glossy magazines that pay extremely well. Their message: The messiahs are at hand, distributing fishes and loaves.

As of July 2002, the delivery of $5.4 billion worth of supplies to Iraq was blocked by the Bush/Blair Pair.[20] It didn't really make the news. But now, under the loving caress of live TV, 230 tons of humanitarian aid—a minuscule fraction of what's actually needed (call it a script prop)—arrived on a British ship, the *Sir Galahad*.[21] Its arrival in the port of Umm Qasr merited a whole day of live TV broadcasts. Barf bag, anyone?

Nick Guttmann, head of emergencies for Christian Aid, writing for the *Independent on Sunday*, said that it would take thirty-two *Sir Galahad*s a day to match the amount of food Iraq was receiving before the bombing began.[22]

We oughtn't to be surprised, though. It's old tactics. They've been at it for years. Remember this moderate proposal by John McNaughton from the Pentagon Papers published during the Vietnam War.

> Strikes at population targets (per se) are likely not only to create a counterproductive wave of revulsion abroad and at home, but greatly to increase the risk of enlarging the war with China or the Soviet Union. Destruction of locks and dams, however—if handled right— might . . . offer promise. Such destruction does not kill or drown

people. By shallow-flooding the rice, it leads after time to widespread starvation (more than a million?) unless food is provided—which we could offer to do "at the conference table."[23]

Times haven't changed very much. The technique has evolved into a doctrine. It's called "Winning Hearts and Minds."

So here's the moral math as it stands: Two hundred thousand Iraqis is estimated to have been killed in the first Gulf War.[24] Hundreds of thousands dead because of the economic sanctions. (At least that lot has been saved from Saddam Hussein.) More being killed every day. Tens of thousands of US soldiers who fought the 1991 war officially declared "disabled" by a disease called Gulf War Syndrome, believed to be caused in part by exposure to depleted uranium.[25] It hasn't stopped the "Allies" from continuing to use depleted uranium.[26]

And now this talk of bringing the United Nations back into the picture.

But that old UN girl—it turns out that she just ain't what she was cracked up to be. She's been demoted (although she retains her high salary). Now she's the world's janitor. She's the Filipina cleaning lady, the Indian jamadarni, the mail-order bride from Thailand, the Mexican household help, the Jamaican au pair. She's employed to clean other people's shit. She's used and abused at will.

Despite Tony Blair's earnest submissions, and all his fawning, George Bush has made it clear that the United Nations will play no independent part in the administration of postwar Iraq. The United States will decide who gets those juicy "reconstruction" contracts.[27] But Bush has appealed to the international community not to "politicize" the issue of humanitarian aid. On March 28, 2003, after Bush called for the immediate resumption of the UN's Oil for Food program, the UN Security Council voted unanimously for the resolution.[28] This means that everybody agrees that Iraqi money (from the sale of Iraqi oil) should be used to feed Iraqi people who are starving because of US-led sanctions and the illegal US-led war.

Contracts for the "reconstruction" of Iraq, we're told, in discussions on the business news, could jump-start the world economy. It's funny how the interests of American corporations are so often, so successfully, and so deliberately confused with the interests of the world economy.

While the American people will end up paying for the war, oil companies, weapons manufacturers, arms dealers, and corporations involved in "reconstruction" work will make direct gains from the war. Many of them are old friends and former employers of the Bush/Cheney/Rumsfeld/ Rice cabal. Bush has already asked Congress for $75 billion.[29] Contracts for "reconstruction" are already being negotiated. The news doesn't hit the stands because much of the US corporate media is owned and managed by the same interests.

Operation Iraqi Freedom, Tony Blair assures us, is about returning Iraqi oil to the Iraqi people. That is, returning Iraqi oil to the Iraqi people via corporate multinationals. Like Shell, like Chevron, like Halliburton. Or are we missing the plot here? Perhaps Halliburton is actually an Iraqi company? Perhaps US Vice President Dick Cheney (who was a former director of Halliburton) is a closet Iraqi?

As the rift between Europe and America deepens, there are signs that the world could be entering a new era of economic boycotts. CNN reported that Americans are emptying French wine into gutters, chanting "We don't need your stinking wine."[30] We've heard about the re-baptism of french fries. Freedom fries, they're called now.[31] There's news trickling in about Americans boycotting German goods.[32] The thing is that if the fallout of the war takes this turn, it is the United States who will suffer the most. Its homeland may be defended by border patrols and nuclear weapons, but its economy is strung out across the globe. Its economic outposts are exposed and vulnerable to attack in every direction. Already the Internet is buzzing with elaborate lists of American and British government products and companies that should be boycotted. These lists are being honed and refined by activists across the world. They could become a practical guide that directs and channels the amorphous but growing fury in the world. Suddenly, the "inevitability" of the project of corporate globalization is beginning to seem more than a little evitable.

It's become clear that the War Against Terror is not really about terror, and the War on Iraq not only about oil. It's about a superpower's self-destructive impulse toward supremacy, stranglehold, global hegemony. The argument is being made that the people of Argentina and Iraq have both been decimated by the same process. Only the weapons used against them differ: In the one case it's an IMF checkbook. In the other, the cruise missiles.

Finally, there's the matter of Saddam Hussein's arsenal of Weapons of Mass Destruction. (Oops, nearly forgot about those!)

In the fog of war one thing's for sure: if the Saddam Hussein regime indeed has weapons of mass destruction, it is showing an astonishing degree of responsibility and restraint in the teeth of extreme provocation. Under similar circumstances (say, if Iraqi troops were bombing New York and laying siege to Washington, DC) could we expect the same of the Bush regime? Would it keep its thousands of nuclear warheads in their wrapping paper? What about its chemical and biological weapons? Its stocks of anthrax, smallpox, and nerve gas? Would it?

Excuse me while I laugh.

In the fog of war we're forced to speculate: Either Saddam Hussein is an extremely responsible tyrant. Or—he simply does not possess Weapons of Mass Destruction. Either way, regardless of what happens next, Iraq comes out of the argument smelling sweeter than the US government.

So here's Iraq—rogue state, grave threat to world peace, paid-up member of the Axis of Evil. Here's Iraq, invaded, bombed, besieged, bullied, its sovereignty shat upon, its children killed by cancers, its people blown up on the streets. And here's all of us watching CNN–BBC, BBC–CNN late into the night. Here's all of us, enduring the horror of the war, enduring the horror of the propaganda, and enduring the slaughter of language as we know and understand it. Freedom now means mass murder (or, in the United States, fried potatoes). When someone says "humanitarian aid" we automatically go looking for induced starvation. "Embedded," I have to admit, is a great find. It's what it sounds like. And what about "arsenal of tactics"? Nice!

In most parts of the world, the invasion of Iraq is being seen as a racist war. The real danger of a racist war unleashed by racist regimes is that it engenders racism in everybody—perpetrators, victims, spectators. It sets the parameters for the debate, it lays out a grid for a particular way of thinking. There is a tidal wave of hatred for the United States rising from the ancient heart of the world. In Africa, Latin America, Asia, Europe, Australia. I encounter it every day. Sometimes it comes from the most unlikely sources. Bankers, businessmen, yuppie students, who bring to it all the crassness of their conservative, illiberal politics. That absurd inability to separate governments from people: America is a nation of morons, a nation of murderers, they say (with the same carelessness with which they say "All Muslims are terrorists"). Even in the grotesque universe of racist insult, the British make their entry as add-ons. Arse-lickers, they're called.

Suddenly, I, who have been vilified for being "anti-American" and "anti-West," find myself in the extraordinary position of defending the people of America. And Britain.

Those who descend so easily into the pit of racist abuse would do well to remember the hundreds of thousands of American and British citizens who protested against their country's stockpile of nuclear weapons. And the thousands of American war resisters who forced their government to withdraw from Vietnam. They should know that the most scholarly, scathing, hilarious critiques of the US government and the "American Way of Life" come from American citizens. And that the funniest, most bitter condemnation of their prime minister comes from the British media. Finally, they should remember that right now, hundreds of thousands of British and American citizens are on the streets protesting the war. The Coalition of the Bullied and Bought consists of governments, not people. More than a third of America's citizens have survived the relentless propaganda they've been subjected to, and many thousands are actively fighting their own government. In the ultra-patriotic climate that prevails in the United States, that's as brave as any Iraqi fighting for his or her homeland.

While the "Allies" wait in the desert for an uprising of Shia Muslims on the streets of Basra, the real uprising is taking place in hundreds of cities across the world. It has been the most spectacular display of public morality ever seen.

Most courageous of all are the hundreds of thousands of American people on the streets of America's great cities—Washington, New York, Chicago, San Francisco. The fact is that the only institution in the world today that is more powerful than the American government is American civil society. American citizens have a huge responsibility riding on their shoulders. How can we not salute and support those who not only acknowledge but act upon that responsibility? They are our allies, our friends.

At the end of it all, it remains to be said that dictators like Saddam

Hussein, and all the other despots in the Middle East, in the Central Asian republics, in Africa, and Latin America, many of them installed, supported, and financed by the US government, are a menace to their own people. Other than strengthening the hand of civil society (instead of weakening it, as has been done in the case of Iraq), there is no easy, pristine way of dealing with them. (It's odd how those who dismiss the peace movement as utopian don't hesitate to proffer the most absurdly dreamy reasons for going to war: to stamp out terrorism, install democracy, eliminate fascism, and, most entertainingly, to "rid the world of evildoers.")[33]

Regardless of what the propaganda machine tells us, these tin-pot dictators are not the greatest threat to the world. The real and pressing danger, the greatest threat of all, is the locomotive force that drives the political and economic engine of the US government, currently piloted by George Bush. Bush-bashing is fun, because he makes such an easy, sumptuous target. It's true that he is a dangerous, almost suicidal pilot, but the machine he handles is far more dangerous than the man himself.

Despite the pall of gloom that hangs over us today, I'd like to file a cautious plea for hope: In time of war, one wants one's weakest enemy at the helm of his forces. And President George W. Bush is certainly that. Any other even averagely intelligent US president would have probably done the very same things but would have managed to smoke up the glass and confuse the opposition. Perhaps even carry the United Nations with him. George Bush's tactless imprudence and his brazen belief that he can run the world with his riot squad has done the opposite. He has achieved what writers, activists, and scholars have striven to achieve for decades. He has exposed the ducts. He has placed on full public view the working parts, the nuts and bolts, of the apocalyptic apparatus of the American Empire.

Now that the blueprint, The Ordinary Person's Guide to Empire, has been put into mass circulation, it could be disabled quicker than the pundits predicted.

Bring on the spanners.

16. The Loneliness of Noam Chomsky

I will never apologize for the United States of America—I don't care what the facts are.
—President George Bush Sr.[1]

Sitting in my home in New Delhi, watching an American TV news channel promote itself ("We report. You decide"), I imagine Noam Chomsky's amused, chipped-tooth smile.

Everybody knows that authoritarian regimes, regardless of their ideology, use the mass media for propaganda. But what about democratically elected regimes in the "free world"?

Today, thanks to Noam Chomsky and his fellow media analysts, it is almost axiomatic for thousands, possibly millions, of us that public opinion in "free market" democracies is manufactured just like any other mass market product—soap, switches, or sliced bread.[2] We know that while, legally and constitutionally, speech may be free, the space in which that freedom can be exercised has been snatched from us and auctioned to the highest bidders. Neoliberal capitalism isn't just about the accumulation of capital (for some). It's also about the accumulation of power (for some), the accumulation of freedom (for some). Conversely, for

Written as an introduction to the second edition of Noam Chomsky, *For Reasons of State* (New York: New Press, 2003).

the rest of the world, the people who are excluded from neoliberalism's governing body, it's about the *erosion* of capital, the *erosion* of power, the *erosion* of freedom. In the "free" market, free speech has become a commodity like everything else—justice, human rights, drinking water, clean air. It's available only to those who can afford it. And naturally, those who can afford it use free speech to manufacture the kind of product, confect the kind of public opinion, that best suits their purpose. (News they can use.) Exactly how they do this has been the subject of much of Noam Chomsky's political writing. Prime Minister Silvio Berlusconi, for instance, has a controlling interest in major Italian newspapers, magazines, television channels, and publishing houses. "The prime minister in effect controls about 90 percent of Italian TV viewership," reports the *Financial Times*.[3] What price free speech? Free speech for *whom*? Admittedly, Berlusconi is an extreme example. In other democracies—the United States in particular—media barons, powerful corporate lobbies, and government officials are imbricated in a more elaborate but less obvious manner. (George Bush Jr.'s connections to the oil lobby, to the arms industry, and to Enron, and Enron's infiltration of US government institutions and the mass media—all this is public knowledge now.)

After the September 11, 2001, terrorist strikes in New York and Washington, the mainstream media's blatant performance as the US government's mouthpiece, its display of vengeful patriotism, its willingness to publish Pentagon press handouts as news, and its explicit censorship of dissenting opinion became the butt of some pretty black humor in the rest of the world.

Then the New York Stock Exchange crashed, bankrupt airline companies appealed to the government for financial bailouts, and there was talk of circumventing patent laws in order to manufacture generic drugs to fight the anthrax scare (*much* more important and urgent of course than the production of generics to fight AIDS in Africa).[4] Suddenly, it began to seem as though the twin myths of Free Speech and the Free Market might come crashing down alongside the Twin Towers of the World Trade Center.

But of course that never happened. The myths live on.

There is, however, a brighter side to the amount of energy and money that the establishment pours into the business of "managing" public opinion. It suggests a very real *fear* of public opinion. It suggests a persistent and valid worry that if people were to discover (and fully comprehend) the real nature of the things that are done in their name, they might *act* upon that knowledge. Powerful people know that ordinary people are not always reflexively ruthless and selfish. (When ordinary people weigh costs and benefits, something like an uneasy conscience could easily tip the scales.) For this reason, they must be guarded against reality, reared in a controlled climate, in an altered reality, like broiler chickens or pigs in a pen.

Those of us who have managed to escape this fate and are scratching about in the backyard no longer believe everything we read in the papers and watch on TV. We put our ears to the ground and look for other ways of making sense of the world. We search for the untold story, the mentioned-in-passing military coup, the unreported genocide, the civil war in an African country written up in a one-column-inch story next to a full-page advertisement for lace underwear.

We don't always remember, and many don't even know, that this way of thinking, this easy acuity, this instinctive mistrust of the mass media, would at best be a political hunch and at worst a loose accusation if it were not for the relentless and unswerving media analysis of one of the world's greatest minds. And this is only *one* of the ways in which Noam Chomsky has radically altered our understanding of the society in which we live. Or should I say, our understanding of the elaborate rules of the lunatic asylum in which we are all voluntary inmates?

Speaking about the September 11 attacks in New York and Washington, President George W. Bush called the enemies of the United States "enemies of freedom." "Americans are asking, why do they hate us?" he said. "They hate our freedoms, our freedom of religion, our freedom of speech, our freedom to vote and assemble and disagree with each other."[5]

If people in the United States want a real answer to that question (as opposed to the ones in the *Idiot's Guide to Anti-Americanism*, that is: "Because they're jealous of us," "Because they hate freedom," "Because they're losers," "Because we're good and they're evil"), I'd say, read Chomsky. Read Chomsky on US military interventions in Indochina, Latin America, Iraq, Bosnia, the former Yugoslavia, Afghanistan, and the Middle East. If ordinary people in the United States read Chomsky, perhaps their questions would be framed a little differently. Perhaps it would be "Why don't they hate us more than they do?" or "Isn't it surprising that September 11 didn't happen earlier?"

Unfortunately, in these nationalistic times, words like *us* and *them* are used loosely. The line between citizens and the state is being deliberately and successfully blurred, not just by governments but also by terrorists. The underlying logic of terrorist attacks, as well as "retaliatory" wars against governments that "support terrorism," is the same: both punish citizens for the actions of their governments.

(A brief digression: I realize that for Noam Chomsky, a US citizen, to criticize his own government is better manners than for someone like myself, an Indian citizen, to criticize the US government. I'm no patriot and am fully aware that venality, brutality, and hypocrisy are imprinted on the leaden soul of every state. But when a country ceases to be merely a country and becomes an empire, then the scale of operations changes dramatically. So may I clarify that I speak as a subject of the US empire? I speak as a slave who presumes to criticize her king.)

If I were asked to choose *one* of Noam Chomsky's major contributions to the world, it would be the fact that he has unmasked the ugly, manipulative, ruthless universe that exists behind that beautiful, sunny word *freedom*. He has done this rationally and empirically. The mass of evidence he has marshaled to construct his case is formidable. Terrifying, actually. The starting premise of Chomsky's method is not ideological, but it *is* intensely political. He embarks on his course of inquiry with an anarchist's instinctive mistrust of power. He takes us on a tour through the bog of the US establishment and leads us through the dizzying maze of corridors that connects the government, big business, and the business of managing public opinion.

Chomsky shows us how phrases like *free speech*, *the free market*, and *the free world* have little, if anything, to do with freedom. He shows us that among the myriad freedoms claimed by the US government are the freedom to murder, annihilate, and dominate other people. The freedom to finance and sponsor despots and dictators across the world. The freedom to train, arm, and shelter terrorists. The freedom to topple democratically elected governments. The freedom to amass and use weapons of mass destruction—chemical, biological, and nuclear. The freedom to go to war against any country whose government it disagrees with. And, most terrible of all, the freedom to commit these crimes against humanity in the name of "justice," in the name of "righteousness," in the name of "freedom."

Attorney General John Ashcroft has declared that US freedoms are "not the grant of any government or document, but . . . our endowment from God."[6] So, basically, we're confronted with a country armed with a mandate from heaven. Perhaps this explains why the US government refuses to judge itself by the same moral standards by which it judges others. (Any attempt to do this is shouted down as "moral equivalence.") Its technique is to position itself as the well-intentioned giant whose good deeds are confounded in strange countries by their scheming natives, whose markets it's trying to free, whose societies it's trying to modernize, whose women it's trying to liberate, whose souls it's trying to save.

Perhaps this belief in its own divinity also explains why the US government has conferred upon itself the right and freedom to murder and exterminate people "for their own good."

When he announced the US air strikes against Afghanistan, President Bush Jr. said, "We're a peaceful nation."[7] He went on to say, "This is the calling of the United States of America, the most free nation in the world, a nation built on fundamental values, that rejects hate, rejects violence, rejects murderers, rejects evil. And we will not tire."[8]

The US empire rests on a grisly foundation: the massacre of millions of indigenous people, the stealing of their lands, and following this, the kidnapping and enslavement of millions of black people from Africa to work that land. Thousands died on the seas while they were being shipped like caged cattle between continents.[9] "Stolen from Africa, brought to America"—Bob Marley's "Buffalo Soldier" contains a whole universe of unspeakable sadness.[10] It tells of the loss of dignity, the loss of wilderness, the loss of freedom, the shattered pride of a people. Genocide and slavery provide the social and economic underpinning of the nation whose fundamental values reject hate, murderers, and evil.

Here is Chomsky, writing in the essay "The Manufacture of Consent," on the founding of the United States of America:

During the Thanksgiving holiday a few weeks ago, I took a walk with some friends and family in a national park. We came across a gravestone, which had on it the following inscription: "Here lies an Indian woman, a Wampanoag, whose family and tribe gave of themselves and their land that this great nation might be born and grow."

Of course, it is not quite accurate to say that the indigenous population gave of themselves and their land for that noble purpose. Rather, they were slaughtered, decimated, and dispersed in the course of one of the greatest exercises in genocide in human history . . . which we celebrate each October when we honor Columbus—a notable mass murderer himself—on Columbus Day.

Hundreds of American citizens, well-meaning and decent people, troop by that gravestone regularly and read it, apparently without reaction; except, perhaps, a feeling of satisfaction that at last we are giving some due recognition to the sacrifices of the native peoples. . . . They might react differently if they were to visit Auschwitz or Dachau and find a gravestone reading: "Here lies a woman, a Jew, whose family and people gave of themselves and their possessions that this great nation might grow and prosper."[11]

How has the United States survived its terrible past and emerged smelling so sweet? Not by owning up to it, not by making reparations, not by apologizing to Black Americans or native Americans, and certainly not by changing its ways (it *exports* its cruelties now). Like most other countries, the United States has rewritten its history. But what sets the United States apart from other countries, and puts it way ahead in the race, is that it has enlisted the services of the most powerful, most successful publicity firm in the world: Hollywood.

In the best-selling version of popular myth as history, US "goodness" peaked during World War II (aka America's War Against Fascism). Lost in the din of trumpet sound and angel song is the fact that when fascism was in full stride in Europe, the US government actually looked away. When Hitler was carrying out his genocidal pogrom against Jews, US officials refused entry to Jewish refugees fleeing Germany. The United States entered the war only *after* the Japanese bombed Pearl Harbor. Drowned out by the noisy hosannas is its most barbaric act, in fact the single most savage act the world has ever witnessed: the dropping of the atomic bomb on civilian populations in Hiroshima and Nagasaki. The war was nearly over. The hundreds of thousands of Japanese people who were killed, the countless others who were crippled by cancers for generations to come, were not a threat to world peace. They were *civilians*. Just as the victims of the World Trade Center and Pentagon bombings were civilians. Just as the hundreds of thousands of people who died in Iraq because of the US-led sanctions were civilians. The bombing of Hiroshima and Nagasaki was a cold, calculated experiment carried out to demonstrate America's power. At the time, President Truman described it as "the greatest thing in history."[12]

The Second World War, we're told, was a "war for peace." The atomic bomb was a "weapon of peace."

We're invited to believe that nuclear deterrence prevented World War III. (That was before President George Bush Jr. came up with the "preemptive strike doctrine.")[13] *Was* there an outbreak of peace after the Second World War? Certainly there was (relative) peace in Europe and America—but does that count as world peace? Not unless savage proxy wars fought in lands where the colored races live (chinks, niggers, dinks, wogs, gooks) don't count as wars at all.

Since the Second World War, the United States has been at war with or has attacked, among other countries, Korea, Guatemala, Cuba, Laos, Vietnam, Cambodia, Grenada, Libya, El Salvador, Nicaragua, Panama, Iraq, Somalia, Sudan, Yugoslavia, and Afghanistan. This list should also include the US government's covert operations in Africa, Asia, and Latin America, the coups it has engineered, and the dictators it has armed and supported. It should include Israel's US-backed war on Lebanon, in which thousands were killed. It should include the key role America has played in the conflict in the Middle East, in which thousands have died fighting Israel's illegal occupation of Palestinian territory. It should include America's role in the civil war in Afghanistan in the 1980s, in which more than one million people were killed.[14] It should include the embargos and sanctions that have led directly and indirectly to the death of hundreds of thousands of people, most visibly in Iraq.[15] Put it all together, and it sounds very much as though there has been a World War III, and that the US government was (or is) one of its chief protagonists.

Most of the essays in Chomsky's *For Reasons of State* are about US aggression in South Vietnam, North Vietnam, Laos, and Cambodia. It was a war that lasted more than twelve years. Fifty-eight thousand Americans and approximately 2 million Vietnamese, Cambodians, and Laotians lost their lives.[16] The US deployed half a million ground troops, dropped more than 6 million tons of bombs.[17] And yet, though you wouldn't believe it if you watched most Hollywood movies, America lost the war.

The war began in South Vietnam and then spread to North Vietnam, Laos, and Cambodia. After putting in place a client regime in Saigon, the US government invited itself in to fight a communist insurgency—Vietcong guerrillas who had infiltrated rural regions of South Vietnam where villagers were sheltering them. This was exactly the model that Russia replicated when, in 1979, it invited itself into Afghanistan. Nobody in the "free world" is in any doubt about the fact that Russia invaded Afghanistan. After glasnost, even a Soviet foreign minister called the Soviet invasion of Afghanistan "illegal and immoral."[18] But there has been no such introspection in the United States. In 1984, in a stunning revelation, Chomsky wrote:

> For the past twenty-two years, I have been searching to find some reference in mainstream journalism or scholarship to an American invasion of South Vietnam in 1962 (or ever), or an American attack against South Vietnam, or American aggression in Indochina—without success. There is no such event in history. Rather, there is an American *defense* of South Vietnam against terrorists supported from the outside (namely from Vietnam).[19]

There is no such event in history!

In 1962 the US Air Force began to bomb rural South Vietnam, where 80 percent of the population lived. The bombing lasted for more than a decade. Thousands of people were killed. The idea was to bomb on a scale colossal enough to induce panic migration from villages into cities, where people could be held in refugee camps. Samuel Huntington referred to this as a process of "urbanization."[20] (I learned about urbanization when I was in architecture school in India. Somehow I don't remember aerial bombing being part of the syllabus.) Huntington—famous today for his essay "The Clash of Civilizations?"—was at the time Chairman of the Council on Vietnamese Studies of the Southeast Asia Development Advisory Group. Chomsky quotes him describing the Vietcong as "a powerful force which cannot be dislodged from its constituency so long as the constituency continues to exist."[21] Huntington went on to advise "direct application of mechanical and conventional power"—in other words, to crush a people's war, eliminate the people.[22] (Or, perhaps, to update the thesis—in order to prevent a clash of civilizations, annihilate a civilization.)

Here's one observer from the time on the limitations of America's mechanical power: "The problem is that American machines are not equal to the task of killing communist soldiers except as part of a scorched-earth policy that destroys everything else as well."[23] That problem has been solved now. Not with less destructive bombs but with more imaginative language. There's a more elegant way of saying "that destroys everything else as well." The phrase is "collateral damage."

And here's a firsthand account of what America's "machines" (Huntington called them "modernizing instruments" and staff officers in the Pentagon called them "bomb-o-grams") can do.[24] This is T. D. Allman flying over the Plain of Jars in Laos:

> Even if the war in Laos ended tomorrow, the restoration of its ecological balance might take several years. The reconstruction of the Plain's totally destroyed towns and villages might take just as long. Even if this was done, the Plain might long prove perilous to human habitation because of the hundreds of thousands of unexploded bombs, mines and booby traps.
>
> A recent flight around the Plain of Jars revealed what less than three years of intensive American bombing can do to a rural area, even after its civilian population has been evacuated. In large areas, the primary tropical colour—bright green—has been replaced by an abstract pattern of black, and bright metallic colours. Much of the remaining foliage is stunted, dulled by defoliants.
>
> Today, black is the dominant colour of the northern and eastern reaches of the Plain. Napalm is dropped regularly to burn off the grass and undergrowth that covers the Plains and fills its many narrow ravines. The fires seem to burn constantly, creating rectangles of black. During the flight, plumes of smoke could be seen rising from freshly bombed areas.
>
> The main routes, coming into the Plain from communist-held territory, are bombed mercilessly, apparently on a non-stop basis.

There, and along the rim of the Plain, the dominant colour is yellow. All vegetation has been destroyed. The craters are countless. . . . The area has been bombed so repeatedly that the land resembles the pocked, churned desert in storm-hit areas of the North African desert.

Further to the southeast, Xieng Khouangville—once the most populous town in communist Laos—lies empty, destroyed. To the north of the Plain, the little resort of Khang Khay also has been destroyed.

Around the landing field at the base of King Kong, the main colours are yellow (from upturned soil) and black (from napalm), relieved by patches of bright red and blue: parachutes used to drop supplies.

. . . The last local inhabitants were being carted into air transports. Abandoned vegetable gardens that would never be harvested grew near abandoned houses with plates still on the tables and calendars on the walls.[25]

(Never counted in the "costs" of war are the dead birds, the charred animals, the murdered fish, incinerated insects, poisoned water sources, destroyed vegetation. Rarely mentioned is the arrogance of the human race toward other living things with which it shares this planet. All these are forgotten in the fight for markets and ideologies. This arrogance will probably be the ultimate undoing of the human species.)

The centerpiece of *For Reasons of State* is an essay called "The Mentality of the Backroom Boys," in which Chomsky offers an extraordinarily supple, exhaustive analysis of the Pentagon Papers, which he says "provide documentary evidence of a conspiracy to use force in international affairs in violation of law."[26] Here, too, Chomsky makes note of the fact that while the bombing of North Vietnam is discussed at some length in the Pentagon Papers, the invasion of South Vietnam barely merits a mention.[27]

The Pentagon Papers are mesmerizing, not as documentation of the history of the US war in Indochina but as insight into the minds of the men who planned and executed it. It's fascinating to be privy to the ideas that were being tossed around, the suggestions that were made, the proposals that were put forward. In a section called "The Asian Mind—the American Mind," Chomsky examines the discussion of the mentality of the enemy that "stoically accept[s] the destruction of wealth and the loss of lives," whereas "we want life, happiness, wealth, power," and for us "death and suffering are irrational choices when alternatives exist."[28] So we learn that the Asian poor, presumably because they cannot comprehend the meaning of happiness, wealth, and power, invite America to carry this "strategic logic to its conclusion, which is genocide." But then "we" balk because "genocide is a terrible burden to bear."[29] (Eventually, of course, "we" went ahead and committed genocide anyway, and then pretended that it never really happened.)

Of course the Pentagon Papers contain some moderate proposals, as well.

> Strikes at population targets (per se) are likely not only to create a counterproductive wave of revulsion abroad and at home but also to greatly increase the risk of enlarging the war with China and the Soviet Union. Destruction of locks and dams, however—if handled right—might offer promise. It should be studied. Such destruction does not kill or drown people. By shallow-flooding the rice, it leads after time to widespread starvation (more than a million?) unless food is provided—which we could offer to do "at the conference table."[30]

Layer by layer, Chomsky strips down the process of decision making by US government officials, to reveal at its core the pitiless heart of the American war machine, completely insulated from the realities of war, blinded by ideology, and willing to annihilate millions of human beings, civilians, soldiers, women, children, villages, whole cities, whole ecosystems—with scientifically honed methods of brutality.

Here's an American pilot talking about the joys of napalm:

> We sure are pleased with those backroom boys at Dow. The original product wasn't so hot—if the gooks were quick they could scrape it off. So the boys started adding polystyrene—now it sticks like shit to a blanket. But then if the gooks jumped under water it stopped burning, so they started adding Willie Peter [white phosphorous] so's to make it burn better. It'll even burn under water now. And just one drop is enough, it'll keep on burning right down to the bone so they die anyway from phosphorous poisoning.[31]

So the lucky gooks were annihilated for their own good. Better Dead than Red.

Thanks to the seductive charms of Hollywood and the irresistible appeal of America's mass media, all these years later, the world views the war as an *American* story. Indochina provided the lush tropical backdrop against which the United States played out its fantasies of violence, tested its latest technology, furthered its ideology, examined its conscience, agonized over its moral dilemmas, and dealt with its guilt (or pretended to). The Vietnamese, the Cambodians, and the Laotians were only script props. Nameless, faceless, slit-eyed humanoids. They were just the people who died. Gooks.

The only real lesson the US government learned from its invasion of Indochina is how to go to war without committing American troops and risking American lives. So now we have wars waged with long-range cruise missiles, Black Hawks, "bunker busters." Wars in which the "Allies" lose more journalists than soldiers.

As a child growing up in the state of Kerala, in South India—where the first democratically elected communist government in the world came to power in 1959, the year I was born—I worried terribly about being a gook. Kerala was only a few thousand miles west of Vietnam. We had jungles and rivers and rice fields, and communists, too. I kept imagining my mother, my brother, and myself being blown out of the bushes by a grenade, or mowed down, like the gooks in the movies, by an American marine with muscled arms and chewing gum and a loud background score. In my dreams, I was the burning girl in the famous photograph taken on the road from Trang Bang.

As someone who grew up on the cusp of both American and Soviet propaganda (which more or less neutralized each other), when I first read Noam Chomsky, it occurred to me that his marshaling of evidence, the volume of it, the relentlessness of it, was a little—how shall I put it?—insane. Even a quarter of the evidence he had compiled would have been enough to convince me. I used to wonder why he needed to do so much *work*. But now I understand that the magnitude and intensity of Chomsky's work is a barometer of the magnitude, scope, and relentlessness of the propaganda machine that he's up against. He's like the wood-borer who lives inside the third rack of my bookshelf. Day and night, I hear his jaws crunching through the wood, grinding it to a fine dust. It's as though he disagrees with the literature and wants to destroy the very structure on which it rests. I call him Chompsky.

Being an American working in America, writing to convince Americans of his point of view must really be like having to tunnel through hard wood. Chomsky is one of a small band of individuals fighting a whole industry. And that makes him not only brilliant, but heroic.

Some years ago, in a poignant interview with James Peck, Chomsky spoke about his memory of the day Hiroshima was bombed. He was sixteen years old:

> I remember that I literally couldn't talk to anybody. There was nobody. I just walked off by myself. I was at a summer camp at the time, and I walked off into the woods and stayed alone for a couple of hours when I heard about it. I could never talk to anyone about it and never understood anyone's reaction. I felt completely isolated.[32]

That isolation produced one of the greatest, most radical public thinkers of our time.

When the sun sets on the American empire, as it will, as it must, Noam Chomsky's work will survive. It will point a cool, incriminating finger at a merciless, Machiavellian empire as cruel, self-righteous, and hypocritical as the ones it has replaced. (The only difference is that it is armed with technology that can visit the kind of devastation on the world that history has never known and the human race cannot begin to imagine.)

As a could've been gook, and who knows, perhaps a potential gook, hardly a day goes by when I don't find myself thinking—for one reason or another—"Chomsky Zindabad."

17. Confronting Empire

I've been asked to speak about "how to confront Empire." It's a huge question, and I have no easy answers.

When we speak of confronting Empire, we need to identify what Empire means. Does it mean the US government (and its European satellites), the World Bank, the International Monetary Fund, the World Trade Organization (WTO), and multinational corporations? Or is it something more than that?

In many countries, Empire has sprouted other subsidiary heads, some dangerous byproducts—nationalism, religious bigotry, fascism, and, of course, terrorism. All these march arm in arm with the project of corporate globalization.

Let me illustrate what I mean. India—the world's biggest democracy—is currently at the forefront of the corporate globalization project. Its "market" of one billion people is being pried open by the WTO. Corporatization and privatization are being welcomed by the government and the Indian elite.

It is not a coincidence that the Prime Minister, the Home Minister, the Disinvestment Minister—the men who signed the deal with Enron in India, the men who are selling the country's infrastructure to corporate multinationals, the men who want to privatize water, electricity, oil,

First presented at the World Social Forum in Porto Alegre, Brazil, January 27, 2003.

coal, steel, health, education, and telecommunication—are all members or admirers of the Rashtriya Swayamsevak Sangh (RSS), a right-wing, ultra-nationalist Hindu guild which has openly admired Hitler and his methods.

The dismantling of democracy is proceeding with the speed and efficiency of a Structural Adjustment Program. While the project of corporate globalization rips through people's lives in India, massive privatization and labor "reforms" are pushing people off their land and out of their jobs. Hundreds of impoverished farmers are committing suicide by consuming pesticide.[1]

Reports of starvation deaths are coming in from all over the country.[2]

While the elite journeys to its imaginary destination somewhere near the top of the world, the dispossessed are spiraling downward into crime and chaos. This climate of frustration and national disillusionment is the perfect breeding ground, history tells us, for fascism.

The two arms of the Indian government have evolved the perfect pincer action. While one arm is busy selling India off in chunks, the other, to divert attention, is orchestrating a howling, baying chorus of Hindu nationalism and religious fascism. It is conducting nuclear tests, rewriting history books, burning churches, and demolishing mosques. Censorship, surveillance, the suspension of civil liberties and human rights, the questioning of who is an Indian citizen and who is not, particularly with regard to religious minorities, are all becoming common practice now.

Last March, in the state of Gujarat, two thousand Muslims were butchered in a state-sponsored pogrom. Muslim women were specially targeted. They were stripped, and gang-raped, before being burned alive. Arsonists burned and looted shops, homes, textile mills, and mosques.[3]

More than a hundred fifty thousand Muslims have been driven from their homes. The economic base of the Muslim community has been devastated.

While Gujarat burned, the Indian Prime Minister was on MTV promoting his new poems. In December 2002, the government that orchestrated the killing was voted back into office with a comfortable majority.[4] Nobody has been punished for the genocide. Narendra Modi, architect of the pogrom, proud member of the RSS, has embarked on his second term as the Chief Minister of Gujarat. If he were Saddam Hussein, of course each atrocity would have been on CNN. But since he's not—and since the Indian "market" is open to global investors—the massacre is not even an embarrassing inconvenience.

There are more than 100 million Muslims in India. A time bomb is ticking in our ancient land.

All this to say that it is a myth that the free market breaks down national barriers. The free market does not threaten national sovereignty, it undermines democracy.

As the disparity between the rich and the poor grows, the fight to corner resources is intensifying. To push through their "sweetheart deals," to corporatize the crops we grow, the water we drink, the air we breathe, and the dreams we dream, corporate globalization needs an international confederation of loyal, corrupt, authoritarian governments in poorer countries to push through unpopular reforms and quell the mutinies.

Corporate globalization—or shall we call it by its name?—Imperialism—needs a press that pretends to be free. It needs courts that pretend to dispense justice.

Meanwhile, the countries of the North harden their borders and stockpile weapons of mass destruction. After all, they have to make sure that it's only money, goods, patents, and services that are globalized. Not the free movement of people. Not a respect for human rights. Not international treaties on racial discrimination or chemical and nuclear weapons or greenhouse gas emissions or climate change or—god forbid—justice.

So this—*all* this—is Empire. This loyal confederation, this obscene accumulation of power, this greatly increased distance between those who make the decisions and those who have to suffer them.

Our fight, our goal, our vision of another world must be to eliminate that distance.

So how do we resist Empire?

The good news is that we're not doing too badly. There have been major victories. Here in Latin America you have had so many—in Bolivia, you have Cochabamba.[5] In Peru, there was the uprising in Arequipa.[6] In Venezuela, President Hugo Chavez is holding on, despite the US government's best efforts.[7]

And the world's gaze is on the people of Argentina, who are trying to refashion a country from the ashes of the havoc wrought by the IMF.[8]

In India the movement against corporate globalization is gathering momentum and is poised to become the only real political force to counter religious fascism.

As for corporate globalization's glittering ambassadors—Enron, Bechtel, WorldCom, Arthur Andersen—where were they last year, and where are they now?

And of course here in Brazil we must ask: Who was the president last year, and who is it now?

Still, many of us have dark moments of hopelessness and despair. We know that under the spreading canopy of the War Against Terrorism, the men in suits are hard at work.

While bombs rain down on us and cruise missiles skid across the skies, we know that contracts are being signed, patents are being registered, oil pipelines are being laid, natural resources are being plundered, water is being privatized, and George Bush is planning to go to war against Iraq.

If we look at this conflict as a straightforward eyeball-to-eyeball confrontation between Empire and those of us who are resisting it, it might seem that we are losing.

But there is another way of looking at it. We, all of us gathered here, have, each in our own way, laid siege to Empire.

We may not have stopped it in its tracks—yet—but we have stripped it down. We have made it drop its mask. We have forced it into the open. It now stands before us on the world's stage in all its brutish, iniquitous nakedness.

Empire may well go to war, but it's out in the open now—too ugly to behold its own reflection. Too ugly even to rally its own people. It won't be long before the majority of American people become our allies.

In Washington, a quarter of a million people marched against the war on Iraq.[9] Each month, the protest is gathering momentum.

Before September 11, 2001, America had a secret history. Secret especially from its own people. But now America's secrets are history, and its history is public knowledge. It's street talk.

Today, we know that every argument that is being used to escalate the war against Iraq is a lie. The most ludicrous of them being the US government's deep commitment to bring democracy to Iraq.

Killing people to save them from dictatorship or ideological corruption is, of course, an old US government sport. Here in Latin America, you know that better than most.

Nobody doubts that Saddam Hussein is a ruthless dictator, a murderer (whose worst excesses were supported by the governments of the United States and Great Britain). There's no doubt that Iraqis would be better off without him.

But, then, the whole world would be better off without a certain Mr. Bush. In fact, he is far more dangerous than Saddam Hussein.

So should we bomb Bush out of the White House?

It's more than clear that Bush is determined to go to war against Iraq, *regardless* of the facts—and regardless of international public opinion.

In its recruitment drive for allies, the United States is prepared to *invent* facts.

The charade with weapons inspectors is the US government's offensive, insulting concession to some twisted form of international etiquette. It's like leaving the "doggie door" open for last-minute "allies" or maybe the United Nations to crawl through.

But for all intents and purposes, the new war against Iraq has begun. What can we do?

We can hone our memory, we can learn from our history. We can continue to build public opinion until it becomes a deafening roar.

We can turn the war on Iraq into a fishbowl of the US government's excesses.

We can expose George Bush and Tony Blair—and their allies—for the cowardly baby killers, water poisoners, and pusillanimous long-distance bombers that they are.

We can reinvent civil disobedience in a million different ways. In other words, we can come up with a million ways of becoming a collective pain in the ass.

When George Bush says "You're either with us, or you are with the terrorists," we can say "No thank you." We can let him know that the people of the world do not need to choose between a Malevolent Mickey Mouse and the Mad Mullahs.

Our strategy should be not only to confront Empire but to lay siege to it. To deprive it of oxygen. To shame it. To mock it. With our art, our music, our literature, our stubbornness, our joy, our brilliance, our sheer relentlessness—and our ability to tell our own stories. Stories that are different from the ones we're being brainwashed to believe.

The corporate revolution will collapse if we refuse to buy what they are selling—their ideas, their version of history, their wars, their weapons, their notion of inevitability.

Remember this: We be many and they be few. They need us more than we need them.

18. Peace Is War

The Collateral Damage of Breaking News

There's been a delicious debate in the Indian press of late. A prominent English daily announced that it would sell space on page 3 (its gossip section) to anyone who was willing to pay to be featured. (The inference is that the rest of the news in the paper is in some way unsponsored, unsullied, "pure news.") The announcement provoked a series of responses—most of them outraged that the proud tradition of impartial journalism could sink to such depths. Personally, I was delighted. For a major mainstream newspaper to introduce the *notion* of "paid-for" news is a giant step forward in the project of educating a largely credulous public about how the mass media operates. Once the idea of "paid-for" news has been mooted, once it's been ushered through the portals of popular imagination, it won't be hard for people to work out that if gossip columns in newspapers can be auctioned, why not the rest of the column space? After all, in this age of the "market" when everything's up for sale—rivers, forests, freedom, democracy, and justice—what's special about news? Sponsored News—what a delectable idea! "This report is brought to you by . . ." There could be a state-regulated sliding scale for rates (headlines, page 1, page 2, sports section, and so on). Or, on second

Speech first delivered at the Center for the Study of Developing Societies, New Delhi, March 7, 2003.

thought, we could leave that to be regulated by the "free market"—as it is now. Why change a winning formula?

The debate about whether mass-circulation newspapers and commercial TV channels are finely plotted ideological conspiracies or apolitical, benign anarchies that bumble along as best they can is an old one and needs no elaboration. After the September 11 attack on the World Trade Center, the US mainstream media's blatant performance as the government's mouthpiece was the butt of some pretty black humor in the rest of the world. It brought the myth of the Free Press in America crashing down. But before we gloat, the Indian mass media behaved no differently during the Pokhran nuclear tests and the Kargil War. There was no bumbling and very little was benign in the shameful coverage of the December 13 attack on the Indian Parliament and the trial of S. A. R. Geelani, who has been sentenced to death after having been the subject of a media trial fueled by a campaign of nationalist hysteria and outright lies. On a more everyday basis: Would anybody who depends on the Indian mass media for information know that eighty thousand people have been killed in Kashmir since 1989, most of them Muslim, most of them by Indian security forces?[1] Most Indians would be outraged if it were suggested to them that the killings and "disappearances" in the Kashmir valley put India on a par with any banana republic.

Modern democracies have been around long enough for neoliberal capitalists to learn how to subvert them. They have mastered the technique of infiltrating the instruments of democracy—the "independent" judiciary, the "free" press, the parliament—and molding them to their purpose. The project of corporate globalization has cracked the code. Free elections, a free press, and an independent judiciary mean little when the free market has reduced them to commodities available on sale to the highest bidder.

To control a democracy, it is becoming more and more vital to control the media. The principal media outlets in America are owned by six major companies.[2] The six largest cable companies have 80 percent of cable television subscribers.[3] Even Internet websites are being colonized by giant media corporations.[4]

It's a mistake to think that the corporate media supports the neoliberal project. It *is* the neoliberal project. It is the nexus, the confluence, the convergence, the union, the chosen medium of those who have power and money. As the project of corporate globalization increases the disparity between the rich and the poor, as the world grows more and more restive, corporations on the prowl for sweetheart deals need repressive governments to quell the mutinies in the servants' quarters. And governments, of course, need corporations. This mutual dependence spawns a sort of corporate nationalism, or, more accurately, a corporate/ nationalism—if you can imagine such a thing. Corporate/nationalism has become the unwavering anthem of the mass media.

One of our main tasks is to expose the complex mess of cables that connect power to money to the supposedly "neutral" free press.

In the last couple of years, New Media has embarked on just such an enterprise. It has descended on Old Media like an annoying swarm of bees buzzing around an old buffalo, going where it goes, stopping where it stops, commenting on and critiquing its every move. New Media has managed not to transform but to create the possibility of transforming conventional mass media from the sophisticated propaganda machine into a vast CD-ROM. Picture it: The old buffalo is the text, the bees are the hyperlinks that deconstruct it. Click a bee, get the inside story.

Basically, for the lucky few who have access to the Internet, the mass media has been contextualized and shown up for what it really is—an elaborate boardroom bulletin that reports and analyzes the concerns of powerful people. For the bees it's a phenomenal achievement. For the buffalo, obviously, it's not much fun.

For the bees (the nice, lefty ones) it's a significant victory but by no means a conquest. Because it's still the annoyed buffalo stumbling across the plains, lurching from crisis to crisis, from war to war, who sets the pace. It's still the buffalo that decides which particular crisis will be the main course on the menu and what's for dessert. So here we are today, the buffalo and the bees—on the verge of a war that could redraw the political map of the world and alter the course of history. As the United States gears up to attack Iraq, the US government's lies are being amplified, its reheated doctrine of preemptive strike talked up, its war machine deployed. There is still no sign of Iraq's so-called arsenal of weapons of mass destruction.

Even before the next phase of the war—the American occupation of Iraq—has begun (the war itself is thirteen years old), thanks to the busy bees the extent and scale, the speed and strength of the mobilization against the war has been unprecedented in history. On February 15, 2003, in an extraordinary display of public morality, millions of people took to the streets in hundreds of cities across the world to protest against the invasion of Iraq.[5] If the US government and its allies choose to ignore this and continue with their plans to invade and occupy Iraq, it could bring about a serious predicament in the modern world's understanding of democracy.

But then again, maybe we'll get used to it. Governments have learned to wait out crises—because they know that crises by definition must be short-lived. They know that a crisis-driven media simply cannot afford to hang about in the same place for too long. It must be off for its next appointment with the next crisis. Like business houses need a cash turnover, the media needs a crisis turnover. Whole countries become old news. They cease to exist. And the darkness becomes deeper than it was before the light was shined on them. We saw that in Afghanistan when the Soviets withdrew. We are being given a repeat performance now.

And eventually, when the buffalo stumbles away, the bees go, too.

Crisis reportage in the twenty-first century has evolved into an independent discipline—almost a science. The money, the technology, and the orchestrated mass hysteria that go into crisis reporting have a curious effect. It isolates the crisis, unmoors it from the particularities of the history, the geography, and the culture that produced it. Eventually it floats free like a hot-air balloon, carrying its cargo of international gadflies—specialists, analysts, foreign correspondents, and crisis photographers with their enormous telephoto lenses.

Somewhere mid-journey and without prior notice, the gadflies auto-eject and parachute down to the site of the next crisis, leaving the crestfallen, abandoned balloon drifting aimlessly in the sky, pathetically masquerading as a current event, hoping it will at least make history.

There are few things sadder than a consumed, spent crisis. (For field research, look up Kabul, Afghanistan, AD 2002, and Gujarat, India, AD 2003.)

Crisis reportage has left us with a double-edged legacy. While governments hone the art of crisis management (the art of waiting out a crisis), resistance movements are increasingly being ensnared in a sort of vortex of crisis production. They have to find ways of precipitating crises, of manufacturing them in easily consumable, spectator-friendly formats.

We have entered the era of crisis as a consumer item, crisis as spectacle, as theater. It's not new, but it's evolving, morphing, taking on new aspects. Flying planes into buildings is its most modern, most extreme form.

The disturbing thing nowadays is that Crisis as Spectacle has cut loose from its origins in genuine, long-term civil disobedience and is gradually becoming an instrument of resistance that is more symbolic than real. Also, it has begun to stray into other territory. Right now, it's blurring the lines that separate resistance movements from campaigns by political parties. I'm thinking here of L. K. Advani's Rath Yatra, which eventually led to the demolition of the Babri Masjid, and of the *kar seva* campaign for the construction of the Ram Temple at Ayodhya, which is brought to a boil by the Sangh Parivar each time elections come around.[6]

Both resistance movements and political election campaigns are in search of spectacle—though, of course, the kind of spectacle they choose differs vastly.

On the occasions when symbolic political theater shades into action that actually breaks the law, then it is the response of the State which usually provides the clarity to differentiate between a campaign by a political party and an action by a people's resistance movement. For instance, the police never opened fire on the rampaging mob that demolished the Babri Masjid, or those who participated in the genocidal campaign by the Congress Party against Sikhs in Delhi in 1984, or the Shiv Sena's massacre of Muslims in Bombay in 1993, or the Bajrang Dal's genocide against Muslims in Gujarat in 2002.[7] Neither the police, nor the courts, nor the government has taken serious action against anybody who participated in this violence.

Yet recently the police have repeatedly opened fire on unarmed people, including women and children, who have protested against the violation of their rights to life and livelihood by the government's "development projects."[8]

In this era of crisis reportage, if you don't have a crisis to call your own, you're not in the news. And if you're not in the news, you don't exist. It's as though the virtual world constructed in the media has become more real than the real world.

Every self-respecting people's movement, every "issue," needs to have its own hot-air balloon in the sky advertising its brand and purpose.

For this reason, starvation deaths are more effective advertisements for drought and skewed food distribution than cases of severe malnutrition—which don't quite make the cut. Standing in the rising water of a reservoir for days on end watching your home and belongings float away to protest against a big dam used to be an effective strategy but isn't anymore. People resisting dams are expected to either conjure new tricks or give up the struggle. In the despair created by the Indian Supreme Court's appalling judgment on the Sardar Sarovar dam, senior activists of the Narmada Bachao Andolan (NBA) began once again to talk of *jal samarpan*—drowning themselves in the rising waters.[9] They were mocked for not really meaning what they said.

Crisis as a blood sport.

The Indian state and the mass media have shown themselves to be benignly tolerant of the phenomenon of Resistance as a Symbolic Spectacle. (It actually helps them to hold down the country's reputation as the world's biggest democracy). But whenever civil resistance has shown the slightest signs of metamorphosing from symbolic acts (dharnas, demonstrations, hunger strikes) into anything remotely resembling genuine civil disobedience—blockading villages, occupying forest land—the State has cracked down mercilessly.

In April 2001 the police opened fire on a peaceful meeting of the Adivasi Mukti Sangathan in Mehndi Kheda, Madhya Pradesh. On February 2, 2001, police fired on a peaceful protest of Munda Adivasis in Jharkhand, who were part of the protest against the Koel Karo hydroelectric, killing eight people and wounding twelve. On April 7, 2000, Gujarat police attacked a peaceful demonstration by the Kinara Bachao Sangharsh Samiti (the Save the Coast Action Committee) against the consortium of Natelco and Unocal who were trying to do a survey for a proposed private port.[10] Lieutenant Colonel Pratap Save, one of the main activists, was beaten to death.[11] In Orissa, three Adivasis were killed for protesting a bauxite mining project in December 2000.[12] In Chilika, police fired on fisherfolk demanding the restoration of their fishing rights. Four people were killed.[13]

The instances of repression go on and on—Jambudweep, Kashipur, Maikanj. The most recent, of course, is the incident in the Muthanga in Wyanad, Kerala. In February 2003, four thousand displaced Adivasis, including women and children, occupied a small part of a wildlife sanctuary, demanding that they be given the land the government had promised them the previous year. The deadline had come and gone, and there had been no sign that the government had any intention of keeping its word. As the tension built up over the days, the Kerala police surrounded the protesters and opened fire, killing one person and severely injuring several others.[14]

Interestingly, when it comes to the poor, and in particular Dalit and Adivasi communities, they get killed for encroaching on forest land (Muthanga), as well as when they're trying to protect forest land from dams, mining operations, steel plants (Koel Karo, Nagarnar).[15]

In almost every instance of police firing, the State's strategy is to say the firing was provoked by an act of violence. Those who have been fired upon are immediately called militant (PWG, MCC, ISI, LTTE) agents.[16] In Muthanga, the police and the government claimed that the Adivasis had staged an armed insurrection and attempted to set up a parallel government. The speaker of the Kerala assembly said that they should have been "suppressed or shot."[17]

At the scene of the firing, the police had put together an "ammunition display." It consisted of some stones, a couple of sickles and axes, bows and arrows, and a few kitchen knives. One of the major weapons used in the uprising was a polythene bag full of bees.[18] (Imagine the young man collecting bees in the forest to protect himself and his little family against the Kerala police. What a delightful parallel government his would be!)

According to the State, when victims refuse to be victims, they become terrorists and are dealt with as such. They're either killed or arrested under POTA (Prevention of Terrorism Act). In states like Orissa, Bihar, and Jharkhand, which are rich in mineral resources and therefore vulnerable to ruthless corporations on the hunt, hundreds of villagers, including minors, have been arrested under POTA and are being held in jail without trial. Some states have special police battalions for "anti-development" activity. This is quite apart from the other use that POTA is being put to—terrorizing Muslims, particularly in states like Jammu and Kashmir and Gujarat. The space for genuine nonviolent civil disobedience is atrophying. In the era of corporate globalization, poverty is a crime, and protesting against further impoverishment is terrorism. In the era of the War on Terror, poverty is being slyly conflated with terrorism.

Calling anyone who protests against the violation of their human and constitutional rights a terrorist can end up becoming a self-fulfilling accusation. When every avenue of nonviolent dissent is closed down, should we really be surprised that the forests are filling up with extremists, insurgents, and militants? Vast parts of the country are already more or less beyond the control of the Indian state—Kashmir, the North East, large parts of Madhya Pradesh, Chhattisgarh, and Jharkhand.

It is utterly urgent for resistance movements and those of us who support them to reclaim the space for civil disobedience. To do this we will have to liberate ourselves from being manipulated, perverted, and headed off in the wrong direction by the desire to feed the media's endless appetite for theater. Because that saps energy and imagination.

There are signs that the battle has been joined. At a massive rally on February 27, 2003, the Nimad Malwa Kisan Mazdoor Sangathan (Nimad Malwa Farmers and Workers' Organization), in its protest against the privatization of power, declared that farmers and agricultural workers would not pay their electricity bills.[19] The Madhya Pradesh government has not yet responded. It'll be interesting to see what happens.

We have to find a way of forcing the real issues back into the news. For example, the real issue in the Narmada valley is not whether people will drown themselves or not. The NBA's strategies, its successes and failures, are an issue, but a separate issue from the problem of big dams.

The real issue is that the privatization of essential infrastructure is essentially undemocratic. The real issue is the towering mass of incriminating evidence against big dams. The real issue is the fact that over the last fifty years in India alone big dams have displaced more than 33 million people.[20] The real issue is the fact that big dams are obsolete. They're ecologically destructive, economically unviable, and politically undemocratic. The real issue is the fact that the Supreme Court of India ordered the construction of the Sardar Sarovar dam to proceed even though it is aware that it violates the fundamental rights to life and livelihood of the citizens of India.[21]

Unfortunately, the mass media, through a combination of ignorance and design, has framed the whole argument as one between those who are pro-development and those who are anti-development. It sly-ly suggests that the NBA is anti-electricity and anti-irrigation. And, of course, anti-Gujarat. This is complete nonsense. The NBA believes that big dams are obsolete. They're not just bad for displaced people, they're bad for Gujarat, too. They're too expensive, the water will not go where it's supposed to, and eventually the area that is supposed to "benefit" will pay a heavy price. Like what is happening in the command area of India's favorite dam—the Bhakra Nangal.[22] The NBA believes that there are more local, more democratic, ecologically sustainable, economically viable ways of generating electricity and managing water systems. It is demanding more modernity, not less. More democracy, not less.

After the Supreme Court delivered what is generally considered to be a knockout blow to the most spectacular resistance movement in India, the vultures are back, circling over the kill. The World Bank's new *Water Resources Sector Strategy* clarifies that the World Bank will return to its policy of funding Big Dams.[23] Meanwhile the Indian government, directed by the venerable Supreme Court, has trundled out an ancient, harebrained, Stalinist scheme of linking India's rivers. The order was given based on no real information or research—just on the whim of an aging judge.[24] The river-linking project makes Big Dams look like enlightenment itself. It will become to the development debate what the Ram Mandir in Ayodhya is to the communal debate—a venal campaign gimmick that can be rolled out just before every election. It is destructive even if it is never realized. It will be used to block every other more local, more effective, more democratic irrigation project. It will be used to siphon off enormous sums of public money.

Linking India's rivers would lead to massive social upheavals and ecological devastation. Any modern ecologist who hears about this plan bursts out laughing. Yet leading papers and journals like *India Today* and *Indian Express* carry laudatory pieces full of absurd information.

Coming back to the tyranny of crisis reportage: one way to cut loose is to understand that for most people in the world, peace is war—a daily battle against hunger, thirst, and the violation of their dignity. Wars are often the end result of a flawed peace, a putative peace. And it is the flaws, the systemic flaws in what is normally *considered* to be "peace," that we ought to be writing about. We have to—at least some of us have to—become peace correspondents instead of war correspondents. We have to lose our terror of the mundane. We have to use our skills and imagination and our art to re-create the rhythms of the endless crisis of normality, and in doing so, expose the policies and processes that make ordinary things—food, water, shelter, and dignity—such a distant dream for ordinary people.

Most important of all, we have to turn our skills toward understanding and exposing the instruments of the State. In India, for instance, the institution that is least scrutinized and least accountable takes every major political, cultural, and executive decision today. The Indian Supreme Court is one of the most powerful courts in the world. It decides whether dams should be built or not, whether slums should be cleared, whether industry should be removed from urban areas. It takes decisions on issues like privatization and disinvestment. On the content of school textbooks. It micro-manages our lives. Its orders affect the lives of millions of people. Whether you agree with the Supreme Court's decisions—all of them, some of them, none of them—or not, as an institution the Supreme Court has to be accountable. In a democracy, you have checks and balances, not hierarchies. And yet because of the Contempt of Court law, we cannot criticize the Supreme Court or call it to account. How can you have an undemocratic institution in a democratic society? It will automatically become a floor trap that accumulates authority, that confers supreme powers on itself. And that's exactly what has happened. We live in a judicial dictatorship. And we don't seem to have even begun to realize it.

The only way to make democracy real is to begin a process of constant questioning, permanent provocation, and continuous public conversation between citizens and the State. That conversation is quite different from the conversation between political parties. (Representing the views of rival political parties is what the mass media thinks of as "balanced" reporting.) Patrolling the borders of our liberty is the only way we can guard against the snatching away of our freedoms. All over the world today, freedoms are being curbed in the name of protecting freedom. Once freedoms are surrendered by civil society, they cannot be retrieved without a struggle. It is so much easier to relinquish them than to recover them.

It is important to remember that our freedoms, such as they are, were never given to us by any government; they have been wrested by us.

If we do not use them, if we do not test them from time to time, they atrophy. If we do not guard them constantly, they will be taken away from us. If we do not demand more and more, we will be left with less and less.

Understanding these things and then using them as tools to interrogate what we consider "normalcy" is a way of subverting the tyranny of crisis reportage.

Finally, there's another worrying kind of collateral damage caused by crisis reportage. Crisis reportage flips history over, turns it belly up. It tells stories back to front. So we begin with the news of a crisis and end (if we're lucky) with an account of the events that led to it. For example, we enter the history of Afghanistan through the debris of the World Trade Center in New York, the history of Iraq through Operation Desert Storm. We enter the story of the Adivasi struggle for justice in Kerala through the news of police firing on those who dared to encroach on a wildlife sanctuary. So crisis reportage forces us to view a complex evolving historical process through the distorting prism of a single current event.

Crises polarize people. They hustle us into making uninformed choices: "You're either with us or with the terrorists." "You're either pro-privatization or pro-State." "If you're not pro-Bush, you're pro–Saddam Hussein." "If you're not good, you're evil."

These are spurious choices. They're not the only ones available to us. But in a crisis, we become like goalkeepers in a penalty shootout of a soccer match. We imagine that we have to commit ourselves to one side or another. We have nothing to go on but instinct and social conditioning. And once we're committed, it's hard to realign ourselves. In this process, those who ought to be natural allies become enemies.

For example, when the police fired on the Adivasis who "encroached" on the wildlife sanctuary in Muthanga, Kerala, environmentalists did not come to their defense because they were outraged that the Adivasis had dared to encroach on a wildlife sanctuary. In actual fact the "sanctuary" was a eucalyptus plantation.[25] Years ago, old-growth forest had been clear-felled by the government to plant eucalyptus for the Birla's Grasim Rayon Factory, set up in 1958. A huge mass of incriminating data accuses the factory of devastating the bamboo forests in the region, polluting the Chaliyar River, emitting toxins into the air, and causing a great deal of suffering to a great number of people.[26] In the name of employing three thousand people, it destroyed the livelihood of what has been estimated to be about three hundred thousand bamboo workers, sand miners, and fisherfolk. The state government did nothing to control the pollution or the destruction of forests and rivers. There were no police firing at the owners or managers of Grasim. But then, they had not committed the crime of being poor, being Adivasi, or being on the brink of starvation. When the natural resources (bamboo, eucalyptus, pulp) ran out, the factory closed down. The workers were abandoned.[27]

Crisis reportage elides these facts and forces people to make uninformed choices.

The real crisis—the dispossession, the disempowerment, the daily violation of the democratic rights and the dignity of not thousands but millions of people, which has been set into motion not by accident but by deliberate design—does not fit into the predetermined format of crisis reporting.

Fifteen years ago, the corrupt, centralized Indian state was too grand, too top-heavy, and too far away for its poor to have access to it—to its institutions of education, of health, of water supply, and of electricity. Even its sewage system was inaccessible, too good for most. Today, the project of corporate globalization has increased the distance between those who take the decisions and those who must suffer them even more. For the poor, the uneducated, the displaced and dispossessed, that distance puts justice out of reach.

So the unrelenting daily grind of injustice goes unreported, and the silent, unformatted battle spreads subcutaneously through our society, ushering us toward a future that doesn't bear thinking about.

But we continue sailing on our *Titanic* as it tilts slowly into the darkened sea. The deckhands panic. Those with cheaper tickets have begun to be washed away. But in the banquet halls, the music plays on. The only signs of trouble are slightly slanting waiters, the kabobs and canapés sliding to one side of their silver trays, the somewhat exaggerated sloshing of the wine in the crystal wineglasses. The rich are comforted by the knowledge that the lifeboats on the deck are reserved for club-class passengers. The tragedy is that they are probably right.

19. Instant-Mix Imperial Democracy

(Buy One, Get One Free)

In these times when we have to race to keep abreast of the speed at which our freedoms are being snatched from us, and when few can afford the luxury of retreating from the streets for a while in order to return with an exquisite, fully formed political thesis replete with footnotes and references, what profound gift can I offer you tonight?

As we lurch from crisis to crisis, beamed directly into our brains by satellite TV, we have to think on our feet. On the move. We enter histories through the rubble of war. Ruined cities, parched fields, shrinking forests, and dying rivers are our archives. Craters left by daisy cutters, our libraries.

So what can I offer you tonight? Some uncomfortable thoughts about money, war, empire, racism, and democracy. Some worries that flit around my brain like a family of persistent moths that keep me awake at night.

Some of you will think it bad manners for a person like me, officially entered in the Big Book of Modern Nations as an "Indian citizen," to come here and criticize the US government. Speaking for myself, I'm no flag-waver, no patriot, and am fully aware that venality, brutality, and hypocrisy are imprinted on the leaden soul of every state. But when a country ceases to be merely a country and becomes an empire, then the

Talk first delivered at the Riverside Church, New York City, May 13, 2003.

scale of operations changes dramatically. So may I clarify that tonight I speak as a subject of the American empire? I speak as a slave who presumes to criticize her king.

Since lectures must be called something, mine tonight is called Instant-Mix Imperial Democracy (Buy One, Get One Free).

Way back in 1988, on July 3, the USS *Vincennes*, a missile cruiser stationed in the Persian Gulf, accidentally shot down an Iranian airliner and killed 290 civilian passengers.[1] George Bush the First, who was at the time on his presidential campaign, was asked to comment on the incident. He said quite subtly, "I will never apologize for the United States. I don't care what the facts are."[2]

I don't care what the facts are. What a perfect maxim for the New American Empire. Perhaps a slight variation on the theme would be more apposite: the facts can be whatever we want them to be.

When the United States invaded Iraq, a *New York Times* / CBS News survey estimated that 42 percent of the American public believed that Saddam Hussein was directly responsible for the September 11 attacks on the World Trade Center and the Pentagon.[3] And an ABC News poll said that 55 percent of Americans believed that Saddam Hussein directly supported Al-Qaeda.[4] None of this opinion is based on evidence (because there isn't any). All of it is based on insinuation, auto-suggestion, and outright lies circulated by the US corporate media, otherwise known as the "Free Press," that hollow pillar on which contemporary American democracy rests.

Public support in the United States for the war against Iraq was founded on a multi-tiered edifice of falsehood and deceit, coordinated by the US government and faithfully amplified by the corporate media.

Apart from the invented links between Iraq and Al-Qaeda, we had the manufactured frenzy about Iraq's Weapons of Mass Destruction. George Bush the Lesser went to the extent of saying it would be "suicide" for the United States not to attack Iraq.[5] We once again witnessed the paranoia that a starved, bombed, besieged country was about to annihilate almighty America. (Iraq was only the latest in a succession of countries—earlier there was Cuba, Nicaragua, Libya, Grenada, Panama.) But this time it wasn't just your ordinary brand of friendly neighborhood frenzy. It was frenzy with a purpose. It ushered in an old doctrine in a new bottle: the doctrine of preemptive strike, aka The United States Can Do Whatever the Hell It Wants, And That's Official.

The war against Iraq has been fought and won, and no Weapons of Mass Destruction have been found. Not even a little one. Perhaps they'll have to be planted before they're discovered. And then the more troublesome amongst us will need an explanation for why Saddam Hussein didn't use them when his country was being invaded.

Of course, there'll be no answers. True believers will make do with those fuzzy TV reports about the discovery of a few barrels of banned chemicals in an old shed. There seems to be no consensus yet about whether they're really chemicals, whether they're actually banned, and whether the vessels they're contained in can technically be called barrels. (There were unconfirmed rumors that a teaspoonful of potassium permanganate and an old harmonica were found there, too.)

Meanwhile, in passing, an ancient civilization has been casually decimated by a very recent, casually brutal nation.

Then there are those who say, so what if Iraq had no chemical and nuclear weapons? So what if there is no Al-Qaeda connection? So what if Osama bin Laden hates Saddam Hussein as much as he hates the United States? Bush the Lesser has said Saddam Hussein was a "Homicidal Dictator."[6] And so, the reasoning goes, Iraq needed a "regime change."

Never mind that forty years ago, the CIA, under President John F. Kennedy, orchestrated a regime change in Baghdad. In 1963, after a successful coup, the Ba'ath Party came to power in Iraq. Using lists provided by the CIA, the new Ba'ath regime systematically eliminated hundreds of doctors, teachers, lawyers, and political figures known to be leftists.[7] An entire intellectual community was slaughtered. (The same technique was used to massacre hundreds of thousands of people in Indonesia and East Timor.)[8] The young Saddam Hussein was said to have had a hand in supervising the bloodbath. In 1979, after factional infighting within the Ba'ath Party, Saddam Hussein became the president of Iraq. In April 1980, while Hussein was massacring Shias, US National Security Adviser Zbigniew Brzezinski declared, "We see no fundamental incompatibility of interests between the United States and Iraq."[9] Washington and London overtly and covertly supported Saddam Hussein. They financed him, equipped him, armed him, and provided him with dual-use materials to manufacture weapons of mass destruction.[10] They supported his worst excesses financially, materially, and morally. They supported the eight-year war against Iran and the 1988 gassing of Kurdish people in Halabja, crimes which fourteen years later were reheated and served up as reasons to justify invading Iraq.[11] After the first Gulf War, the "Allies" fomented an uprising of Shias in Basra and then looked away while Saddam Hussein crushed the revolt and slaughtered thousands in an act of vengeful reprisal.[12]

The point is, if Saddam Hussein was evil enough to merit the most elaborate, openly declared assassination attempt in history (the opening move of Operation Shock and Awe), then surely those who supported him ought at least to be tried for war crimes? Why aren't the faces of US and UK government officials on the infamous pack of cards of wanted men and women?

Because when it comes to Empire, facts don't matter.

Yes, but all that's in the past, we're told. Saddam Hussein is a monster who must be stopped now. And only the United States can stop him. It's an effective technique, this use of the urgent morality of the present to obscure the diabolical sins of the past and the malevolent plans for the future. Indonesia, Panama, Nicaragua, Iraq, Afghanistan—the list goes on and on. Right now there are brutal regimes being groomed for the future—Egypt, Saudi Arabia, Turkey, Pakistan, the Central Asian republics.

US Attorney General John Ashcroft recently declared that US freedoms are "not the grant of any government or document, but . . . our endowment from God."[13] (Why bother with the United Nations when God himself is on hand?)

So here we are, the people of the world, confronted with an Empire armed with a mandate from heaven (and, as added insurance, the most formidable arsenal of weapons of mass destruction in history). Here we are, confronted with an Empire that has conferred upon itself the right to go to war at will and the right to deliver people from corrupting ideologies, from religious fundamentalists, dictators, sexism, and poverty, by the age-old, tried-and-tested practice of extermination. Empire is on the move, and Democracy is its sly new war cry. Democracy, home-delivered to your doorstep by daisy cutters. Death is a small price for people to pay for the privilege of sampling this new product: Instant-Mix Imperial Democracy (bring to a boil, add oil, then bomb).

But then perhaps chinks, negroes, dinks, gooks, and wogs don't really qualify as real people. Perhaps our deaths don't qualify as real deaths. Our histories don't qualify as history. They never have.

Speaking of history, in these past months, while the world watched, the US invasion and occupation of Iraq was broadcast on live TV. Like Osama bin Laden and the Taliban in Afghanistan, the regime of Saddam Hussein simply disappeared. This was followed by what analysts called a "power vacuum."[14] Cities that had been under siege, without food, water, or electricity for days, cities that had been bombed relentlessly, people who had been starved and systematically impoverished by the UN sanctions regime for more than a decade, were suddenly left with no semblance of urban administration. A seven-thousand-year-old civilization slid into anarchy. On live TV.

Vandals plundered shops, offices, hotels, and hospitals. American and British soldiers stood by and watched.[15] They said they had no orders to act. In effect, they had orders to kill people but not to protect them. Their priorities were clear. The safety and security of Iraqi people was not their business. The security of whatever little remained of Iraq's infrastructure was not their business. But the security and safety of Iraq's oil fields were. Of course they were. The oil fields were "secured" almost before the invasion began.[16]

On CNN and the BBC the scenes of the rampage were played and replayed. TV commentators, army and government spokespersons, portrayed it as a "liberated people" venting their rage at a despotic regime. US Defense Secretary Donald Rumsfeld said: "It's untidy. . . . Freedom's untidy. And free people are free to make mistakes and commit crimes and do bad things."[17] Did anybody know that Donald Rumsfeld was an anarchist? I wonder—did he hold the same view during the riots in Los Angeles following the beating of Rodney King? Would he care to share his thesis about the Untidiness of Freedom with the 2 million people being held in US prisons right now?[18] (The world's "freest" country has one of the highest numbers of prisoners per capita in the world.)[19] Would he discuss its merits with young African American men, 28 percent of whom will spend some part of their adult lives in jail?[20] Could he explain why he serves under a president who oversaw 152 executions when he was governor of Texas?[21]

Before the war on Iraq began, the Office of Reconstruction and Humanitarian Assistance (ORHA) sent the Pentagon a list of sixteen crucial sites to protect. The National Museum was second on that list.[22] Yet the museum was not just looted, it was desecrated. It was a repository of an ancient cultural heritage. Iraq as we know it today was part of the river valley of Mesopotamia. The civilization that grew along the banks of the Tigris and the Euphrates produced the world's first writing, first calendar, first library, first city, and, yes, the world's first democracy. King Hammurabi of Babylon was the first to codify laws governing the social life of citizens.[23] It was a code in which abandoned women, prostitutes, slaves, and even animals had rights. The Hammurabi Code is acknowledged not just as the birth of legality but the beginning of an understanding of the concept of social justice. The US government could not have chosen a more inappropriate land in which to stage its illegal war and display its grotesque disregard for justice.

At a Pentagon briefing during the days of looting, Secretary Rumsfeld, Prince of Darkness, turned on his media cohorts who had served him so loyally through the war. "The images you are seeing on television, you are seeing over and over and over, and it's the same picture, of some person walking out of some building with a vase. And you see it twenty times. And you think, 'My goodness, were there that many vases? Is it possible that there were that many vases in the whole country?'"[24]

Laughter rippled through the press room. Would it be all right for the poor of Harlem to loot the Metropolitan Museum? Would it be greeted with similar mirth?

The last building on the ORHA list of sixteen sites to be protected was the Ministry of Oil.[25] It was the only one that was given adequate protection.[26] Perhaps the occupying army thought that in Muslim countries lists are read upside down?

Television tells us that Iraq has been "liberated" and that Afghanistan is well on its way to becoming a paradise for women—thanks to Bush and Blair, the twenty-first century's leading feminists. In reality, Iraq's infrastructure has been destroyed. Its people brought to the brink of starvation. Its food stocks depleted. And its cities devastated by a complete administrative breakdown. Iraq is being ushered in the direction of a civil war between Shias and Sunnis. Meanwhile, Afghanistan has lapsed back into the pre-Taliban era of anarchy, and its territory has been carved up into fiefdoms by hostile warlords.[27]

Undaunted by all this, on May 2, 2003, Bush the Lesser launched his 2004 campaign hoping to be finally elected US president. In what probably constitutes the shortest flight in history, a military jet landed on an aircraft carrier, the USS *Abraham Lincoln*, which was so close to shore that, according to the Associated Press, administration officials "acknowledged positioning the massive ship to provide the best TV angle for Bush's speech, with the vast sea as his background instead of the very visible San Diego coastline."[28] President Bush, who never served his term in the military,[29] emerged from the cockpit in fancy dress—a US military bomber jacket, combat boots, flying goggles, helmet. Waving to his cheering troops, he officially proclaimed victory over Iraq. He was careful to say that it was just "one victory in a war on terror ... [which] still goes on."[30]

It was important to avoid making a straightforward victory announcement, because under the Geneva Convention a victorious army is bound by the legal obligations of an occupying force, a responsibility that the Bush administration does not want to burden itself with.[31] Also, closer to the 2004 elections, in order to woo wavering voters, another victory in the "War on Terror" might become necessary. Syria is being fattened for the kill.

It was Hermann Goering, that old Nazi, who said, "People can always be brought to the bidding of the leaders. . . . All you have to do is tell them they're being attacked and denounce the pacifists for a lack of patriotism and exposing the country to danger. It works the same way in any country."[32]

He's right. It's dead easy. That's what the Bush regime banks on. The distinction between election campaigns and war, between democracy and oligarchy, seems to be closing fast.

The only caveat in these campaign wars is that US lives must not be lost. It shakes voter confidence. But the problem of US soldiers being killed in combat has been licked. More or less.

At a media briefing before Operation Shock and Awe was unleashed, General Tommy Franks announced, "This campaign will be like no other in history."[33] Maybe he's right.

I'm no military historian, but when was the last time a war was fought like this?

As soon as the war began, the governments of France, Germany, and Russia, which refused to allow a final resolution legitimizing the war to be passed in the UN Security Council, fell over each other to say how much they wanted the United States to win. President Jacques Chirac offered French airspace to the Anglo-American air force.[34] US military bases in Germany were open for business.[35] German foreign minister Joschka Fischer publicly hoped that Saddam Hussein's regime would "collapse as soon as possible."[36] Vladimir Putin publicly hoped for the same.[37] These are governments that colluded in the enforced disarming of Iraq before their dastardly rush to take the side of those who attacked it. Apart from hoping to share the spoils, they hoped Empire would honor their pre-war oil contracts with Iraq. Only the very naive could expect old Imperialists to behave otherwise.

Leaving aside the cheap thrills and the lofty moral speeches made in the UN during the run-up to the war, eventually, at the moment of crisis, the unity of Western governments—despite the opposition from the majority of their people—was overwhelming.

When the Turkish government temporarily bowed to the views of 90 percent of its population and turned down the US government's offer of billions of dollars of blood money for the use of Turkish soil, it was accused of lacking "democratic credentials."[38] According to a Gallup International poll, in no European country was support for a war carried out "unilaterally by America and its allies" higher than 11 percent.[39] But the governments of England, Italy, Spain, Hungary, and other countries of Eastern Europe were praised for disregarding the views of the majority of their people and supporting the illegal invasion. That, presumably, was fully in keeping with democratic principles. What's it called? New Democracy? (Like Britain's New Labour?)

In stark contrast to the venality displayed by their governments, on February 15, 2003, weeks before the invasion, in the most spectacular display of public morality the world has ever seen, more than 10 million people marched against the war on five continents.[40] Many of you, I'm sure, were among them. They—we—were disregarded with utter disdain. When asked to react to the antiwar demonstrations, President Bush said,

"It's like deciding, well, I'm going to decide policy based upon a focus group. The role of a leader is to decide policy based upon the security, in this case, the security of the people."[41]

Democracy, the modern world's holy cow, is in crisis. And the crisis is a profound one. Every kind of outrage is being committed in the name of democracy. It has become little more than a hollow word, a pretty shell, emptied of all content or meaning. It can be whatever you want it to be. Democracy is the Free World's whore, willing to dress up, dress down, willing to satisfy a whole range of tastes, available to be used and abused at will.

Until quite recently, right up to the 1980s, democracy did seem as though it might actually succeed in delivering a degree of real social justice.

But modern democracies have been around for long enough for neoliberal capitalists to learn how to subvert them. They have mastered the technique of infiltrating the instruments of democracy—the "independent" judiciary, the "free" press, the parliament—and molding them to their purpose. The project of corporate globalization has cracked the code. Free elections, a free press, and an independent judiciary mean little when the free market has reduced them to commodities on sale to the highest bidder.

To fully comprehend the extent to which democracy is under siege, it might be an idea to look at what goes on in some of our contemporary democracies. The world's largest: India (which I have written about at some length and, therefore, will not speak about tonight). The world's most interesting: South Africa. The world's most powerful: the United States of America. And, most instructive of all, the plans that are being made to usher in the world's newest: Iraq.

In South Africa, after three hundred years of brutal domination of the black majority by a white minority through colonialism and apartheid, a nonracial, multi-party democracy came to power in 1994. It was a phenomenal achievement. Within two years of coming to power, the African National Congress had genuflected with no caveats to the Market God. Its massive program of structural adjustment, privatization, and liberalization has only increased the hideous disparities between the rich and the poor. Official unemployment among blacks has increased from 40 percent to 50 percent since the end of apartheid.[42]

The corporatization of basic services—electricity, water, and housing—has meant that 10 million South Africans, almost a quarter of the population, have been disconnected from water and electricity.[43] Two million have been evicted from their homes.

Meanwhile, a small white minority that has been historically privileged by centuries of brutal exploitation is more secure than ever before. They continue to control the land, the farms, the factories, and the abundant natural resources of that country. For them, the transition from apartheid to neoliberalism barely disturbed the grass. It's apartheid with a clean conscience. And it goes by the name of democracy.

Democracy has become Empire's euphemism for neoliberal capitalism.

In countries of the first world, too, the machinery of democracy has been effectively subverted. Politicians, media barons, judges, powerful corporate lobbyists, and government officials are imbricated in an elaborate underhand configuration that completely undermines the lateral arrangement of checks and balances between the constitution, courts of law, parliament, the administration, and, perhaps most important of all, the independent media that form the structural basis of a parliamentary democracy. Increasingly, the imbrication is neither subtle nor elaborate.

Italian Prime Minister Silvio Berlusconi, for instance, has a controlling interest in major Italian newspapers, magazines, television channels, and publishing houses. The *Financial Times* reported that he controls about 90 percent of Italy's TV viewership.[44] Recently, during a trial on bribery charges, while insisting he was the only person who could save Italy from the Left, he said, "How much longer do I have to keep living this life of sacrifices?"[45] That bodes ill for the remaining 10 percent of Italy's TV viewership. What price free speech? Free speech for whom?

In the United States, the arrangement is more complex. Clear Channel Communications is the largest radio station owner in the country. It runs more than twelve hundred channels, which together account for 9 percent of the market.[46] When hundreds of thousands of American citizens took to the streets to protest against the war on Iraq, Clear Channel organized pro-war patriotic "Rallies for America" across the country.[47] It used its radio stations to advertise the events and then sent correspondents to cover them as though they were breaking news. The era of manufacturing consent has given way to the era of manufacturing news.

Soon media newsrooms will drop the pretense and start hiring theater directors instead of journalists.

As America's show business gets more and more violent and warlike, and America's wars get more and more like show business, some interesting crossovers are taking place. The designer who built the $250,000 set in Qatar from which General Tommy Franks stage-managed news coverage of Operation Shock and Awe also built sets for Disney, MGM, and *Good Morning America*.[48]

It is a cruel irony that the United States, which has the most ardent, vociferous defenders of the idea of free speech, and (until recently) the most elaborate legislation to protect it, has so circumscribed the space in which that freedom can be expressed. In a strange, convoluted way, the sound and fury that accompany the legal and conceptual defense of free speech in America serve to mask the process of the rapid erosion of the possibilities of actually exercising that freedom.

The news and entertainment industry in the United States is for the most part controlled by a few major corporations—AOL Time Warner, Disney, Viacom, News Corporation.[49] Each of these corporations owns and controls TV stations, film studios, record companies, and publishing ventures. Effectively, the exits are sealed.

America's media empire is controlled by a tiny coterie of people. Chairman of the Federal Communications Commission Michael Powell, the son of Secretary of State Colin Powell, has proposed even further deregulation of the communications industry, which will lead to even greater consolidation.[50]

So here it is—the world's greatest democracy, led by a man who was not legally elected. America's Supreme Court gifted him his job. What price have American people paid for this spurious presidency?

In the three years of George Bush the Lesser's term, the American economy has lost more than 2 million jobs.[51] Outlandish military expenses, corporate welfare, and tax giveaways to the rich have created a financial crisis for the US educational system. According to a survey by the National Conference of State Legislatures, US states cut $49 billion in public services, health, welfare benefits, and education in 2002. They plan to cut another $25.7 billion this year.[52] That makes a total of $75 billion. Bush's initial budget request to Congress to finance the war in Iraq was $80 billion.[53]

So who's paying for the war? America's poor. Its students, its unemployed, its single mothers, its hospital and home-care patients, its teachers, and its health workers.

And who's actually fighting the war?

Once again, America's poor. The soldiers who are baking in Iraq's desert sun are not the children of the rich. Only one of all the representatives in Congress and the Senate has a child fighting in Iraq.[54] America's "volunteer" army in fact depends on a poverty draft of poor whites, Blacks, Latinos, and Asians looking for a way to earn a living and get an education. Federal statistics show that African Americans make up 21 percent of the total armed forces and 29 percent of the US Army. They account for only 12 percent of the general population.[55] It's ironic, isn't it—the disproportionately high representation of African Americans in the army and prison? Perhaps we should take a positive view and look at this as affirmative action at its most effective. Nearly 4 million Americans (2 percent of the population) have lost the right to vote because of felony convictions.[56] Of that number, 1.4 million are African Americans, which means that 13 percent of all voting-age Black people have been disenfranchised.[57]

For African Americans there's also affirmative action in death. A study by the economist Amartya Sen shows that African Americans as a group have a lower life expectancy than people born in China, in the Indian state of Kerala (where I come from), Sri Lanka, or Costa Rica.[58] Bangladeshi men have a better chance of making it to the age of sixty-five than African American men from here in Harlem.[59]

This year, on what would have been Martin Luther King Jr.'s seventy-fourth birthday, President Bush denounced the University of Michigan's affirmative action program favoring Blacks and Latinos. He called it "divisive," "unfair," and unconstitutional.[60] The successful effort to keep Blacks off the voting rolls in the state of Florida in order that George Bush be elected was of course neither unfair nor unconstitutional. I don't suppose affirmative action for White Boys From Yale ever is.

So we know who's paying for the war. We know who's fighting it. But who will benefit from it? Who is homing in on the reconstruction contracts estimated to be worth up to $100 billion?[61] Could it be America's poor and unemployed and sick? Could it be America's single mothers? Or America's Black and Latino minorities?

Consider this: The Defense Policy Board advises the Pentagon on defense policy. Its members are appointed by the Under Secretary of Defense and approved by Donald Rumsfeld. Its meetings are classified. No information is available for public scrutiny.

The Washington-based Center for Public Integrity found that nine out of the thirty members of the Defense Policy Board are connected to companies that were awarded defense contracts worth $76 billion between the years 2001 and 2002.[62] One of them, Jack Sheehan, a retired Marine Corps general, is a senior vice president at Bechtel, the giant international engineering outfit.[63] Riley Bechtel, the company chairman, is on the President's Export Council.[64] Former Secretary of State George Shultz, who is also on the board of directors of the Bechtel Group, is the chairman of the advisory board of the Committee for the Liberation of Iraq.[65] When asked by the *New York Times* whether he was concerned about the appearance of a conflict of interest, he said, "I don't know that Bechtel would particularly benefit from it. But if there's work to be done, Bechtel is the type of company that could do it."[66]

Bechtel has been awarded a $680 million reconstruction contract in Iraq.[67] According to the Center for Responsive Politics, Bechtel contributed $1.3 million toward the 1999–2000 Republican campaign.[68]

Arcing across this subterfuge, dwarfing it by the sheer magnitude of its malevolence, is America's anti-terrorism legislation. The USA Patriot Act, passed on October 12, 2001, has become the blueprint for similar anti-terrorism bills in countries across the world. It was passed in the US House of Representatives by a majority vote of 337–79. According to the *New York Times*, "Many lawmakers said it had been impossible to truly debate, or even read, the legislation."[69]

The Patriot Act ushers in an era of systemic automated surveillance. It gives the government the authority to monitor phones and computers and spy on people in ways that would have seemed completely unacceptable a few years ago.[70] It gives the FBI the power to seize all of the circulation, purchasing, and other records of library users and bookstore customers on the suspicion that they are part of a terrorist network.[71] It blurs the boundaries between speech and criminal activity, creating the space to construe acts of civil disobedience as violating the law.

Already hundreds of people are being held indefinitely as "unlawful combatants."[72] (In India, the number is also in the hundreds.[73] In Israel, five thousand Palestinians are now being detained.[74]) Noncitizens, of course, have no rights at all. They can simply be "disappeared" like the people of Chile under Washington's old ally General Pinochet. More than one thousand people, many of them Muslim or of Middle Eastern origin, have been detained, some without access to legal representatives.[75]

Apart from paying the actual economic costs of war, American people are paying for these wars of "liberation" with their own freedoms. For the ordinary American, the price of New Democracy in other countries is the death of real democracy at home.

Meanwhile, Iraq is being groomed for "liberation." (Or did they mean "liberalization" all along?) The *Wall Street Journal* reports that "the Bush administration has drafted sweeping plans to remake Iraq's economy in the U.S. image."[76]

Iraq's constitution is being redrafted. Its trade laws, tax laws, and intellectual property laws rewritten in order to turn it into an American-style capitalist economy.[77]

The United States Agency for International Development has invited US companies to bid for contracts that range from road building and water systems to textbook distribution and cell-phone networks.[78]

Soon after Bush the Second announced that he wanted American farmers to feed the world, Dan Amstutz, a former senior executive of Cargill, the biggest grain exporter in the world, was put in charge of agricultural reconstruction in Iraq. Kevin Watkin, Oxfam's policy director, said, "Putting Dan Amstutz in charge of agricultural reconstruction in Iraq is like putting Saddam Hussein in the chair of a human rights commission."[79]

The two men who have been shortlisted to run operations for managing Iraqi oil have worked with Shell, BP, and Fluor. Fluor is embroiled in a lawsuit by black South African workers who have accused the company of exploiting and brutalizing them during the apartheid era.[80] Shell, of course, is well known for its devastation of the Ogoni tribal lands in Nigeria.[81]

Tom Brokaw (one of America's best-known TV anchors) was inadvertently succinct about the process. "One of the things we don't want to do," he said, "is to destroy the infrastructure of Iraq because in a few days we're going to own that country."[82]

Now that the ownership deeds are being settled, Iraq is ready for New Democracy.

So, as Lenin used to ask: What Is To Be Done? Well . . . We might as well accept the fact that there is no conventional military force that can successfully challenge the American war machine. Terrorist strikes only give the US government an opportunity that it is eagerly awaiting to further tighten its stranglehold. Within days of an attack you can bet that Patriot II would be passed. To argue against US military aggression by saying that it will increase the possibilities of terrorist strikes is futile. It's like threatening Brer Rabbit that you'll throw him into the bramble bush. Anybody who has read the document called "The Project for the New American Century" can attest to that. The government's suppression of the congressional Joint Inquiry into Intelligence Community Activities before and after the terrorist attacks of September 11, 2001, which found that there was intelligence warning of the strikes that was ignored,[83] also attests to the fact that, for all their posturing, the terrorists and the Bush regime might as well be working as a team. They both hold people responsible for the actions of their governments. They both believe in the doctrine of collective guilt and collective punishment. Their actions benefit each other greatly.

The US government has already displayed in no uncertain terms the range and extent of its capability for paranoid aggression. In human psychology, paranoid aggression is usually an indicator of nervous insecurity. It could be argued that it's no different in the case of the psychology of nations. Empire is paranoid because it has a soft underbelly.

Its homeland may be defended by border patrols and nuclear weapons, but its economy is strung out across the globe. Its economic outposts are exposed and vulnerable.

Yet it would be naive to imagine that we can directly confront Empire. Our strategy must be to isolate Empire's working parts and disable them one by one. No target is too small. No victory too insignificant. We could reverse the idea of the economic sanctions imposed on poor countries by Empire and its Allies. We could impose a regime of Peoples' Sanctions on every corporate house that has been awarded a contract in postwar Iraq, just as activists in this country and around the world targeted institutions of apartheid. Each one of them should be named, exposed, and boycotted. Forced out of business. That could be our response to the Shock and Awe campaign. It would be a great beginning.

Another urgent challenge is to expose the corporate media for the boardroom bulletin that it really is. We need to create a universe of alternative information. We need to support independent media like *Democracy Now*, Alternative Radio, South End Press.

The battle to reclaim democracy is going to be a difficult one. Our freedoms were not granted to us by any governments. They were wrested from them by us. And once we surrender them, the battle to retrieve them is called a revolution. It is a battle that must range across continents and countries. It must not acknowledge national boundaries, but if it is to succeed, it has to begin here. In America. The only institution more powerful than the US government is American civil society. The rest of us are subjects of slave nations. We are by no means powerless, but you have the power of proximity. You have access to the Imperial Palace and the Emperor's chambers. Empire's conquests are being carried out in your name, and you have the right to refuse. You could refuse to fight. Refuse to move those missiles from the warehouse to the dock. Refuse to wave that flag. Refuse the victory parade.

You have a rich tradition of resistance. You need only read Howard Zinn's *A People's History of the United States* to remind yourself of this.[84]

Hundreds of thousands of you have survived the relentless propaganda you have been subjected to, and are actively fighting your own government. In the ultra-patriotic climate that prevails in the United States, that's as brave as any Iraqi or Afghan or Palestinian fighting for his or her homeland.

If you join the battle, not in your hundreds of thousands but in your millions, you will be greeted joyously by the rest of the world. And you will see how beautiful it is to be gentle instead of brutal, safe instead of scared. Befriended instead of isolated. Loved instead of hated.

I hate to disagree with your president. Yours is by no means a great nation. But you could be a great people.

History is giving you the chance. Seize the time.

20. Do Turkeys Enjoy Thanksgiving?

Last January thousands of us from across the world gathered in Porto Alegre in Brazil and declared—reiterated—that "Another World Is Possible." A few thousand miles north, in Washington, George Bush and his aides were thinking the same thing.

Our project was the World Social Forum. Theirs, to further what many call "the Project for the New American Century."[1]

In the great cities of Europe and America, where a few years ago these things would only have been whispered, now people are openly talking about the good side of imperialism and the need for a strong empire to police an unruly world. The new missionaries want order at the cost of justice. Discipline at the cost of dignity. And ascendancy at any price. Occasionally some of us are invited to "debate" the issue on "neutral" platforms provided by the corporate media. Debating imperialism is a bit like debating the pros and cons of rape. What can we say? That we really miss it?

In any case, New Imperialism is already upon us. It's a remodeled, streamlined version of what we once knew. For the first time in history, a single empire with an arsenal of weapons that could obliterate the world in an afternoon has complete, unipolar economic and military hegemony. It uses different weapons to break open different markets. Argentina's

Speech delivered at the World Social Forum, Bombay, India, January 14, 2004.

the model if you want to be the poster child of neoliberal capitalism, Iraq if you're the black sheep.

Poor countries that are geopolitically of strategic value to empire, or have a "market" of any size, or infrastructure that can be privatized, or, god forbid, natural resources of value—oil, gold, diamonds, cobalt, coal—must do as they're told or become military targets. Those with the greatest reserves of natural wealth are most at risk. Unless they surrender their resources willingly to the corporate machine, civil unrest will be fomented, or war will be waged. In this new age of empire, when nothing is as it appears to be, executives of concerned companies are allowed to influence foreign policy decisions.

This brutal blueprint has been used over and over again, across Latin America, Africa, Central and Southeast Asia. It has cost millions of lives. It goes without saying that every war Empire wages becomes a just war. This, in large part, is due to the role of the corporate media. It's important to understand that the corporate media doesn't just support the neoliberal project. It *is* the neoliberal project. This is not a moral position it has chosen to take, it's structural. It's intrinsic to the economics of how the mass media works.

Most nations have adequately hideous family secrets. So it isn't often necessary for the media to lie. It's all in the editing—what's emphasized and what's ignored. Say, for example, India was chosen as the target for a righteous war. The fact that about eighty thousand people have been killed in Kashmir since 1989, most of them Muslim, most of them by Indian security forces (making the average death toll about six thousand a year); the fact that in March of 2003 more than two thousand Muslims were murdered on the streets of Gujarat, that women were gang-raped and children were burned alive and one hundred fifty thousand people were driven from their homes while the police and administration watched, and sometimes actively participated; the fact that no one has been punished for these crimes and the government that oversaw them was reelected—all of this would make perfect headlines in international newspapers in the run-up to war.

Next we know, our cities will be leveled by cruise missiles, our villages fenced in with razor wire, US soldiers will patrol our streets, and Narendra Modi, Pravin Togadia, or any of our popular bigots could, like

Saddam Hussein, be in US custody, having their hair checked for lice and the fillings in their teeth examined on primetime TV.

But as long as our "markets" are open, as long as corporations like Enron, Bechtel, Halliburton, Arthur Andersen are given a free hand, our "democratically elected" leaders can fearlessly blur the lines between democracy, majoritarianism, and fascism.

Our government's craven willingness to abandon India's proud tradition of being non-aligned, its rush to fight its way to the head of the queue of the completely aligned (the fashionable phrase is "natural ally"—India, Israel, and the United States are "natural allies"), has given it the legroom to turn into a repressive regime without compromising its legitimacy.

A government's victims are not only those whom it kills and imprisons. Those who are displaced and dispossessed and sentenced to a lifetime of starvation and deprivation must count among them too. Millions of people have been dispossessed by "development" projects.

In the era of the War Against Terror, poverty is being slyly conflated with terrorism. In the era of corporate globalization, poverty is a crime. Protesting against further impoverishment is terrorism. And now, the Indian Supreme Court says that going on strike is a crime.[2] Criticizing the court of course is a crime, too.[3] They're sealing the exits.

Like Old Imperialism, New Imperialism too relies for its success on a network of agents—corrupt local elites who service empire. We all know the sordid story of Enron in India. The then-Maharashtra government signed a power purchase agreement that gave Enron profits that amounted to 60 percent of India's entire rural development budget. A single American company was guaranteed a profit equivalent to funds for infrastructural development for about 500 million people!

Unlike in the old days, the New Imperialist doesn't need to trudge around the tropics risking malaria or diarrhea or early death. New Imperialism can be conducted on e-mail. The vulgar, hands-on racism of Old Imperialism is outdated. The cornerstone of New Imperialism is New Racism.

The tradition of "turkey pardoning" in the United States is a wonderful allegory for New Racism. Every year since 1947, the National Turkey Federation has presented the US president with a turkey for Thanksgiving. Every year, in a show of ceremonial magnanimity, the president spares that particular bird (and eats another one). After receiving the presidential pardon, the Chosen One is sent to Frying Pan Park in Virginia to live out its natural life. The rest of the fifty million turkeys raised for Thanksgiving are slaughtered and eaten on Thanksgiving Day. ConAgra Foods, the company that has won the Presidential Turkey contract, says it trains the lucky birds to be sociable, to interact with dignitaries, schoolchildren, and the press. (Soon they'll even speak English!)

That's how New Racism in the corporate era works. A few carefully bred turkeys—the local elites of various countries, a community of wealthy immigrants, investment bankers, the occasional Colin Powell or Condoleezza Rice, some singers, some writers (like myself)—are given absolution and a pass to Frying Pan Park. The remaining millions lose their jobs, are evicted from their homes, have their water and electricity connections cut, and die of AIDS. Basically they're for the pot. But the Fortunate Fowls in Frying Pan Park are doing fine. Some of them even work for the IMF and the WTO—so who can accuse those organizations of being anti-turkey? Some serve as board members on the Turkey Choosing Committee—so who can say that turkeys are against Thanksgiving? They participate in it! Who can say the poor are anti–corporate globalization? There's a stampede to get into Frying Pan Park. So what if most perish on the way?

As part of the project of New Racism we also have New Genocide. New Genocide in this new era of economic interdependence can be facilitated by economic sanctions. New Genocide means creating conditions that lead to mass death without actually going out and killing people. Denis Halliday, who was the UN humanitarian coordinator in Iraq between 1997 and 1998 (after which he resigned in disgust), used the term *genocide* to describe the sanctions in Iraq.[4] In Iraq the sanctions outdid Saddam Hussein's best efforts by claiming more than half a million children's lives.[5]

In the new era, apartheid as formal policy is generally considered antiquated and unnecessary. International instruments of trade and finance oversee a complex system of multilateral trade laws and financial agreements that keep the poor in their Bantustans anyway. Its whole purpose is to institutionalize inequity. Why else would it be that the United States taxes a garment made by a Bangladeshi manufacturer twenty times more than it taxes a garment made in the United Kingdom?[6] Why else would it be that countries that grow 90 percent of the world's cocoa bean produce only 5 percent of the world's chocolate? Why else would it be that countries that grow cocoa bean, like the Ivory Coast and Ghana, are taxed out of the market if they try and turn it into chocolate?[7] Why else would it be that rich countries that spend over a billion dollars a day on subsidies to farmers demand that poor countries like India withdraw all agricultural subsidies, including subsidized electricity? Why else would it be that after having been plundered by colonizing regimes for more than half a century, former colonies are steeped in debt to those same regimes and repay them some $382 billion a year?[8]

For all these reasons, the derailing of trade agreements at Cancún was crucial for us.[9] Though our governments try and take the credit, we know that it was the result of years of struggle by many millions of people in many, many countries. What Cancún taught us is that in order to inflict real damage and force radical change, it is vital for local resistance movements to make international alliances. From Cancún we learned the importance of globalizing resistance.

No individual nation can stand up to the project of corporate globalization on its own. Time and again we have seen that when it comes to the neoliberal project, the heroes of our times are suddenly diminished. Extraordinary, charismatic men, giants in the opposition, when they seize power and become heads of state, they become powerless on the global stage. I'm thinking here of President Lula of Brazil. Lula was the hero of the World Social Forum (WSF) last year. This year he's busy implementing IMF guidelines, reducing pension benefits, and purging radicals from the Workers' Party. I'm thinking also of ex-president of South Africa Nelson Mandela. He instituted a program of privatization and structural adjustment, leaving millions of people homeless, jobless, and without water and electricity.

Why does this happen? There's little point in beating our breasts and feeling betrayed. Lula and Mandela are, by any reckoning, magnificent men. But the moment they cross the floor from the opposition into government, they become hostage to a spectrum of threats—most malevolent among them the threat of capital flight, which can destroy any government overnight. To imagine that a leader's personal charisma and a résumé of struggle will dent the corporate cartel is to have no understanding of how capitalism works, or for that matter how power works. Radical change will not be negotiated by governments; it can only be enforced by people.

At the WSF, some of the best minds in the world come together to exchange ideas about what is happening around us. These conversations refine our vision of the kind of world we're fighting for. It is a vital process that must not be undermined. However, if all our energies are diverted into this process at the cost of real political action, then the WSF, which has played such a crucial role in the movement for global justice, runs the risk of becoming an asset to our enemies. What we need to discuss urgently are strategies of resistance. We need to aim at real targets, wage real battles, and inflict real damage. Gandhi's Salt March was not just political theater. When, in a simple act of defiance, thousands of Indians marched to the sea and made their own salt, they broke the salt tax laws. It was a direct strike at the economic underpinning of the British Empire. It was *real*. While our movement has won some important victories, we must not allow nonviolent resistance to atrophy into ineffectual, feel-good political theater. It is a very precious weapon that needs to be constantly honed and reimagined. It cannot be allowed to become a mere spectacle, a photo opportunity for the media.

It was wonderful that on February 15, 2003, in a spectacular display of public morality, 10 million people in five continents marched against the war on Iraq. It was wonderful, but it was not enough. February 15 was a weekend. Nobody had to so much as miss a day of work. Holiday protests don't stop wars. George Bush knows that. The confidence with which he disregarded overwhelming public opinion should be a lesson to us all. Bush believes that Iraq can be occupied and colonized—as Afghanistan has been, as Tibet has been, as Chechnya is being, as East Timor once was and Palestine still is. He thinks that all he has to do is hunker down and wait until a crisis-driven media, having picked this crisis to the bone, drops it, and moves on. Soon the carcass will slip off the best-seller charts and all of us outraged folks will lose interest. Or so he hopes.

This movement of ours needs a major, global victory. It's not good enough to be right. Sometimes, if only in order to test our resolve, it's important to win something. In order to win something, we need to agree on something. That something does not need to be an overarching, preordained ideology into which we force-fit our delightfully factious, argumentative selves. It does not need to be an unquestioning allegiance to one or another form of resistance to the exclusion of everything else. It could be a minimum agenda.

If all of us are indeed against imperialism and against the project of neoliberalism, then let's turn our gaze on Iraq. Iraq is the inevitable culmination of both. Plenty of antiwar activists have retreated in confusion since the capture of Saddam Hussein. Isn't the world better off without Saddam Hussein? they ask timidly.

Let's look this thing in the eye once and for all. To applaud the US Army's capture of Saddam Hussein and therefore, in retrospect, justify its invasion and occupation of Iraq is like deifying Jack the Ripper for disemboweling the Boston Strangler. And that after a quarter-century partnership in which the ripping and strangling was a joint enterprise. It's an in-house quarrel. They're business partners who fell out over a dirty deal. Jack's the CEO.

So if we are against imperialism, shall we agree that we are against the US occupation and that we believe that the United States must withdraw from Iraq and pay reparations to the Iraqi people for the damage that the war has inflicted?

How do we begin to mount our resistance? Let's start with something really small. The issue is not about *supporting* the resistance in Iraq against the occupation or discussing who exactly constitutes the resistance. (Are they old Killer Ba'athists, are they Islamic Fundamentalists?) We have to become the global resistance to the occupation.

Our resistance has to begin with a refusal to accept the legitimacy of the US occupation of Iraq. It means acting to make it materially impossible for Empire to achieve its aims. It means soldiers should refuse to fight, reservists should refuse to serve, workers should refuse to load ships and aircraft with weapons. It certainly means that in countries like India and Pakistan we must block the US government's plans to have Indian and Pakistani soldiers sent to Iraq to clean up after them.

I suggest we choose by some means two of the major corporations that are profiting from the destruction of Iraq. We could then list every project they are involved in. We could locate their offices in every city and every country across the world. We could go after them. We could shut them down. It's a question of bringing our collective wisdom and experience of past struggles to bear on a single target. It's a question of the desire to win.

"The Project for the New American Century" seeks to perpetuate inequity and establish American hegemony at any price, even if it's apocalyptic. The World Social Forum demands justice and survival.

For these reasons, we must consider ourselves at war.

21. Public Power in the Age of Empire

When language has been butchered and bled of meaning, how do we understand "public power"? When freedom means occupation, when democracy means neoliberal capitalism, when reform means repression, when words like *empowerment* and *peacekeeping* make your blood run cold—why, then, *public power* could mean whatever you want it to mean. A biceps building machine, or a Community Power Shower. So, I'll just have to define "public power" as I go along, in my own self-serving sort of way.

In India, the word *public* is now a Hindi word. It means *people*. In Hindi, we have *sarkar* and *public*, the government and the people. Inherent in this use is the underlying assumption that the government is quite separate from "the people." This distinction has to do with the fact that India's freedom struggle, though magnificent, was by no means revolutionary. The Indian elite stepped easily and elegantly into the shoes of the British imperialists. A deeply impoverished, essentially feudal society became a modern, independent nation-state. Even today, fifty-seven years on to the day, the truly vanquished still look upon the government as *mai-baap*, the parent and provider. The somewhat more radical, those who still have fire in their bellies, see it as *chor*, the thief, the snatcher-away of all things.

Public address delivered at the American Sociological Association's 99th Annual Meeting, San Francisco, August 16, 2004.

Either way, for most Indians, *sarkar* is very separate from *public*. However, as you make your way up India's complex social ladder, the distinction between *sarkar* and *public* gets blurred. The Indian elite, like the elite anywhere in the world, finds it hard to separate itself from the State. It sees like the State, thinks like the State, speaks like the State.

In the United States, on the other hand, the blurring of the distinction between *sarkar* and *public* has penetrated far deeper into society. This could be a sign of a robust democracy, but unfortunately, it's a little more complicated and less pretty than that. Among other things, it has to do with the elaborate web of paranoia generated by the US *sarkar* and spun out by the corporate media and Hollywood. Ordinary people in the United States have been manipulated into imagining they are a people under siege whose sole refuge and protector is their government. If it isn't the Communists, it's Al-Qaeda. If it isn't Cuba, it's Nicaragua. As a result, this the most powerful nation in the world—with its unmatchable arsenal of weapons, its history of having waged and sponsored endless wars, and of being the only nation in history to have actually used nuclear bombs—is peopled by a terrified citizenry, jumping at shadows. A people bonded to the state not by social services, or public health care, or employment guarantees, but by fear.

This synthetically manufactured fear is used to gain public sanction for further acts of aggression. And so it goes, building into a spiral of self-fulfilling hysteria, now formally calibrated by the US government's Amazing Technicolored Terror Alerts: fuchsia, turquoise, salmon pink.

To outside observers, this merging of *sarkar* and *public* in the United States sometimes makes it hard to separate the actions of the government from the people. It is this confusion that fuels anti-Americanism in the world. Anti-Americanism is then seized upon and amplified by the US government and its faithful media outlets. You know the routine: "Why do they hate us? They hate our freedoms," et cetera. This enhances the sense of isolation among people in the United States and makes the embrace between *sarkar* and *public* even more intimate. Like Red Riding Hood looking for a cuddle in the wolf's bed.

Two thousand one was not the first year that the US government declared a "war on terrorism." As Noam Chomsky reminds us, the first "war on terrorism" was declared by President Ronald Reagan in the

1980s during the US-sponsored terrorist wars across Central America, the Middle East, and Africa. The Reagan administration called terrorism a "plague spread by depraved opponents of civilization itself." In keeping with this sentiment, in 1987 the United Nations General Assembly proposed a strongly worded condemnation of terrorism. One hundred fifty-three countries voted for it. Only the United States and Israel voted against it. They objected to a passage that referred to "the right to self-determination, freedom, and independence . . . of people forcibly deprived of that right . . . particularly peoples under colonial and racist regimes and foreign occupation." Remember that in 1987, the United States was a staunch ally of apartheid South Africa. The African National Congress and Nelson Mandela were listed as "terrorists." The term *foreign occupation* was taken to mean Israel's occupation of Palestine.

Over the last few years, the "war on terrorism" has mutated into the more generic "war on terror." Using the threat of an external enemy to rally people behind you is a tired old horse that politicians have ridden into power for centuries. But could it be that ordinary people are fed up with that poor old horse and are looking for something different? There's an old Hindi film song that goes *yeh public hai, yeh sab jaanti hai* (the public, she knows it all). Wouldn't it be lovely if the song were right and the politicians wrong?

Before Washington's illegal invasion of Iraq, a Gallup International poll showed that in no European country was the support for a unilateral war higher than 11 percent. On February 15, 2003, weeks before the invasion, more than 10 million people marched against the war on different continents, including North America. And yet the governments of many supposedly democratic countries still went to war.

The question is: Is "democracy" still democratic?

Are democratic governments accountable to the people who elected them? And, critically, is the *public* in democratic countries responsible for the actions of its *sarkar*?

If you think about it, the logic that underlies the war on terrorism and the logic that underlies terrorism are exactly the same. Both make ordinary citizens pay for the actions of their government. Al-Qaeda made the people of the United States pay with their lives for the actions of their government in Palestine, Saudi Arabia, Iraq, and Afghanistan.

The US government has made the people of Afghanistan pay in the thousands for the actions of the Taliban, and the people of Iraq pay in the hundreds of thousands for the actions of Saddam Hussein.

The crucial difference is that nobody really elected Al-Qaeda, the Taliban, or Saddam Hussein. But the president of the United States was elected (well . . . in a manner of speaking).

The prime ministers of Italy, Spain, and the United Kingdom were elected. Could it then be argued that citizens of these countries are more responsible for the actions of their government than Iraqis were for the actions of Saddam Hussein or Afghans for the Taliban?

Whose God decides which is a "just war" and which isn't? George Bush Sr. once said: "I will never apologize for the United States. I don't care what the facts are." When the president of the most powerful country in the world doesn't *need* to care what the facts are, then we can at least be sure we have entered the Age of Empire.

So what does public power mean in the Age of Empire? Does it mean anything at all? Does it actually *exist*?

In these allegedly democratic times, conventional political thought holds that public power is exercised through the ballot. Scores of countries in the world will go to the polls this year. Most (not all) of them will get the governments they vote for. But will they get the governments they want?

In India this year, we voted the Hindu nationalists out of office. But even as we celebrated, we knew that on nuclear bombs, neoliberalism, privatization, censorship, Big Dams—on every major issue other than overt Hindu nationalism—the Congress and the BJP have no major ideological differences. We know that it is the fifty-year legacy of the Congress Party that prepared the ground culturally and politically for the Far Right. It was also the Congress Party that first opened India's markets to corporate globalization. It passed legislation that encouraged the privatization of water and power, the dismantling of the public sector, and the denationalization of public companies. It enforced cutbacks in government spending on education and health, and weakened labor laws that protected workers' rights. The BJP took this process forward with pitiless abandon.

In its election campaign, the Congress Party indicated that it was prepared to rethink some of its earlier economic policies. Millions of India's poorest people came out in strength to vote in the elections. The spectacle of the great Indian democracy was telecast live—the poor farmers, the old and infirm, the veiled women with their beautiful silver jewelry, making quaint journeys to election booths on elephants and camels and bullock carts. Contrary to the predictions of all India's experts and pollsters, Congress won more votes than any other party.

India's communist parties won the largest share of the vote in their history. India's poor had clearly voted against neoliberalism's economic "reforms" and growing fascism. As soon as the votes were counted, the corporate media dispatched them like badly paid extras on a film set. Television channels featured split screens. Half the screen showed the chaos outside the home of Sonia Gandhi, the leader of the Congress Party, as the coalition government was cobbled together. The other half showed frenzied stockbrokers outside the Bombay Stock Exchange, panicking at the thought that the Congress Party might actually honor its promises and implement its electoral mandate. We saw the Sensex stock index move up and down and sideways. The media, whose own publicly listed stocks were plummeting, reported the stock market crash as though Pakistan had launched ICBMs on New Delhi.

Even before the new government was formally sworn in, senior Congress politicians made public statements reassuring investors and the media that privatization of public utilities would continue. Meanwhile the BJP, now in opposition, has cynically, and comically, begun to oppose foreign direct investment and the further opening of Indian markets.

This is the spurious, evolving dialectic of electoral democracy.

As for the Indian poor, once they've provided the votes, they are expected to bugger off home. Policy will be decided despite them.

And what of the US elections? Do US voters have a real choice?

It's true that if John Kerry becomes president, some of the oil tycoons and Christian fundamentalists in the White House will change. Few will be sorry to see the back of Dick Cheney or Donald Rumsfeld or John Ashcroft or an end to their blatant thuggery. But the real concern is that in the new administration their policies will continue. That we will have Bushism without Bush.

Those positions of real power—the bankers, the CEOs—are not vulnerable to the vote (and in any case, they fund both sides).

Unfortunately, US elections have deteriorated into a sort of personality contest, a squabble over who would do a better job of overseeing Empire. John Kerry believes in the idea of Empire as fervently as George Bush does.

The US political system has been carefully crafted to ensure that no one who questions the natural goodness of the military-industrial-corporate structure will be allowed through the portals of power.

Given this, it's no surprise that in this election you have two Yale University graduates, both members of Skull and Bones, the same secret society, both millionaires, both playing at soldier-soldier, both talking up war and arguing almost childishly about who will lead the war on terror more effectively.

Like President Bill Clinton before him, Kerry will continue the expansion of US economic and military penetration into the world. He says he would have voted to authorize Bush to go to war in Iraq even if he had known that Iraq had no weapons of mass destruction. He promises to commit more troops to Iraq. He said recently that he supports Bush's policies toward Israel and Ariel Sharon "completely." He says he'll retain 98 percent of Bush's tax cuts.

So, underneath the shrill exchange of insults, there is almost absolute consensus. It looks as though even if people in the United States vote for Kerry, they'll still get Bush. President John Kerbush or President George Berry.

It's not a real choice. It's an *apparent* choice.

Like choosing a brand of detergent. Whether you buy Ivory Snow or Tide, they're both owned by Procter & Gamble.

This doesn't mean that one takes a position that is without nuance, that the Congress and the BJP, New Labor and the Tories, the Democrats and Republicans are the same. Of course they're not. Neither are Tide and Ivory Snow. Tide has oxyboosting and Ivory Snow is a gentle cleanser.

In India, there is a difference between an overtly fascist party (the BJP) and a party that slyly pits one community against another (Congress) and sows the seeds of communalism that are then so ably harvested by the BJP.

There are differences in the IQs and levels of ruthlessness between this year's US presidential candidates. The anti-war movement in the United States has done a phenomenal job of exposing the lies and venality that led to the invasion of Iraq, despite the propaganda and intimidation it faced. This was a service not just to people here but to the whole world.

But why is it that the Democrats do not even have to pretend to be against the invasion and occupation of Iraq? If the anti-war movement openly campaigns for Kerry, the rest of the world will think that it approves of his policies of "sensitive" imperialism. Is US imperialism preferable if it is supported by the United Nations and European countries? Is it preferable if the UN asks Indian and Pakistani soldiers to do the killing and dying in Iraq instead of US soldiers? Is the only change that Iraqis can hope for that French, German, and Russian companies will share in the spoils of the occupation of their country?

Is this actually better or worse for those of us who live in subject nations? Is it better for the world to have a smarter emperor in power or a stupider one? Is that our only choice?

I'm sorry, I know that these are uncomfortable, even brutal questions, but they must be asked.

The fact is that electoral democracy has become a process of cynical manipulation. It offers us a very reduced political space today. To believe that this space constitutes real choice would be naive.

The crisis in modern democracy is a profound one. Free elections, a free press, and an independent judiciary mean little when the free market has reduced them to commodities available on sale to the highest bidder.

On the global stage, beyond the jurisdiction of sovereign governments, international instruments of trade and finance oversee a complex system of multilateral laws and agreements that have entrenched a system of appropriation that puts colonialism to shame. This system allows the unrestricted entry and exit of massive amounts of speculative capital—hot money—into and out of third world countries, which then effectively dictates their economic policy. Using the threat of capital flight as a lever, international capital insinuates itself deeper and deeper into these economies. Giant transnational corporations are taking control of their essential infrastructure and natural resources, their minerals, their water, their electricity. The World Trade Organization, the World Bank, the International Monetary Fund, and other financial institutions like the Asian Development Bank virtually write economic policy and parliamentary legislation. With a deadly combination of arrogance and ruthlessness, they take their sledgehammers to fragile, interdependent, historically complex societies, and devastate them.

All this goes under the fluttering banner of "reform."

As a consequence of this reform, in Africa, Asia, and Latin America, thousands of small enterprises and industries have closed down, millions of workers and farmers have lost their jobs and land.

Anyone who criticizes this process is mocked for being "anti-reform," anti-progress, anti-development. Somehow a Luddite.

The *Spectator* newspaper in London assures us that "we live in the happiest, healthiest and most peaceful era in human history."

Billions wonder: Who's "we"? Where does he live? What's his Christian name?

Once the economies of third world countries are controlled by the free market, they are enmeshed in an elaborate, carefully calibrated system of economic inequality. For example, Western countries that together spend more than a billion dollars a *day* on subsidies to farmers demand that poor countries withdraw all agricultural subsidies, including subsidized electricity. Then they flood the markets of poor countries with their subsidized agricultural goods and other products with which local producers cannot possibly compete.

Countries that have been plundered by colonizing regimes are steeped in debt to these same powers, and have to repay them at the rate of about $382 *billion* a year. Ergo, the rich get richer and the poor get poorer—not accidentally but by *design*. By *intention*.

To put a vulgar point on all of this—the truth is getting more vulgar by the minute—the combined wealth of the world's billionaires in 2004 (587 "individuals and family units"), according to *Forbes* magazine, is $1.9 trillion. This is more than the gross domestic product of the world's 135 poorest countries combined. The good news is that there are 111 more billionaires this year than there were in 2003. Isn't that fun?

The thing to understand is that modern democracy is safely premised on an almost religious acceptance of the nation-state. But corporate globalization is not. Liquid capital is not. So even though capital needs the coercive powers of the nation-state to put down revolts in the servants' quarters, this setup ensures that no individual nation can oppose corporate globalization on its own.

Time and again we have seen the heroes of our times, giants in opposition, suddenly diminished. President Lula of Brazil was the hero of the World Social Forum in January 2002. Now he's busy implementing IMF guidelines, reducing pension benefits, and purging radicals from the Workers' Party. Lula has a worthy predecessor in the former president of South Africa, Nelson Mandela, who instituted a massive program of privatization and structural adjustment that has left thousands of people homeless, jobless, and without water and electricity. When Harry Oppenheimer died in August 2000, Mandela called him "one of the great South Africans of our time." Oppenheimer was the head of Anglo-American, one of South Africa's largest mining companies, which made its money exploiting cheap Black labor made available by the repressive apartheid regime.

Why does this happen? It is neither true nor useful to dismiss Mandela and Lula as weak or treacherous people. It's important to understand the nature of the beast they were up against. The moment they crossed the floor from the opposition into government, they became hostage to a spectrum of threats—most malevolent among them the threat of capital flight, which can destroy any government overnight. To imagine that a leader's personal charisma and history of struggle will dent the corporate cartel is to have no understanding of how capitalism works, or for that matter, how power works.

Radical change cannot and will not be negotiated by governments; it can only be enforced by people. By the *public*. A public who can link hands *across* national borders.

So when we speak of public power in the age of Empire, I hope it's not presumptuous to assume that the only thing that is worth discussing seriously is the power of a *dissenting* public. A public that *disagrees* with the very concept of Empire. A public that has set itself against incumbent power—international, national, regional, or provincial governments and institutions that support and service Empire.

Of course those of us who live in Empire's subject nations are aware that in the great cities of Europe and the United States, where a few years ago these things would only have been whispered, there is now open talk about the benefits of imperialism and the need for a strong empire to police an unruly world. It wasn't long ago that colonialism also sanctified itself as a "civilizing mission." So we can't give these pundits high marks for originality.

We are aware that New Imperialism is being marketed as a "lesser evil" in a less-than-perfect world. Occasionally some of us are invited to "debate" the merits of imperialism on "neutral" platforms provided by the corporate media. It's like debating slavery. It isn't a subject that deserves the dignity of a debate.

What are the avenues of protest available to people who wish to resist Empire? By *resist* I don't mean only to *express* dissent but to effectively force change.

Empire has a range of calling cards. It uses different weapons to break open different markets. There isn't a country on God's earth that is not caught in the crosshairs of the US cruise missile and the IMF checkbook. Argentina's the model if you want to be the poster boy of neoliberal capitalism, Iraq if you're the black sheep.

For poor people in many countries, Empire does not always appear in the form of cruise missiles and tanks, as it has in Iraq or Afghanistan or Vietnam. It appears in their lives in very local avatars—losing their jobs, being sent unpayable electricity bills, having their water supply cut, being evicted from their homes and uprooted from their land. All this overseen by the repressive machinery of the State, the police, the army, the judiciary. It is a process of relentless impoverishment with which the poor are historically familiar. What Empire does is to further entrench and exacerbate already existing inequalities.

Even until quite recently, it was sometimes difficult for people to see themselves as victims of Empire. But now local struggles have begun to see their role with increasing clarity. However grand it might sound, the fact is, they *are* confronting Empire in their own, very different ways. Differently in Iraq, in South Africa, in India, in Argentina, and differently, for that matter, on the streets of Europe and the United States.

Mass resistance movements, individual activists, journalists, artists, and filmmakers have come together to strip Empire of its sheen. They have connected the dots, turned cash-flow charts and boardroom speeches into real stories about real people and real despair. They have shown how the neoliberal project has cost people their homes, their land, their jobs, their liberty, their dignity. They have made the intangible tangible. The once seemingly incorporeal enemy is now corporeal.

This is a huge victory. It was forged by the coming together of disparate political groups, with a variety of strategies. But they all recognized that the target of their anger, their activism, and their doggedness is the same. This was the beginning of *real* globalization. The globalization of dissent.

Broadly speaking, there are two kinds of mass resistance movements in third world countries today. The landless peoples' movement in Brazil, the anti-dam movement in India, the Zapatistas in Mexico, the Anti-Privatization Forum in South Africa, and hundreds of others are fighting their own sovereign governments, which have become agents of the neoliberal project. Most of these are radical struggles, fighting to change the structure and chosen model of "development" of their own societies.

Then there are those fighting formal and brutal neocolonial occupations in contested territories whose boundaries and fault lines were often arbitrarily drawn last century by the imperialist powers. In Palestine, Tibet, Chechnya, Kashmir, and several states in India's northeast provinces, people are waging struggles for self-determination.

Several of these struggles might have been radical, even revolutionary, when they began, but often the brutality of the repression they face pushes them into conservative, even retrogressive spaces where they use the same violent strategies and the same language of religious and cultural nationalism used by the states they seek to replace.

Many of the foot soldiers in these struggles will find, like those who fought apartheid in South Africa, that once they overcome overt occupation, they will be left with another battle on their hands—a battle against covert economic colonialism.

Meanwhile, the rift between rich and poor is being driven deeper and the battle to control the world's resources intensifies. Economic colonialism through formal military aggression is staging a comeback.

Iraq today is a tragic illustration of this process. An illegal invasion. A brutal occupation in the name of liberation. The rewriting of laws that allow the shameless appropriation of the country's wealth and resources by corporations allied to the occupation, and now the charade of a local "Iraqi government."

For these reasons, it is absurd to condemn the resistance to the US occupation in Iraq as being masterminded by terrorists or insurgents or supporters of Saddam Hussein. After all, if the United States were invaded and occupied, would everybody who fought to liberate it be a terrorist or an insurgent or a Bushite?

The Iraqi resistance is fighting on the frontlines of the battle against Empire. And therefore that battle is our battle.

Like most resistance movements, it combines a motley range of assorted factions. Former Baathists, liberals, Islamists, fed-up collaborationists, communists, etc. Of course, it is riddled with opportunism, local rivalry, demagoguery, and criminality. But if we are only going to support pristine movements, then no resistance will be worthy of our purity.

A whole industry of development experts, academics, and consultants have built an industry on the back of global social movements in which they are not direct participants. Many of these "experts," who earn their livings studying the struggles of the world's poor, are funded by groups like the Ford Foundation, the World Bank, and wealthy universities such Harvard, Stanford, and Cornell. From a safe distance, they offer us their insightful critiques. But the same people who tell us that we can reform the World Bank from within, that we change the IMF by working inside it, would not themselves seek to reform a resistance movement by working within it.

This is not to say that we should never criticize resistance movements. Many of them suffer from a lack of democracy, from the iconization of their "leaders," a lack of transparency, a lack of vision and direction. But most of all they suffer from vilification, repression, and lack of resources.

Before we prescribe how a pristine Iraqi resistance must conduct a secular, feminist, democratic, nonviolent battle, we should shore up our end of the resistance by forcing the US government and its allies to withdraw from Iraq.

The first militant confrontation in the United States between the global justice movement and the neoliberal junta took place famously at the WTO conference in Seattle in December 1999. To many mass movements in developing countries that had long been fighting lonely, isolated battles, Seattle was the first delightful sign that their anger and their vision of another kind of world was shared by people in the imperialist countries.

In January 2001, in Porto Alegre, Brazil, twenty thousand activists, students, filmmakers—some of the best minds in the world—came together to share their experiences and exchange ideas about confronting Empire. That was the birth of the now historic World Social Forum. It was the first formal coming together of an exciting, anarchic, unindoctrinated, energetic, new kind of "public power." The rallying cry of the WSF is "Another World Is Possible." The forum has become a platform where hundreds of conversations, debates, and seminars have helped to hone and refine a vision of what kind of world it should be. By January 2004, when the fourth WSF was held in Mumbai, India, it attracted two hundred thousand delegates. I have never been part of a more electrifying gathering. It was a sign of the Social Forum's success that the mainstream media in India ignored it completely. But now the WSF is threatened by its own success. The safe, open, festive atmosphere of the Forum has allowed politicians and nongovernmental organizations that are imbricated in the political and economic systems that the Forum opposes to participate and make themselves heard.

Another danger is that the WSF, which has played such a vital role in the movement for global justice, runs the risk of becoming an end unto itself. Just organizing it every year consumes the energies of some of the best activists. If *conversations* about resistance replace real civil disobedience, then the WSF could become an asset to those whom it was created to oppose. The Forum must be held and must grow, but we have to find ways to channel our conversations there back into concrete action.

As resistance movements have begun to reach out across national borders and pose a real threat, governments have developed their own strategies of how to deal with them. They range from co-optation to repression.

I'm going to speak about three of the contemporary dangers that confront resistance movements: the difficult meeting point between mass movements and the mass media, the hazards of the NGO-ization of resistance, and the confrontation between resistance movements and increasingly repressive states.

The place in which the mass media meets mass movements is a complicated one.

Governments have learned that a crisis-driven media cannot afford to hang about in the same place for too long. Like a business needs cash turnover, the media need crisis turnover. Whole countries become old news. They cease to exist, and the darkness becomes deeper than before the light was briefly shined on them. We saw it happen in Afghanistan when the Soviets withdrew. And now, after Operation Enduring Freedom put the CIA's Hamid Karzai in place, Afghanistan has been thrown to its warlords once more.

Another CIA operative, Iyad Allawi, has been installed in Iraq, so perhaps it's time for the media to move on from there, too.

While governments hone the art of waiting out crises, resistance movements are increasingly being ensnared in a vortex of crisis production, seeking to find ways of manufacturing them in easily consumable, spectator-friendly formats.

Every self-respecting people's movement, every "issue," is expected to have its own hot air balloon in the sky advertising its brand and purpose.

For this reason, starvation deaths are more effective advertisements for impoverishment than millions of malnourished people, who don't quite make the cut. Dams are not newsworthy until the devastation they wreak makes good television. (And by then, it's too late.)

Standing in the rising water of a reservoir for days on end, watching your home and belongings float away to protest against a big dam, used to be an effective strategy but isn't any more. The media is dead bored of that one. So the hundreds of thousands of people being displaced by dams are expected to either conjure new tricks or give up the struggle.

Resistance as spectacle, as political theater, has a history. Gandhi's Salt March in 1931 to Dandi is among the most exhilarating examples. But the Salt March wasn't theater alone. It was the symbolic part of a larger act of real civil disobedience. When Gandhi and an army of freedom fighters marched to Gujarat's coast and made salt from seawater, thousands of Indians across the country began to make their own salt, openly defying imperial Britain's salt tax laws, which banned local salt production in favor of British salt imports. It was a direct strike at the economic underpinning of the British Empire.

The disturbing thing nowadays is that resistance as spectacle has cut loose from its origins in genuine civil disobedience and is beginning to become more symbolic than real. Colorful demonstrations and weekend marches are vital but alone are not powerful enough to stop wars. Wars will be stopped only when soldiers refuse to fight, when workers refuse to load weapons onto ships and aircraft, when people boycott the economic outposts of Empire that are strung across the globe.

If we want to reclaim the space for civil disobedience, we will have to liberate ourselves from the tyranny of crisis reportage and its fear of the mundane. We have to use our experience, our imagination, and our art to interrogate those instruments of state that ensure that "normality" remains what it is: cruel, unjust, unacceptable. We have to expose the policies and processes that make ordinary things—food, water, shelter, and dignity—such a distant dream for ordinary people. The real preemptive strike is to understand that wars are the end result of a flawed and unjust peace.

As far as mass resistance movements are concerned, the fact is that no amount of media coverage can make up for mass strength on the ground. There is no option, really, to old-fashioned, backbreaking political mobilization. Corporate globalization has increased the distance between those who make decisions and those who have to suffer the effects of those decisions. Forums like the WSF enable local resistance movements to reduce that distance and to link up with their counterparts in rich countries. That alliance is a formidable one. For example, when India's first private dam, the Maheshwar dam, was being built, the Narmada Bachao Andolan (the NBA), the German organization Urgewald, the Berne Declaration in Switzerland, and the International Rivers Network in Berkeley worked together to push a series of international banks and corporations out of the project. This would not have been possible had there not been a rock-solid resistance movement on the ground. The voice of that local movement was amplified by supporters on the global stage, embarrassing investors and forcing them to withdraw.

An infinite number of similar alliances, targeting specific projects and specific corporations, would help to make another world possible.

We should begin with the corporations that did business with Saddam Hussein and now profit from the devastation and occupation of Iraq.

A second hazard facing mass movements is the NGO-ization of resistance. It will be easy to twist what I'm about to say into an indictment of all NGOs. That would be a falsehood. In the murky waters of fake NGOs set up to siphon off grant money or as tax dodges (in states like Bihar, they are given as dowry), of course there are NGOs doing valuable work. But it's important to turn our attention away from the positive work being done by some individual NGOs and consider the NGO phenomenon in a broader political context.

In India, for instance, the funded NGO boom began in the late 1980s and 1990s. It coincided with the opening of India's markets to neoliberalism. At the time, the Indian State, in keeping with the requirements of Structural Adjustment, was withdrawing funding from rural development, agriculture, energy, transport, and public health. As the State abdicated its traditional role, NGOs moved in to work in these very areas. The difference, of course, is that the funds available to them are a minuscule fraction of the actual cut in public spending. Most large, well-funded NGOs are financed and patronized by aid and development agencies, which are in turn funded by Western governments, the World Bank, the UN, and some multinational corporations. Though they may not be the very same agencies, they are certainly part of the same loose political formation that oversees the neoliberal project and demands the slash in government spending in the first place.

Why should these agencies fund NGOs? Could it be just old-fashioned missionary zeal? Guilt? It's a little more than that.

NGOs give the *impression* that they are filling the vacuum created by a retreating state. And they are, but in a materially inconsequential way. Their *real* contribution is that they defuse political anger and dole out as aid or benevolence what people ought to have by right. They alter the public psyche. They turn people into dependent victims and blunt the edges of political resistance. NGOs form a sort of buffer between the *sarkar* and *public*. Between Empire and its subjects. They have become the arbitrators, the interpreters, the facilitators of the discourse. They play out the role of the "reasonable man" in an unfair, unreasonable war.

In the long run, NGOs are accountable to their funders, not to the people they work among. They're what botanists would call an indicator species. It's almost as though the greater the devastation caused by neoliberalism, the greater the outbreak of NGOs. Nothing illustrates this more poignantly than the phenomenon of the US preparing to invade a country and simultaneously readying NGOs to go in and clean up the devastation.

In order to make sure their funding is not jeopardized and that the governments of the countries they work in will allow them to function, NGOs have to present their work—whether it's in a country devastated by war, poverty, or an epidemic of disease—within a shallow framework more or less shorn of a political or historical context. At any rate, an *inconvenient* historical or political context. It's not for nothing that the "NGO perspective" is becoming increasingly respected.

Apolitical (and therefore, actually, extremely political) distress reports from poor countries and war zones eventually make the (dark) people of those (dark) countries seem like pathological victims. *Another malnourished Indian, another starving Ethiopian, another Afghan refugee camp, another maimed Sudanese* . . . in need of the white man's help. They unwittingly reinforce racist stereotypes and reaffirm the achievements, the comforts, and the compassion (the tough love) of Western civilization, minus the guilt of the history of genocide, colonialism, and slavery. They're the secular missionaries of the modern world.

Eventually—on a smaller scale but more insidiously—the capital available to NGOs plays the same role in alternative politics as the speculative capital that flows in and out of the economies of poor countries. It begins to dictate the agenda.

It turns confrontation into negotiation. It depoliticizes resistance. It interferes with local peoples' movements that have traditionally been self-reliant. NGOs have funds that can employ local people who might otherwise be activists in resistance movements but now can feel they are doing some immediate, creative good (and earning a living while they're at it). Charity offers instant gratification to the giver, as well as the receiver, but its side effects can be dangerous. Real political resistance offers no such shortcuts.

The NGO-ization of politics threatens to turn resistance into a well-mannered, reasonable, salaried, 9-to-5 job. With a few perks thrown in.

Real resistance has real consequences. And no salary.

This brings us to a third danger I want to speak about tonight: the deadly nature of the actual confrontation between resistance movements and increasingly repressive states. Between public power and the agents of Empire.

Whenever civil resistance has shown the slightest signs of evolving from symbolic action into anything remotely threatening, the crackdown is merciless. We've seen what happened in the demonstrations in Seattle, in Miami, in Gothenburg, in Genoa.

In the United States, you have the USA Patriot Act, which has become a blueprint for anti-terrorism laws passed by governments around the world. Freedoms are being curbed in the name of protecting freedom. And once we surrender our freedoms, to win them back will take a revolution.

Some governments have vast experience in the business of curbing freedoms and still smelling sweet. The government of India, an old hand at the game, lights the path.

Over the years the Indian government has passed a plethora of laws that allow it to call almost anyone a terrorist, an insurgent, a militant. We have the Armed Forces Special Powers Act, the Public Security Act, the Special Areas Security Act, the Gangster Act, the Terrorist and Disruptive Areas Act (which has formally lapsed, but under which people are still facing trial), and, most recently, POTA (the Prevention of Terrorism Act), the broad-spectrum antibiotic for the disease of dissent.

There are other steps that are being taken, such as court judgments that in effect curtail free speech, the right of government workers to go on strike, the right to life and livelihood. Courts have begun to micro-manage our lives in India. And criticizing the courts is a criminal offense.

But coming back to the counterterrorism initiatives, over the last decade the number of people who have been killed by the police and security forces runs into the tens of thousands. In the state of Andhra Pradesh (the pin-up girl of corporate globalization in India), an average of about two hundred "extremists" are killed in what are called "encounters" every year. The Bombay police boast of how many "gangsters" they have killed in "shootouts." In Kashmir, in a situation that almost amounts to war, an estimated eighty thousand people have been killed since 1989. Thousands have simply "disappeared." In the northeastern provinces, the situation is similar.

In recent years, the Indian police have opened fire on unarmed people at peaceful demonstrations, mostly Dalit and Adivasi. The preferred method is to kill them and then call them terrorists. India is not alone, though. We have seen similar things happen in countries such as Bolivia and Chile. In the era of neoliberalism, poverty is a crime, and protesting against it is more and more being defined as terrorism.

In India, the Prevention of Terrorism Act is often called the *Production* of Terrorism Act. It's a versatile, hold-all law that could apply to anyone from an Al-Qaeda operative to a disgruntled bus conductor. As with all anti-terrorism laws, the genius of POTA is that it can be whatever the government wants. For example, in Tamil Nadu it has been used to imprison and silence critics of the state government. In Jharkhand 3,200 people, mostly poor Adivasis accused of being Maoists, have been named in criminal complaints under POTA. In Gujarat and Mumbai, the act is used almost exclusively against Muslims. After the 2002 state-assisted pogrom in Gujarat, in which an estimated 2,000 Muslims were savagely killed by Hindu mobs and 150,000 driven from their homes, 287 people have been accused under POTA. Of these, 286 are Muslim and *one* is a Sikh.

POTA allows confessions extracted in police custody to be admitted as judicial evidence. In effect, torture tends to replace investigation. The South Asia Human Rights Documentation Center reports that India has the highest number of torture and custodial deaths in the world. Government records show that there were 1,307 deaths in judicial custody in 2002 alone.

A few months ago, I was a member of a peoples' tribunal on POTA. Over a period of two days, we listened to harrowing testimonies of what is happening in our wonderful democracy. It's everything—from people being forced to drink urine, being stripped, humiliated, given electric shocks, burned with cigarette butts, having iron rods put up their anuses, to people being beaten and kicked to death.

The new government has promised to repeal POTA. I'd be surprised if that happens before similar legislation under a different name is put in place.

When every avenue of nonviolent dissent is closed down, and everyone who protests against the violation of their human rights is called a terrorist, should we really be surprised if vast parts of the country are overrun by those who believe in armed struggle and are more or less beyond the control of the State: in Kashmir, the northeastern provinces, large parts of Madhya Pradesh, Chattisgarh, Jharkhand, and Andhra Pradesh? Ordinary people in these regions are trapped between the violence of the militants and the state.

In Kashmir, the Indian army estimates that three to four thousand militants are operating at any given time. To control them, the Indian government deploys about five hundred thousand soldiers. Clearly it isn't just the militants the army seeks to control, but a whole population of humiliated, unhappy people who see the Indian army as an occupation force. The primary purpose of laws like POTA is not to target real terrorists or militants, who are usually simply shot. Anti-terrorism laws are used to intimidate civil society. Inevitably, such repression has the effect of fueling discontent and anger.

The Armed Forces Special Powers Act allows not just officers but even junior commissioned officers and noncommissioned officers of the army to use force and even kill any person on *suspicion* of disturbing public order. It was first imposed on a few districts in the state of Manipur in 1958. Today it applies to virtually all of the northeast and Kashmir. The documentation of instances of torture, disappearances, custodial deaths, rape, and summary execution by security forces is enough to turn your stomach.

In Andhra Pradesh, in India's heartland, the militant Marxist-Leninist Peoples' War Group—which for years has been engaged in a violent armed struggle and has been the principal target of many of the Andhra police's fake "encounters"—held its first public meeting in years on July 28, 2004, in the town of Warangal.

The former Chief Minister of Andhra Pradesh, Chandrababu Naidu, liked to call himself the CEO of the state. In return for his enthusiasm in implementing Structural Adjustment, Andhra Pradesh received millions of dollars of aid from the World Bank and development agencies such as Britain's Department for International Development. As a result of Structural Adjustment, Andhra Pradesh is now best known for two things: the hundreds of suicides by farmers who were steeped in debt and the spreading influence and growing militancy of the Peoples' War Group. During Naidu's term in office, the PWG were not arrested or captured, they were summarily shot.

In response, the PWG campaigned actively, and, let it be said, violently, against Naidu. In May the Congress won the state elections. The Naidu government didn't just lose, it was humiliated in the polls.

When the PWG called a public meeting, it was attended by hundreds of thousands of people. Under POTA, all of them are considered terrorists.

Are they all going to be detained in some Indian equivalent of Guantánamo Bay?

The whole of the northeast and the Kashmir valley is in ferment. What will the government do with these millions of people?

One does not endorse the violence of these militant groups. Neither morally nor strategically. But to condemn it without first denouncing the much greater violence perpetrated by the State would be to deny the people of these regions not just their basic human rights but even the right to a fair hearing. People who have lived in situations of conflict are in no doubt that militancy and armed struggle provokes a massive escalation of violence from the State. But living as they do, in situations of unbearable injustice, can they remain silent forever?

There is no discussion taking place in the world today that is more crucial than the debate about strategies of resistance. And the choice of strategy is not entirely in the hands of the *public*. It is also in the hands of *sarkar*.

After all, when the US invades and occupies Iraq in the way it has done, with such overwhelming military force, can the resistance be expected to be a conventional military one? (Of course, even if it *were* conventional, it would still be called terrorist.) In a strange sense, the US government's arsenal of weapons and unrivaled air and fire power makes terrorism an all-but-inescapable response. What people lack in wealth and power, they will make up for with stealth and strategy.

In the twenty-first century, the connection between corporate globalization, religious fundamentalism, nuclear nationalism, and the pauperization of whole populations is becoming impossible to ignore. The unrest has myriad manifestations: terrorism, armed struggle, nonviolent mass resistance, and common crime.

In this restive, despairing time, if governments do not do all they can to honor nonviolent resistance, then by default they privilege those who turn to violence. No government's condemnation of terrorism is credible if it cannot show itself to be open to change by nonviolent dissent. But instead nonviolent resistance movements are being crushed. Any kind of mass political mobilization or organization is being bought off, broken, or simply ignored.

Meanwhile, governments and the corporate media, and let's not forget the film industry, lavish their time, attention, funds, technology, research, and admiration on war and terrorism. Violence has been deified.

The message this sends is disturbing and dangerous: if you seek to air a public grievance, violence is more effective than nonviolence.

As the rift between the rich and poor grows, as the need to appropriate and control the world's resources to feed the great capitalist machine becomes more urgent, the unrest will only escalate.

For those of us who are on the wrong side of Empire, the humiliation is becoming unbearable.

Each of the Iraqi children killed by the United States was our child. Each of the prisoners tortured in Abu Ghraib was our comrade. Each of their screams was ours. When they were humiliated, we were humiliated.

The US soldiers fighting in Iraq—mostly volunteers in a poverty draft from small towns and poor urban neighborhoods—are victims, just as much as the Iraqis, of the same horrendous process, which asks them to die for a victory that will never be theirs.

The mandarins of the corporate world, the CEOs, the bankers, the politicians, the judges and generals, look down on us from on high and shake their heads sternly. "There's no alternative," they say, and let slip the dogs of war.

Then, from the ruins of Afghanistan, from the rubble of Iraq and Chechnya, from the streets of occupied Palestine and the mountains of Kashmir, from the hills and plains of Colombia and the forests of Andhra Pradesh and Assam, comes the chilling reply: "There's no alternative but terrorism." Terrorism. Armed struggle. Insurgency. Call it what you want.

Terrorism is vicious, ugly, and dehumanizing for its perpetrators as well as its victims. But so is war. You could say that terrorism is the privatization of war. Terrorists are the free marketers of war. They are people who don't believe that the State has a monopoly on the legitimate use of violence.

Human society is journeying to a terrible place.

Of course, there is an alternative to terrorism. It's called justice.

It's time to recognize that no amount of nuclear weapons, or full-spectrum dominance, or daisy cutters, or spurious governing councils and *loya jirgas*, can buy peace at the cost of justice.

The urge for hegemony and preponderance by some will be matched with greater intensity by the longing for dignity and justice by others.

Exactly what form that battle takes, whether it's beautiful or blood-thirsty, depends on us.

Notes

My Seditious Heart: An Unfinished Diary of Nowadays

1. Dr. Gokarakonda Naga Saibaba s/o G. Satayanarayana Murthy v. State of Maharashtra, Criminal Application No. 785 (2015).
2. B. R. Ambedkar, *The Annihilation of Caste*, ed. S. Anand (London: Verso, 2014), 241–42.
3. Mohd Haroon & Ors. v. Union of India & Anr., Writ Petition (Criminal) No. 155 (2013), 2.
4. Sruthisagar Yamunan, "IIT-Madras Derecognises Student Group," *Hindu*, May 28, 2015, http://www.thehindu.com/news/national/tamil-nadu/iitmadras -derecognises-student-group/article7256712.ece.
5. "My Birth Is My Fatal Accident: Full Text of Dalit Student Rohith's Suicide Letter, *Indian Express*, January 19, 2016, http://indianexpress.com/article/india /india-news-india/dalit-student-suicide-full-text-of-suicide-letter-hyderabad/.
6. Dalit Panthers, "Dalit Panthers Manifesto" (Bombay, 1973), quoted in Barbara R. Joshi, ed., *Untouchable!: Voices of the Dalit Liberation Movement* (London: Zed Books, 1986), p. 145. For further discussion, see Roy, "The Doctor and the Saint," in *Annihilation of Caste*, p. 116.
7. "The Case against Afza," *Hindu*, February 10, 2013, http://www.thehindu.com /news/national/the-case-against-afzal/article4397845.ece.
8. Mohammad Ali, "BJP MP Sakshi Maharaj Courts Controversy over JNU Unrest," *Hindu*, February 15, 2016, http://www.thehindu.com/news/national /other-states/bjp-mp-sakshi-maharaj-courts-controversy-over-jnu-unrest /article8237932.ece; Abhinav Malhotra, "Sakshi Maharaj Demands Strict Action against Those behind JNU Incident," February 14, 2016, http://timesofindia. indiatimes.com/city/kanpur/Sakshi-Maharaj-demands-strict-action-against -those-behind-JNU-incident/articleshow/50979831.cms.
9. Samreena Mushtaq, Essar Batool, Natasha Rather, Munaza Rashid, and Ifrah Butt, *Do You Remember Kunan Poshpura? The Story of a Mass Rape* (New Delhi:

Zubaan Books, 2016).

10. "From the Delhi HC Order Granting Bail to Kanhaiya: 'Those Shouting Anti-national Slogans May Not Be Able to Withstand Siachen for an Hour,'" *Indian Express*, March 3, 2016, http://indianexpress.com/article/india/india-news-india/jnu-row-from-the-high-court-order-granting-bail-to-kanhaiya-those-shouting-anti-national-slogans-may-not-be-able-to-withstand-siachen-for-an-hour/.

2. Democracy: Who Is She When She's at Home?

1. Her name has been changed.
2. Violence was directed especially at women. See, for example, the following report by Laxmi Murthy: "A doctor in rural Vadodara said that the wounded who started pouring in from February 28 had injuries of a kind he had never witnessed before even in earlier situations of communal violence. In a grave challenge to the Hippocratic oath, doctors have been threatened for treating Muslim patients, and pressurised to use the blood donated by RSS volunteers only to treat Hindu patients. Sword injuries, mutilated breasts and burns of varying intensity characterised the early days of the massacre. Doctors conducted post-mortems on a number of women who had been gang raped, many of whom had been burnt subsequently. A woman from Kheda district who was gang raped had her head shaved and 'Om' cut into her head with a knife by the rapists. She died after a few days in the hospital. There were other instances of 'Om' engraved with a knife on women's backs and buttocks." From Laxmi Murthy, "In the Name of Honour," CorpWatch India, April 23, 2002.
3. See "Stray Incidents Take Gujarat Toll to 544," *Times of India*, March 5, 2002.
4. Edna Fernandes, "India Pushes Through Anti-terror Law," *Financial Times* (London), March 27, 2002, 11; "Terror Law Gets President's Nod," *Times of India*, April 3, 2002; Scott Baldauf, "As Spring Arrives, Kashmir Braces for Fresh Fighting," *Christian Science Monitor*, April 9, 2002, 7; Howard W. French and Raymond Bonner, "At Tense Time, Pakistan Starts to Test Missiles," *New York Times*, May 25, 2002, A1; Edward Luce, "The Saffron Revolution," *Financial Times* (London), May 4, 2002, 1; Martin Regg Cohn, "India's 'Saffron' Curriculum," *Toronto Star*, April 14, 2002, B4; and Pankaj Mishra, "Holy Lies," *Guardian* (London), April 6, 2002, 24.
5. See Edward Luce, "Battle over Ayodhya Temple Looms," *Financial Times* (London), February 2, 2002, 7.
6. "Gujarat's Tale of Sorrow: 846 Dead," *Economic Times*, April 18, 2002; see also Celia W. Dugger, "Religious Riots Loom over Indian Politics," *New York Times*, July 27, 2002, A1; Edna Fernandes, "Gujarat Violence Backed by State, Says EU Report," *Financial Times* (London), April 30, 2002, 12; and Human Rights Watch, "'We Have No Orders to Save You': State Participation and Complicity in Communal Violence in Gujarat," vol. 14, no. 3(C), April 2002, www.hrw.org/reports/2002/india/ (hereafter HRW Report). See also Human Rights Watch, "India: Gujarat Officials Took Part in Anti-Muslim Violence," press release, New York, April 30, 2002.
7. "A Tainted Election," *Indian Express*, April 17, 2002; Meena Menon, "A Divided

Gujarat Not Ready for Snap Poll," Inter Press Service, July 21, 2002.

8. See HRW Report, 27–31. Dugger, "Religious Riots Loom over Indian Politics," A1; "Women Relive the Horrors of Gujarat," *Hindu*, May 18, 2002; Harbaksh Singh Nanda, "Muslim Survivors Speak in India," United Press International, April 27, 2002; and "Gujarat Carnage: The Aftermath—Impact of Violence on Women," 2002, www.onlinevolunteers.org/gujarat/women/index.htm.

9. HRW Report, 15–16, 31; Justice A. P. Ravani, Submission to the National Human Rights Commission, New Delhi, March 21, 2002, appendix 4. See also Dugger, "Religious Riots Loom over Indian Politics," A1.

10. HRW Report, 31; and "Artists Protest Destruction of Cultural Landmarks," Press Trust of India, April 13, 2002.

11. HRW Report, 7, 45. Rama Lakshmi, "Sectarian Violence Haunts Indian City: Hindu Militants Bar Muslims from Work," *Washington Post*, April 8, 2002, A12.

12. *Communalism Combat* (March–April 2002) recounted Jaffri's final moments: "Ehsan Jaffri is pulled out of his house, brutally treated for 45 minutes, stripped, paraded naked, and asked to say, 'Vande Maataram!' and 'Jai Shri Ram!' He refuses. His fingers are chopped off, he is paraded around in the locality, badly injured. Next, his hands and feet are chopped off. He is then dragged, a fork-like instrument clutching his neck, down the road before being thrown into the fire." See also "50 Killed in Communal Violence in Gujarat, 30 of Them Burnt," Press Trust of India, February 28, 2002.

13. HRW Report, 5. See also Dugger, "Religious Riots Loom over Indian Politics," A1.

14. "ML Launches Frontal Attack on Sangh Parivar," *Times of India*, May 8, 2002.

15. HRW Report, 21–27. See also the remarks of Kamal Mitra Chenoy of Jawaharlal Nehru University, who led an independent fact-finding mission to Gujarat, "Can India End Religious Revenge?" CNN International, "Q&A with Zain Verjee," April 4, 2002.

16. See Tavleen Sigh, "Out of Tune," *India Today*, April 15, 2002, 21. See also Sharad Gupta, "BJP: His Excellency," *India Today*, January 28, 2002, 18.

17. Khozem Merchant, "Gujarat: Vajpayee Visits Scene of Communal Clashes," *Financial Times* (London), April 5, 2002, 10. See also Pushpesh Pant, "Atal at the Helm, or Running on Auto?" *Times of India*, April 8, 2002.

18. See Bharat Desai, "Will Vajpayee See through All the Window Dressing?" *Economic Times*, April 5, 2002.

19. Agence France-Press, "Singapore, India to Explore Closer Economic Ties," April 8, 2002.

20. See "Medha Files Charges against BJP Leaders," *Economic Times*, April 13, 2002.

21. HRW Report, 30. See also Burhan Wazir, "Militants Seek Muslim-Free India," *Observer* (London), July 21, 2002, 20.

22. See Mishra, "Holy Lies," 24.

23. The Home Minister, L. K Advani, made a public statement claiming that the burning of the train was a plot by Pakistan's Inter Services Intelligence (ISI). Months later, the police have not found a shred of evidence to support that claim. The Gujarat government's forensic report says that sixty liters of petrol were poured onto the floor by someone who was inside the carriage. The doors were

locked, possibly from the inside. The burned bodies of the passengers were found in a heap in the middle of the carriage. So far, nobody knows who started the fire. There are theories to suit every political position: It was a Pakistani plot. It was Muslim extremists who managed to get into the train. It was the angry mob. It was a VHP / Bajrang Dal plot staged to set off the horror that followed. No one really knows. See HRW Report, 13–14; Siddharth Srivastava, "No Proof Yet on ISI Link with Sabarmati Attack: Officials," *Times of India*, March 6, 2002; "ISI behind Godhra Killings, Says BJP," *Times of India*, March 18, 2002; Uday Mahurkar, "Gujarat: Fuelling the Fire," *India Today*, July 22, 2002, 38; "Bloodstained Memories," *Indian Express*, April 12, 2002; and Celia W. Dugger, "After Deadly Firestorm, India Officials Ask Why," *New York Times*, March 6, 2002, A3.

24. "Blame It on Newton's Law: Modi," *Times of India*, March 3, 2002. See also Fernandes, "Gujarat Violence Backed by State," 12.

25. "RSS Cautions Muslims," Press Trust of India, March 17, 2002. See also Sanghamitra Chakraborty, "Minority Guide to Good Behaviour," *Times of India*, March 25, 2002.

26. P. R. Ramesh, "Modi Offers to Quit as Gujarat CM," *Economic Times*, April 13, 2002; "Modi Asked to Seek Mandate," *Statesman* (India), April 13, 2002.

27. See M. S. Golwalkar, *We, or Our Nationhood Defined* (Nagpur: Bharat, 1939); Vinayak Damodar Savarkar, *Hindutva* (New Delhi: Bharti Sadan, 1989). See also "Saffron Is Thicker Than . . . ," editorial, *Hindu*, October 22, 2000; David Gardner, "Hindu Revivalists Raise the Question of Who Governs India," *Financial Times* (London), July 13, 2000, 12.

28. See Arundhati Roy, *Power Politics*, 2nd ed. (Cambridge, MA: South End Press, 2001), 57 and notes (p. 159).

29. See Noam Chomsky, "Militarizing Space 'to Protect U.S. Interests and Investment,'" *International Socialist Review* 19 (July–August 2001), www.isreview.org/issues/19/NoamChomsky.shtml.

30. Pankaj Mishra, "A Mediocre Goddess," *New Statesman*, April 9, 2001, a review of Katherine Frank, *Indira: A Life of Indira Nehru Gandhi* (London: HarperCollins, 2001).

31. William Claiborne, "Gandhi Urges Indians to Strengthen Union," *Washington Post*, November 20, 1984, A9. See also Tavleen Singh, "Yesterday, Today, Tomorrow," *India Today*, March 30, 1998, 24.

32. HRW Report, 39–44.

33. President George W. Bush, "September 11, 2001, Terrorist Attacks on the United States," address to Joint Session of Congress, Federal News Service, September 20, 2001.

34. John Pilger, "Pakistan and India on Brink," *Mirror* (London), May 27, 2002, 4.

35. Alison Leigh Cowan, Kurt Eichenwald, and Michael Moss, "Bin Laden Family, with Deep Western Ties, Strives to Re-establish a Name," *New York Times*, October 28, 2001, 1, 9.

36. Sanjeev Miglani, "Opposition Keeps Up Heat on Government over Riots," Reuters, April 16, 2002.

37. "Either Govern or Just Go," *Indian Express*, April 1, 2002. Parekh is CEO of

HDFC, the Housing Development Finance Corporation Limited.

38.   "It's War in Drawing Rooms," *Indian Express*, May 19, 2002.

39.   Ranjit Devraj, "Pro-Hindu Ruling Party Back to Hardline Politics," Inter Press Service, July 1, 2002; "An Unholy Alliance," *Indian Express*, May 6, 2002.

40.   Nilanjana Bhaduri Jha, "Congress [Party] Begins Oust-Modi Campaign," *Economic Times*, April 12, 2002.

41.   Richard Benedetto, "Confidence in War on Terror Wanes," *USA Today*, June 25, 2002, 19A; David Lamb, "Israel's Invasions, 20 Years Apart, Look Eerily Alike," *Los Angeles Times*, April 20, 2002, A5.

42.   See "The End of Imagination," above.

43.   "I would say it is a weapon of peace guarantee, a peace guarantor," said Abdul Qadeer Khan of Pakistan's nuclear bomb. See Imtiaz Gul, "Father of Pakistani Bomb Says Nuclear Weapons Guarantee Peace," Deutsche Presse-Agentur, May 29, 1998. See also Raj Chengappa, *Weapons of Peace: The Secret Story of India's Quest to Be a Nuclear Power* (New Delhi: HarperCollins, 2000).

44.   The 1999 Kargil War between India and Pakistan claimed hundreds of lives. See Edward Luce, "Fernandes Hit by India's Coffin Scandal," *Financial Times* (London), December 13, 2001, 12.

45.   See "Arrested Growth," *Times of India*, February 2, 2000.

46.   Dugger, "Religious Riots Loom over Indian Politics," A1.

47.   Edna Fernandes, "EU Tells India of Concern over Violence in Gujarat," *Financial Times* (London), May 3, 2002, 12; Alex Spillius, "'Please Don't Say This Was a Riot. It Was Genocide, Pure and Simple,'" *Daily Telegraph* (London), June 18, 2002, 13.

48.   "Gujarat is an internal matter and the situation is under control," said Jaswant Singh, India's foreign affairs minister. See Shishir Gupta, "The Foreign Hand," *India Today*, May 6, 2002, 42 and sidebar.

49.   "Laloo Wants Use of POTA [Prevention of Terrorism Act] against VHP, RSS," *Times of India*, March 7, 2002.

3. When the Saints Go Marching Out: The Strange Fate of Martin, Mohandas, and Mandela

1.   See "Democracy: Who Is She When She's at Home?" in *War Talk*, 65–79, above.

2.   "Cong[ress Party] Ploy Fails, Modi Steals the Show in Pain," *Indian Express*, August 16, 2003.

3.   Agence France-Presse, "Indian Activists Urge Mandela to Snub Gujarat Government Invite," August 4, 2003; "Guj[arat]–Mandela," Press Trust of India, August 5, 2003; and "Battle for Gujarat's Image Now on Foreign Soil," *Times of India*, August 7, 2003.

4.   Agence France-Presse, "Relax, Mandela Isn't Coming, He's Working on a Book," August 5, 2003.

5.   Michael Dynes, "Mbeki Can Seize White Farms under New Law," *Times* (London), January 31, 2004, 26.

6.   Ibid.

7. Patrick Laurence, "South Africa Fights to Put the Past to Rest," *Irish Times*, December 28, 2000, 57.
8. Anthony Stoppard, "South Africa: Water, Electricity Cutoffs Affect 10 Million," Inter Press Service, March 21, 2002.
9. Henri E. Cauvin, "Hunger in Southern Africa Imperils Lives of Millions," *New York Times*, April 26, 2002, A8; James Lamont, "Nobody Says 'No' to Mandela," *Financial Times* (London), December 10, 2002, 4; and Patrick Laurence, "South Africans Sceptical of Official Data," *Irish Times*, June 6, 2003, 30.
10. See Ashwin Desai, *We Are the Poors: Community Struggles in Post-Apartheid South Africa* (New York: Monthly Review Press, 2002).
11. South African Press Association, "Gauteng Municipalities to Target Service Defaulters," May 4, 1999; Alison Maitland, "Combining to Harness the Power of Private Enterprise," *Financial Times* (London), August 23, 2002, survey: "Sustainable Business," 2.
12. Nicol Degli Innocenti and John Reed, "SA Govt Opposes Reparations Lawsuit," *Financial Times* (London), May 19, 2003, 15.
13. South African Press Association, "SAfrica Asks US Court to Dismiss Apartheid Reparations Cases," BBC Worldwide Monitoring, July 30, 2003.
14. Martin Luther King, Jr., *A Testament of Hope: The Essential Writings and Speeches of Martin Luther King, Jr.*, ed. James M. Washington (New York: HarperCollins, 1991), 233.
15. Ibid., 233.
16. "Men of Vietnam," *New York Times*, April 9, 1967, Week in Review, 2E. Quoted in Mike Marqusee, *Redemption Song: Muhammad Ali and the Spirit of the Sixties* (New York: Verso, 1999), 217.
17. King, *Testament of Hope*, 245.
18. David M. Halbfinger and Steven A. Holmes, "Military Mirrors a Working-Class America," *New York Times*, March 30, 2003, A1; Darryl Fears, "Draft Bill Stirs Debate over the Military, Race and Equity," *Washington Post*, February 4, 2003, A3.
19. David Cole, "Denying Felons Vote Hurts Them, Society," *USA Today*, February 3, 2000, 17A; "From Prison to the Polls," editorial, *Christian Science Monitor*, May 24, 2001, 10.
20. King, *Testament of Hope*, 239.
21. Quoted in Marqusee, *Redemption Song*, 218.
22. King, *Testament of Hope*, 250.
23. Marqusee, *Redemption Song*, 1–4, 292.

4. In Memory of Shankar Guha Niyogi

1. Human Rights Watch, "India: Human Rights Developments," *Human Rights Watch World Report 1993*, www.hrw.org/reports/1993/WR93/Asw-06.htm.

5. How Deep Shall We Dig?

1. Hina Kausar Alam and P. Balu, "J&K [Jammu and Kashmir] Fudges DNA Samples to Cover Up Killings," *Times of India*, March 7, 2002.

2. See "Democracy: Who Is She When She's at Home?" 65–79, above.

3. Somit Sen, "Shooting Turns Spotlight on Encounter Cops," *Times of India*, August 23, 2003.

4. W. Chandrakanth, "Crackdown on Civil Liberties Activists in the Offing?" *Hindu*, October 4, 2003: "Several activists have gone underground fearing police reprisals. Their fears are not unfounded, as the State police have been staging encounters at will. While the police frequently release the statistics on naxalite violence, they avoid mentioning the victims of their own violence. The Andhra Pradesh Civil Liberties Committee (APCLC), which is keeping track of the police killings, has listed more than 4,000 deaths, 2,000 of them in the last eight years alone." See also K. T. Sangameswaran, "Rights Activists Allege Ganglord-Cop Nexus," *Hindu*, October 22, 2003.

5. David Rohde, "India and Kashmir Separatists Begin Talks on Ending Strife," *New York Times*, January 23, 2004, A8; Deutsche Presse-Agentur, "Thousands Missing, Unmarked Graves Tell Kashmir Story," October 7, 2003.

6. Unpublished reports from the Association of Parents of Disappeared People (APDP), Srinagar.

7. See also Edward Luce, "Kashmir's New Leader Promises 'Healing Touch,'" *Financial Times* (London), October 28, 2002, 12.

8. Ray Marcelo, "Anti-terrorism Law Backed by India's Supreme Court," *Financial Times* (London), December 17, 2003, 2.

9. People's Union for Civil Liberties, "In Jharkhand All the Laws of the Land Are Replaced by POTA," Delhi, India, May 2, 2003, www.pucl.org/Topics/Law/2003/poto-jharkhand.htm.

10. "People's Tribunal Highlights Misuse of POTA," *Hindu*, March 18, 2004.

11. "People's Tribunal." See also "Human Rights Watch Ask Centre to Repeal POTA," Press Trust of India, September 8, 2002.

12. Leena Misra, "240 POTA Cases, All against Minorities," *Times of India*, September 15, 2003; "People's Tribunal." The *Times of India* misreported the testimony presented. As the Press Trust of India article notes, in Gujarat "the only non Muslim in the list is a Sikh, Liversingh Tej Singh Sikligar, who figured in it for an attempt on the life of Surat lawyer Hasmukh Lalwala, and allegedly hung himself in a police lock-up in Surat in April [2003]." On Gujarat, see "Democracy: Who Is She," above.

13. "A Pro-Police Report," *Hindu*, March 20, 2004; Amnesty International, "India: Report of the Malimath Committee on Reforms of the Criminal Justice System: Some Comments," September 19, 2003 (ASA 20/025/2003).

14. "J&K [Jammu and Kashmir] Panel Wants Draconian Laws Withdrawn," *Hindu*, March 23, 2003. See also South Asian Human Rights Documentation Center, "Armed Forces Special Powers Act: A Study in National Security Tyranny," November 1995.

15. "Growth of a Demon: Genesis of the Armed Forces (Special Powers) Act, 1958" and related documents in *Manipur Update*, December 1999.

16. On the lack of any convictions for the massacres in Gujarat, see Edward Luce, "Master of Ambiguity," *Financial Times* (London), April 3–4, 2004, 16. On the March 31, 1997, murder of Chandrashekhar Prasad, see Andrew Nash, "An

Election at JNU," *Himāl*, December 2003. For more information on the additional crimes listed here, see 313–15, above.

17. N. A. Mujumdar, "Eliminate Hunger Now, Poverty Later," *Business Line*, January 8, 2003.

18. "Foodgrain Exports May Slow Down This Fiscal [Year]," *India Business Insight*, June 2, 2003; "India—Agriculture Sector: Paradox of Plenty," *Business Line*, June 26, 2001; and Ranjit Devraj, "Farmers Protest against Globalization," Inter Press Service, January 25, 2001.

19. Utsa Patnaik, "Falling Per Capita Availability of Foodgrains for Human Consumption in the Reform Period in India," *Akhbar* 2 (October 2001); P. Sainath, "Have Tornado, Will Travel," *Hindu Magazine*, August 18, 2002; Sylvia Nasar, "Profile: The Conscience of the Dismal Science," *New York Times*, January 9, 1994, 8; and Maria Misra, "Heart of Smugness: Unlike Belgium, Britain Is Still Complacently Ignoring the Gory Cruelties of Its Empire," *Guardian* (London), July 23, 2002, 15. See also Utsa Patnaik, "On Measuring 'Famine' Deaths: Different Criteria for Socialism and Capitalism?" *Akhbar* 6 (November–December 1999), www.indowindow.com/akhbar/article.php?article=74&category=8&issue=9.

20. Amartya Sen, *Development as Freedom* (New York: Alfred A. Knopf, 1999).

21. "The Wasted India," *Statesman* (India), February 17, 2001; "Child-Blain," *Statesman* (India), November 24, 2001.

22. Utsa Patnaik, "The Republic of Hunger," lecture, Jawaharlal Nehru University, New Delhi, April 10, 2004, macroscan.com/fet/apr04/fet210404Republic _Hunger.htm.

23. Praful Bidwai, "India amidst Serious Agrarian Crisis," *Central Chronicle* (Bhopal), April 9, 2004.

24. See "Power Politics," 151–76, above.

25. See Mike Davis, *Late Victorian Holocausts: El Niño Famines and the Making of the Third World* (New York: Verso, 2002).

26. Among other sources, see Edwin Black, *IBM and the Holocaust: The Strategic Alliance between Nazi Germany and America's Most Powerful Corporation* (New York: Three Rivers, 2003).

27. "For India Inc., Silence Protects the Bottom Line," *Times of India*, February 17, 2003; "CII Apologises to Modi," *Hindu*, March 7, 2003.

28. In May 2004, the right-wing BJP-led coalition was not just voted out of power, it was humiliated by the Indian electorate. None of the political pundits had predicted this decisive vote against communalism and neoliberalism's economic "reforms." Yet even as we celebrate, we know that on every major issue other than overt Hindu nationalism—nuclear bombs, Big Dams, privatization—the newly elected Congress Party and the BJP have no major ideological differences. We know that it was the legacy of the Congress that led us to the horror of the BJP. Still we celebrated, because surely a darkness has passed. Or has it? Even before it formed a government, the Congress made overt reassurances that "reforms" would continue. Exactly what kind of reforms, we'll have to wait and see. Fortunately the Congress will be hobbled by the fact that it needs the support of left parties—the only parties to be overtly (if ineffectively) critical of the reforms—to

make up a majority in order to form a government. The Left parties have been given an unprecedented mandate. Hopefully, things will change. A little. It's been a pretty hellish six years.

29. India was the only country to abstain on December 22, 2003, from UN General Assembly Resolution, "Protection of Human Rights and Fundamental Freedoms While Countering Terrorism," A/RES/58/187, http://www.un.org/en/ga/search/view_doc.asp?symbol=A/RES/58/187&Area=UNDOC. Quoted in Amnesty International India, "Security Legislation and State Accountability: A Presentation for the POTA People's Hearing, March 13–14, New Delhi."

6. The Greater Common Good

1. Jawaharlal Nehru, *Modern Temples of India: Selected Speeches of Jawaharlal Nehru at Irrigation and Power Projects*, ed. C. V. J. Sharma (Delhi: Central Board of Irrigation and Power, 1989), 40–49.

2. Patrick McCully, *Silenced Rivers: The Ecology and Politics of Large Dams* (Hyderabad: Orient Longman, 1998), 80.

3. From (uncut) film footage of Bargi dam oustees, Anurag Singh and Jharana Jhaveri, Jan Madhyam, New Delhi, 1995.

4. J. Nehru, *Modern Temples*, 52–56. In a speech given before the Twenty-Ninth Annual Meeting of the Central Board of Irrigation and Power (November 17, 1958) Nehru said, "For some time past, however, I have been beginning to think that we are suffering from what we may call 'the disease of gigantism.' We want to show that we can build big dams and do big things. This is a dangerous outlook developing in India . . . the idea of big—having big undertakings and doing big things for the sake of showing that we can do big things—is not a good outlook at all." And "it is . . . the small irrigation projects, the small industries and the small plants for electric power, which will change the face of the country far more than half a dozen big projects in half a dozen places."

5. Centre for Science and Environment, *Dying Wisdom: Rise, Fall and Potential of India's Traditional Water Harvesting Systems* (New Delhi: CSE, 1997), 399; Madhav Gadgil and Ramachandra Guha, *Ecology and Equity* (New Delhi: Penguin India, 1995), 39.

6. Indian Water Resources Society, *Five Decades of Water, Resources Development in India* (1998), 7.

7. World Resource Institute, *World Resources 1998–99* (Oxford: Oxford University Press, 1998), 251.

8. McCully, *Silenced Rivers*, 26–29. See also *The Ecologist Asia* 6, no. 5 (September–October 1998): 50–51 for excerpts of speech by Bruce Babbitt, US interior secretary, in August 1998.

9. Besides McCully, *Silenced Rivers*, see the CSE's *State of India's Environment*, 1999, 1985, and 1982; Nicholas Hildyard and Edward Goldsmith, 1984, *The Social and Environmental Impacts of Large Dams* (Cornwall, UK: Wadebridge Ecological Centre, 1984); Satyajit Singh, *Taming the Waters: The Political Economy of Large Dams* (New Delhi: Oxford University Press, 1997); World Bank, *India:*

Irrigation Sector Review (1991); and Anthony H. J. Dorcey, ed., *Large Dams: Learning from the Past, Looking to the Future* (1997).

10. Mihir Shah, Debashis Banerji, P. S. Vijayshankar, and Pramathesh Ambasta, *India's Drylands: Tribal Societies and Development through Environmental Regeneration* (New Delhi: Oxford University Press, 1998), 51–103.

11. Ann Danaiya Usher, *Dams as Aid: A Political Anatomy of Nordic Development Thinking* (London: Routledge, 1997).

12. $1 US = Rs 43.35. A crore is 10 million. Equal to Rs 2,200,000 crore, at constant 1996–97 prices.

13. D. K. Mishra and R. Rangachari, *The Embankment Trap and Some Disturbing Questions*, Seminar 478 (June 1999), 46–48 and 62–63, respectively; CSE, *Floods, Floodplains and Environmental Myths*.

14. Shah et al., *India's Drylands*, 51–103.

15. Singh, *Taming the Waters*, 188–90; also, government of India (GOI) figures for actual displacement.

16. At a January 21, 1999, meeting in New Delhi organized by the Union Ministry of Rural Areas and Employment, for discussions on the draft National Resettlement and Rehabilitation Policy and the amendment to the draft Land Acquisition Act.

17. Bradford Morse and Thomas Berger, *Sardar Sarovar: The Report of the Independent Review* (Ottawa: Resource Futures International [RFI], 1992), 62.

18. GOI, *28th and 29th Report of the Commissioner for Scheduled Castes and Scheduled Tribes* [New Delhi, 1988–89].

19. *Indian Express* (New Delhi), April 10, 1999, front page.

20. GOI, *Ninth Five Year Plan, 1997–2002* (1999), 2:437.

21. Siddharth Dube, *Words like Freedom* (New Delhi: Harper Collins, 1998); Centre for Monitoring the Indian Economy, 1996. See also *World Bank Poverty Update*, quoted in *Business Line*, June 4, 1999.

22. National Human Rights Commission, *Report of the Visit of the Official Team of the NHRC to the Scarcity Affected Areas of Orissa*, December 1996.

23. GOI, *Award of the Narmada Water Disputes Tribunal*, 1978–79.

24. GOI, *Report of the FMG-2 on SSP* (1995); also see various affidavits of the goverment of India and government of Madhya Pradesh before the Supreme Court of India, 1994–98.

25. Central Water Commission, *Monthly Observed Flows of the Narmada at Garudeshwar* (New Delhi: Hydrology Studies Organisation, Central Water Commission, 1992).

26. Written Submission on Behalf of Union of India, February 1999, p. 7, clause 1.7.

27. *Tigerlink News* 5, no. 2 (June 1999): 28.

28. *World Bank Annual Reports*, 1993–98.

29. McCully, *Silenced Rivers*, 274.

30. Ibid., 21. The World Bank started funding dams in China in 1984. Since then it has lent around $3.4 billion (not adjusted for inflation) to finance thirteen Big Dams that will cause the displacement of 360,000 people. The centerpiece of the World Bank's dam financing in China is the Xiaolangdi dam on the Yellow River, which will singlehandedly displace 181,000 people.

31. Ibid., 278.

32. J. Vidal and N. Cumming-Bruce, "The Curse of Pergau," *Economist,* March 5, 1994; "Dam Price Jumped 81 Million Pounds Days after Deal," *Guardian,* January 19, 1994; "Whitehall Must Not Escape Scot Free," *Guardian,* February 12, 1994; quoted in McCully, *Silenced Rivers,* 291.

33. McCully, *Silenced Rivers,* 62.

34. For example, see Sardar Sarovar Narmada Nigam (SSNNL), *Planning for Prosperity* (1989); Babubhai J. Patel, *Progressing amidst Challenges* (1992); C. C. Patel, *SSP, What It Is and What It Is Not* (1991); and P. A. Raj, *Facts: Sardar Sarovar Project* (Gujarat: Sardar Sarovar Narmada Nigam, 1989, 1990, 1991 editions).

35. Ibid.; also Rahul Ram, *Muddy Waters: A Critical Assessment of the Benefits of the Sardar Sarovar Project* (New Delhi: Kalpavriksh, 1993).

36. Morse and Berger, *Sardar Sarovar,* 319. According to official statistics (Narmada Control Authority, *Benefits to Saurashtra and Kutch Areas in Gujarat* [Indore: NCA, 1992]), 948 villages in Kutch and 4,877 villages in Saurashtra are to get drinking water from the Sardar Sarovar Projects. However, according to the 1981 census there are only 887 inhabited villages in Kutch and 4,727 villages in the whole of Saurashtra. The planners had simply hoovered up the names of villages from a map, thereby including the names of 211 deserted villages! Cited in Ram, *Muddy Waters.*

37. For example, the minutes of the various meetings of the Rehabilitation and Resettlement subgroups of the Narmada Control Authority, 1998 99. Also, Morse and Berger, *Sardar Sarovar,* 51.

38. Ram, *Muddy Waters,* 34.

39. See for example, the petition filed by the NBA in the Supreme Court, 1994.

40. SSNNL, *Planning for Prosperity;* government of Gujarat.

41. S. Dharmadhikary, "Hydropower at Sardar Sarovar: Is It Necessary, Justified, and Affordable?" in *Towards Sustainable Development? Struggling over India's Narmada River,* ed. William F. Fisher (Armonk, NY: M. F. Sharpe, 1995), 141.

42. McCully, *Silenced Rivers,* 87.

43. Ibid., 185.

44. World Bank, *Resettlement and Development: The Bankwide Review of Projects Involving Resettlement 1986–1993* (Washington, DC, 1994).

45. World Bank, *Resettlement and Rehabilitation of India: A Status Update of Projects Involving Involuntary Resettlement* (Washington, DC, 1994).

46. Ibid.

47. Letter to the president in Morse and Berger, *Sardar Sarovar,* xii, xxiv, xxv.

48. Morse and Berger, *Sardar Sarovar,* xxv.

49. Minimum conditions included unfinished appraisal of social and environmental impacts. For details, see Lori Udall, "The International Narmada Campaign," in *Toward Sustainable Development? Struggling over India's Narmada River,* ed. William F. Fisher (Armonk, NY: M. F. Sharpe, 1995); Patrick McCully, "Cracks in the Dam: The World Bank in India," *Multinational Monitor,* December 1992, http://www.multinationalmonitor.org/hyper/issues/1992/12/mm1292_08.html.

50. See the letter from the GOI to the World Bank, March 29, 1993; press release of the World Bank dated March 30, 1993, a copy of which can be found in the

campaign information package of International Rivers Network, *Narmada Valley Development Project* 1 (August 1998).

51. The date was November 14, 1992. Venue: outside the Taj Mahal Hotel, Bombay, where Lewis Preston, president of the World Bank, was staying. See Lawyers Committee for Human Rights, *Unacceptable Means: India's Sardar Sarovar Project and Violations of Human Rights: Oct. 1992–Feb. 1993*, 10–12.

52. On the night of March 20, 1994, the NBA Office at Baroda was attacked by hoodlums simply because of a (baseless) rumor that one member of the Five Member Group Committee was sitting inside with members of the NBA. Some NBA activists were manhandled, and a large collection of NBA documents was burned and destroyed.

53. Ministry of Water Resources, GOI, *Report of the Five Member Group on Sardar Sarovar Project*, 1994.

54. Writ Petition 319 of 1994 argued that the Sardar Sarovar Projects violated the fundamental rights of those affected by the project and that the project was not viable on social, environmental, technical (including seismic and hydrological), financial, or economic grounds. The Writ Petition asked for a comprehensive review of the project, pending which construction on the project should cease.

55. *Frontline*, January 27, 1995, and January 21, 1995.

56. In January 1995 the Supreme Court took on record the statement of the Counsel for the Union of India that no further work on the Sardar Sarovar dam would be done without informing the Court in advance. On May 4, 1995, the Court allowed construction of "humps" on the dam, on the plea of the Union of India that they were required for reasons of safety. The Court, however, reiterated its order of January 1995 that no further construction will be done without the express permission of the Court.

57. *Report of the Narmada Water Disputes Tribunal with Its Decision* (1979), 2:102; cited in Morse and Berger, *Sardar Sarovar*, 250.

58. Morse and Berger, *Sardar Sarovar*, 323–29.

59. Raj, *Facts: Sardar Sarovar Project*.

60. Medha Patkar, "The Struggle for Participation and Justice: A Historical Narrative," in *Toward Sustainable Development? Struggling over India's Narmada River*, ed. William F. Fisher (Armonk, NY: M. F. Sharpe, 1995), 159–78; S. Parasuraman, "The Anti-Dam Movement and Rehabilitation Policy," in *The Dam and the Nation*, edited by Jean Drèze, Meera Samson, and Satyajit Singh (Oxford: Oxford University Press, 1997), 26–65; and minutes of various meetings of the R & R subgroup of the Narmada Control Authority.

61. On my visit to the valley in March 1999, I was told this by villagers at Mokhdi who had returned from their resettlement colonies.

62. *Kaise Jeebo Re*, documentary film directed by Anurag Singh and Jharana Jhaveri, Jan Madhyam, 1997; also, unedited footage in the NBA archives.

63. Letter to *Independent Review* from a resident of Parveta resettlement colony, cited in https://www.facebook.com/attn/videos/1006281599407299/159-160.

64. Narmada Manavadhikar Yatra, which traveled from the Narmada Valley to Delhi via Bombay. It reached Delhi on April 7, 1999.

65. Told to me by Mohan Bhai Tadvi, in Kevadia Colony, March 1999.
66. Morse and Berger, *Sardar Sarovar*, 89–94; NBA interviews, March 1999.
67. NBA interviews, March 1999.
68. Morse and Berger, *Sardar Sarovar*, 277–94.
69. McCully, *Silenced Rivers*, 46–49.
70. For a discussion on the subject, see the World Bank, *India Irrigation Sector Review* (1991); A. Vaidyanathan, *Food, Agriculture and Water* (Madras: MIDS, 1994); and McCully, *Silenced Rivers*, 182–207.
71. World Bank, *India Irrigation Sector Review*, 2:7.
72. Cited in McCully, *Silenced Rivers*, 187.
73. Shaheen Rafi Khan, "The Kalabagh Controversy" (Pakistan, 1998), http://www.sanalist.org/kalabagh/a-14.htm; E. Goldsmith, "Learning to Live with Nature: The Lessons of Traditional Irrigation," *Ecologist* 6, no. 5 (September–October 1998).
74. Shah et al., *India's Drylands*, 51; also in Goldsmith, "Learning to Live with Nature."
75. Operations Research Group (ORG), *Critical Zones in Narmada Command: Problems and Prospects* (Baroda, 1981); ORG, *Regionalisation of Narmada Command* (Gandhinagar, 1982); World Bank, *Staff Appraisal Report, India, Narmada River Development—Gujarat, Water Delivery and Drainage Project*, Report 5108-IN (1985); Core Consultants, *Main Report: Narmada Mahi Doab Drainage Study*, commissioned by Narmada Planning Group, government of Gujarat (1985).
76. Robert Wade, "Greening the Bank. The Struggle over the Environment, 1970–1995," in *The World Bank: Its First Half Century*, ed. Devesh Kapur, John P. Lewis, and Richard Webb (Washington, DC: Brookings Institution Press, 1997), 661–62.
77. Khan, "Kalabagh Controversy."
78. CES, *Pre-feasibility Level Drainage Study for SSP Command beyond River Mahi* (New Delhi: CES Water Resources Development and Management Consultancy for government of Gujarat, 1992).
79. Rahul Ram, "The Best-Laid Plans . . . ," *Frontline*, July 14, 1995, 78.
80. Core Consultants, *Main Report*, 66.
81. Ibid.
82. For example, see GOI, *Report of the FMG-2*; or Ram, "Best-Laid Plans."
83. Called the Economic Regeneration Programme, formulated to generate funds for the cash-strapped Sardar Sarovar Narmada Nigam. Under the program, land along the main canal of the Narmada Project will be acquired and sold for tourist facilities, hotels, water parks, fun world sites, garden restaurants, etc. Cf. *Times of India* (Ahmedabad), May 17, 1998.
84. World Bank, *India Irrigation Sector Review*.
85. Written Submissions on Behalf of the Petitioners (NBA) in the Supreme Court, January 1999, 63; *Times of India* (Ahmedabad), May 23, 1999.
86. Ismail Serageldin, 1994, *Water Supply, Sanitation and Environmental Sustainability* (Washington, DC: World Bank, 1994), 4.
87. Morse and Berger, *Sardar Sarovar*, xxiii.
88. Ibid., 317–19.
89. McCully, *Silenced Rivers*, 167.

7. Power Politics: The Reincarnation of Rumpelstiltskin

1. Stephen Fidler and Khozem Merchant, "US, India Announce Deals of Dollars 4bn," *Financial Times*, March 25, 2000, 10.

2. Peter Popham, "Clinton's Visit Seals Future for Controversial Indian Dam," *Independent*, March 28, 2000, 16; "S. Kumars Ties Up with Ogden for MP Project," *Economic Times of India*, December 14, 1999.

3. See 119–20, above; World Commission on Dams, *Dams and Development: A New Framework for Decision-Making—The Report of the World Commission on Dams* (London: Earthscan, 2000), 117 (hereafter WCD Report); Steven A. Brandt and Fekri Hassan, "Dams and Cultural Heritage Management: Final Report—August 2000," WCD Working Paper, http://www.dams.org/docs/html /contrib/soc212.htm; and WCD, "Flooded Fortunes: Dams and Cultural Heritage Management," press release, September 26, 2000. See also "Do or Die: The People versus Development in the Narmada Valley," *New Internationalist* 336 (July 2001), http://newint.org/issues/2001/07/01/; documentation at the Friends of the River Narmada site, http://www.narmada.org/nvdp.dams/.

4. Second World Water Forum: From Vision to Action, The Hague, March 17–22, 2000.

5. One billion people in the world have no access to safe drinking water: United Nations Development Program, *Human Development Report 2000: Human Rights and Human Development* (New York: Oxford University Press, 2000), 4 (hereafter UNDP 2000).

6. See chapter 8, note 5, above.

7. "Bolivian Water Plan Dropped after Protests Turn into Melees," *New York Times*, April 11, 2000.

8. "Develop Infrastructure to Cope with Digital Revolution: John Welch," *Hindu*, September 17, 2000; "Welch Makes a Power Point," *Economic Times of India*, September 17, 2000.

9. World Resource Institute, *World Resources 1998–1999* (Oxford: Oxford University Press, 1998), 251; UNDP 2000, table 4, Human Poverty in Developing Countries, 170.

10. Peter Marsh, "Big Four Lead the Field in Power Stakes: The Main Players," *Financial Times*, June 4, 2001, 2.

11. US Department of Energy, Energy Information Administration, *International Energy Outlook 1998*, Electricity Report (DOE/EIA-0484[98]), http://www.eia .doe.gov/oiaf/archive/ieo98/elec.html.

12. "India: Bharat Heavy Electricals–GE's Refurbishment Centre," *Hindu*, March 17, 2001; "BHEL Net Rises 10% to Rs 599 Crore," *Economic Times of India*, September 30, 2000.

13. Abhay Mehta, *Power Play: A Study of the Enron Project* (Hyderabad, India: Orient Longman, 2000), 15; Irfan Aziz, "The Supreme Court Upheld the Ruling That the Jain Diary Constituted Insufficient Evidence," Rediff.com, July 22, 2000, http://www.rediff.com/news/2000/jul/22spec.htm; and Ritu Sarin, "Ex-CBI Official Accuses Vijaya Rama Rao," *Financial Express*, May 11, 1997.

14. See figures in "Clinton's India Sojourn: Industry Hopes Doubling of FDI, Better

Access to US Markets," DHAN.com News Track, March 27, 2000; and George Pickart (senior adviser, Bureau for South Asian Affairs), "Address to the Network of South Asian Professionals," Washington, DC, August 9, 1997 http://www.indiainc.org.in/h0809971.htm.

15. P. R. Kumaramangalam, speech at the Conference of the Power Minister of India, March 2, 2000. See also "India: Power Problems," *Business Line*, June 21, 2000.

16. Ritu Sarin, "Disappearing Power," *Indian Express*, March 28, 2000. Hereafter Sarin, "Disappearing Power."

17. Neeraj Mishra, "Megawatt Thieves," *Outlook*, July 31, 2000, 54; Sarin, "Disappearing Power"; "India: Power Problems," *Business Line*, June 21, 2000; Louise Lucas, "Survey—India: Delays and Bureaucracy Force Investors to Flee: Power," *Financial Times*, November 6, 2000; and "India's Power Generation to Increase over Next 3 Years: Minister," *Asia Pulse*, April 27, 2001.

18. Sarin, "Disappearing Power"; "Red Tape and Blue Sparks," *Economist* 359, no. 8224 (June 2–8, 2001); "A Survey of India's Economy," *Economist* 359, no. 8224 (June 2–8, 2001), 9–10; and Sunil Saraf, "At Last, the Selloff Gets Underway," Survey—Power in Asia 1996, *Financial Times*, September 16, 1996, 5.

19. Mehta, *Power Play*; Human Rights Watch, *The Enron Corporation: Corporate Complicity in Human Rights Violations* (New York: Human Rights Watch, 1999), https://www.hrw.org/report/1999/01/01/enron-corporation/corporate-complicity-human-rights-violations; Tony Allison, "Enron's Eight-Year Power Struggle in India," Asia Times Online, January 18, 2001, http://www.atimes.com/reports/CA13Ai01.html; Scott Baldauf, "Plug Pulled on Investment in India," *Christian Science Monitor*, July 9, 2001, 9; S. N. Vasuki, "The Search for a Middle Ground," *Business Times* (Singapore), August 6, 1993; Agence France-Presse, "Work to Start in December on India's Largest Power Plant," September 14, 1993; and Agence France-Presse, "Work on Enron Power Project to Resume on May 1," February 23, 1996.

20. Scott Neuman, "More Power Reviews Likely in India," United Press International, August 5, 1995.

21. Agence France-Presse, "India, Enron Deny Payoff Charges over Axed Project," August 7, 1995, which acknowledges "a remark by an Enron official that the company spent 20 million dollars on 'educating Indians' about the controversial deal."

22. "Former US Amabassador to India Joins Enron Oil Board," *Asia Pulse*, October 30, 1997; Girish Kuber, "US Delegation to Meet Ministers on Enron Row," *Economic Times of India*, January 23, 2001; and Vijay Prashad, "The Power Elite: Enron and Frank Wisner," *People's Democracy*, November 16, 1997.

23. Mark Nicholson, "Elections Cloud Investment in India: Opening the Economy Has Wide Support Despite Recent Events," *Financial Times*, August 21, 1995; Agence France-Presse, "Hindu Leader Ready for Talks on Scrapped Enron Project," August 31, 1995; BBC Summary of World Broadcasts, "Maharashtra Government Might Consider New Enron Proposal," September 2, 1995; Suzanne Goldenberg, "India Calls on Left Bloc as BJP Cedes Power," *Guardian*, May 29, 1996; Mark Nicholson, "Delhi Clears Way for Dollars 2.5bn Dabhol Power Plant," *Financial Times*, July 10, 1996, 4; and Associated Press, "Enron Can Re-

sume Big Indian Power Project," *New York Times*, July 10, 1996, D19.

24. Mehta, *Power Play*, xv, 20–21, 151–58; Agence France-Presse, "Massive US-Backed Power Project Awaits Indian Court Ruling," August 25, 1996; Kenneth J. Cooper, "Foreign Power Plant Blooms; Low-Key India Venture Avoids Enron's Woes," *International Herald Tribune*, September 11, 1996; Praful Bidwai, "Enron Judgment: Blow to Energy Independence," *Times of India*, May 22, 1997; and Praful Bidwai, "The Enron Deal Must Go: Albatross round Public's Neck," *Times of India*, May 4, 1995.

25. Agence France-Presse, "Enron Power Project Survives Court Challenge," May 3, 1997.

26. "The Dabhol Backlash," *Business Line*, December 5, 2000; Sucheta Dalai, "No Power May End Up Being Better Than That High Cost Power," *Indian Express*, December 3, 2000; Soma Banerjee, "State Plans to Move Court on Tariff Revision Proposal," *Economic Times of India*, May 26, 2000; Madhu Nainan, "Indian State Says It Has No Money to Pay Enron for Power," Agence France-Presse, January 8, 2001; Khozem Merchant, "Enron Invokes Guarantee to Retrieve Fees from Local Unit," *Financial Times*, January 31, 2001, 7; S. N. Roy, "The Shocking Truth about Power Reforms," *Indian Express*, February 28, 2000; and Anthony Spaeth, "Bright Lights, Big Bill," *Time* (Asian edition) 157 (February 26, 2001): 8, http://www.time.com/time/asia/biz/magazine/0,9754,99899,00.html.

27. "India: Maharashtra State Electricity Board Stops Buying Power," *Hindu*, May 30, 2001; Celia W. Dugger, "High-Stakes Showdown: Enron's Fight over Power Plant Reverberates beyond India," *New York Times*, March 20, 2001, C1 (hereafter Dugger, "High-Stakes Showdown").

28. Mehta, *Power Play*, 3; Dugger, "High-Stakes Showdown"; "Red Tape and Blue Sparks"; "A Survey of India's Economy," 9–10; GOI, *Ninth Five Year Plan, 1997–2002*; and GOI, Press Information Bureau, fact sheet.

29. S. Balakrishnan, "FIS in U.S. Press Panic Button as MSEB Fails to Pay Enron," *Times of India*, January 7, 2001; Madhu Nainan, "Indian State Says It Has No Money to Pay Enron for Power," Agence France-Presse, January 8, 2001; and Khozem Merchant, "Enron Invokes Guarantee to Retrieve Fees from Local Unit," *Financial Times*, January 31, 2001, 7.

30. Pratap Chatterjee, "Meet Enron, Bush's Biggest Contributor," *Progressive* 64 (September 2000): 9. See also Dugger, "High-Stakes Showdown."

31. Dugger, "High-Stakes Showdown"; Praful Bidwai, "Congentrix = (Equals) Bullying Tricks," *Kashmir Times*, December 27, 1999.

32. Center for Science and Environment, *State of India's Environment: The Citizens' Fifth Report*, pt. 2, *Statistical Database* (New Delhi: Center for Science and Environment, 1999), 203; Union Power Minister Suresh Prabhu, press conference, Hyderabad, cited in *Business Line*, July 21, 2001; and Abusaleh Shariff, *India: Human Development Report—A Profile of Indian States in the 1990s* (New Delhi: National Council of Applied Economic Research / Oxford University Press, 1999), 238.

33. UNDP 2000, table 18, Aid and Debt by Recipient Country, p. 221. See also ENS Economic Bureau, "India Inching towards Debt Trap," *Indian Express*, February 23, 1999. See also Economist Intelligence Unit, "India: External Debt."

34. WCD Report, p. 11 and table 1.2.

35. See 110–12, above; WCD Report, table 1.1, Dams Currently under Construc-
     tion, p. 10, and table V.1, Top 20 Countries by Number of Large Dams, p. 370;
     and the website of the International Commission on Large Dams, http://www.
     icold-cigb.org/home.asp.

36. *Modern Temples of India: Selected Speeches of Jawaharlal Nehru at Irrigation and
     Power Projects*, ed. C. V. J. Sharma (Delhi: Central Board of Irrigation and Power,
     1989), 40–49. See 107, 110, above.

37. PTI News Agency (New Delhi), "India: Construction Begins on 'Controversial'
     Narmada Dam," BBC Worldwide Monitoring, October 31, 2000; Vinay Kumar,
     "People Cheer as Work on Narmada Dam Resumes," *Hindu*, November 1, 2000;
     "Violence Mars Gujarat Govt's Narmada Bash," *Times of India*, November 1,
     2000; and "Ministers Attacked, Cars Burnt at Narmada Dam Site," *Hindustan
     Times*, November 1, 2000.

38. WCD Fact Sheet, "Dams and Water: Global Statistics: India: 4,291 Large Dams
     and 9% of the World Dam Population." See also Himanshu Thakker, "Perfor-
     mance of Large Dams in India: The Case of Irrigation and Flood Control," paper
     presented at the World Commission on Dams Regional Consultation, Sri Lanka,
     December 1998.

39. R. Rangachari et al., "Large Dams—India's Experience: A WCD Case Study
     Prepared as an Input to the Word Commission on Dams," World Commission
     on Dams Country Review Paper, November 2000 (hereafter Rangachari et al.,
     "Large Dams—India's Experience").

40. Ibid., 25.

41. Ashok Gulati, "Overflowing Granaries, Empty Stomachs," *Economic Times of
     India*, April 27, 2000; UNDP 2000, table 4, Human Poverty in Developing
     Countries, p. 170.

42. Gail Omvedt, "Editorial: Rotting Food," *Hindu*, October 23, 1999. See also Shri
     Sriram Chuahan, Minister of States for Food and Public Distribution, Ministry
     of Consumer Affairs, Food, and Public Distribution, GOI, "Loss of Foodgrains,"
     press release, August 8, 2000.

43. See 113, above; "Indian Govt to Protest World Commission on Dams Report," *Asia
     Pulse*, February 5, 2001; Kalpana Sharma, "Misconceptions about Dams Commis-
     sion," *Hindu*, September 11, 1998; "Keshubhai Warns Dam Inspection Team May Be
     Held," *Indian Express*, September 9, 1998; "Gujarat Bans Visit of 'Anti-dam' Body,"
     Hindu, September 5, 1998; Kalpana Sharma, "Damning All Dissent," *Hindu*, Sep-
     tember 21, 1998; WCD website, http://www.internationalrivers
     .org/; "Medium and Large Dams Damned," *Business Standard*, September 23, 2000;
     "SC Wants Time Limit on Closure of Polluting Units," *Times of India*, January 25,
     2001; and Rangachari et al., "Large Dams—India's Experience," 116.

44. Ibid.

45. US Department of Energy, Energy Information Administration, *International
     Energy Outlook 1998*; see 111, 142–43, above; and Rangachari et al., "Large
     Dams—India's Experience," 132.

46. "The Human Cost of the Bargi Dam," http://www.narmada.org/nvdp.dams/

bargi/bargi.html; "Dam Ousters to Go on Hunger-Strike," *Statesman*, August 13, 1997.

47. WCD Report, 106–07; Sanjay Sangvai, *The River and Life: People's Struggle in the Narmada Valley* (Mumbai: Earthcare Books, 2000), 28; and "Human Cost of the Bargi Dam."

48. See 123, above.

49. WCD Report, 104–05; see 122–23, above; Robert Marquand, "Indian Dam Protests Evoke Gandhi," *Christian Science Monitor*, August 5, 1999, 1; "The Sardar Sarovar Dam: A Brief Introduction," http://www.narmada.org /sardarsarovar.html; Narmada Bachao Andolan (NBA), "Displacement, Submergence and Rehabilitation in Sardar Sarovar Project: Ground Reality Indicating Utter Injustice," http://www.narmada.org/sardar-sarovar/sc.ruling/Displacement .rehab.html; and Free the Narmada Campaign, India, "Who Pays? Who Profits? A Short Guide to the Sardar Sarovar Project," http://www.narmada.org/sardar -sarovar/faq/whopays.html.

50. International Rivers Network, "Confidential World Bank Evaluation Admits Future of Narmada Dam Uncertain," press release, May 16, 1995; Office of Director-General, Operations Evaluation, World Bank, Memorandum to the Executive Directors and the President, March 29, 1995; MNC Masala, "The World Bank and Sardar Sarovar Project: A Story of Unacceptable Means towards Unacceptable Ends," CorpWatch, n.d.; WCD Report, 26; and Morse and Berger, *Sardar Sarovar*.

51. Celia W. Dugger, "Opponents of India Dam Project Bemoan Green Light from Court," *New York Times*, October 20, 2000, A9.

52. Free the Narmada Campaign, "Who Pays? Who Profits?"

53. "The Maheshwar Dam: A Brief Introduction" and related links, http://www. narmada.org/maheshwar.html; Meena Menon, "Damned by the People: The Maheshwar Hydro-Electricity Project in Madhya Pradesh," *Business Line*, June 15, 1998; Sangvai, *River and Life*, 81–84; and Richard E. Bissell, Shekhar Singh, and Hermann Warth, *Maheshwar Hydroelectric Project: Resettlement and Rehabilitation—An Independent Review Conducted for the Ministry of Economic Cooperation and Development (BMZ), Government of Germany*, June 15, 2000 (hereafter Bissell Report).

54. Mardana Resolution, http://www.narmada.org/maheshwar/mardana.declaration .html; NBA, "Hundreds of Maheshwar Dam Affected People Demonstrate at IFCI, Delhi," press note, November 16, 2000, http://www.narmada.org/nba -press-releases/november-2000/ifci.demo.html; and Sangvai, *River and Life*, Annexure 4, 194–97, and Annexure 6, 200–201.

55. Heffa Schücking, "The Maheshwar Dam in India," March 1999, http://www. narmada.org/urg990421.3.html.

56. Menon, "Damned by the People."

57. "S. Kumars Forays into Ready-to-Wear Apparel," *India Info*, December 10, 2000, and "S. Kumars Ups Ads-Spend by 66% with Kapil Dev on Board," *India Express*, July 8, 1999.

58. Menon, "Damned by the People"; "Do or Die: The People versus Development

in the Narmada Valley."

59. "German Firms Pull Out of MP Dam Project," *Statesman*, April 21, 1999. See also Desikan Thirunarayanapuram, "Siemens Role in Dam Project Doubtful," *Statesman*, June 30, 2000.

60. Bissell Report.

61. "Leaked Letter Shows German Company Quits Bid for Dam Credit," *Deutsche Presse-Agentur*, August 25, 2000; "US Firm Pulls Out of Narmada Hydel Project," *Statesman*, December 13, 2000.

62. "PM's Is Going to Be a 'Power Trip,'" *Indian Express*, September 4, 2000.

63. "Ogden Pulls Out from Maheshwar Hydel Unit," *Indian Express*, December 8, 2000.

64. Mark Landler, "Hi, I'm in Bangalore (But I Can't Say So)," *New York Times*, March 21, 2001, A1.

65. David Gardiner, "Impossible India's Improbable Chance," in *The World in 2001* (London: Economist, 2000), 46.

66. Prabhakar Sinha, "Tatas Plan Foray into Call Centre Business," *Times of India*, October 7, 2000.

8. The Ladies Have Feelings, So . . . Shall We Leave It to the Experts?

1. Roger Cohen, "Germans Seek Foreign Labor for New Era of Computers," *New York Times*, April 9, 2000, 1.

2. Report at Rediff.com, http://www.rediff.com/news/2001/may/26pic3.htm.

3. For data on poverty and illiteracy in India, see UNDP 2000, table 1, Human Development Index, p. 159; table 4, Human Poverty in Developing Countries, p. 170; and table 19, Demographic Trends, p. 225. Reports also available online at http://www.undp.org and at the site of the UNDP Program in India, http://www.undp.org.in/.

4. Arundhati Roy, *The Cost of Living* (New York: Modern Library, 1999), which includes "The End of the Imagination," published in *Outlook* and *Frontline* magazines in August 1998, and "The Greater Common Good," published by *Outlook* and *Frontline* in May–June 1999. "Power Politics: The Reincarnation of Rumpelstiltskin," the seventh chapter in this volume, appeared originally in *Outlook*, November 27, 2000. See http://www.frontlineonline.com and http://www.outlookindia.com/ Arundhati Roy, *The God of Small Things* (New York: Harper-Perennial, 1998).

5. UNDP 2000, table 19, Demographic Trends, p. 225.

6. Ashok Gulati, "Overflowing Granaries, Empty Stomachs," *Economic Times of India*, April 27, 2000.

7. UNDP 2000, table 4, Human Poverty in Developing Countries, p. 170, and table 19, Demographic Trends, p. 225. See also Gardiner, "Impossible India's Improbable Chance," 46.

8. Joseph Kahn, "U.S.-India Agreement," *New York Times*, January 11, 2000, 4.

9. Dev Raj, "Land Acquisition Bill Worse Than Colonial Law," Inter Press Service,

December 3, 1998; S. Gopikrishna Warrier, "India: NGOs for Including Relief, Rehab Provisions in Land Act," *Business Line*, February 13, 2001.

10. Associated Press, "Anti-dam Activists Vow to Protest India's Supreme Court Ruling," October 20, 2000. For more on the Sardar Sarovar dam project, see "The Greater Common Good"; "The Sardar Sarovar Dam: A Brief Introduction," Friends of the River Narmada, http://www.narmada.org/sardarsarovar.html, and related links; and Sangvai, *River and Life*.

11. Frederick Noronha, "Dam Protesters Battle Police for Access to World Bank President," Environment News Service, Global News Wire, November 13, 2000.

12. See 113, above; Rangachari et al., "Large Dams—India's Experience," 116–17, 130–31. For additional information on Big Dams, see Patrick McCully, *Silenced Rivers: The Ecology and Politics of Large Dams*, enlarged and updated edition (London: Zed Books, 2001), and the website of the International Rivers Network, http://www.internationalrivers.org/.

13. For more information on displacement from Sardar Sarovar, see WCD Report, box 4.3, p. 104. See also Rangachari et al., "Large Dams—India's Experience," 116–17; Planning Commission, GOI, "Irrigation, Flood Control and Command Area Development: Rehabilitation and Resettlement," chap. 4 in *Mid-term Appraisal of the Ninth Five Year Plan: Final Document (1997–2002)* (Delhi: Planning Commission, 2000), 89, para. 68; see 114, above; Morse and Berger, *Sardar Sarovar*, 62; and GOI, *28th and 29th Report of the Commissioner for Scheduled Castes and Scheduled Tribes* (New Delhi: Government of India, 1988).

14. "Indian Govt to Protest World Commission on Dams Report"; Sharma, "Misconceptions about Dams Commission"; "Keshubhai Warns Dam Inspection Team May Be Held"; "Gujarat Bans Visit of 'Anti-dam' Body"; and Sharma, "Damning All Dissent."

15. WCD Report. See the WCD website, http://www.internationalrivers.org/; "Medium and Large Dams Damned."

16. Peter Popham, "Squalid, Disgusting, Toxic: Is This the Dirtiest City on the Planet?" *Independent*, October 27, 1997, E9; World Bank, "World Bank Says World's Worst Slums Can Be Transformed," press release, June 3, 1996, web.worldbank.org/WBSITE/EXTERNAL/NEWS/0,,contentMDK:20011723~pagePK:64257043~piPK:437376~theSitePK:4607,00.html.

17. GOI, Ministry of Environment and Forests, *White Paper on Pollution in Delhi: With an Action Plan* (New Delhi: Ministry of Environment and Forests, 1997), http://envfor.nic.in/divisions/cpoll/delpolln.html.

18. WCD Report, p. 11 and table 1.2.

19. "NBA Case: Supreme Court Adjourns Hearing on Gujarat Plea," *Hindu*, July 30, 1999; T. Padmanabha Rao, "India: Supreme Court Unhappy with NBA Leaders, Arundhati Roy," *Hindu*, October 16, 1999.

9. On Citizens' Rights to Express Dissent

1. Nadja Vancauwenberghe and Maurice Frank, "New Media: If You Take a Bribe, We'll Nail You," *Guardian*, June 4, 2001; "Egg on Congress's Face," *Statesman*,

April 10, 2001; "Chief Justice Turns Down Request for Sitting Judge for Arms Scandal Inquiry," BBC Summary of World Broadcasts, March 20, 2001; and "CJI Refuses to Spare Sitting Judge," *Times of India*, March 20, 2001.

2. PTI, "Ex-SC Judge to Hold Probe," *Tribune*, March 19, 2001, http://www.tribuneindia.com/20010320/main3.htm.

10. Ahimsa (Nonviolent Resistance)

1. The government of India plans to build 30 large, 135 medium, and 3,000 small dams on the Narmada to generate electricity, displacing 400,000 people in the process. For
    more information, see www.narmada.org.
2. The activists ended their fast on June 18, 2002, after an
    independent committee was set up to look into the issue of resettlement. For more information, see www
    .narmada.org/nba-press-releases/jun-2002/fast.ends.html.

11. The Algebra of Infinite Justice

1. Fox News, September 17, 2001.
2. Marc Levine, "New Suspect Arrested, but Doubts Grow over Terrorists' Identities," Agence France-Presse, September 21, 2001.
3. President George W. Bush, "September 11, 2001, Terrorist Attacks on the United States."
4. Elsa Brenner, "Hoping to Fill the Need for Office Space," *New York Times*, Westchester Weekly ed., September 23, 2001, 3.
5. Leslie Stahl, "Punishing Saddam," produced by Catherine Olian, *60 Minutes*, CBS, May 12, 1996.
6. Tamim Ansary, "Bomb Afghanistan Back to Stone Age? It's Been Done," *Providence Journal-Bulletin*, September 22, 2001, B7.
7. Thomas E. Ricks, "Land Mines, Aging Missiles Pose Threat," *Washington Post*, September 25, 2001, A15. See also Danna Harman, "Digging up Angola's Deadly Litter," *Christian Science Monitor*, July 27, 2001, 6.
8. Barry Bearak, "Misery Hangs over Afghanistan after Years of War and Drought," *New York Times*, September 24, 2001, B3; Rajiv Chandrasekaran and Pamela Constable, "Panicked Afghans Flee to Border Area," *Washington Post*, September 23, 2001, A30; Catherine Solyom, "Exhibit a Glimpse into Refugee Life," *Gazette* (Montreal), September 21, 2001, A13; and Raymond Whitaker, Agence France-Presse, "Pakistan Fears for Seven Million Refugees as Winter Looms," *Independent* (London), September 27, 2001, 4.
9. BBC, "Aid Shortage Adds to Afghan Woes," September 22, 2001, http://news.bbc.co.uk/2/hi/south_asia/1556117.stm.
10. Ansary, "Bomb Afghanistan Back to Stone Age?"
11. Paul Leavitt, "Maps of Afghanistan Now in Short Supply," *USA Today*, September 18, 2001, 13A.

12. *Washington Post*, February 7, 1985, quoted in Raja Anwar, *The Tragedy of Afghan-istan: A First-Hand Account*, trans. Khalid Hasan (New York: Verso, 1988), 232; "Inside the Taliban: U.S. Helped Cultivate the Repressive Regime Sheltering bin Laden," *Seattle Times*, September 19, 2001, A3; and Andrew Duffy, "Geographic Warriors," *Ottawa Citizen*, September 23, 2001, C4.

13. On the CIA connection, see Steve Coll, "Anatomy of a Victory: CIA's Covert Afghan War," *Washington Post*, July 19, 1992, A1; Steve Coll, "In CIA's Covert Afghan War, Where to Draw the Line Was Key," *Washington Post*, July 20, 1992, A1; Tim Weiner, "Blowback from the Afghan Battlefield," *New York Times Magazine*, March 13, 1994, 6: 53; and Ahmed Rashid, "The Making of a Terrorist," *Straits Times* (Singapore), September 23, 2001, 26.

14. Scott Baldauf, "Afghans Try Opium-Free Economy," *Christian Science Monitor*, April 3, 2001, 1.

15. David Kline, "Asia's 'Golden Crescent' Heroin Floods the West," *Christian Science Monitor*, November 9, 1982, 1; David Kline, "Heroin's Trail from Poppy Fields to the West," *Christian Science Monitor*, November 10, 1982, 1; and Rahul Bedi, "The Assassins and Drug Dealers Now Helping US Intelligence," *Daily Telegraph* (London), September 26, 2001, 10.

16. Peter Popham, "Taliban Monster That Was Launched by the US," *Independent* (London), September 17, 2001, 4.

17. Suzanne Goldenberg, "Mullah Keeps Taliban on a Narrow Path," *Guardian* (London), August 17, 1998, 12.

18. David K. Willis, "Pakistan Seeks Help from Abroad to Stem Heroin Flow," *Christian Science Monitor*, February 28, 1984, 11.

19. Farhan Bokhari, survey in "Pakistan: Living in Shadow of Debt Mountain," *Financial Times* (London), March 6, 2001, 4.

20. Douglas Frantz, "Sentiment in Pakistani Town Is Ardently Pro-Taliban," *New York Times*, September 27, 2001, B1; Rahul Bedi, "The Assassins and Drug Dealers Now Helping US Intelligence," *Daily Telegraph* (London), September 26, 2001, 10.

21. Edward Luce, "Pakistan Nervousness Grows as Action Nears," *Financial Times* (London), September 27, 2001, 6.

22. Angus Donald and Khozem Merchant, "Concern at India's Support for US," *Financial Times* (London), September 21, 2001, 14.

23. Jeff Greenfield and David Ensor, "America's New War: Weapons of Terror," *Greenfield at Large*, CNN, September 24, 2001.

24. Jim Drinkard, "Bush Vows to 'Rid the World of Evildoers,'" *USA Today*, September 17, 2001, 1A.

25. Secretary of Defense Donald Rumsfeld, "Developments concerning Attacks on the Pentagon and the World Trade Center Last Week," special defense briefing, Federal News Service, September 20, 2001.

26. Robert Fisk, "This Is Not a War on Terror, It's a Fight against America's Enemies," *Independent* (London), September 25, 2001, 4.

27. George Monbiot, "The Need for Dissent," *Guardian* (London), September 18, 2001, 17.

28. Michael Slackman, "Terrorism Case Illustrates Difficulty of Drawing Tangible Ties to Al Qaeda," *Los Angeles Times*, September 22, 2001, A1.

29. Tim Russert, "Secretary of State Colin Powell Discusses America's Preparedness for the War on Terrorism," *Meet the Press*, NBC, September 23, 2001.

30. T. Christian Miller, "A Growing Global Chorus Calls for Proof," *Los Angeles Times*, September 24, 2001, A10; Dan Rather, "President Bush's Address to Congress and the Nation," *CBS News Special Report*, September 20, 2001.

31. Nityanand Jayaraman and Peter Popham, "Work Halts at Indian Unilever Factory after Poisoning Alert," *Independent* (London), March 11, 2001, 19.

32. Jack Hitt, "Battlefield: Space," *New York Times Magazine*, August 5, 2001, 6.

33. Colin Nickerson and Indira A. R. Lakshmanan, "America Prepares the Global Dimension," *Boston Globe*, September 27, 2001, A1; Barbara Crossette, "Taliban's Ban on Poppy a Success, U.S. Aides Say," *New York Times*, May 20, 2001, 1, 7; and Christopher Hitchens, "Against Rationalization," *Nation* 273, no. 10 (October 8, 2001): 8.

34. Bush, "September 11, 2001, Terrorist Attacks on the United States."

12. War Is Peace

1. Alexander Nicoll, "US Warplanes Can Attack at All Times, Says Forces Chief," *Financial Times* (London), October 10, 2001, 2.

2. Noam Chomsky, "US Iraq Policy: Motives and Consequences," in *Iraq under Siege: The Deadly Impact of Sanctions and War*, ed. Anthony Arnove (Cambridge, MA: South End; London: Pluto, 2000), 54.

3. Slackman, "Terrorism Case Illustrates Difficulty of Drawing Tangible Ties to Al Qaeda," A1.

4. "Bush's Remarks on U.S. Military Strikes on Afghanistan," *New York Times*, October 8, 2001, B6; Ellen Hale, "'To Safeguard Peace, We Have to Fight,' Blair Emphasizes to Britons," *USA Today*, October 8, 2001, 6A.

5. "Remarks by President George W. Bush at an Anti-terrorism Event," Washington, DC, Federal News Service, October 10, 2001.

6. Tom Pelton, "A Graveyard for Many Armies," *Baltimore Sun*, September 18, 2001, 2A.

7. Dave Newbart, "Nowhere to Go but Up," *Chicago Sun-Times*, September 18, 2001, 10.

8. Edward Epstein, "U.S. Seizes Skies over Afghanistan," *San Francisco Chronicle*, October 10, 2001, A1.

9. Steven Mufson, "For Bush's Veteran Team, What Lessons to Apply?" *Washington Post*, September 15, 2001, A5.

10. Donald H. Rumsfeld, "Defense Department Special Briefing Re: Update on U.S. Military Campaign in Afghanistan," Arlington, VA, Federal News Service, October 9, 2001.

11. Epstein, "U.S. Seizes Skies over Afghanistan."

12. Human Rights Watch, "Military Assistance to the Afghan Opposition: Human Rights Watch Backgrounder," October 2001, http://www.hrw.org/background-

er/asia/afghan-bck1005.htm. See also Gregg Zoroya, "Northern Alliance Has Bloody Past, Critics Warn," *USA Today*, October 12, 2001, 1A.

13. David Rohde, "Visit to Town Where 2 Linked to bin Laden Killed Afghan Rebel," *New York Times*, September 26, 2001, B4.

14. Zahid Hussain and Stephen Farrell, "Tribal Chiefs See Chance to Be Rid of Taliban," *Times* (London), October 2, 2001.

15. Alan Cowell, "Afghan King Is Courted and Says, 'I Am Ready,'" *New York Times*, September 26, 2001, A4.

16. Said Mohammad Azam, "Civilian Toll Mounts as Bush Signals Switch to Ground Assault," Agence France-Presse, October 19, 2001; Indira A. R. Lakshmanan, "UN's Peaceful Mission Loses 4 to War," *Boston Globe*, October 10, 2001, A1; and Steven Lee Myers and Thom Shanker, "Pilots Told to Fire at Will in Some Zones," *New York Times*, October 17, 2001, B2.

17. UN documents and reports summarized in Center for Economic and Social Rights, "Afghanistan Fact Sheet 3: Key Human Vulnerabilities," http://www.cesr. org/downloads/Afghanistan%20Fact%20Sheet%203.pdf.

18. David Rising, "U.S. Military Defends Its Food Drops in Afghanistan from Criticism by Aid Organizations," Associated Press, October 10, 2001; Luke Harding, "Taliban Say Locals Burn Food Parcels," *Guardian* (London), October 11, 2001, 9; and Tyler Marshall and Megan Garvey, "Relief Efforts Trumped by Air War," *Los Angeles Times*, October 17, 2001, A1.

19. Martin Merzer and Jonathan S. Landay, Knight Ridder News Service, "Second Phase of Strikes Begins," *Milwaukee Journal Sentinel*, October 10, 2001, 1A.

20. Jennifer Steinhauer, "Citing Comments on Attack, Giuliani Rejects Saudi's Gift," *New York Times*, October 12, 2001, B13.

21. Robert Pear, "Arming Afghan Guerrillas: A Huge Effort Led by U.S.," *New York Times*, April 18, 1988, A1. See also Coll, "Anatomy of a Victory," A1; Coll, "In CIA's Covert Afghan War, Where to Draw the Line Was Key," A1; Weiner, "Blowback from the Afghan Battlefield"; and Rashid, "Making of a Terrorist," 26.

22. "Voices of Dissent and Police Action," *Hindu*, October 13, 2001.

23. "Vajpayee Gets Tough, Says No Compromise with Terrorism," *Economic Times of India*, October 15, 2001.

24. Howard Fineman, "A President Finds His True Voice," *Newsweek*, September 24, 2001, 50.

25. Aaron Pressman, "Former FCC Head Follows the Money," *IndustryStandard .com*, May 2, 2001.

26. Alice Cherbonnier, "Republican-Controlled Carlyle Group Poses Serious Ethical Questions for Bush Presidents, but *Baltimore Sun* Ignores It," *Baltimore Chronicle and Sentinel*, n.d. See also Leslie Wayne, "Elder Bush in Big G.O.P. Cast Toiling for Top Equity Firm," *New York Times*, March 5, 2001, A1.

27. "America, Oil and Afghanistan," editorial, *Hindu*, October 13, 2001.

28. Tyler Marshall, "The New Oil Rush: High Stakes in the Caspian," *Los Angeles Times*, February 23, 1998, A1.

29. Ahmed Rashid, *Taliban: Militant Islam, Oil and Fundamentalism in Central Asia* (New Haven, CT: Yale Nota Bene / Yale University Press, 2001), 143–82.

13. War Talk: Summer Games with Nuclear Bombs

1. *Prophecy*, directed by Susumu Hani (1982; Nagasaki, Japan: Nagasaki Publishing Committee), 16mm.

2. See Aruna Roy and Nikhil Dey, "Words and Deeds," *India Together*, June 2002, and "Stand-Off at Maan River: Dispossession Continues to Stalk the Narmada Valley," *India Together*, May 2002, www.indiatogether.org/campaigns/narmada/. See also "Maan Dam," Friends of River Narmada, www.narmada.org/nvdp.dams/maan/.

3. "Nobel laureate Amartya Sen may think that health and education are the reasons why India has lagged behind in development in the past 50 years, but I think it is because of defence," said Home Minister L.K. Advani. See "Quote of the Week, Other Voices," *India Today*, June 17, 2002, 13.

4. See Human Rights Watch, "Behind the Kashmir Conflict: Abuses by Indian Security Forces and Militant Groups Continue," 1999, www.hrw.org/reports/1999/kashmir/summary.htm.

5. See Pilger, "Pakistan and India on Brink," 4; Neil Mackay, "Cash from Chaos: How Britain Arms Both Sides," *Sunday Herald* (Scotland), June 2, 2002, 12.

6. See Richard Norton-Taylor, "UK Is Selling Arms to India," *Guardian* (London), June 20, 2002, 1; Tom Baldwin, Philip Webster, and Michael Evans, "Arms Export Row Damages Peace Mission," *Times* (London), May 28, 2002; and Agence France-Presse, "Blair Peace Shuttle Moves from India to Pakistan," January 7, 2002.

7. Pilger, "Pakistan and India on Brink."

14. Come September

1. See John Berger, *G.* (New York: Vintage International, 1991), 123.

2. See Damon Johnston, "U.S. Hits Back Inspirations," *Advertiser*, September 22, 2001, 7.

3. See John Pomfret, "Chinese Working Overtime to Sew U.S. Flags," *Washington Post*, September 20, 2001, A14.

4. See "Democracy: Who Is She When She's at Home?" above.

5. See David E. Sanger, "Bin Laden Is Wanted in Attacks, 'Dead or Alive,' President Says," *New York Times*, September 18, 2001, A1; John F. Burns, "10-Month Afghan Mystery: Is bin Laden Dead or Alive?" *New York Times*, September 30, 2002, A1.

6. See the Associated Press list, available on the website of the *Toledo Blade*, of those confirmed dead, reported dead, or reported missing in the September 11 terrorist attacks, www.toledoblade.com/Nation/2011/09/11/list-of-2977-victims-of-Sept-11-2001-terror-attacks.html.

7. Quoted in Seymour M. Hersh, *The Price of Power: Kissinger in the Nixon White House* (New York: Summit Books, 1983), 265.

8. See Pilar Aguilera and Ricardo Fredes, eds., *Chile: The Other September 11* (New York: Ocean, 2002); Amnesty International, "The Case of Augusto Pinochet."

9. Clifford Krauss, "Britain Arrests Pinochet to Face Charges by Spain," *New York Times*, October 18, 1998, 1; National Security Archive, "Chile: 16,000 Secret

U.S. Documents Declassified," press release, November 13, 2000, nsarchive.gwu
.edu/news/20001113/; and selected documents on the National Security Archive
website, nsarchive.gwu.edu/news/20001113/#docs.

10. Kissinger told this to Pinochet at a meeting of the Organization of American
States in Santiago, Chile, on June 8, 1976. See Lucy Kosimar, "Kissinger Covered
Up Chile Torture," *Observer*, February 28, 1999, 3.

11. Among other histories, see Eduardo Galeano, *Open Veins of Latin America: Five
Centuries of the Pillage of a Continent*, 2nd ed., trans. Cedric Belfrage (New York:
Monthly Review Press, 1998); Noam Chomsky, *Turning the Tide: U.S. Intervention in Central America and the Struggle for Peace*, 2nd ed. (Boston: South End,
1985); Noam Chomsky, *The Culture of Terrorism* (Boston: South End, 1983); and
Gabriel Kolko, *Confronting the Third World: United States Foreign Policy, 1945–
1980* (New York: Pantheon, 1988).

12. In a public relations move, the SOA renamed itself the Western Hemisphere
Institute for Security Cooperation (WHINSEC) on January 17, 2001. See Jack
Nelson-Pallmeyer, *School of Assassins: Guns, Greed, and Globalization*, 2nd ed.
(New York: Orbis Books, 2001); Michael Gormley, "Army School Faces Critics
Who Call It Training Ground for Assassins," Associated Press, May 2, 1998; and
School of the Americas Watch, www.soaw.org.

13. On these interventions, see, among other sources, Noam Chomsky, *American
Power and the New Mandarins*, 2nd ed. (New York: New Press, 2002); Noam
Chomsky, *At War with Asia* (New York: Vintage Books, 1970); and Howard Zinn,
Vietnam: The Logic of Withdrawal, 2nd ed. (Cambridge, MA: South End, 2002).

14. See Samih K. Farsoun and Christina E. Zacharia, *Palestine and the Palestinians*
(Boulder, CO: Westview, 1997), 10.

15. The Balfour Declaration is included in ibid., appendix 2, 320.

16. Quoted in Noam Chomsky, *Fateful Triangle: The United States, Israel, and the
Palestinians*, 2nd ed. (Cambridge, MA: South End, 2000), 90.

17. Quoted in "Scurrying towards Bethlehem," editorial, *New Left Review* 10 (July/
August 2001), 9n5.

18. Quoted in Farsoun and Zacharia, *Palestine and the Palestinians*, 10, 243.

19. Ibid., 111, 123.

20. Ibid., 116.

21. See Chomsky, *Fateful Triangle*, 103–07, 118–32, 156–60.

22. From 1987 to 2002 alone, more than two thousand Palestinians were killed. See
statistics from B'Tselem (Israeli Information Center for Human Rights in the
Occupied Territories) at www.btselem.org/statistics.

23. See Naseer H. Aruri, *Dishonest Broker: The United States, Israel, and the Palestinians* (Cambridge MA: South End, 2003); Noam Chomsky, *World Orders Old and
New*, 2nd ed. (New York: Columbia University Press, 1996).

24. In addition to more than $3 billion annually in official Foreign Military Financ-
ing, the US government supplies Israel with economic assistance, loans, technology transfers, and arms sales. See Nick Anderson, "House Panel Increases Aid
for Israel, Palestinians," *Los Angeles Times*, May 10, 2002, A1; Aruri, *Dishonest
Broker*; and Anthony Arnove and Ahmed Shawki, foreword to *The Struggle for*

Palestine, ed. Lance Selfa (Chicago: Haymarket Books, 2002), xxv.

25. Article 27 of the Charter of the Islamic Resistance Movement (Hamas), quoted in Farsoun and Zacharia, *Palestine and the Palestinians*, appendix 13, 339.

26. George H. W. Bush, "Text of Bush's Speech: 'It Is Iraq against the World,'" *Los Angeles Times*, September 12, 1990, A7.

27. See Glenn Frankel, "Iraq Long Avoided Censure on Rights," *Washington Post*, September 22, 1990, A1.

28. See Christopher Dickey and Evan Thomas, "How Saddam Happened," *Newsweek*, September 23, 2002, 35–37.

29. See Anthony Arnove, introduction to *Iraq under Siege*, 20.

30. Arnove, *Iraq under Siege*, 221–22.

31. Ibid., 17, 205.

32. See Thomas J. Nagy, "The Secret behind the Sanctions: How the U.S. Intentionally Destroyed Iraq's Water Supply," *Progressive* 65, no. 9 (September 2001).

33. See Arnove, *Iraq under Siege*, 121, 185–203. See also Nicholas D. Kristof, "The Stones of Baghdad," *New York Times*, October 4, 2002, A27.

34. Leslie Stahl, "Punishing Saddam," produced by Catherine Olian, *60 Minutes*, CBS, May 12, 1996.

35. Elisabeth Bumiller, "Bush Aides Set Strategy to Sell Policy on Iraq," *New York Times*, September 7, 2002, A1.

36. Richard Perle, "Why the West Must Strike First against Saddam Hussein," *Daily Telegraph* (London), August 9, 2002, 22.

37. See Alan Simpson and Glen Rangwala, "The Dishonest Case for a War on Iraq," September 27, 2002, www.grassrootspeace.org/counter-dossier.html; Glen Rangwala, "Notes Further to the Counter-Dossier," September 29, 2002, grassrootspeace.org/archivecounter-dossierII.html.

38. George Bush, "Bush's Remarks on U.S. Military Strikes in Afghanistan," *New York Times*, October 8, 2001, B6.

39. See Paul Watson, "Afghanistan Aims to Revive Pipeline Plans," *Los Angeles Times*, May 30, 2002, A1; Ilene R. Prusher, Scott Baldauf, and Edward Girardet, "Afghan Power Brokers," *Christian Science Monitor*, June 10, 2002, 1.

40. See Lisa Fingeret et al., "Markets Worry That Conflict Could Spread in Area That Holds Two-Thirds of World Reserves," *Financial Times* (London), April 2, 2002, 1.

41. Thomas L. Friedman, "Craziness Pays," *New York Times*, February 24, 1998, A21.

42. ———, *The Lexus and the Olive Tree: Understanding Globalization* (New York: Farrar, Strauss, and Giroux, 1999), 373.

43. Statistics from Joseph E. Stiglitz, *Globalization and Its Discontents* (New York: W. W. Norton, 2002), 5; Noam Chomsky, *Rogue States: The Rule of Law in World Affairs* (Cambridge, MA: South End, 2000), 214; and Noreena Hertz, "Why Consumer Power Is Not Enough," *New Statesman*, April 30, 2001.

44. Among the many treaties and international agreements the United States has not signed, ignores, violates, or has broken are the UN International Covenant on Economic, Social and Cultural Rights (1966); the UN Convention on the Rights of the Child (CRC); the UN Convention on the Elimination of All Forms of Discrimination Against Women (CEDAW); agreements setting the

jurisdiction for the International Criminal Court (ICC); the 1972 Anti-Ballistic Missile Treaty with Russia; the Comprehensive Test Ban Treaty (CTBT); and the Kyoto Protocol regulating greenhouse gas emissions.

45. See David Cole and James X. Dempsey, *Terrorism and the Constitution: Sacrificing Civil Liberties in the Name of National Security* (New York: New Press, 2002).

46. Luke Harding, "Elusive Mullah Omar 'Back in Afghanistan,'" *Guardian* (London), August 30, 2002, 12.

47. See Human Rights Watch, "Opportunism in the Face of Tragedy: Repression in the Name of Anti-terrorism," http://www.hrw.org/legacy/campaigns/september11/opportunismwatch.htm.

48. See "Power Politics," 151–76, above, and related notes.

15. An Ordinary Person's Guide to Empire

1. CNN International, March 21, 2003.

2. Ibid.

3. Ibid. See also Dexter Filkins, "In the Field Marines: Either Take a Shot or Take a Chance," *New York Times*, March 29, 2003, A1. Filkins interviewed Sergeant Eric Schrumpf, aged twenty-eight, of the Fifth Marine Regiment. "'We had a great day,' Sergeant Schrumpf said. 'We killed a lot of people.' . . . 'We dropped a few civilians, . . . but what do you do?' . . . He recalled watching one of the women standing near the Iraqi soldier go down. 'I'm sorry,' the sergeant said. 'But the chick was in the way.'"

4. Patrick E. Tyler and Janet Elder, "Threats and Responses—The Poll: Poll Finds Most in U.S. Support Delaying a War," *New York Times*, February 14, 2003, A1.

5. Maureen Dowd, "The Xanax Cowboy," *New York Times*, March 9, 2003, 4, 13.

6. George W. Bush, joint statement with Tony Blair after the Azores summit. See "Excerpts from Remarks by Bush and Blair: 'Iraq Will Soon Be Liberated,'" *New York Times*, April 9, 2003, B7.

7. "You Cannot Hide, Hoon Tells Saddam," *Birmingham Evening Mail*, March 20, 2003, 2; Charles Reiss, "We Had No Option But to Use Force to Disarm Saddam, Says Straw," *Evening Standard* (London), March 20, 2003, 11.

8. General Vince Brooks, deputy director of operations, United States Central Command Daily Press Briefing, Federal News Service, March 27, 2003.

9. CNN International, March 25, 2003.

10. Remarks by President George W. Bush to Troops at MacDill Air Force Base, Tampa, FL, Federal News Service, March 26, 2003.

11. See David Cole, *Enemy Aliens: Double Standards and Constitutional Freedoms in the War on Terrorism* (New York: New Press, 2003).

12. Charles Lane, "Justices to Rule on Detainees' Rights; Court Access for 660 Prisoners at Issue," *Washington Post*, November 11, 2003, 1; David Rohde, "U.S. Rebuked on Afghans in Detention," *New York Times*, March 8, 2004, A6. See also Cole, *Enemy Aliens*, 39–45.

13. Jeremy Armstrong, "Field of Death—Total Slaughter: Amnesty [International] Demands Probe Be over Bloody Massacre of Taliban Prisoners," *Mirror* (Lon-

don), November 29, 2001, 6.

14. "Injustice in Afghanistan," editorial, *Washington Post*, March 21, 2004, B6.

15. Bill O'Reilly, "Talking Points Memo," *The O'Reilly Factor*, Fox News, March 24, 2003. See also Bill O'Reilly, "Unresolved Problems: Interview with Kenneth Roth," *The O'Reilly Factor*, Fox News, March 27, 2003.

16. See Rageh Omaar, *Revolution Day: The Human Story of the Battle for Iraq* (London: Viking, 2004).

17. Martin Bright, Ed Vulliamy, and Peter Beaumont, "Revealed: US Dirty Tricks to Win Vote on Iraq War," *Observer* (London), March 2, 2003, 1.

18. Marc Santora, "Aid Workers Fear Dangers of Delay: Basra, without Power and Water, Is at Risk," *International Herald Tribune*, March 25, 2003, 1; John Pilger, "Gulf War 2: Six Days of Shame," *Mirror* (London), March 26, 2003, 14.

19. Patrick Nicholson, "The Cans and Buckets Are Empty and People Are Desperate," *Independent* (London), April 5, 2003, 8.

20. Agence France-Presse, "Iraq's Weekly Oil Production Reaches New Levels," July 23, 2002.

21. Mark Nicholson, "Troops Prepare to Deliver Supplies," *Financial Times* (London), March 27, 2003, 2.

22. Nick Guttmann, "Humanitarian Aid—Wanted: 32 Galahads a Day," *Independent on Sunday* (London), March 30, 2003, 26.

23. Quoted in Noam Chomsky, *For Reasons of State* (New York: New Press, 2003), 67–69.

24. Juan J. Walte, "Greenpeace: 200,000 Died in Gulf," *USA Today*, May 30, 1991, 1A.

25. Kim Cobb, "Vets Warn of Risks to Soldiers' Health: Critics Fear Repeat of Gulf War Illnesses," *Houston Chronicle*, February 9, 2003, 1.

26. James Meikle, "'Health Will Suffer for Years,'" *Guardian* (London), November 12, 2003, 17.

27. Joel Brinkley, "American Companies Rebuilding Iraq Find They Are Having to Start from the Ground Up," *New York Times*, February 22, 2004, 11; Tucker Carlson, "Hired Guns," *Esquire*, March 2004, 130–38.

28. Felicity Barringer, "Security Council Votes to Revive Oil-for-Food Program in Iraq," *New York Times*, March 29, 2003, B7.

29. Dan Morgan and Karen DeYoung, "Hill Panels Approve War Funds, with Curbs: Most Restrictions Aimed at Pentagon," *Washington Post*, April 2, 2003, A26.

30. Lou Dobbs, *Lou Dobb's Moneyline*, CNN, March 27, 2003.

31. Greg Wright, "French Fries? Mais Non, Congress Calls Em Freedom Fries," Gannett News Service, March 12, 2003, www.gannettonline.com/gns/faceoff2/20030312-18100.shtml.

32. Serge Bellanger, "Of Wal-Marts, BMWs and Brie," *Chicago Tribune*, April 27, 2003, 9.

33. George W. Bush, Camp David, Maryland, press briefing, September 16, 2001: "We're going to do it. We will rid the world of the evildoers. We will call together freedom-loving people to fight terrorism. And so on this day of—on the Lord's day, I say to my fellow Americans, thank you for your prayers, thank you for your compassion, thank you for your love for one another, and tomorrow

when you get back to work, work hard like you always have. But we've been warned. We've been warned there are evil people in this world. We've been warned so vividly and we'll be alert. Your government is alert. The governors and mayors are alert that evil folks still lurk out there."

16. The Loneliness of Noam Chomsky

1. R. W. Apple, Jr., "Bush Appears in Trouble despite Two Big Advantages," *New York Times*, August 4, 1988, A1. Bush made this remark in refusing to apologize for the shooting down of an Iranian passenger plane, killing 290 passengers. See Lewis Lapham, *Theater of War* (New York: New Press, 2002), 126.

2. Chomsky would be the first to point out that other pioneering media analysts include his frequent coauthor Edward Herman, Ben Bagdikian (whose 1983 classic *The Media Monopoly* recounts the suppression of Chomsky and Herman's *Counter-Revolutionary Violence: Bloodbaths in Fact and Propaganda*), and Herbert Schiller.

3. Paul Betts, "Ciampi Calls for Review of Media Laws," *Financial Times* (London), July 24, 2002, 8. For an overview of Berlusconi's holdings, see Ketupa.net Media Profiles: www.ketupa.net/berlusconi1.htm.

4. See Sabin Russell, "U.S. Push for Cheap Cipro Haunts AIDS Drug Dispute," *San Francisco Chronicle*, November 8, 2001, A13; Frank Swoboda and Martha McNeil Hamilton, "Congress Passes $15 Billion Airline Bailout," *Washington Post*, September 22, 2001, A1.

5. President George W. Bush, Jr., "President Bush's Address on Terrorism before a Joint Meeting of Congress," *New York Times*, September 21, 2001, B4.

6. Dan Eggen, "Ashcroft Invokes Religion in U.S. War on Terrorism," *Washington Post*, February 20, 2002, A2.

7. President George W. Bush, Jr., "Bush's Remarks on U.S. Military Strikes in Afghanistan," *New York Times*, October 8, 2001, B6.

8. President George W. Bush, Jr., remarks at FBI Headquarters, Washington, DC, October 10, 2001, Federal Document Clearinghouse.

9. See Howard Zinn, *A People's History of the United States: 1492–Present*, 20th anniv. ed. (New York: HarperCollins, 2001).

10. Bob Marley and N. G. Williams (aka King Sporty), "Buffalo Soldier."

11. Noam Chomsky, "The Manufacture of Consent," in *The Chomsky Reader*, ed. James Peck (New York: Pantheon, 1987), 121–22.

12. See Jim Miller, "Report from the Inferno," *Newsweek*, September 7, 1981, 72; review of Committee for the Compilation of Materials on Damage Caused by the Atomic Bombs in Hiroshima and Nagasaki, *Hiroshima and Nagasaki: The Physical, Medical, and Social Effects of the Atomic Bombings* (New York: Basic, 1981).

13. David E. Sanger, "Bush to Formalize a Defense Policy of Hitting First," *New York Times*, June 17, 2002, A1; David E. Sanger, "Bush Renews Pledge to Strike First to Counter Terror Threats," *New York Times*, July 20, 2002, A3.

14. See Terence O'Malley, "The Afghan Memory Holds Little Room for Trust in U.S.," *Irish Times*, October 15, 2001, 16.

15. Arnove, *Iraq under Siege*.

16. See Noam Chomsky, "Memories," review of *In Retrospect* by Robert McNamara (New York: Times Books, 1995), *Z Magazine* (July–August 1995), www.zmag.org/.

17. "Myth and Reality in Bloody Battle for the Skies," *Guardian* (London), October 13, 1998, 15.

18. Bill Keller, "Moscow Says Afghan Role Was Illegal and Immoral," *New York Times*, October 24, 1989, A1.

19. Noam Chomsky, "Afghanistan and South Vietnam," in *Chomsky Reader*, ed. Peck, 225.

20. Samuel P. Huntington, "The Bases of Accommodation," *Foreign Affairs* 46, no. 4 (1968): 642–56. Quoted in Noam Chomsky, *At War with Asia* (New York: Vintage Books, 1970), 87.

21. Samuel P. Huntington, "The Clash of Civilizations?" *Foreign Affairs* 72, no. 3 (Summer 1993): 22–49.

22. Huntington, "The Bases of Accommodation," quoted in Chomsky, *At War with Asia*, 87.

23. T. D. Allman, "The Blind Bombers," *Far Eastern Economic Review* 75, no. 5 (January 29, 1972): 18–20, quoted in Chomsky, *For Reasons of State*, 72.

24. Chomsky, *For Reasons of State*, 72; Chomsky, *At War with Asia*, 87; and Lapham, *Theater of War*, 145.

25. T. D. Allman, "The War in Laos: Plain Facts," *Far Eastern Economic Review* 75, no. 2 (January 8, 1972): 16ff.

26. Chomsky, *For Reasons of State*, 18. See also Noam Chomsky, "The Pentagon Papers as Propaganda and as History," in *The Pentagon Papers: The Defense Department History of United States Decisionmaking on Vietnam; The Senator Gravel Edition—Critical Essays*, ed. Noam Chomsky and Howard Zinn (Boston: Beacon, 1971–72), 5:79–201.

27. Chomsky, *For Reasons of State*, 67, 70.

28. William Pfaff, *Condemned to Freedom: The Breakdown of Liberal Society* (New York: Random House, 1971), 75–77, quoted in Chomsky, *For Reasons of State*, 94.

29. Pfaff, *Condemned to Freedom*, 75–77, quoted in Chomsky, *For Reasons of State*, 94–95.

30. *Pentagon Papers*, 4:43, quoted in Chomsky, *For Reasons of State*, 67.

31. Philip Jones Griffiths, *Vietnam Inc.*, 2nd ed. (New York: Phaidon, 2001), 210. First edition quoted in Chomsky, *For Reasons of State*, 3–4.

32. Noam Chomsky, interview with James Peck, in *Chomsky Reader*, ed. Peck, 14.

17. Confronting Empire

1. See Ranjit Devraj, "Asia's 'Outcast' Hurt by Globalization," Inter Press Service, January 6, 2003; Statesman News Service, "Farm Suicide Heat on Jaya," *Statesman* (India), January 9, 2003; and "'Govt. Policies Driving Farmers to Suicide,'" *Times of India*, February 4, 2002.

2. See "Govt.'s Food Policy Gets a Reality Check from States," *Indian Express*, January 11, 2003; Parul Chandra, "Victims Speak of Hunger, Starvation across Country," *Times of India*, January 11, 2003.

3. See "Democracy: Who Is She When She's at Home?" 65–79, above; see also Pan-

kaj Mishra, "The Other Face of Fanaticism," *New York Times*, February 2, 2003, 42–46; Concerned Citizens Tribunal, *Crime against Humanity: An Inquiry into the Carnage in Gujarat*, 2 vols. (Mumbai: Citizens for Justice and Peace, 2002).

4. See Edward Luce, "Gujarat Win Likely to Embolden Hindu Right," *Financial Times* (London), December 16, 2002, 8.

5. Oscar Olivera, "The War over Water in Cochabamba, Bolivia," trans. Florencia Belvedere, presented at "Services for All?" Municipal Services Project Conference, South Africa, May 15–18, 2002.

6. Tom Lewis, "Contagion in Latin America," *International Socialist Review* 24 (July–August 2002).

7. Julian Borger and Alex Bellos, "U.S. 'Gave the Nod' to Venezuelan Coup," *Guardian* (London), April 17, 2002, 13.

8. David Sharrock, "Thousands Protest in Buenos Aires as Economic Woes Persist," *Times* (London), December 21, 2002, 18.

9. See Mary McGrory, "'A River of Peaceful People,'" *Washington Post*, January 23, 2003, A21.

18. Peace Is War: The Collateral Damage of Breaking News

1. Mohammed Shehzad, "'Killing Hindus' Better than Dialogue with India: Lashkar-e-Taiba Chief," Agence France-Presse, April 3, 2003.

2. Ben H. Bagdikian, *The New Media Monopoly* (Boston: Beacon, 2004).

3. Edward Helmore, "Who Sets the TV Control? Battle Is Raging over a Decision to Allow US Media Giants to Own Even More," *Observer* (London), June 8, 2003, 6.

4. Howard Rheingold, "From the Screen to the Streets," *In These Times*, November 17, 2003, 34; Stephen Labaton, "Debate/Monopoly on Information: It's a World of Media Plenty; Why Limit Ownership?" *New York Times*, October 12, 2003, 4.

5. See Connie Koch, *2/15: The Day the World Said No to War* (New York: Hello NYC; Oakland: AK Press, 2004).

6. See Edward Luce, "Battle over Ayodhya Temple Looms," *Financial Times* (London), February 2, 2002, 7.

7. Pankaj Mishra, "A Mediocre Goddess," *New Statesman*, April 9, 2001; John Ward Anderson, "The Flame That Lit An Inferno: Hindu Leader Creates Anti-Muslim Frenzy," *Washington Post*, August 11, 1993, A14. See also "Democracy: Who Is She When She's at Home?" 65–79, above.

8. See "In Memory of Shankar Guha Niyogi."

9. Raja Bose, "A River Runs Through It," *Times of India*, February 25, 2001.

10. C. Rammanohar Reddy, "At Loggerheads over Resources," *Hindu*, May 27, 2001; Kata Lee (Project Coordinator of Hotline Asia), "India: Unarmed Tribals Killed by Jharkhand Police," Asian Center for the Progress of Peoples, Asian Human Rights Commission, March 3, 2003.

11. Gurbir Singh, "Guj[arat] Police Cane Protesters of NATELCO-UNOCAL Port," *Economic Times*, April 12, 2000; "Human Rights Defenders Persecuted in India:

Amnesty [International]," Press Trust of India, April 26, 2000. See also Rosa Basanti, "Villagers Take On Giant Port Project," Inter Press Service, June 7, 2000.

12. Sanjay Kumar, "The Adivasis of Orissa," *Hindu*, November 6, 2001; Anu Kumar, "Orissa: A Continuing Denial of Adivasi Rights," InfoChange News and Features, Centre for Communication and Development Studies, November 2003. See also "When Freedom Is Trampled Upon," *Hindu*, January 24, 1999.

13. Danielle Knight, "The Destructive Impact of Fish Farming," Inter Press Service, October 13, 1999.

14. "Eviction of Tribals by Force in Kerala to Be Taken Up with NHRC," *Hindu*, February 26, 2003.

15. On the Nagarnar attacks, see Kuldip Nayar, "Pushing the POTO," *Hindu*, November 28, 2001.

16. People's War Group (PWG), Maoist Communist Centre (MCC), Pakistan's Inter-Services Intelligence (ISI), and the Liberation Tigers of Tamil Eelam (LTTE).

17. "Mr. [Vakkom] Purushothaman said he was of the view that the Adivasis who had 'tried to establish a parallel government should have been suppressed or shot.'" Quoted in "Opposition Boycotts Assembly," *Hindu*, February 22, 2003.

18. Mari Marcel Thekaekara, "What Really Happened," *Frontline*, March 15–28, 2003.

19. Sanjay Nigam, Mangat Verma, and Chittaroopa Palit, "Fifteen Thousand Farmers Gather in Mandleshwar to Protest against Electricity Tariff Hikes in Madhya Pradesh," Nimad Malwa Kisan Mazdoor Sangathan press release, February 27, 2003, www.narmada.org/nba-press-releases/february-2003/antitariff.html.

20. WCD Report, box 4.3, 104.

21. "The Greater Common Good" and "Power Politics," above.

22. L. S. Aravinda, "Supreme Court Majority Judgment: Mockery of Modern India," Association for India's Development.

23. World Bank Water Resources Management Group, *Water Resources Sector Strategy: Strategic Directions for World Bank Engagement* (Washington, DC: International Bank for Reconstruction and Development/World Bank, 2004), documents.worldbank.org/curated/en/2004/01/3030614/water-resources-sector-strategy-strategic-directions-world-bank-engagement; Peter Bosshard et al., "Gambling with People's Lives: What the World Bank's New 'High-Risk/High-Reward' Strategy Means for the Poor and the Environment," Environmental Defense, Friends of the Earth and International Rivers Network, September 19, 2003. See also Carrieann Davies, "From the Editor: Back to the Future," *Water Power and Dam Construction*, April 30, 2003, 3.

24. "Major Rivers to Be Linked by 2016," Press Trust of India, December 17, 2002. See also Medha Patkar, ed., *River Linking: A Millennium Folly?* (Pune, India: National Alliance of People's Movements/Initiative, 2004).

25. See "Tribals' Promised Land Is Kerala Sanctuary," *Indian Express*, February 6, 2003.

26. "Call to Prosecute Grasim Management for Pollution," *Business Line*, February 1, 1999.

27. R. Krishnakumar, "Closure of Grasim Industries," *Frontline*, July 21–August 3, 2001.

19. Instant-Mix Imperial Democracy
(Buy One, Get One Free)

1. Molly Moore, "The USS *Vincennes* and a Deadly Mistake: Highly Sophisticated Combat Ship at Center of Defense Department Investigation," *Washington Post*, July 4, 1988, A23.

2. Apple, "Bush Appears in Trouble," A1. See Lapham, *Theater of War*, 126.

3. Tyler and Elder, "Threats and Responses," A1.

4. Dowd, "The Xanax Cowboy," 13.

5. President George W. Bush, address to the nation, State Floor Cross Hallway, the White House, Federal News Service, March 17, 2003.

6. President George W. Bush, speech at the Cincinnati Museum Center, Cincinnati, Ohio, Federal News Service, October 7, 2002.

7. See Saïd K. Aburish, *Saddam Hussein: The Politics of Revenge* (London: Bloomsbury, 2001). See also the PBS *Frontline* interview with Aburish, "Secrets of His Life and Leadership," from *The Survival of Saddam*, www.pbs.org/wgbh/pages /frontline/shows/saddam/interviews/aburish.html.

8. See Anthony Arnove, "Indonesia: Crisis and Revolt," *International Socialist Review* 5 (Fall 1998).

9. Originally stated in a May 1980 interview on the *MacNeil/Lehrer Report* on PBS. Quoted in Philip Geyelin, "Forget Gunboat Diplomacy," *Washington Post*, September 29, 1980, A13.

10. See Arnove, *Iraq under Seige*, especially the chapter by Noam Chomsky, "US Iraq Policy: Consequences and Motives," 65–74, and Arnove's introduction, 11–31.

11. See, among many other of Bush's speeches, his address to the Wings over the Rockies Air and Space Museum, Denver, Colorado, Federal News Service, October 28, 2002, in which he reminded his audience that Hussein "is a person who has gassed his own people. . . . He's anxious to have, once again to develop a nuclear weapon. He's got connections with al Qaeda." Bush also commented: "We love life, everybody matters as far as we're concerned, everybody is precious. They have no regard for innocent life whatsoever. (Applause.) They hate the fact that we love freedom. We love our freedom of religion, we love our freedom of speech, we love every aspect of freedom. (Applause.) And we're not changing. (Applause.) We're not intimidated. As a matter of fact, the more they hate our freedoms, the more we love our freedoms. (Applause.)"

12. See Arnove, *Iraq under Siege*, 68–69.

13. "We are a nation called to defend freedom—a freedom that is not the grant of any government or document, but is our endowment from God." See Eggen, "Ashcroft Invokes Religion," A2.

14. Michael R. Gordon, "Baghdad's Power Vacuum Is Drawing Only Dissent," *New York Times*, April 21, 2003, A10.

15. Peter Beaumont, "Anger Rises as US Fails to Control Anarchy," *Observer* (London), April 13, 2003, 3.

16. Jim Dwyer, "Troops Endure Blowing Sands and Mud Rain," *New York Times*, March 26, 2003, A1; Neela Banerjee, "Army Depots in Iraqi Desert Have Names of Oil Giants," *New York Times*, March 27, 2003, C14.

17. Secretary of Defense Donald H. Rumsfeld, Defense Department operational update briefing, Pentagon Briefing Room, Arlington, VA, Federal News Service, April 11, 2003.

18. Reuters, "Number Imprisoned Exceeds 2 Million, Justice Dept. Says," *Washington Post*, April 7, 2003, A4; Sentencing Project, "U.S. Prison Populations: Trends and Implications," May 2003, 1.

19. Sentencing Project, "U.S. Prison Populations."

20. Fox Butterfield, "Prison Rates among Blacks Reach a Peak, Report Finds," *New York Times*, April 7, 2003, A12.

21. Richard Willing, "More Seeking President's Pardon," *USA Today*, December 24, 2002, 3A.

22. Paul Martin, Ed Vulliamy, and Gaby Hinsliff, "US Army Was Told to Protect Looted Museum," *Observer* (London), April 20, 2003, 4; Frank Rich, "And Now: 'Operation Iraqi Looting,'" *New York Times*, April 27, 2003, 2.

23. See Scott Peterson, "Iraq: Saladin to Saddam," *Christian Science Monitor*, March 4, 2003, 1.

24. Rumsfeld, Defense Department briefing.

25. Martin, Vulliamy, and Hinsliff, "US Army Was Told to Protect Looted Museum," 4.

26. See Robert Fisk, "Americans Defend Two Untouchable Ministries from the Hordes of Looters," *Independent* (London), April 14, 2003, 7:

> Iraq's scavengers have thieved and destroyed what they have been allowed to loot and burn by the Americans—and a two-hour drive around Baghdad shows clearly what the US intends to protect. After days of arson and pillage, here's a short but revealing scorecard. US troops have sat back and allowed mobs to wreck and then burn the Ministry of Planning, the Ministry of Education, the Ministry of Irrigation, the Ministry of Trade, the Ministry of Industry, the Ministry of Foreign Affairs, the Ministry of Culture and the Ministry of Information. They did nothing to prevent looters from destroying priceless treasures of Iraq's history in the Baghdad Archaeological Museum and in the museum in the northern city of Mosul, or from looting three hospitals.
>
> The Americans have, though, put hundreds of troops inside two Iraqi ministries that remain untouched—and untouchable—because tanks and armoured personnel carriers and Humvees have been placed inside and outside both institutions. And which ministries proved to be so important for the Americans? Why, the Ministry of Interior, of course—with its vast wealth of intelligence information on Iraq—and the Ministry of Oil.

27. Carlotta Gall, "In Afghanistan, Violence Stalls Renewal Effort," *New York Times*, April 26, 2003, A1. See also Rohde, "U.S. Rebuked on Afghans in Detention," A6.

28. Scott Lindlaw, "Accommodating TV-Friendly Presidential Visit Caused a Few Changes in Navy Carrier's Routine," Associated Press, May 2, 2003.

29. Walter V. Robinson, "1-Year Gap in Bush's Guard Duty: No Record of Airman

at Drills in 1972–73," *Boston Globe*, May 23, 2000, A1.

30. David E. Sanger, "Bush Declares 'One Victory in a War on Terror,'" *New York Times*, May 2, 2003, A1.

31. James Harding, "Bush to Hail Triumph but Not Declare a US Victory," *Financial Times* (London), May 1, 2003, 8.

32. Quoted in John R. MacArthur, "In the Psychological Struggle, Nations Wield Their Weapons of Mass Persuasion," *Boston Globe*, March 9, 2003, D12.

33. General Tommy Franks, *Sunday Morning*, CBS, March 23, 2003.

34. "'Non' Campaigner Chirac Ready to Address French," *Daily Mail* (London), March 20, 2003, 13.

35. Robert J. McCartney, "Germany Stops Short of Saying 'I Told You So': Opposition to War Vindicated, Officials Say," *Washington Post*, April 3, 2003, A33: "Although Germany formally opposes the war, it is supporting the U.S. effort through such steps as overflight rights and special security at U.S. bases in Germany. Officials say Germany is doing more for the war than any country except Britain." See also Giles Tremlett and John Hooper, "War in the Gulf: Clampdown on Coverage of Returning Coffins," *Guardian* (London), March 27, 2003, 3.

36. Judy Dempsey and Robert Graham, "Paris Gives First Signs of Support to Coalition," *Financial Times* (London), April 4, 2003, 4.

37. Interfax, "Putin Wants US Victory," *Hobart Mercury* (Australia), April 4, 2003.

38. Morton Abramowitz, "Turkey and Iraq, Act II," *Wall Street Journal*, January 16, 2003, A12.

39. Noam Chomsky, *Hegemony or Survival: America's Quest for Global Dominance* (New York: Metropolitan Books, 2004), 131.

40. Angelique Chrisafis et al., "Millions Worldwide Rally for Peace," *Guardian* (London), February 17, 2003, 6, http://www.theguardian.com/world/2003/feb/17/politics.uk.

41. Richard W. Stevenson, "Antiwar Protests Fail to Sway Bush on Plans for Iraq," *New York Times*, February 19, 2003, A1.

42. David McDonald and John Pape, "South Africa: Cost Recovery Is Not Sustainable," Africa News, August 30, 2002; David McDonald and John Pape, eds., *Cost Recovery and the Crisis of Service Delivery in South Africa* (London: Zed Press, 2002). See also Ashwin Desai, *We Are the Poors: Community Struggles in Post-Apartheid South Africa* (New York: Monthly Review Press, 2002).

43. "Africa's Engine," *Economist*, January 17, 2004.

44. Betts, "Ciampi Calls for Review of Media Laws," 8. For an overview of Berlusconi's holdings, see Ketupa.net Media Profiles: www.ketupa.net/berlusconi1.htm.

45. Frank Bruni, "Berlusconi, in a Rough Week, Says Only He Can Save Italy," *New York Times*, May 10, 2003, A1.

46. Tim Burt, "Mays on a Charm Offensive: The Clear Channel Chief Is Seeking to Answer His Group's Critics," *Financial Times* (London), October 27, 2003, 27. See also John Dunbar and Aron Pilhofer, "Big Radio Rules in Small Markets," Center for Public Integrity, October 1, 2003, https://www.publicintegrity.org/2003/10/01/6587/big-radio-rules-in-small-markets.

47. Douglas Jehl, "Across Country, Thousands Gather to Back U.S. Troops and Poli-

cy," *New York Times*, March 24, 2003, B15.

48. Frank Rich, "Iraq around the Clock," *New York Times*, March 30, 2003, 2.

49. Bagdikian, *New Media Monopoly*.

50. Tom Shales, "Michael Powell and the FCC: Giving Away the Marketplace of Ideas," *Washington Post*, June 2, 2003, C1; Paul Davidson and David Lieberman, "FCC Eases Rules for Media Mergers," *USA Today*, June 3, 2003, 1A.

51. David Leonhardt, "Bush's Record on Jobs: Risking Comparison to a Republican Ghost," *New York Times*, July 3, 2003, C1.

52. Robert Tanner, "Report Says State Budget Gaps Jumped by Nearly 50 Percent, with Next Year Looking Worse," Associated Press, February 5, 2003.

53. Dana Milbank and Mike Allen, "Bush to Ask Congress for $80 Billion: Estimate of War's Cost Comes as Thousands March in Protest," *Washington Post*, March 23, 2003, A1.

54. Sheryl Gay Stolberg, "Senators' Sons in War: An Army of One," *New York Times*, March 22, 2003, B10. See also David M. Halbfinger and Steven A. Holmes, "Military Mirrors a Working-Class America," *New York Times*, March 30, 2003, A1.

55. Darryl Fears, "Draft Bill Stirs Debate over the Military, Race and Equity," *Washington Post*, February 4, 2003, A3.

56. David Cole, "Denying Felons Vote Hurts Them, Society," *USA Today*, February 3, 2000, 17A; "From Prison to the Polls," editorial, *Christian Science Monitor*, May 24, 2001, 10.

57. See Cole, "Denying Felons" and sidebar, "Not at the Ballot Box."

58. Kenneth J. Cooper, "In India's Kerala, Quality of Life Is High but Opportunity Is Limited," *Washington Post*, January 3, 1997, A35; Amartya Sen, *Development as Freedom* (New York: Alfred A. Knopf, 1999). See also Fareed Zakaria, "Beyond Money," *New York Times Book Review*, November 28, 1999, 14.

59. Linda Villarosa, "As Black Men Move into Middle Age, Dangers Rise," *New York Times*, September 23, 2002, F1.

60. Amy Goldstein and Dana Milbank, "Bush Joins Admissions Case Fight: U-Mich. Use of Race Is Called 'Divisive,'" *Washington Post*, January 16, 2003, A1; James Harding, "Bush Scrambles to Bolster Civil Rights Credibility," *Financial Times* (London), January 21, 2003, 10.

61. Elizabeth Becker and Richard A. Oppel, Jr., "Bechtel Top Contender In Bidding over Iraq," *New York Times*, March 29, 2003, B6.

62. André Verlöy and Daniel Politi, with Aron Pilhofer, "Advisors of Influence: Nine Members of the Defense Policy Board Have Ties to Defense Contractors," Center for Public Integrity, March 28, 2003, https://www.publicintegrity.org /2003/03/28/3157/advisors-influence-nine-members-defense-policy-board -have-ties-defense-contractors.

63. Laura Peterson, "Bechtel Group Inc.," Center for Public Integrity, http://www. publicintegrity.org/wow/bio.aspx?act=pro&ddlC=6.

64. Ibid.

65. Bob Herbert, "Spoils of War," *New York Times*, April 10, 2003, A27.

66. Quoted in ibid.

67. Karen DeYoung and Jackie Spinner, "Contract for Rebuilding of Iraq Awarded

to Bechtel: U.S. Firm 1 of 6 Invited to Bid for $680 Million Project," *Washington Post*, April 18, 2003, A23. In December 2003 the contract was raised by $350 million, to $1.03 billion. In January 2004 Bechtel won a contract worth another $1.8 billion. See Elizabeth Douglass and John Hendren, "Bechtel Wins Another Iraq Deal," *Los Angeles Times*, January 7, 2004, C2.

68. Stephen J. Glain, "Bechtel Wins Pact to Help Rebuild Iraq: Closed-Bid Deal Could Total $680M," *Boston Globe*, April 18, 2003, A1.

69. Robin Toner and Neil A. Lewis, "House Passes Terrorism Bill Much Like Senate's, but with 5-Year Limit," *New York Times*, October 13, 2001, B6.

70. See Cole, *Enemy Aliens*, 57–69.

71. Evelyn Nieves, "Local Officials Rise Up to Defy the Patriot Act," *Washington Post*, April 21, 2003, A1.

72. See Cole, *Enemy Aliens*.

73. Amnesty International, "India: Abuse of the Law in Gujarat: Muslims Detained Illegally in Ahmedabad," November 6, 2003, AI index no. ASA 20/029/2003, https://www.amnesty.org/en/documents/asa20/029/2003/en/. See also "People's Tribunal"; Sanghamitra Chakraborty et al., "Slaves in Draconia: Ordinary Folks—Minors, Farmers, Minorities—Fall Prey to POTA for No Fault of Theirs," *Outlook India*, March 22, 2004.

74. Greg Myre, "Shootout in West Bank Kills an Israeli Soldier and a Palestinian," *New York Times*, March 13, 2003, A5.

75. Wayne Washington, "More Opposition to Detentions in Terror Probe," *Boston Globe*, May 13, 2002, A1; Tamar Lewin, "As Authorities Keep Up Immigration Arrests, Detainees Ask Why They Are Targets," *New York Times*, February 3, 2002, 14.

76. Neil King, Jr., "Bush Officials Draft Broad Plan for Free-Market Economy in Iraq," *Wall Street Journal*, May 1, 2003, A1.

77. Naomi Klein, "Iraq Is Not America's to Sell," *Guardian* (London), November 7, 2003, 27. See also Jeff Madrick, "The Economic Plan for Iraq Seems Long on Ideology, Short on Common Sense," *New York Times*, October 2, 2003, C2.

78. David Usborne, "US Firm Is Hired to Purge Schools of Saddam's Doctrine," *Independent* (London), April 22, 2003, 10; Steve Johnson, "Scramble to Win the Spoils of War," *Financial Times* (London) April 23, 2003, 27; and Paul Richter and Edmund Sanders, "Contracts Go to Allies of Iraq's Chalabi," *Los Angeles Times*, November 7, 2003, A1.

79. Heather Stewart, "Iraq—After the War: Fury at Agriculture Post for US Grain Dealer," *Guardian* (London), April 28, 2003, 11.

80. Alan Cowell, "British Ask What a War Would Mean for Business," *New York Times*, March 18, 2003, W1; "Spoils of War," editorial, *San Francisco Chronicle*, March 29, 2003, A14; Jan Hennop, "S. African Apartheid Victims File Lawsuit in US Court, Name Companies," Agence France-Presse, November 12, 2002; and Nicol Degli Innocenti, "African Workers Launch Dollars 100bn Lawsuit," *Financial Times* (London), October 13, 2003, 9.

81. John Vidal, "Shell Fights Fires as Strife Flares in Delta," *Guardian* (London), September 15, 1999, 15; Vidal, "Oil Wealth Buys Health in Country within a

Country," *Guardian* (London), September 16, 1999, 19. See also Ike Okonta and Oronto Douglas, *Where Vultures Feast: Shell, Human Rights, and Oil* (New York: Verso, 2003); Al Gedicks, *Resource Rebels: Native Challenges to Mining and Oil Corporations* (Cambridge, MA: South End, 2001).

82. Tom Brokaw, speaking to Vice Admiral Dennis McGinn, *NBC News Special Report: Target Iraq*, March 19, 2003.

83. Bryan Bender, "Roadblocks Seen in Sept. 11 Inquiry," *Boston Globe*, July 9, 2003, A2. See also Josh Meyer, "Terror Not a Bush Priority before 9/11, Witness Says," *Los Angeles Times*, March 25, 2004, A1; Edward Alden, "Tale of Intelligence Failure Above and Below," *Financial Times* (London), March 26, 2004, 2.

84. Zinn, *A People's History of the United States*. See also Anthony Arnove and Howard Zinn, *Voices of a People's History of the United States* (New York: Seven Stories, 2004).

20. Do Turkeys Enjoy Thanksgiving?

1. See André Verlöy and Daniel Politi, with Aron Pilhofer, "Advisors of Influence: Nine Members of the Defense Policy Board Have Ties to Defense Contractors," Center for Public Integrity, March 28, 2003, https://www.publicintegrity.org/2003/03/28/3157/advisors-influence-nine-members-defense-policy-board-have-ties-defense-contractors.

2. "Strike Not Your Right Anymore: SC [Supreme Court] to Govt Staff," *Indian Express*, August 7, 2003; "Trade Unions Protest against SC [Supreme Court] Order on Strikes," *Times of India*, August 8, 2003.

3. See "On Citizens' Rights to Express Dissent," in the current volume.

4. Michael Jensen, "Denis Halliday: Iraq Sanctions Are Genocide," *Daily Star*, Lebanon, July 7, 2000. See also the interview with Halliday and Phyllis Bennis in *Iraq under Siege*, 53–64.

5. Arnove, *Iraq under Siege*, 103–04.

6. Joseph E. Stiglitz, *Globalization and Its Discontents* (New York: W. W. Norton, 2002), 7, 61, 253–54.

7. "World Trade Special Report," *Independent* (London), September 10, 2003, 1; Thompson Ayodele, "Last Chance for Fair Go on Trade," *Australian Financial Review*, September 11, 2003, B63.

8. George Monbiot, *The Age of Consent* (New York: New Press, 2004), 158. See also UN General Assembly, *External Debt Crisis and Development: Report to the Secretary-General*, A/57/253, 2003, 2, https://documents-dds-ny.un.org/doc/UN-DOC/GEN/N02/503/65/PDF/N0250365.pdf?OpenElement.

9. The Fifth WTO Ministerial Conference was held in Cancún, Mexico, September 10–14, 2003. Sue Kirchhoff and James Cox, "WTO Talks Break Down, Threatening Future Pact," *USA Today*, September 15, 2003, 1B.

Sources

The End of Imagination
First published in *Outlook* and *Frontline*, July 27, 1998.

Democracy
Who Is She When She's at Home?
First published in the May 6, 2002, issue of *Outlook* magazine (India). A shorter version of this essay appeared under the title "Fascism's Firm Footprint in India" in *The Nation* magazine on September 30, 2002, and in *Nothing Sacred: Women Respond to Religious Fundamentalism and Terror*, edited by Betsy Reed (New York: Nation Books, 2002).

When the Saints Go Marching Out
The Strange Fate of Martin, Mohandas, and Mandela
This text is an expanded version of an essay originally broadcast by BBC Radio 4, August 25, 2003. By request of the BBC, which had determined that copyright restrictions prohibited it from broadcasting direct quotations from King's public speeches, the original used only paraphrases of King's words. In this version, direct quotations have been used.

In Memory of Shankar Guha Niyogi
This talk was delivered in Raipur, India, September 28, 2003, and first

published in Hindi in Hindustan on October 13, 2003. Shankar Guha Niyogi was a popular trade union leader of Chhattisgarh.

How Deep Shall We Dig?

This is the full text of the first I. G. Khan Memorial Lecture, delivered at Aligarh Muslim University in Aligarh, India, on April 6, 2004. It was first published in Hindi in Hindustan, April 23–24, 2004, and in English in *The Hindu*, April 25, 2004. An excerpt also appeared in the *Los Angeles Times*, April 25, 2004. On the February 14, 2003, murder of I. G. Khan, see Parvathi Menon, "A Man of Compassion," *Frontline*, March 29–April 11, 2003, www.frontline.in/static/html/fl2007/stories /20030411004511400.htm.

The Greater Common Good

First published in *Outlook* and *Frontline*, June 4, 1999.

Power Politics
The Reincarnation of Rumpelstiltskin

First Published in *Outlook*, November 27, 2000.

The Ladies Have Feelings, So...

Based on a talk given as the Third Annual Eqbal Ahmad Lecture, February 15, 2001, at Hampshire College, Amherst, Massachusetts.

On Citizens' Rights to Express Dissent

Court affadavit filed April 23, 2001. First published in Arundhati Roy, *Power Politics*, 2nd ed. (South End Press, 2001).

Ahimsa (Nonviolent Resistance)

First published in the *Hindustan Times* (India), June 12, 2002. This version is based on the version published in the *Christian Science Monitor* on July 5, 2002, as "Listen to the Nonviolent Poor: Allow for Peaceful Change, Before Violent Change Becomes Inevitable."

The Algebra of Infinite Justice

First published in the *Guardian*, September 29, 2001, and *Outlook*, October 8, 2001.

War Is Peace

First published in *Outlook*, October 29, 2001.

War Talk

First appeared in *Frontline* (India) 19, no. 12 (June 8–21, 2002).

Come September

First presented as a lecture in Santa Fe, New Mexico, at the Lensic Performing Arts Center, September 18, 2002. Sponsored by Lannan Foundation: www.lannan.org.

An Ordinary Person's Guide to Empire

The original version of this essay was first published in the *Guardian* (London), April 2, 2003.

The Loneliness of Noam Chomsky

Written as an introduction to the new edition of Noam Chomsky's *For Reasons of State* (New York: New Press, 2003).

Confronting Empire

First presented at the closing rally of the World Social Forum in Porto Alegre, Brazil, January 27, 2003.

Peace Is War
The Collateral Damage of Breaking News

This is the text of a speech first delivered March 7, 2003, at the Center for the Study of Developing Societies (CSDS), New Delhi, at a workshop organized by Sarai: The New Media Initiative, CSDS, and the Waag Society in Delhi. It was first published in the *Sarai Reader 4: Crisis/Media* (New Delhi: Sarai, 2004). See http://www.sarai.net for additional information on Sarai.

Instant-Mix Imperial Democracy
(Buy One, Get One Free)

This talk was first delivered May 13, 2003, at the Riverside Church, New York City, and broadcast live on Pacifica Radio. The lecture, sponsored by Lannan Foundation and the Center for Economic and Social Rights, was delivered as an acceptance speech for the 2002 Lannan Prize for Cultural Freedom.

Do Turkeys Enjoy Thanksgiving?

This speech was delivered at the World Social Forum in Bombay, India, on January 14, 2004.

Public Power in the Age of Empire

This text is based on a public address delivered to an overflow crowd at the American Sociological Association's 99th Annual Meeting in San Francisco on August 16, 2004. The theme of the conference was "Public Sociologies." The talk quickly aired on C-SPAN *Book TV*, *Democracy Now!*, and *Alternative Radio*, reaching audiences throughout North America and beyond, and was circulated via e-mail around the world.

Index